# DATE DUE

| | | | |
|---|---|---|---|
| | | | |
| | | | |
| | | | |
| | | | |
| | | | |
| | | | |
| | | | |
| | | | |
| | | | |
| | | | |
| | | | |
| | | | |
| | | | |
| | | | |
| | | | |
| | | | |
| | | | |
| | | | PRINTED IN U.S.A. |

# WITHOUT COPYRIGHTS

## Modernist Literature & Culture

*Kevin J. H. Dettmar & Mark Wollaeger, Series Editors*

# WITHOUT
# COPYRIGHTS

## PIRACY, PUBLISHING, AND
## THE PUBLIC DOMAIN

## ROBERT SPOO

OXFORD
UNIVERSITY PRESS

# OXFORD
## UNIVERSITY PRESS

Oxford University Press is a department of the University of Oxford.
It furthers the University's objective of excellence in research, scholarship,
and education by publishing worldwide.

Oxford    New York
Auckland    Cape Town    Dar es Salaam    Hong Kong    Karachi
Kuala Lumpur    Madrid    Melbourne    Mexico City    Nairobi
New Delhi    Shanghai    Taipei    Toronto

With offices in
Argentina    Austria    Brazil    Chile    Czech Republic    France    Greece
Guatemala    Hungary    Italy    Japan    Poland    Portugal    Singapore
South Korea    Switzerland    Thailand    Turkey    Ukraine    Vietnam

Oxford is a registered trademark of Oxford University Press
in the UK and certain other countries.

Published in the United States of America by
Oxford University Press
198 Madison Avenue, New York, NY 10016

Library of Congress Cataloging-in-Publication Data
Spoo, Robert E.
Without copyrights : piracy, publishing, and the public domain / Robert Spoo.
p. cm. – (Modernist literature & culture)
Includes bibliographical references and index.
ISBN 978-0-19-992787-6 – ISBN 978-0-19-992788-3    1. Copyright–United States–History.
2. Copyright, International–History.    3. Law and literature.    I. Title.
KF2994.S65 2013
346.7304'82–dc23
2012040019

1 3 5 7 9 8 6 4 2
Printed in the United States of America
on acid-free paper

*For the Three Tolerant Graces: Marjorie, Sophie, and Virginia*

# CONTENTS

6

*ULYSSES* AUTHORIZED: RANDOM HOUSE
AND COURTESY 233

EPILOGUE—DISTURBING THE AMERICAN
PUBLIC DOMAIN 263

# SERIES EDITORS' FOREWORD

In publishing Paul Saint-Amour's edited collection *Modernism and Copyright* in 2011 (which includes an early version of chapter 3 of this book), we hoped to set the stage for a more thorough and sophisticated conversation about the role intellectual property issues played in the construction of modernism. Further, we believed that the Modernist Literature & Culture series might be an attractive venue for the kind of vibrant work on IP modernism sketched out in that volume. (Indeed, the series had already tapped into new work in law and modern literature with Sean Latham's *The Art of Scandal* in 2009.) In the back of our minds, we also knew that Robert Spoo was at work on an important study of the topic, work that reached back into the nineteenth-century tradition of "trade courtesy" and bore the impress of his careful legal scholarship; for many of us, the earliest inkling of this work came with the 1998 publication of his *Yale Law Journal* article "Copyright Protectionism and Its Discontents: The Case of James Joyce's *Ulysses* in America."

But we think it's fair to say that no one—not even Bob—knew back then how this story would turn out. In *Without Copyrights: Piracy, Publishing, and the Public Domain*, Spoo traces the shifting and dynamic relationship between intellectual property law, informal "gentlemen's" publishing traditions, and the practices of modernist literary production—"the story," as he describes it, "of transatlantic modernism's encounter with U.S. copyright law, lawful piracy, and the American public domain." The book's thesis, to pick up on just one of Spoo's artful formulations, is that "the fear of failed copyrights lay behind many developments of modernism."

It's hard to write this foreword without dropping a lot of "spoilers": you'll learn things that will fundamentally unsettle your understanding of modernist authorship. Without giving too much away here, one comes away from

*Without Copyrights* with a profound (and completely unexpected) respect for the poster boy of modernist literary piracy, Samuel Roth—and with a much complicated understanding of the legality of the "piracy" of Roth and others, a piracy enabled, if not created, by protectionist American copyright law. Ezra Pound's thoughtful and systematic response to the predations of a publisher like Roth resulted in his somewhat quixotic proposal for perpetual copyrights combined with requirements to keep works in print, a proposal that begins to make sense for the first time in Spoo's account; as he writes, "Pound was the theorist of modernism's encounter with copyright and piracy."

As was demonstrated rather dramatically by the internet leak in 2003 of Radiohead's album *Hail to the Thief* ten weeks prior to its commercial release, piracy can in fact generate publicity, and have a beneficial, not parasitic, effect on sales: the album sold 300,000 copies in its first week of U.S. release, a debut aided, according to many commentators, by the bootlegged preview. (See, for instance, Jonathan Cohen, "Web Leak Fails to Deter Capitol's Radiohead Setup," *Billboard* 14 June 2003.) But similar parables date back to at least the late nineteenth century; Spoo tells of the U.S. lecture tours of Oscar Wilde and W. B. Yeats, for instance, both of whom benefitted commercially from being "pirated."

Finally (for now), it's impossible to read through this careful and even-handed work without having one's conception of Joyce significantly complicated. We won't ruin the suspense, but suffice it to say that while he was "shocked, shocked!" by Roth's piracy, Joyce was hardly a naïf when it came to the hard realities of the U.S.'s refusal to sign on to international copyright accords. "Pirate," as Spoo succinctly puts it, "was a term that could expand and contract with the nature of the perceived outrage."

As a professor of modernist literature (and former editor of the *James Joyce Quarterly*) turned law-school professor of intellectual property, Spoo is, to a degree that gives new life to the cliché, "uniquely qualified" to tell the story set out in this study. He reads belles lettres and the law with equal sensitivity and flair and insight—he reads the law with a literary scholar's wide imaginative sympathies, and reads literary texts (and their paratexts) with a forensic eye. In another's hands, these literary texts would be rendered mere evidence, or the legal literature sprinkled in as a dilettantish, titillating garnish. In Spoo's careful weave, the two become mutually constitutive, mutually suspicious, quarrelling yet loving twin brothers: Shem the Penman, say, and Shaun the Post.

We count ourselves lucky to have *Without Copyrights* for the Modernist Literature & Culture series, and we're excited to bring it to you. But please read with caution: the pages that follow are bound to upend some received wisdom.

—Kevin J. H. Dettmar & Mark Wollaeger

# ACKNOWLEDGMENTS

I began work on this book more than a decade ago when I was in the thick of law school and the early years of legal practice. It was hard to get sustained writing done during those hectic times; much of the development of my theme was carried out, necessarily and I fear compulsively, in conversations with colleagues and friends. Any attempt at recording the multitude of my debts here is bound to be incomplete. Ideas, inspirations, sudden shifts and detours of thought, confirmations of hunches—I owe these and more to many persons I have known in law school, practice, and the literary and legal academy. I can list only a few of those debts here, but my gratitude to everyone is profound and abiding.

To begin with, I wish to thank Oxford University Press for its interest in this project from the start. I am grateful to Shannon McLachlan for beginning the journey with me and to Brendan O'Neill for seeing it through with such thoughtfulness and care. Kevin Dettmar and Mark Wollaeger, friends and colleagues of long standing, saw how this book might fit into their Modernist Literature & Culture series, and I thank them for their support. I wish also to thank my hawkeyed yet compassionate copyeditor, Leslie Watkins.

I have had the benefit of discerning responses to portions of this book presented at academic institutions, societies, and conferences. These include Arizona State University Law School; University at Buffalo, the UB Humanities Institute, and the Baldy Center for Law and Social Policy; University of Connecticut at Storrs; Cornell University; the Fleur Cowles Flair Symposium, University of London; the International James Joyce Symposium, Dublin, Ireland; the James Joyce Research Colloquium, sponsored by University College Dublin and the National Library of Ireland;

John Jay College of Criminal Justice; University of Miami; the Modern Language Association; the Ohio State University; the Penn Humanities Forum, the Department of English, and the Cinema Studies Program at the University of Pennsylvania; the Law and Humanities Workshop at the University of Toronto Faculty of Law; and the Society of American Archivists. Scholars and students at all these places helped light my way and refine my arguments.

The intertwining plots of this book could not have been recovered and told without data mined from many libraries and archives. I am grateful for the patient assistance of the following institutions and their staff: Arthur W. Diamond Law Library, Columbia University; Beinecke Library, Yale University; Henry W. and Albert A. Berg Collection of English and American Literature, New York Public Library; The Poetry Collection, University at Buffalo, State University of New York; Chadbourne & Parke LLP; Rare Book and Manuscript Library, Columbia University; Appellate Division Law Library, M. Dolores Denman Courthouse, Rochester, New York; Harry Ransom Humanities Research Center, University of Texas at Austin; Lilly Library, Indiana University; National Library of Ireland; New York County Clerk archives; New York County Lawyers Association; New York University School of Law Library; Manuscripts and Archives Division, New York Public Library; Department of Rare Books and Special Collections, Princeton University Library; Schaffer Law Library, Albany Law School; Special Collections Research Center, Southern Illinois University Carbondale; Department of Special Collections and University Archives, University of Tulsa; Albert and Shirley Small Special Collections Library, University of Virginia; Archives Department, University of Wisconsin Milwaukee Libraries; Yale Law School; and Zurich James Joyce Foundation.

I must thank in particular certain individuals who made it possible for me to track down crucial portions of the story of James Joyce's dispute with Samuel Roth. Jay Gertzman, who has done more scholarly work on Roth than anyone, generously helped me again and again with details of Roth's career and steered me through the then unprocessed Samuel Roth Papers at Columbia University. Our lunches and dinners at that Cuban restaurant on Broadway are a treasured memory. Charles K. O'Neill, partner in the New York office of Chadbourne & Parke LLP, kindly made available to me the unprivileged portions of the *Joyce v. Roth* litigation file, preserved by that firm since its days as Chadbourne, Stanchfield & Levy. I wish to note that the firm scrupulously withheld any privileged attorney–client communications and other confidential material; the communications between Joyce and his lawyers that I cite in the book were found in other archives. Jacob ("Jay") Padgug helped make his father, Nathan Mordechai Padgug, come alive for me through stories and photographs. I wish him and his wife the best in their new life in Israel.

For permission to quote from or reproduce textual and photographic materials, I am grateful to Chadbourne & Parke LLP, Robert Cox, James Kugel, Jay Padgug, and Anne Roiphe. Unpublished letters and other writings by Ezra Pound: Copyright © 2013 by Mary de Rachewiltz and the Estate of Omar S. Pound. Used by permission of New Directions Publishing Corp.

Financial support for this project was provided by the University of Tulsa College of Law. Most especially, I wish to thank Dean Janet K. Levit for making summer research funds and other support available to me and the donors of the Chapman Distinguished Chair for their generosity.

Many individuals have read portions of this book or have discussed its claims with me and have contributed ideas, criticisms, or corrections. Others have provided critical research leads or spared me from blundering down blind alleys. Although I will probably omit some names unintentionally, I wish to record my thanks to Charles Adams, John Ashley, Laura Barnes, Mark Bartholomew, Michael Birnhack, Philip Bishop, William S. Brockman, Frank Callanan, Jean-Christophe Cloutier, Luca Crispi, Ronan Crowley, Melba Cuddy-Keane, Jeffrey P. Cunard, Peter Decherney, Sally Dennison, Kenneth Durr, Lars Engle, Michael J. Everton, Mike Groden, Ben Gutman, Sam Halabi, Justice Adrian Hardiman, Peter B. Hirtle, Richard Hix, Merlin Holland, Nancy Horan, Dennis S. Karjala, Bruce P. Keller, Joseph A. Kestner, Carlton Larson, Sean Latham, Lawrence Lessig, James Levine, Janet K. Levit, William Manz, Jim McCue, Margaret Melcher, Sue Melcher, John Nyhan, Edward P. O'Hanlon, Judy Padgug, Tamara R. Piety, Paul K. Saint-Amour, Amanda Sigler, Simon Stern, Lior Strahilevitz, Karin Thieme, Rebecca Tushnet, Joseph Van Nostrand, Jolanta Wawrzycka, David Weir, Hannah Wiseman, Sam Wiseman, Martha Woodmansee, and Richard Workman.

I also wish to thank my research assistants at the University of Tulsa College of Law—Melissa Eick, Lindsey Snedden, Philip Tinker, and Derek Weinbrenner—for their excellent and dedicated work. Gina Bradley and Chris Farwell provided invaluable technical help.

Incalculable support, day and night, obvious and subtle, has come from the members of my family: my wife Marjorie and my daughters Sophie and Virginia. No book gets written without sacrifice and tolerance on the part of loved ones who live through the process with the author. My deepest thanks go to these three.

Early versions of chapter 3 were published in the *UCLA Law Review* 56 (2009): 1775–1834 and in the collection of essays edited by Paul K. Saint-Amour, *Modernism and Copyright* (New York: Oxford University Press, 2011), 39–64. Portions of chapter 4 first appeared as "Copyright Protectionism and Its Discontents: The Case of James Joyce's *Ulysses* in America," *Yale Law Journal* 108 (1998): 633–67. A few paragraphs in chapters 2 and 5 originated in my monograph, *Three Myths for Aging Copyrights: Tithonus, Dorian Gray, Ulysses* (Dublin: National Library of Ireland, Joyce Studies Series No. 6, 2004).

# WITHOUT COPYRIGHTS

# PROLOGUE

## Growing the American Public Domain

*All this chaos and uncertainty, all these feuds and enmities, have one and the same cause,—the existence in the world of a kind of property which is at once the most precious, the easiest stolen, and the worst protected.*
*—James Parton (1867)*[1]

Late in September of 1918, a miscellaneous troupe of actors—some professionals, some rank novices—launched a series of performances of George Bernard Shaw's *Mrs. Warren's Profession* for audiences in Zurich, Switzerland. The actors called themselves the English Players. They had been assembled, in part, to assist in promoting British culture during wartime, and they performed Shaw's controversial play in English, without permission from the playwright. A year later, with the dust of war still settling in Europe, G. Herbert Thring, secretary of the Society of Authors in London, wrote to chide the English Players for mounting the play without Shaw's consent and without paying him any royalties. The unauthorized production and the troupe's evasiveness were creating "a very bad impression" on the Society of Authors, Thring warned, and the society was considering pressing "legal claims to the utmost."[2]

Thring's menacing letter found its way to James Joyce, cofounder of the English Players, but Joyce was a hard man to intimidate. Instead of hastening to placate the society, he responded with a string of legal theories designed to excuse the alleged outrage. First, he coolly hinted that there could be no enforceable rights in a play like Shaw's, whose indecency had caused the Lord Chamberlain to deny a license for its public performance in Britain. Second, he claimed that the production of English-language plays on the Continent was "an exceptional case not foreseen" by the Berne Convention for the Protection of Literary and Artistic Works, the agreement that governed copyright relations among many nations. Performing the play in Switzerland was "free" because the Berne Convention did not expressly forbid such an act. The most Joyce would concede was that his company might have given the appearance of infringing "literary courtesy."[3]

The tables turned seven years later when Joyce, now a victim of piracy himself, was treated to uncannily similar defenses by Samuel Roth, a New York publisher who had begun reprinting unauthorized magazine installments of *Ulysses* in July 1926. Roth told Joyce's lawyers that *Ulysses* was "not copyrighted" in the United States and was therefore "the property of anyone wishing to use it."[4] At that time, America was still isolationist in copyright matters, a tainted wether of the international flock, prevented by its hyper-formalistic laws from joining the Berne Convention. The 1909 U.S. Copyright Act, which determined what was and what was not protected within the borders of the United States, specified that, to enjoy full copyright, foreign works written in English had to be reset, printed, and bound on American soil within a fixed number of days after they had been published abroad. Works like *Ulysses* that suffered from the stigma of immorality often failed to find a legitimate publisher in time to satisfy these requirements, known collectively as "the manufacturing clause." The penalty was loss of copyright. Perversely, copyright and obscenity statutes worked at cross purposes in this respect: books that vice crusaders sought to ban from circulation could more easily reappear under the imprints of unauthorized publishers simply because one of the chief restraints on promiscuous distribution—the authorial monopoly conferred by copyright—had been withheld by federal law on technical grounds. Joyce in 1919 and Roth in 1926 each appealed to the law to justify their doubtful activities. Copyright codes, they argued, authorized their unauthorized acts.

Around the time that Thring's accusatory letter reached Joyce in Zurich, Roth in New York mailed off a check for $500 to Edwin Arlington Robinson, whose long poem *Lancelot* had won the cash and a promise of publication in a contest arranged by Roth through the Lyric Society.[5] The donor of the prize had reneged, so Roth made good the $500 out of his own pocket. The gesture was characteristically flamboyant, a combination of generosity and showmanship. He was a romantic when it came to his literary passions, a determined disseminator of the authors he loved. Several years later he realized another of his dreams by reprinting *Ulysses*, though his reward would be to wear a scarlet "P" for the rest of his life.

Roth, too, learned what it was to be pirated within the law. During a sojourn in London in 1921, hungry and low on funds, he visited the office of *The Jewish Chronicle* in the hope of selling some articles. The editor, who had previously reprinted Roth's contributions to the American Jewish press without permission or compensation, looked him in the eye and told him it was the *Chronicle*'s policy never to pay for what it could get for nothing; once Roth's new articles appeared in the States, the *Chronicle* could freely reprint them with the blessing of British law, which, given America's non-Berne status, granted no automatic protections for the published writings of U.S. citizens.[6] Roth was shocked by "the discourtesy of this indecent old reprobate and his piratical magazine."[7] Later, he looked back on the encounter as a sort of primal scene foreshadowing his own lawful depredations. Like the old editor of the *Chronicle*, he admitted to using "a great deal of matter in the public domain" during his long career.[8]

This is a book about the convergence of lawful piracy and transatlantic modernism within what I call the American public domain, a vast, opportunistic literary commons assembled from the legal have-nots of foreign authorship and reflecting the protectionist policies of a developing nation in quest of instant and assured culture. Created by U.S. copyright laws, the American public domain was nothing less than an aggressively legislated commons, an invitation to piracy that served the interests of domestic publishers, typesetters, printers, binders, and the book-buying public. For the first century of federal copyright protection and well into the twentieth century, the American public domain grew daily through the influx of new works by foreign-domiciled authors. By operation of the law, these works were claimed, immediately or soon after they were issued abroad, by a preternaturally premature, or forced, commons.

One of my goals is to reframe literary piracy and its role in modernism within an accurate understanding of copyright law and the realities of publishing in the period. The typical and uncritical use of the term *piracy*—detached from the legal conditions that permitted and even encouraged it—gives a false aura of illegality to a practice that, though inconsistent with strict business morality or what was then called "the courtesy of the trade," was a lawful form of cultural diffusion well into the twentieth century. Joyce's retaliatory campaign to discredit Roth for exploiting *Ulysses* was a continuation, by other means, of the traditional extralegal sanctions of trade courtesy, but it was not the upbraiding of a violator of the copyright law. What Joyce brashly asserted concerning Shaw's play in Zurich—that it was free for common use—was really true of *Ulysses* in the United States. This study seeks to disentangle the coarse weave of the rhetoric of piracy as used by modernism's contemporaries as well as by today's commentators and to reveal piracy's role in transatlantic modernism.[9] My use of the term *pirate* varies from context to context, sometimes denoting a breaker of the law, at other times indicating a deviant from courtesy or a transgressor of other informal norms. Context gives the appropriate coloration; I have avoided intrusive glosses of my every use of *pirate*.[10]

The story I tell concerns the disseminative conditions of transatlantic modernism, the practice and rhetoric of lawful piracy, the counter-rhetoric and retaliations of its outraged victims, and the courteous code by which some publishers justified exploiting the free booty of the American public domain. My methodology combines traditional legal and literary history with an intense focus on the particular rules of U.S. copyright law as they affected foreign-domiciled authors. I bring to bear the discourses of law, economics, protectionism, and piracy as they were produced in the nineteenth century and were carried over, in familiar and altered forms, into the twentieth. My perspective is sociolegal and interdisciplinary, historical in mood, narrative in style, and grounded in three decades of literary and legal study and more than a decade of practicing and teaching copyright law. My accounts of law and courtesy are woven from many archival sources, including the recently acquired Samuel Roth Papers at Columbia University, documents uncovered in New York court archives, the litigation file preserved by the law firm that represented Joyce in his 1927–28 lawsuit against Roth, and materials located in a score of other libraries and private collections throughout the world.

Chapter 1, "The American Public Domain and the Courtesy of the Trade in the Nineteenth Century," explores the founding rules of a protectionist copyright law that openly encouraged the unauthorized reprinting of new foreign works, generated frenzied competition for those free resources, and set in motion a counter-practice of self-restraint among American publishers that came to be called the courtesy of the trade. As a way of regulating ruinous competition for unprotected titles, and to give themselves an aura of respectability and fairness, the major publishers adopted trade courtesy whereby, in its simplest form, the first publisher to announce plans to issue an American edition of an unprotected foreign work acquired informal title to that work—a kind of makeshift copyright grounded on tacit trade agreements and community-based norms. Drawing on the insights of scholars of social norms and common-pool regulation, I offer a detailed account of nineteenth-century courtesy and its regime of entitlements, exceptions, and penalties. Courtesy restored a fragile order to the publishing scene by imitating the main features of copyright law and permitting both publishers and authors to benefit, though inconsistently, from the wholly informal exclusive rights recognized by this self-interested chivalry.

Chapter 2, "Transatlantic Modernism in the American Public Domain," moves into the twentieth century and traces the same forces—copyright law, legalized piracy, and trade courtesy—as they shaped the production and consumption of modernism in the United States. Here I show how the dreaded manufacturing clause and other strict formalities of U.S. copyright law, persisting from the previous century, claimed works by many foreign-domiciled authors for the American public domain. The stringent law and the high costs of American printing combined to drive such writers as Ezra Pound to publish in Europe and thereby to sacrifice their U.S. copyrights. The fear of failed copyrights lay behind many developments of modernism, including Pound's editorial work for *The Little Review* and *The Dial*, foreign authors' efforts to place their writings in American magazines and to print special limited editions of their works, and the role of the New York lawyer and cultural patron John Quinn in building a legal infrastructure for the transatlantic avant-garde in America.

Chapter 2 also introduces Samuel Roth as a central figure in the unauthorized production of modernism in America and traces the quiet persistence of trade courtesy among other American publishers, such as B. W. Huebsch and Bennett Cerf. A variety of legal and social pressures had caused courtesy to decline from its extrovert prominence in the nineteenth century, but it continued on in the new century, more an ethical assumption of doing business than a boasted badge of probity. An echo of the old courtesies can be heard in Joyce's halfhearted assurance to Thring that, though the English Players had violated no legal rights, they wished to avoid the appearance of transgressing "literary courtesy." Roth's protest over the "discourtesy" of the editor of *The Jewish Chronicle* likewise alluded to an ethical impropriety that did not rise to outright unlawfulness. Courtesy was a voluntary affirmation of moral solidarity with authors and fellow publishers. To operate outside of courtesy was to declare oneself dead to the higher ideals of the trade. Deviants from the practice were branded as pirates, a second-order piracy that could leave a permanent stain on a publisher's reputation. Roth never fully recovered from Joyce's campaign to fix him as an unscrupulous thief beyond the courtesy pale.

Ezra Pound hated literary piracy, lawful or unlawful, and was a sworn enemy of the copyright-defeating technicalities of U.S. law. For decades he railed against statutes that "favour[ed] the printer at the expense of the author."[11] Although he thought Roth was a "bloody crook" for reprinting uncopyrighted works without permission, he considered "the American copyright law ... a worse crook than he is."[12] The law made the man, Pound thought, and Roth was merely a symptom. Chapter 3, "Ezra Pound's Copyright Statute: Perpetual Rights and Unfair Competition with the Dead," traces Pound's detailed proposals for copyright reform and his rigorously ambivalent attitudes toward authors' legal rights and disseminative piracy. At the very moment that the English Players were presenting Shaw's play to Zurich audiences without a license, Pound was publishing his proposals in the London weekly *The New Age*. His program for reform envisioned the granting of strong authorial entitlements—indeed, he urged a perpetual copyright—but at the same time he worried over the power that such entitlements would place in the hands of authors and their heirs. His solution was to install various checks and balances that would enable publishers to reprint authors' works without permission if authors or their heirs failed or refused to keep works in circulation. Pound's idea of a literature without borders, a utopia of fluid international communication, existed in conscious tension with his desire to fortify authors' rights and to combat literary piracy.

Chapter 4, "*Ulysses* Unauthorized: Protectionism, Piracy, and Protest," tells how U.S. copyright law forced Joyce's masterpiece into the American public domain within months of its publication in France in 1922. The chief reason for the book's unprotected status was Joyce's inability to comply with the 1909 copyright act's manufacturing clause. The law's willingness to trade protection for protectionism enabled Roth to use his *Two Worlds* magazines as a force for diffusing an archly eroticized version of modernism in a country bound by moral prohibitions and conventional reading habits. Here and in the following chapter I discuss Roth's reprinting of Joyce, T. S. Eliot, and Pound and show that the international protest over Roth's *Ulysses* piracy, organized by Joyce and his supporters, employed one of the familiar penalties of trade courtesy: the ritual ostracism of a violator of informal publishing norms. Pound's refusal to sign the protest was not a personal crotchet, as Joyce liked to believe. It reflected instead a principled distaste for pillorying an individual who was acting in conformity with an admittedly objectionable law and who in any case was circulating a great work that had frightened off other American publishers. The law, Pound thought, not its inevitable product, should have been the focus of Joyce's organized army of protesters.

Chapter 5, "*Joyce v. Roth*: Authors' Names and Blue Valley Butter," turns to Joyce's lawsuit against Samuel Roth in 1927–28. The litigation has never been recounted in anything like sufficient or accurate detail, and its implications for Joyce's career have gone unnoticed. Joyce's lawyers, unable to sue for copyright infringement, chose a New York civil rights statute to combat Roth's reprinting of *Ulysses*. The lawsuit, which alleged that Roth had unlawfully exploited Joyce's name for commercial and advertising purposes, was an early example of a publicity-rights claim couched in the legal idiom of privacy rights. The litigation became a means by which Joyce altered public perception of *Ulysses* and furthered his growing reputation as an avant-garde innovator. Together with the international protest, the lawsuit marked a significant moment in the development of modernism as an engine for generating authorial celebrity. The injunction against Roth that Joyce eventually obtained—a product of the parties' agreement as much as the judgment of a tribunal—was in many ways a fitting conclusion to this rather free-form experiment in litigation, but even a diminished remedy served Joyce as an additional piece of the courtesy machinery he was assembling and the fame he was crafting.

The final chapter, "*Ulysses* Authorized: Random House and Courtesy," revisits the efforts of the lawyer Morris L. Ernst to remove the customs ban on *Ulysses* and to prepare the way for Random House's authorized edition of the novel. But my perspective is not the usual one of focusing on the legal strategies and arguments that persuaded Judge John M. Woolsey to declare

Joyce's masterpiece safe for admission into the United States. Rather, I tell the much less familiar story of how the uncopyrighted status of *Ulysses* in America created additional legal obstacles for Random House and how Bennett Cerf shrewdly employed trade courtesy to fend off what he feared would be a feeding frenzy of lawful piracy following Judge Woolsey's removal of the last legal barrier—the strictures of obscenity law—to unchecked reproduction of what was widely known to be a public domain work. Free riding publishers were Cerf's chief concern, once vice crusaders had been chased from the scene. So effective was his strategy that the exclusivity of Random House's claim to *Ulysses* went unchallenged for decades after its publication in 1934.

The American public domain has not been static. It has evolved remarkably during recent decades into a much less acquisitive, more author-friendly commons, especially after the United States joined the international Berne Convention in 1989 and adopted laws to safeguard the rights of foreign authors. Laws have been enacted, and upheld, that restore protection to foreign works that lost their U.S. copyrights through the operation of the manufacturing clause or other formalities. The epilogue, "Disturbing the American Public Domain," examines this changing public domain and legislators' quest for international harmonization of copyright rules. Far from unifying the global public domain, however, recent laws enacted in the United States and Europe only guarantee its continuing disharmony and fragmentation. Worldwide availability of modernist works is threatened by a tragedy of the uncoordinated global commons, a congestion of divergent durational terms and other rules that impede the free use of works created nearly a century ago. How the American public domain will fit its voice into this copyright cacophony is a story that continues to unfold.

At the heart of modernism, as of all creativity, lurks a mystery that challenges the received rationale for copyright laws. The Anglo-American theory of copyright holds that the prospect of an enforceable property right encourages authors to trouble themselves to produce because they know they will not be giving their creative offspring as hostages to free riders. This is the incentive theory of copyright, and it requires us to think of an author as a rational actor who responds with dutiful scribbling when the invisible hand of interest beckons. People get down to creating, the theory says, when they can descry a monetary carrot in the offing; if you promise to build their bank account, they will come. Abraham Lincoln encapsulated the idea when he remarked of patents that they add "the fuel of *interest* to the *fire* of genius, in the discovery and production of new and useful things."[13]

Yet even lawyers know this is only a partial account of creativity. Creativity is "messy," writes Rebecca Tushnet, "in ways that copyright law and theory have often ignored to their detriment."[14] Authors produce for many reasons that have little to do with immediate material gain; their lives attest to other compulsions: joy, competitiveness, prestige, celebrity, the lure of aesthetic pleasure, the dream of building a beautiful mousetrap. Tushnet sees desire as central to the experience of creators, including "desire for reciprocal gift relationships between authors and audiences."[15] Arguments for copyright have often relied on the figure of the Romantic author—the embodiment of originality standing apart from soulless capitalism and faceless markets—as a justification for awarding a monopoly for creativity. But when it comes to theories of incentive, copyright law abandons Keats and substitutes *homo economicus*—the rational artist who produces with dollar signs dancing in his head—and argues that more protection will always incentivize more creativity.[16] In those places where I draw upon the incentive theory, I am ever mindful of the incompleteness of its explanatory power.

Pound wrote of the artist's "inherent activity." He recalled that his grandfather had built a railroad "probably less from a desire to make money or an illusion that he could make more that way than some other, than from inherent activity, artist's desire to MAKE something, the fun of constructing and the play of outwitting and overcoming obstruction."[17] Modernist writing was undoubtedly motivated by the marketplace, yet copyrights played a complex and varied role in the lives of many writers. These authors were prompted as much by a desire to accumulate cultural capital as by a need to secure immediate monetary benefits, and they made striking property-related sacrifices in their quest for textual ideality. Joyce was willing to forgo copyright in the United States for the opportunity to issue an unexpurgated *Ulysses* in France, even though he knew that judicious revision would have made the work acceptable to some American publishers. W. B. Yeats so longed for collected editions by which he could shape and reshape his artistic image that he reluctantly gave an exclusive license for publishing his collected works to a New York publisher.[18] These authors had their reward. Yeats joyfully remade himself over and over in successive editions. Joyce kept his text inviolate, and he later turned his legal disability into a loss leader by using his quarrel with Roth to accelerate his growing celebrity, all the while that

Roth's unauthorized installments were seeding the American market for an authorized *Ulysses*. The pursuit of fame and the quest for artistic perfection, together with inherent activity, drove these writers as much as the hope of monetizing each new story or poem.

In addition to the mysteries of motivation, the existence of cultural patrons complicates the picture of modernists' copyright incentives. Patronage is usually viewed as historically and structurally distinct from copyright regimes,[19] but it coexisted with copyright for the modernists. Numerous authors—Pound, Eliot, H.D., Wyndham Lewis, to name a few—enjoyed the benefactions of patrons for brief or lengthy periods of time. John Quinn served as a clearinghouse for gifts (his own and those of others), and he provided pro bono legal and publishing services to Joyce, Pound, Yeats, and others. In 1919, Harriet Shaw Weaver settled an enormous sum of money on Joyce and later added more, sustaining him and his family for more than twenty years. Copyright and patronage inhabited the same cultural moment that saw the convergence, as Lawrence Rainey has shown, of collectors, investors, little reviews, limited editions, and other institutions of modernism that courted commodification while resisting it.[20] According to strict economic logic, the kind of financial assistance that Joyce received should have lessened the urgency to protect his works as property. As public goods, they were reaching readers by fair means or foul, through appointed publishers or self-appointed reprinters, and Joyce was being amply rewarded for his creativity by his English patron (and receiving handsome royalties from the Paris edition of *Ulysses*, protected by copyright in France at least). Yet that was not enough for him; he clung to his copyrights, whether they existed or not.

Modernist authors thought of their work as ownable and resented assaults on it, even when the work lay squarely in the American public domain, stripped of all incidents of legal property. The idea of literary property was talismanic, emblematic of respect for artistic labor, an acknowledgment of the dignity of the attic. For some, it was a question of honor. When in 1953 Margaret Anderson published the retrospective *Little Review Anthology*, she included Eliot's prose dialogue "Eeldrop and Appleplex" from a 1917 number of *The Little Review*. Anderson's editor, having satisfied himself that the piece was "free to use" because it lacked U.S. copyright protection, had not sought Eliot's permission but had simply forwarded him a "courtesy payment" after the fact. Eliot coldly returned the check, remarking that acceptance of payment might be construed as permission to reprint.[21] Anderson was chagrined, but Eliot had made his point: authors deserved better than to be treated to the sterile letter of the law, and courtesy was not courteous if it failed to acknowledge authors' moral rights to dispose of their work as they pleased. Whether they were acting from pride, the need for royalties, or the desire to control the quality and placement of their texts, transatlantic modernists worried over their copyrights; and when copyrights did not exist, they expected full-blooded courtesy.

The American public domain could be merciless, but it could also be a writer's friend. Lawful piracies helped build the success of the American tours of Oscar Wilde, Arthur Conan Doyle, and Yeats, spreading the fame of those authors and others throughout the United States.[22] Unauthorized reprinting was, in important respects, an involuntary boon to such writers as Joyce and Pound, in a time when the costs of American printing were prohibitive and the mores of the parlor and the vigilance of vice societies often foreclosed legitimate avenues of publishing. Pound knew the value of dissemination, even though he condemned piracy. His attitude toward Samuel Roth was complex; he publicly denounced the New York publisher's thefts while reserving a measure of respect for his courage. They were secret sharers.

At the core of the events I relate are three very different figures of high modernism: Pound, Joyce, and Roth. Although I show how dozens of transatlantic writers, from Virginia Woolf to Edgar Wallace, struggled with the American public domain, these three men, with their sharply divergent attitudes toward literary property, most vividly illustrate the scope and intensity of the commons decreed by U.S. copyright law. Roth was a bold pragmatist, the bad boy of magazine publishing who cynically acted within the letter of a discriminatory law and used the public domain to promote his libidinous confections of the avant-garde. He was, in a sense, U.S. copyright law luridly personified, shorn of courtesies and dedicated to a louche, bullying sort of public service. Joyce, in contrast, was the preacher of *droit d'auteur*, a self-righteous property scold who, even as he launched protests and lawsuits, quietly benefited from the network effects of enhanced fame and expanded markets that lawful piracies created.[23] He was Roth's inevitable adversary, the avenging fury of authors' moral and natural entitlements.

Pound was the theorist of modernism's encounter with copyright and piracy. Unafraid to articulate the contradictions within literary property, he believed in strong authorial rights as long as they did not interfere with free trade in books and ideas. My emphasis on Anglophone modernism is equally a product of the law. From 1909 on, U.S. copyright status extended protection to works published abroad in foreign languages even when they were not reprinted and bound on American soil, but those statutes continued to subject all English-language works to manufacturing requirements that were in some respects even more stringent than formerly. The rise of modernism was coterminous with the U.S. manufacturing clause; transatlantic authors, particularly those who wrote in English, were bound and defined by American copyright protectionism, an inescapable part of the mode of literary production.

"[A]rt is more ancient than copyright laws," Roth once wrote in defense of his actions.[24] Alongside a desire to cash in on his peculiar blend of modernism and erotica, a part of him believed that art was a gift to the world and that he had a right and a duty to keep that gift in motion, the "constant donation" of which Lewis Hyde has written.[25] If he failed to observe courtesy, or if he bent it to his needs, it was because his temperament and finances prevented him from climbing above his pariah status and joining Alfred Knopf, Bennett Cerf, and other new publishers in their quest for respectability. Courtesy was mostly a game for insiders anyway. Roth preferred the periphery.

This is a book about the periphery, the elusive point at which law and piracy traded places, legitimacy shaded off into lawlessness, courtesy grew discourteous, and gifts to the world were deemed encroachments on authorial entitlement. Amid an abundance of unowned riches, law-abiding reprinters were viewed as international thieves held together by a precarious code of honor, and buccaneers boasted of being Johnny Appleseeds. In some ways, it was a world turned upside down. It was the American public domain.

# THE AMERICAN PUBLIC DOMAIN AND THE COURTESY OF THE TRADE IN THE NINETEENTH CENTURY

*[A] literary pirate is not only not an outlaw; he is protected by the law.*
*He is the product of law.*
—*The Publishers' Weekly (1882)*[1]

*[Trade courtesy] was a brief realization of the ideals of philosophical anarchism—*
*self-regulation without law.*
—*Henry Holt (1908)*[2]

In 1891, at the age of thirty-nine, Thomas Bird Mosher of Portland, Maine, began a career of fine book publishing. The small volumes he lovingly designed in his shop on Exchange Street were tasteful and elegant, printed on fine paper, stamped with a dolphin-and-anchor device borrowed from Aldus Manutius, and surprisingly affordable. Books in his Old World Series were limited to 925 copies printed on Van Gelder paper and 100 copies on Japan Vellum, with white parchment wrappers. In 1897, these volumes sold for between $1 and $2.50, net, postage included. Mosher's various series—the Old World, the Bibelot, the Brocade, the English Reprint—offered writings and translations by noted British and French writers of recent decades: Robert Bridges, Edward Fitzgerald, Richard Jefferies, Andrew Lang, George Meredith, William Morris, Gérard de Nerval, Walter Pater, Dante Gabriel Rossetti, George William Russell ("A.E."), John Addington Symonds, and A. C. Swinburne.[3]

Mosher was often praised for his outpouring of tasteful books—more than 300 separate titles and 750 volumes before his death in 1923.[4] He was also attacked, mostly from the other side of the Atlantic, for his unapologetic literary "piracies." It is no exaggeration to say that Mosher built his list and his business on unauthorized publication, or what the American publishing trade was pleased to call reprinting. Mosher was dubbed the Pirate of Portland, but the epithet sacrificed legal accuracy for colorful disapprobation. American copyright law permitted and even encouraged Mosher's buccaneering; works authored by non-U.S. citizens or nonresidents received no copyright protection in the United States for most of the nineteenth century. Mosher was simply doing what many American publishers had done before him: helping himself to a free resource that had been placed at his disposal by statutory command. And since he added elegance and affordability to his product, why should authors complain?

Yet complain they did. When in 1895 Mosher issued Andrew Lang's translation of *Aucassin et Nicolete* in his Old World Series without the permission of Lang or his London publisher, the Scottish author took Mosher to task publicly for his "discourteous" act, carried out for his "own emolument."[5] Mosher gamely replied in the pages of the New York–based periodical *The Critic* that American copyright law authorized his conduct and that he would not waste time debating the "ethics of reprinting" because the reprinting of uncopyrighted works was a recognized calling in the United States: "I am neither singular, nor is my procedure a new one. It began before I was born; it will continue when I am dead."[6] Besides, Mosher noted, he had offered Lang's publisher, apparently after the fact, an "*honorarium*, open to refusal, but surely suggested in good faith." Why not "accept a solatium when the deed was done?"[7] Mosher had chosen this mock-legalistic thrust carefully. A solatium is a kind of damages paid, not for pecuniary loss, but for injured feelings.[8] Legally, Mosher owed nothing by way of financial compensation; he had made a gentlemanly offer, ex gratia, to smooth ruffled pride.

Taking up Lang's piracy taunt, Mosher retorted that he had "laid hold" of Lang's translation as an attractive piece of literature: "because you and your publisher abandoned it on the high seas, as flotsam and jetsam, I rescued it and brought it into port, that it might not become forever derelict and lost. It is mine because I found it!"[9] Playfully alluding to the law of marine salvage (as a boy, he had accompanied his father on sea voyages), Mosher likened public domain works like Lang's *Aucassin and Nicolete* to "flotsam and jetsam," cargo floating on the sea or cast adrift from an imperiled vessel, offering a fair opportunity for reward to any hardy salvor. Carried away by his metaphor, Mosher wrote as though Lang and his publisher had been remiss in not taking steps to secure an American copyright for *Aucassin and Nicolete*. But no such neglect could properly be imputed; in 1887, the year Lang published his translation in London, there was virtually no way for him to obtain U.S. copyright protection.[10]

Mosher then moved on from the simple question of reprinters' rights under the law to the moral propriety of issuing Lang's translation without having obtained permission. Mosher's chief justification was that he had made a scarce, expensive volume available to ordinary American readers at an affordable price. Wasn't the true source of irritation, he wondered aloud, the fact that Lang was "accustomed himself to see, unmoved, copies of his *rarissimus* quoted among bibliophiles at five-guinea rates" and had awakened "to find a reprint quite as choice as the original, selling for less than one-twenty-fifth of that sum?" More brashly still, Mosher reminded Lang that he had no basis for any grievance, at law or in conscience: "Legal rights there were none; moral rights I take to have been forfeited when the needy scholar could not buy your book."[11] In a bold stroke, Mosher had cast himself as a literary Robin Hood, snatching an elegant book, with the help of American copyright law, from the well-heeled book collector and handing it to the poor student and the poetry lover. The skeptical editors of *The Critic* were not charmed by Mosher's confident preening. Conceding that his legal right was "beyond question," they objected that his moral claim was "essentially that of the gentleman of the road who, having 'held up' a banker, lends his victim's money, for his own benefit, at a lower rate of interest than the owner would have asked for it, and perhaps gives a part of it to the poor."[12]

The dispute in the pages of *The Critic* rang the changes on the piracy question as it had been debated over the previous six decades. Positions had become polarized, and moralized. By the 1880s, the anti-piracy camp viewed reprinters like Mosher as "gentlemen of the road," lining their pockets at the expense of helpless European authors. The pro-reprinting contingent disagreed, hailing Mosher as a "kind of 'literary Johnny Appleseed,' disseminating to a mass audience the seeds of literary appreciation and cultural revival."[13] Anyway, his supporters insisted, Mosher was only exercising his legal rights under American law.

The anti-pirates rejected these apologetics as grossly insensitive to the moral rights of authors. Surely, they reasoned, an ethical obligation to honor writers' creative labors trumped mere legal opportunism. Scrambling for the high ground, the pro-reprinters countered that no appeal to moral rights could justify an enforced scarcity of letters. British authors and publishers had only themselves to blame if they issued appealing books in small print runs at high prices. Mosher and his brethren were doing nothing more than lawfully serving the "impecunious republic of booklovers";[14] ordinary Americans had a right to cheap, good books. The anti-pirates, immune to the romance of dissemination, replied that an author deserves some remuneration for creative effort; Mosher may have offered honoraria, but he did so insolently and only after he had raked in profits from his furtive enterprise. These entrenched positions, set forth so colorfully in the Lang–Mosher dispute, typified the decades-long controversy over the practice of unauthorized though lawful reprinting of European authors in the United States.

Thomas Bird Mosher was a transitional figure in American publishing. He plied his reprint trade during a period of enormous change in American copyright law and in the publishing industry. The year in which he commenced operations, 1891, was the same year in which the U.S. Congress enacted the Chace International Copyright Act. The Chace Act made copyright protection available, for the first time, to non-U.S. authors, though on stringent conditions that often defeated their efforts to obtain rights, and in the service of a policy that openly protected the interests of American typesetters and platemakers. As of 1923, the year of Mosher's death, subsequent legislation—the 1909 copyright act—continued to erect obstacles for foreign authors and preserved many of the protectionist features of the 1891 act. The controversy over literary piracy had declined from its

**Figure 1.1** Thomas Bird Mosher, the Pirate of Portland, 1901. (*Courtesy Philip R. Bishop, Thomas Bird Mosher Collection*)

pre-1900 intensity, but it had not entirely subsided. Certain transatlantic writers—notably and vociferously, Ezra Pound—protested U.S. copyright law and policy and denounced the license it continued to give to unauthorized reprinting in the United States. By 1926, James Joyce and T. S. Eliot, who had recently achieved fame with *Ulysses* and *The Waste Land*, respectively, were complaining that their writings were being pirated by the New York magazine publisher Samuel Roth. Roth, a devout practitioner of what had been called the Mosher Method, responded to their charges with a brazenness and panache worthy of the Pirate of Portland himself. I will explore the modernist encounter with literary piracy, and Roth's central role in it, in later chapters.

Mosher, despite his self-contented buccaneering, occasionally paid for his booty—and not just with the kind of post hoc honorarium he offered to Andrew Lang. Mosher gave one of his favorite authors, the Scottish writer William Sharp ("Fiona MacLeod"), $32 outright for the reprinting of *By Sundown Shores: Studies in Spirituality* (1902) and $100 for *The Divine Adventure* (1903)—both previously published in London. He paid $50 for Edward McCurdy's collection of essays on Italy and medieval themes, *Roses of Paestum* (1912), first issued in London in 1900. Instead of a flat payment,

Mosher sometimes offered a royalty on copies sold. For example, he gave a ten percent royalty to George William Russell ("A.E.") for a 1904 reprinting of his *Homeward: Songs by the Way*, originally published in Dublin in 1894.[15] All of these works probably lacked copyright protection in the United States, despite the conditional protections extended to foreign books under the 1891 Chace Act.

But why would Mosher pay, even occasionally, for what U.S. copyright law gave him for free? The answer lies, in part, in the professional mores of nineteenth-century American publishers. Up to 1891, and even after, prominent publishers attempted to repair the defects of America's isolationist copyright law by practicing an informal, norms-based system of self-regulation they called the courtesy of the trade, or trade courtesy. Trade courtesy was a voluntary, extralegal system in which many of the larger publishing houses behaved as if rights in foreign works existed and could be enforced against a publisher who reprinted without authorization. In obedience to courtesy, publishers assumed a virtue they lacked under the governing law. By paying foreign authors or their publishers a sum—token or substantial, as circumstances permitted—for synthetic rights to reprint authorized editions, publishers mimicked the salient features of copyright law, making a show of respectability and fairness to authors and avoiding ruinous competition among themselves for unprotected books. Trade courtesy was good business as well as good manners.

Mosher's occasional payments of lump sums and royalties to his European authors show that he recognized the principles of courtesy. Yet he observed these principles fitfully and idiosyncratically for the simple reason that he could take or leave them. His operation was too small and specialized to offer competition to, or to invite reprisal from, the major houses that depended on courtesy to get along with each other. And by 1900, the courtesy system had receded from the American publishing scene as a visibly active form of self-regulation. It did not vanish, however. Throughout the first half of the twentieth century it persisted as a publishing ethic and an occasional informal remedy, just as long as American copyright law failed to offer uniform and complete protection to non-U.S. authors. Most important for the present study, trade courtesy was seized upon and adapted by Joyce and his representatives as a strategy for combating the piracies of Samuel Roth and, later, for securing informal, extralegal protection for *Ulysses* in the United States. The story of courtesy's role in the history of *Ulysses* and in literary modernism generally will be told in later chapters of this book. The present chapter traces the nineteenth-century backgrounds of the modernist encounter with U.S. copyright law: the law's creation of an aggressive public domain, the rise of legalized piracy of unprotected foreign works, and the courtesy of the trade.

## Legal and Moral Piracy: The 1790 Copyright Act and After

As inhabitants of the digital age, we usually think of the word *pirate* as naming the violator of a formal, legally enforceable right—a copyright, a patent, a trade secret. The specter of widespread and promiscuous piracy has hovered behind much of the febrile property talk and eager lawmaking of recent years. Starting from the premise that digital technology, if left unchecked, would destroy incentives to produce and distribute intellectual property, Congress enacted the Digital Millennium Copyright Act of 1998, which provided expansive protections for copy-prevention technologies and copyright management information. The Senate Judiciary Committee summarized the prevailing dread: "Due to the ease with which digital works can be copied and distributed worldwide virtually instantaneously, copyright owners will hesitate to make their works readily available on the Internet without reasonable assurance that they will be protected against massive piracy."[16] The phrase "massive piracy" has emotional force in excess of its denotative capacity. Applied, as it often is today, to unauthorized file sharing by countless anonymous or pseudonymous users in decentralized peer-to-peer networks,[17] the phrase conjures up conspiratorial intent to break the law—a gigantic, orchestrated music heist—when in fact the very nature of decentralized file sharing scatters concerted intent and *mens rea* over the vast reaches of the World Wide Web. This is why the music and movie industries have focused much of their litigation efforts on the purveyors of peer-to-peer technologies and services: Napster, Aimster, Grokster, Kazaa, LimeWire, BitTorrent, and, of course, The Pirate Bay. Piracy, in the digital era, as in the past, must have a local habitation and a name, and the pirate is almost invariably thought of as a wicked lawbreaker, a violator of legislated or common law rights.

The concept of the pirate as a foe of the formal copyright law is not new.[18] As long ago as 1936, Judge Learned Hand, writing for a panel of the U.S. Court of Appeals for the Second Circuit, rejected the idea that a work could not be infringing just because portions of it owed nothing to the infringed work. In holding that Metro-Goldwyn's film *Letty Lynton* infringed a copyrighted play entitled *Dishonored Lady*, Judge Hand famously wrote, "[I]t is enough that substantial parts [of the play] were lifted; no plagiarist can excuse the wrong by showing how much of his work he did not pirate."[19] Here, Judge Hand used the verb "to pirate" in a sense familiar to contemporary ears: to trespass upon a statutory copyright. That meaning has a long history stretching back to the nineteenth century and before. In 1839, Supreme Court Justice Joseph Story, sitting on the U.S. Circuit Court of Massachusetts, concluded in *Gray v. Russell* that the defendants had infringed the copyright in a revised edition of an old Latin grammar. Likening the modified grammar to an improved map that enjoys copyright protection by virtue of the skill and labor that have gone into updating public domain materials, Justice Story observed that it would be "downright piracy" to copy the whole of the revised map.[20] Copyright piracy could occur in a variety of forms, added Story. For example, "if in one of the large encyclopaedias of the present day, the whole or a large portion of a scientific treatise of another author … should be incorporated, it would be just as much a piracy upon the copyright, as if it were published in a single volume." Like Judge Hand, Justice Story was using "piracy" in its familiar modern sense: the invasion of an enforceable, state-supplied legal right.

Throughout the nineteenth century, however, running alongside this sense of *piracy* was another meaning of the word: the unauthorized copying of works that were *not* protected by copyright in the United States. This seemingly paradoxical usage was mostly reserved for impugning American reprinters who took advantage of Congress's refusal to grant copyright protection to foreign authors. It is this meaning that Andrew Lang intended when he questioned Thomas Bird Mosher's honor for "pirating" his translation of *Aucassin et Nicolete*. Joining forces with Lang in the pages of *The Academy*, the English poet and critic Lionel Johnson leveled the additional charge that Mosher had "perpetrated a triple piracy" two years earlier when he issued an unauthorized reprint of one of Johnson's essays together with Robert Bridges' sonnet sequence *The Growth of Love* under the "emblem and imprint" used by Bridges' Oxford publisher.[21] It was no consolation that Mosher professed admiration for the essay. "I would beg Mr. Mosher to cease paying sugared compliments to his victims," Johnson wrote. "If a footpad steal my watch, I am not consoled by his approval of its merits."[22] This doubly false analogy—comparing the lawful use of an intangible work to the unlawful taking of tangible property—was typical of the rhetoric of outraged authorship in this period. As Catherine Seville has shown, the moralistic use of such terms as *pirate* and *footpad* to describe the lawful reprinting of unprotected literature became increasingly intense as the nineteenth century wore on and the call for congressional action to protect foreign authors grew more strident.[23]

Pirate, footpad, gentleman of the road—all were epithets that, when accurately employed, condemned actual criminal activity on land or the high seas. The theft of a watch was, and still is, a crime against property. Highway robbery was defined as a crime against the person as well as against property because typically it involved harm or a threat of imminent harm to the victim. Yet the Pirate of Portland had committed no such offenses and had infringed no copyrights in reprinting Johnson's essay and Bridges' sonnet sequence. The works he published in his Old World and English Reprint series lay squarely in the American public domain, and not by some quirk of legislative negligence. Congress had intended that they be there.

The express lack of protection for foreign authors' works had been inscribed into the law as early as the first federal copyright act of 1790: "[N]othing in this act shall be construed to extend to prohibit the importation or vending, reprinting, or publishing within the United States, of any map, chart, book or books, written, printed, or published by any person not a citizen of the United States, in foreign parts or places without the jurisdiction of the United States."[24] This provision, which Meredith L. McGill has called an "extraordinary license [for] the unrestricted republication of foreign texts,"[25] was as unequivocal as it was expansive. No map, chart, or book produced by a non-U.S. citizen or nonresident was protected by copyright within the United States, and the act forbade any contrary construction of its language. Quite simply, Americans were permitted, even encouraged, to import, reprint, publish, or sell foreign works without the permission of their authors or publishers. The law did nothing less than immunize acts that, if committed on U.S. soil against American authors enjoying copyright protection, could have resulted in damages and fines along with forfeiture and destruction of infringing copies.[26]

Over the course of the nineteenth century, Congress enhanced the rights and remedies of American authors but continued to withhold protection from foreign authors. (U.S. patent law, in contrast, was friendlier to foreign inventors.)[27] A revision of the copyright law in 1831 sharpened the text of the 1790 act to stress that no copyright protection existed for any person not "a citizen of the United States nor resident within the jurisdiction thereof."[28] A major revision of 1870 repeated the language of the previous acts and expanded the legal disability of foreign authors to include any "dramatic or musical composition, print, cut, engraving, or photograph."[29] Here the law stood until the passage of the Chace Act of 1891, which at last extended copyright protection, conditionally, to foreign authors, as discussed below.

During the nineteenth century, accusations of piracy of foreign works often carried a double and shifting valence. On one level, critics might be assailing the particular American publisher responsible for an unauthorized reprint, as Andrew Lang and Lionel Johnson were in protesting the activities of Mosher. On another level, critics might be attacking Congress or the nation itself for failing to protect foreign authors. Protests sometimes blurred the target, making it unclear whether the inertia of politicians or the moral failing of businessmen was more to blame. The ambivalence can be seen in an 1888 essay by the publisher Henry Holt, who, on the one hand, pointed to "the overwhelming competition of foreign stolen goods which our laws encourage" and, on the other, blamed "pirate" publishers who sought to excuse their conduct "because their proceedings are within the law."[30] Some critics distinguished more sharply between legislative and individual responsibility. Though a strong advocate of copyright protection for foreign authors, Samuel Clemens conceded in testimony before a U.S. Senate committee on patents in 1886 that it was wrong to accuse American reprinters of dishonesty:

> I do consider that those persons who are called "pirates" ... were made pirate by the collusion of the United States Government.... Congress, if anybody, is to blame for their action. It is not dishonesty. They have that right, and they have been working under that right a long time, publishing what is called "pirated books." They have invested their money in that way, and they did it in the confidence that they would be supported and no injustice done them.[31]

Clemens recognized, pragmatically, that the American publishing industry had grown up under conditions created by the copyright law and that a dramatic change in the law would undoubtedly upset settled expectations.

Like Clemens, British commentators sometimes took the position that American publishers should not be assailed for simply acting in conformity with the law of the land. The London publisher Grant Richards, charmed by Mosher's attractive and scholarly reprints, wrote,

> It is difficult to see why the word "pirate" should be used in any oppro-
> brious sense, since all that he did was to avail himself of his legal rights.
> Besides, much of what Mosher printed was "chosen from scarce editions
> and from sources not generally known," while at all times he used material
> that was, according to the law of his country, within the public domain.[32]

The English writer Richard Le Gallienne went even further and declared that it seemed to him "mere childishness ... to complain if some one exercises his undoubted legal right of taking a fancy to [an uncopyrighted work]. Actually, I rejoice no little that so much exquisite literature would seem to have been thus left unprotected."[33] In essence, Richards and Le Gallienne, like Clemens, were insisting on the disambiguation of the term *pirate*, refusing to impute ethical impropriety where no criminal or civil liability could be charged. The American copyright authority Eaton S. Drone summed up these exonerating distinctions in his 1879 treatise:

> In the law of copyright, piracy is the use of literary property in violation of
> the legal rights of the owner.... [I]t is not piracy to take without authority
> either a part or the whole of what another has written, if neither a stat-
> ute nor the common law is thereby violated.... Hence, there may be an
> unauthorized appropriation of literary property which is neither piracy
> nor plagiarism, as the republication in the United States of the work of a
> foreign author. This is not piracy, because no law is violated; and, without
> misrepresentation as to authorship, it is not plagiarism.[34]

Many American reprinters could not accurately be called pirates or plagiarists. Yet those who persisted in railing against pirate reprinters swept away such distinctions in their indignation. The rhetoric of piracy in the nineteenth century was burdened with the outrage of these moralists, and the system of trade courtesy added further lexical freight, as shown below.

## Lawful American Book Piracy in the Nineteenth Century

Throughout the nineteenth century, protests against so-called Yankee pirates issued from both sides of the Atlantic.[35] By the 1830s, the practice of reprinting British books and periodicals without permission had become widespread in the American book trade. A decade earlier, the recently founded Harper publishing house in New York was already competing with the Carey firm of Philadelphia for *Guy Mannering, Kenilworth, The Pirate*, and other popular novels by Sir Walter Scott.[36] The Harper editions of Scott's unprotected novels sold in America for a fraction of the price charged in Britain and gained a wider readership than they enjoyed abroad.[37] The reprinting of British titles was both a business and a game, an exuberant scramble to exploit a large and utterly free resource.[38] Over the years, many popular British writers were seized upon—Tennyson, Thackeray, the Brownings, George Eliot, Thomas Carlyle, Edward Bulwer-Lytton, and Wilkie Collins, to name just a few.

Charles Dickens was a fiercely contested prize. Hundreds of thousands of pirated copies of his works circulated in the United States.[39] In the frenzied competition for new English fiction among the weekly and daily periodicals of the 1830s and 1840s, firms like Harpers that regarded themselves as Dickens's authorized publishers retaliated by issuing his novels in unbound parts at twelve-and-a-half cents and six cents.[40] In 1842, the year of his first American tour, Dickens denounced the "scoundrel-booksellers" who "grow rich [in the United States] from publishing books, the authors of which do not reap one farthing from their issue," along with the "vile, blackguard, and detestable newspaper[s]" that also reprinted British writings without authorization or remuneration.[41] Writing to Dickens in the same year, Thomas Carlyle adopted decalogic tones to express his disgust with American pirates: "That thou belongest to a different 'Nation' and canst steal without being certainly hanged for it, gives thee no permission to steal. Thou shalt not in any wise steal at all! So it is written down for Nations and for Men, in the Law Book of the Maker of this Universe."[42]

Carlyle was not the only author to appeal to God's law for the confounding of rascally reprinters. Later in the century, the American poet James Russell Lowell put his frustration with book piracy into a single uncompromising quatrain, which became the motto of the American Copyright League and the chant of advocates of international copyright:

> In vain we call old notions fudge,
> And bend our conscience to our dealing;
> The Ten Commandments will not budge,
> And stealing will continue stealing.[43]

Even Walt Whitman, usually a lyrical advocate of the interests of American multitudes, lamented his compatriots' exploitation of British authors:

> Do not our publishers fatten quicker and deeper? (helping themselves, under shelter of a delusive and sneaking law, or rather absence of law, to most of their forage, poetical, pictorial, historical, romantic, even comic, without money and without price—and fiercely resisting the timidest proposal to pay for it.)[44]

Like Henry Holt, Whitman trained his criticism on two targets, the "delusive and sneaking law" and the publishers that gorged themselves on free literary "forage," without deciding which was the more culpable.

In the latter part of the nineteenth century, American publishers continued to be aggressive in reprinting popular British authors without authorization and often without payment. In the fierce competition for foreign titles in the 1880s, which led to the overproduction of cheap paper-covered books and a ruinous glutting of the market, Robert Louis Stevenson's uncopyrighted works were widely reproduced, as were Mrs. Humphry Ward's *Robert Elsmere* and Rider Haggard's *Cleopatra*, the latter appearing in ten different editions.[45] When Holt published an authorized edition of *The Mayor of Casterbridge* in 1886, he assured Thomas Hardy that although the market was overrun with pirates, "[w]e will do the best we can with it in these distressing times when it seems next to impossible to do anything with anything."[46] Alexander Grosset brought out a string of unprotected works by Rudyard Kipling in 1899, including *Barrack Room Ballads, Departmental Ditties, and Other Ballads and Verses*; *The Light That Failed*; *The City of Dreadful Night*; *Child Stories*; *The Vampire*; and several of his popular poems done up as booklets selling for fifteen cents a copy. As

Grosset's partner George T. Dunlap later explained, the young firm justified this spate of titles on the seemingly paradoxical ground that these already uncopyrighted works had become a kind of "public property . . . having been reprinted indiscriminately by about everyone else in the business."[47]

Oscar Wilde learned that he was the victim of American pirates while on his famous lecture tour of the United States in 1882. A 10 cent edition of his *Poems*, printed together with his lecture on the English Renaissance, had appeared in a pamphlet in George P. Munro's Seaside Library. Imitations of Munro's edition quickly appeared. Wilde complained to the American press that "in all your [railroad] cars I find newsmen selling my poems—stolen! I never can resist the impulse to read out a lesson on the heinousness of the offense." What concerned him most was that the piracies were eroding attendance at his lectures: "'The English Renaissance' is printed in the 'Sea Side,'" he lamented, "so people think they know it and stay away."[48] Yet the piracies also helped to spread Wilde's fame. He earned thousands of dollars as his share of the tour receipts.[49]

W. B. Yeats, too, was pirated during his lecture tour of America in 1903–4. Mosher, who reprinted Yeats's *The Land of Heart's Desire* through several unauthorized editions, issued a 1903 text of the play in his Lyric Garland Series, for which he claimed to have had Yeats's consent. The success of the Irish author's tour, which netted him over three thousand dollars, had been helped by the circulation of his play, though he apparently received no ex gratia payment from Mosher.[50] Others pirated Yeats as well, at least through 1926: Walter H. Baker, The Thomas Y. Crowell Co., The Little Leather Library Corp. of New York, and The Shrewsbury Publishing Co.[51]

Literary piracy in nineteenth-century America was a complex activity intimately bound up with legitimate publishing and the copyright law. As one commentator put it in 1882, piracy was "the product of law."[52] Respectable houses and pirate firms were not always distinguishable. Just as the U.S. copyright acts of 1790, 1831, and 1870 openly encouraged the unauthorized reprinting of foreign authors, so reprinting was an enabling condition of much legitimate publishing in the United States. Not only did the low overhead of reprinting underwrite publishers' more expensive, authorized undertakings; promiscuous freebooting allowed many startup firms to acquire lists and capital that propelled them to power and respectability. The profits from reprinting Kipling helped build the financial foundation of Grosset & Dunlap.[53] The Harper firm, which came to dominate the American

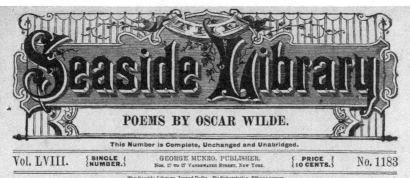

## Seaside Library

### POEMS BY OSCAR WILDE.

**This Number is Complete, Unchanged and Unabridged.**

| Vol. LVIII. | { SINGLE } { NUMBER.} | GEORGE MUNRO, PUBLISHER, Nos. 17 to 27 VANDEWATER STREET, NEW YORK. | { PRICE } { 10 CENTS.} | No. 1183 |

The Seaside Library, Issued Daily.—By Subscription, $36 per annum.
Copyrighted 1882, by GEORGE MUNRO.—Entered at the Post Office at New York at Second Class Rates.—January 19, 1882.

# Poems by Oscar Wilde.

ALSO, HIS LECTURE ON THE ENGLISH RENAISSANCE.

## THE POEMS.

ELEUTHERIA:—
  Sonnet to Liberty.
  Ave Imperatrix.
  To Milton.
  Louis Napoleon.
  Sonnet on the Massacre of the Christians in Bulgaria.
  Quantum Mutata.
  Libertatis Sacra Fames.
  Theoretikos.
THE GARDEN OF EROS.
ROSA MYSTICA:—
  Requiescat.
  Sonnet on approaching Italy.
  San Miniato.
  Ave Maria plena Gratia.
  Italia.
  Sonnet written in Holy Week at Genoa.
  Rome Unvisited.
  Urbs Sacra Æterna.
  Sonnet on hearing the Dies Iræ sung in the Sistine Chapel.

Easter Day.
E Tenebris.
Vita Nuova.
Madonna Mia.
The New Helen.
THE BURDEN OF ITYS.
IMPRESSION DU MATIN.
MAGDALEN WALKS.
ATHANASIA.
SERENADE.
ENDYMION.
LA BELLA DONNA DELLA MIA MENTE
CHANSON.
CHARMIDES.
IMPRESSIONS. I. Les Silhouettes.
            II. La Fuite de la Lune.
THE GRAVE OF KEATS.
THEOCRITUS: A VILLANELLE.
IN THE GOLD ROOM: A HARMONY.
BALLADE DE MARGUERITE.
THE DOLE OF THE KING'S DAUGHTER.
AMOR INTELLECTUALIS.

SANTA DECCA.
A VISION.
IMPRESSION DU VOYAGE.
THE GRAVE OF SHELLEY.
BY THE ARNO.
IMPRESSIONS DU THEATRE:—
  Fabien di Franchi.
  Phèdre.
  Portia.
  Henrietta Maria.
  Camma.
PANTHEA.
IMPRESSION: LE REVEILLON.
AT VERONA.
APOLOGIA.
QUIA MULTUM AMAVI.
SILENTIUM AMORIS.
HER VOICE.
MY VOICE.
TÆDIUM VITÆ
HUMANITAD.
ΓΛΥΚΥΠΙΚΡΟΣ · ΕΡΩΣ

NEW YORK:
## GEORGE MUNRO, PUBLISHER
17 to 27 VANDEWATER STREET.

**Figure 1.2** Pirate reprint of Wilde's *Poems*, New York, Seaside Library, 1882. *(Courtesy Merlin Holland)*

publishing scene, was well known for its early piratical aggressions, selling British reprints at much lower prices than in England, where lending libraries depressed sales and raised prices.[54] As McGill has shown, a decentralized reprint industry in the antebellum years reflected the republican ideals of cultural diffusion and widespread learning, fostering a depersonalized print culture at the expense of individual authors' rights.[55] Legislators built piracy into the copyright law as a way of accommodating the democratic values of "ready access to literature, information, education, and other conduits for achieving equality of opportunity."[56]

Much later in the century, the energetic New York publisher John W. Lovell, who had openly defied trade courtesy and become known as "Book-A-Day Lovell" for the millions of inexpensive copies he issued each year, formed a "book trust" of cheap reprinters, called the United States Book Co., with the objective of establishing uniform prices and discounts and stabilizing the chaotic competition in cheap foreign reprints.[57] The Lovell book trust thus sought to accomplish by overt cartel behavior what trade courtesy had achieved through less formal methods. Indeed, so destructive had the competition in cheap reprints become during the 1880s that Lovell and others briefly tried to carry on a kind of trade courtesy among themselves, paying honoraria to foreign authors and royalties on copyrighted American works. Although the book trust was short-lived, *The Publishers' Weekly* wrote,

> From a "predatory" beginning—in this respect not much unlike many who consider themselves their betters—the Lovells have gradually worked their way up from indifferently-made to better-made novels; from pirated work to books published by arrangement with foreign authors and publishers, and to American copyright literature.[58]

Once established, Lovell—in this respect like Mosher—adopted the graces of the courtesy publishers, entering into agreements with foreign authors, obtaining advance sheets, and paying honoraria. Lovell's uninhibited publication of cheap books in his salad days, called piracy by established publishers, had laid the foundation for his later prosperity and ambitions.

Piracy was more than an enabling condition of legitimate publishing, however; it was also a necessary condition of American literary culture in the nineteenth century. Throughout much of the century, the United States was a net importer of works of fiction, and British books were eagerly sought by an increasingly literate populace.[59] Publishers and book manufacturers depended on a flow of production that might be impeded "unless there was a reservoir of English works to draw upon when the American streams ran dry."[60] According to David Saunders, the Harper firm's first catalogue contained 234 titles of which ninety percent were English reprints, "the same pattern being true for Wiley and for Putnam."[61] Prior to the Civil War, approximately fifty percent of all fiction best sellers in America were unauthorized foreign works.[62] The Report of the 1876–78 Royal British Commission on Copyrights observed, "[T]he original works published in America are, as yet, less numerous than those published in Great Britain. This naturally affords a temptation to the Americans to take advantage of the works of the older country, and at the same time tends to diminish the inducement to publish original works."[63] The commission was especially concerned that American publishers were able to issue British books "at cheap rates to a population of forty millions, perhaps the most active readers in the world."[64]

The cheap libraries launched by American publishers in the 1880s give an idea of the dominance of British fiction in the United States only a few years before Congress enacted international copyright reform. Brander Matthews, a strong proponent of copyright protection for foreign authors, reported that of the fifty-four numbers of Harper & Brothers' Franklin Square Library published in 1886, only one was by an American author. Forty-six of the fifty-three foreign-authored numbers were works of fiction. Of the sixty-two numbers issued in Harper's Handy Series in the same year, fifty-eight were by foreign authors, and fifty-two of these were fiction.[65] Volumes in these series sold for twenty or twenty-five cents each.[66] Observing that books published in the United States on other subjects, such as law, science, and theology, were mostly authored by Americans and were therefore protected by copyright, Matthews concluded that passage of a reform bill would "remove the premium of cheapness which now serves to make the American public take imported novels instead of native wares" and would reduce the "well-nigh exclusive diet of English fiction full of the feudal ideas and superstitions and survivals of which we have been striving for a century to rid ourselves."[67] During the late 1880s, the popularity of foreign novels noticeably declined, and the number of copyrighted American books spiked, due in part to a change in popular taste and to the poor quality of foreign reprints.[68] But even after Congress added international copyright protections in 1891, fiction by foreign authors remained a powerful presence. In 1895, foreign authors still accounted for eight of the top ten best sellers in the United States, though this changed by 1910, when nine of the top ten were authored by Americans.[69]

## The Cultural Commons and the Public Goods Problem

The 1790 copyright act was captioned "An act for the encouragement of learning, by securing the copies of maps, charts, and books, to the authors and proprietors of such copies, during the times therein mentioned."[70] The statute's grant of federal copyrights aimed to stimulate American authorship, while its creation of a copyright vacuum for foreign authors no less clearly benefited American publishers, printers, and book manufacturers, together with readers who could purchase foreign works at a fraction of the original cost. Both of these congressional fiats—the giving and the withholding of copyright protection—encouraged learning in the United States, the first by offering a stimulus to creativity, the second by providing incentives and windfalls to the reprint trade. These two faces of copyright law were defining features of the American public domain from its inception.

Although meanings of the term vary, the public domain may be defined, for present purposes, as the common pool of works that are not protected by copyright in a given country, either because they were created before the advent of copyright laws or because the copyrights they once enjoyed have naturally expired or because they have prematurely forfeited or do not qualify for copyright protection. The 1790 act and subsequent acts of Congress primarily drew upon two of these approaches for creating the American public domain. The first was to grant to American authors copyrights that would eventually expire. Under the 1790 act, federal copyrights in works by U.S. citizens and residents endured for a maximum of twenty-eight years from the recording of the work's title in a district court.[71] (Later enactments increased this term.) The second approach was expressly to deny copyrights to foreign-authored works from their inception; these works lacked copyright protection whether they were "written, printed, or published."[72] Thus, the American public domain was, from the beginning, a two-tiered resource consisting largely of expired copyrights and withheld copyrights.

Economists and legal scholars refer to intangible, infinitely reproducible things, such as works of authorship, as public goods. Other examples of public goods are air, fireworks, lighthouses, and national defense; as with authors' writings, the benefits offered by these things can be shared by many persons without being depleted. By their nature, public goods are nonexcludable and nonrivalrous—that is, they cannot be fenced off in the manner of private property, and one person's consumption of a public good does not prevent a second person from consuming the same good. Paul A. Samuelson classically defined public goods as *"collective consumption goods ... which all enjoy in common in the sense that each individual's consumption of such a good leads to no subtraction from any other individual's consumption of that good."*[73] Wendy J. Gordon has noted that intangible works of authorship are public goods that are "susceptible to freeriding, and thus difficult to produce in a normal competitive market."[74] A public goods problem arises when free riding becomes so prevalent that the producer of the good loses the incentive to continue to produce it—a consequence that economists refer to as a type of market failure. In recent years, the recording industry has frequently raised the specter of market failure by warning that if unlawful online file sharing continues unchecked, musicians and record companies will simply cease creating and recording music; they will have no incentive to continue producing what they cannot control. Intellectual property laws can be viewed as attempts to prevent market failure by placing an invisible legal fence around the intrinsically open and unbounded public good of authorship.[75]

To the extent that nineteenth-century authors may be said to have produced public goods, unauthorized reprinting of their writings may be viewed as a vast free rider problem (or an easy rider problem, since reprinting involved printing costs and other overhead). But if reprinters free rode so heavily on foreign authors, why did those authors continue to write and publish? In part because the copyright laws of their own countries solved free rider problems for their publishing markets, allowing them to capture the domestic benefits of their labors. Although free or easy riding was rampant in the United States, foreign authors could live with those losses. They might hope for ex gratia payments from American publishers and complain bitterly about scoundrel reprinters, but American piracies did not undermine their incentives to create so long as they could look to their own markets for remuneration. Such an arrangement was irresistible to American publishers: they had access to a free, valuable, and continuously replenished resource that no amount of exploitation could noticeably deplete. The American public domain was parasitic in this regard; it annexed a vast free resource of foreign innovation without running the risk of losing that resource through failure to incentivize it. With respect to the creation of foreign works, the public domain was not haunted by the public goods problem.

But publishers, too, are producers; like authors, they require economic incentives to go on producing. Why would a publishing firm in New York invest in advance sheets of a Dickens novel when a firm across town or in Philadelphia could free or easy ride by bringing out a competing edition within a few days? The publishing industry faced this public goods problem throughout the nineteenth century; reprinting spawned reprinting, and publishers had no more legal recourse against each other than foreign authors had against them. Why, then, did the threat of uncontrolled reprinting not result in widespread market failure within the American publishing industry and the early abandonment of foreign literature as a profitable good?

This question was of critical importance to publishers. What the commons gave them, the commons might easily take away by eroding their incentives to go to the expense of reprinting foreign works. Competing editions of the same uncopyrighted work might result in ruinous price-cutting that would drive revenues down below the point at which a reasonable profit could be extracted. Unrestrained predatory pricing of cheap reprints threatened to tear the American publishing industry apart in the 1840s, and it resulted in a sharp decline in the reprinting of foreign works in the late 1880s.[76] How could publishers regulate this resource so as to make it a paying commons? The answer, intricately and ingeniously evolved over the nineteenth century, was the courtesy of the trade.

## Regulating the Cultural Commons: The Law of Courtesy

Looking back over forty years of American publishing, Henry Holt in 1893 laconically defined the courtesy of the trade as the duty "[n]ot to jump another publisher's claim."[77] A few years earlier, he had been more expansive. "[T]here grew up," he wrote, "between, say, 1850 and 1876, the unwritten law ... of 'trade courtesy.' It not only prevented ruinous competition between American publishers, but also secured to foreign authors most of their rights."[78] Trade courtesy, in its fully developed form, thus had a horizontal and a vertical axis. By requiring participating publishers to respect the claim of the first publisher to announce its intention to reprint a foreign title, courtesy horizontally regulated what might otherwise have disintegrated into destructive competition for the new foreign work. Holt acknowledged that this aspect of the courtesy system was "simply the result of an enlightened self-interest."[79] Vertically, the system ordered relations between American publishers and foreign authors by encouraging payments to the authors or their publishers. Again, self-interest was at work. Payments helped cement relationships with foreign authors and signaled to other publishers that the paying firm was a responsible member of the trade. What is most immediately striking about trade courtesy is that it was an unwritten law, an entirely voluntary system of informal norms that mimicked the basic features and purposes of copyright law. Courtesy evolved a complex set of exclusive rights, rules for securing those rights, and sanctions for violating them. These synthetic rights helped to regulate the American public domain and stabilize the book market during much of the nineteenth century.

Holt praised trade courtesy as a system that grew to possess "the essential features of an International Copyright Law," despite the "gaps and defects" that were typical of "all usages, and for that matter ... all laws."[80] A few years earlier, the Harper firm had acknowledged that courtesy "has enabled American publishers to grant to foreign authors many of the benefits which would accrue to them under the operation of a copyright treaty."[81] In 1855, the Board of Music Trade of the United States of America, which had been established to bring order to the volatile American market for sheet music, organized a form of courtesy by which music publishers agreed to refrain from reprinting uncopyrighted music that had previously been issued by a participating publisher. This practice, observed the *New-York Musical Review and Gazette*, "is supposed to place copyright, or American compositions, on an equal business footing with non-copyright, or foreign compositions, inasmuch as the latter will hereafter have but one publisher instead of half a dozen or more, as formerly."[82] Trade courtesy encouraged participants to treat publishers' prior claims to foreign works as a kind of virtual property, on the basis of which firms could invest in the production of books and music, make contracts with authors and with each other, and transfer "rights" in the works to which they held courtesy title. The practice bridged the protection gap created by U.S. copyright law, but no American court ever treated these norms as actual legal entitlements. A court in 1865 noted that the system confessedly rests upon no common law of the country, recognized and administered by judicial tribunals. If it has any foundation at all, it stands on the mere will, or ... the "courtesy" of the trade.... It can, therefore, hardly be called property at all—certainly not in any sense known to the law.[83]

Yet within the charmed circle of participants, the courtesy claim of one publisher, if properly secured, was recognized as a kind of property. Some scholars trace the origins of American trade courtesy to the self-regulating practices of Irish publishers prior to the extension of English copyright law to Ireland in 1801.[84] Similar norms-based observances are known to have existed in Scotland in the eighteenth and early nineteenth centuries before English works were protected by copyright there.[85] Even in England, regulated cartels, referred to as printing congers, arose to protect publishers' vested interests in uncopyrighted works by Shakespeare, Henry Fielding, Samuel Johnson, and other authors.[86] After the enactment of the Statute of Anne in 1709, which conferred limited statutory terms of copyright, some English publishers continued to trade and hold shares in perpetual common law copyrights, as if these had never been abolished by Parliament's enactment.[87] Other publishers were permitted, by courtesy, to ignore the expiration of a work's copyright after its statutory term and to continue to print the book as their exclusive property.[88] Well into the nineteenth century a few English publishers observed a kind of courtesy with respect to books by American authors, though the system was not as cohesive and efficient as its American counterpart, and American books that had been paid for by one English publisher were, "in a large number of cases, promptly reissued in cheaper rival editions by other houses."[89] A common feature of all these extralegal practices is that they took place within close-knit communities that shared economic interests.

Scholars in various disciplines have noted that informal, norms-based conservation of common resources has succeeded best within relatively small, cohesive groups.[90] Notable examples include the norms and sanctions that have evolved within the community of Maine lobstermen—particularly the lobstermen of Matinicus Island, twenty miles off Maine—to preserve customary trapping boundaries. Local customs and practices, not law, have fixed the areas where lobster traps may be employed as well as the number of traps that may be set. Lobstermen's informal rules range from cutting trap lines on traps set by unauthorized outsiders to notching the tails of egg-bearing female lobsters in order to conserve the lobster population.[91]

Today, as in nineteenth-century America, informal norms operate within certain defined communities to fill lacunae within intellectual property laws. For example, the lack of copyright protection for chefs' recipes and preparations has given rise to a collection of social norms within the culinary industry. These informal rules are uniform and strictly observed: a chef must not copy another chef's recipe exactly; if a chef reveals a secret recipe to a colleague, that colleague must not pass the secret on to others without permission; and chefs must give credit to the developers of significant recipes or techniques.[92] Stand-up comedy is another area in which scholarship has unearthed a community governed by informal rules. Here, social norms—including rules for establishing the priority of gags, prohibitions on copying premises and punch-lines, and shaming sanctions for violators—have taken the place of formal, enforceable laws.[93] Fashion design is yet another industry that has evolved an informal, norms-based system of entitlements and sanctions.[94]

In each of these industries—culinary art, stand-up comedy, and fashion design—the absence or inadequacy of legal protections has stimulated a close-knit community to establish a framework of informal rules and punishments that allows the community to police itself and to manage an essentially free, common-pool resource of intangible, easily copied creations. This is precisely what American publishers did in the nineteenth century when they developed the consensual system of trade courtesy. The community of participating publishers was a small, cohesive one. Although estimates vary, the extant correspondence of Charles Scribner's Sons reveals that at least nine major publishing firms, in addition to Scribner's, observed the principles of courtesy during the 1870s: J. B. Lippincott & Co., J. R. Osgood & Co., D. Appleton & Co., Roberts Brothers, G. P. Putnam's Sons, Harper & Brothers, Macmillan & Co., E. P. Dutton & Co., and Henry Holt & Co.[95] Although other publishing houses dabbled in courtesy—Mosher, for example, employed some of its rules, as did certain cheap reprint houses during the chaotic competition of the 1880s—some firms did not. Novice publishers and small firms had strong incentives to resist the gentlemanly code and to reprint freely as a way of establishing book lists, and courtesy failed to gain a foothold in the aggressive cheap paper-book trade of the 1870s and 1880s.

The practice of courtesy is a vivid example of what Robert C. Ellickson has called "order without law," a system of folkways peculiar to a close-knit group or community in which informal norms have come to take the place of formal legal rules. Ellickson has argued that "[m]uch of the glue of a society comes not from law enforcement ... but rather from the informal enforcement of social mores by acquaintances, bystanders, trading partners, and others."[96] In rewarding conformity and punishing deviancy, American publishers employed the carrots and sticks of Ellickson's taxonomy of remedial norms. As "unofficial enforcers," they used "punishments such as negative gossip and ostracism to discipline malefactors and bounties such as esteem and enhanced trading opportunities to reward the worthy."[97] Ellickson grounds his conclusions in an empirical study of the norms used for dealing with animal trespass in rural Shasta County, California; "trespass conflicts," writes Ellickson, "are generally resolved not 'in the shadow of the law' but, rather, *beyond* that shadow. Most rural residents are consciously committed to an overarching norm of cooperation among neighbors."[98] Other scholars have explored the informal norms operating, for example, in the American cotton industry, the grain and feed industry, and the diamond trade in New York.[99]

Of course, the publishing world in the nineteenth century, though cohesive enough to evolve an extralegal code of conduct, was more heterogeneous and volatile than the close-knit rural community of Ellickson's study. And, unlike his resourceful cattlemen who employ flexible social mores as an alternative to unwieldy or unfamiliar legal remedies, American publishers did not have the luxury of choosing between informal norms and legal entitlements, since the foreign authors whom they reprinted enjoyed no legal entitlements at all in the United States. These publishers were confronted instead with a starker choice between informal self-regulation and no regulation at all. The choice was not between order with law and order without law, but, more fundamentally, between order and chaos. Anticipating Ellickson by eighty years, Henry Holt, a proud chronicler of courtesy, described it as "a brief realization of the ideals of philosophical anarchism— self-regulation without law."[100] Operating beyond the shadow of the law— indeed, in its absence—publishers sought to avert destructive competition by evolving informal modes of cooperating to manage a free, unprotected resource. With striking though intermittent success over the decades, the elaborate rules of courtesy staved off a public goods problem and a ruinous overuse of the commons of foreign works.

## Trade Courtesy: Entitlements

In its simplest outlines, the courtesy of the trade granted an informal exclusive right of publication to the first American publisher to announce plans to issue an uncopyrighted foreign book. Participating houses recognized this right and refrained from what they called "printing on" the announcing firm. Later, in order to ensure official notice, publishers agreed among themselves that the announcement had to be made in some recognized medium, and the *New York Commercial Advertiser* became the primary organ for "in press" announcements. *The Publishers' Weekly, The Weekly Trade Circular*, and other organs reprinted the *Commercial Advertiser's* announcements of forthcoming foreign books. Eager publishers began to exploit this notice mechanism, however, by announcing any title that seemed promising, whether it was actually in hand or only contemplated. To remedy such "courtesy creep,"[101] which was leading to simultaneous announcements and confusion over priority, the rule emerged that the announcing firm, to secure its rights, must actually have purchased advance sheets of the foreign edition for use as setting copy or have entered into an agreement with the author for permission to reprint. "If a publisher had the advance sheets in his possession, such right or claim overrode a simple announcement."[102] By supplementing its announcement with the purchase of advance sheets or an author's contract, the publisher perfected its otherwise bare title to the foreign work.

The rules of courtesy recognized fastidious distinctions. The mere purchase of copies of a foreign edition did not secure an exclusive right to the American market; there was a difference between setting up an edition from advance sheets and importing books from abroad.[103] A firm looked more like a distributor than a publisher when it simply purchased premanufactured copies. No Locke-like property entitlements could be claimed by those who performed no real labor in the commons.[104] The perfection of courtesy rights did not always require the purchase of advance sheets, but some affirmative act beyond mere announcement had to be performed.

Only when an American publisher decided to take the risk of publishing a new or unknown foreign author was it permissible to rely on announcement alone; in such cases, other houses respected the publisher's willingness to try its luck with an uncertain prospect. Books by "new and uncertain authors," explained Holt, "are a field for experiment, and if a publisher concluded that one was worth experimenting with, though not worth paying for in advance of experiment, the rights from first announcement were intended to secure him the fruits of his experiment, if successful."[105] Here, risk and adventure played the role that honoraria and author agreements ordinarily played in securing courtesy title. A further advantage was that the experimenting firm might obtain a right to the author's future books.[106] Simultaneous announcements in such cases were settled by arrangement between the competing houses.

Trade courtesy also developed a kind of option system, based on what the trade referred to as the rule of association. Once an American publisher reprinted a foreign title and paid its author, it was generally understood that the author was associated with that house, which could then expect to have the first refusal of the author's next effort. For example, after William D. Ticknor built a claim to Tennyson's *Poems* in 1842, other publishers respected the Boston firm's right to publish Tennyson's later works.[107] Houses that observed trade courtesy usually resisted the temptation to interfere with other houses' associations. Ticknor & Fields, the authorized American publisher of Robert Browning, would gladly have added Elizabeth Barrett Browning to its list but recognized the superior claim of her New York publisher, C. S. Francis & Co. Reluctant to meddle with a prior claim, Ticknor & Fields wryly remarked to Robert Browning, "We are a funny set of christians over the waves."[108] Joseph Henry Harper recalled publishers' punctilio in matters of association: "An offer received by a publisher from an author already identified with another house was by courtesy first submitted to the house which had already published the author's works, and publishers abstained from entering into competition for books which were recognized as the special province of another house."[109] There were additional refinements. For example, if a publisher reprinted the work of an untried author as an experiment, the publisher would have the refusal of the author's later books only if it made satisfactory payment to the author for the first publication.[110]

With variations, the foregoing rules evolved over time into a coherent and elaborate system of informal property norms. Holt noted the system's law-like imbrication of rules and subrules: "Trade courtesy is as full of exceptions as the law itself. It has grown up as a mass of decisions in particular cases, just as the common law has."[111] Fully developed, courtesy provided bright-line rules for securing title to foreign works by announcement; a method for recording claims in a recognized public medium, so that disputes over priority could be settled objectively; a basis for making payments to foreign authors or their publishers; and further rules for associating an author with a house by obtaining an option on his or her future work. As publishers recognized, this system imitated the broad features of copyright law: acquisition of exclusive publishing rights, registration of rights with a public authority, and payment of outright sums or royalties to copyright owners.

Publishers sometimes paid handsome, even extraordinary, sums for advance sheets of popular books. As early as the 1820s and 1830s, the Philadelphia firm of Carey & Lea was making payments to Sir Walter Scott or his publisher.[112] Scott received £75 for advance sheets of each of the Waverley novels and £300 for his *Life of Napoleon Bonaparte*.[113] In 1835, Harper & Brothers paid Bulwer-Lytton for early proofs "at the rate of £50 per volume of a new English novel, or £150 for the usual 'three decker.'"[114] In 1849, the Harpers brought out Thomas Babington Macaulay's famous *History of England, from the Accession of James II* after announcing the book and paying his English publisher £200 for first proofs.[115] The Harpers paid Charles Dickens £360 for *Bleak House*, £250 for *Little Dorrit*, £1,000 each for *A Tale of Two Cities* and *Our Mutual Friend*, £1,250 for *Great Expectations*, and £2,000 for the never-finished *Mystery of Edwin Drood*.[116] Until fierce competition from cheap reprints made it difficult to pay honoraria in the 1880s, the Appleton firm paid the Welsh author Rhoda Broughton a thousand dollars for each of her novels.[117] Writing to the Scottish novelist Mrs. Oliphant in 1873, the Harpers described the courtesy practice of purchasing advance sheets from foreign authors or their agents or publishers:

> In the absence of an international copyright, it is the custom for an English author, or his agent in London, to send early sheets to some American publisher, fixing a price therefor, and by a law of courtesy the American publisher who has issued the previous works of an author is entitled to the first consideration of that author's new book. If such publisher cannot arrange satisfactorily and upon reasonable terms for the book, obviously he cannot object to its offer to some of his neighbors. In many cases when the English authors send us early sheets of their books, and for some reason we fail to use them, we endeavor to sell them on the author's account to other American houses.[118]

The Harpers here touched on a further way in which courtesy approximated principles of copyright law: a publisher, once it had acquired courtesy title, enjoyed the power to transfer it.

Publishers frequently issued announcements that skillfully combined in press notices with advertising, thereby addressing fellow publishers and book buyers at the same time. In 1841, the publishers of the New York periodical *The New World* had "the pleasure to announce that they have purchased at great expense, the advance proof-sheets of the new Swedish novel by Frederika Bremer, translated by Mary Howitt, entitled The Home: or, Family Cares and Family Joys."[119] *Harper's New Monthly Magazine* in 1855 printed a notice stating that "Harper and Brothers have in press and will publish, from advance sheets," works by Sir Walter Scott, Anne Marsh-Caldwell, James Silk Buckingham, and Lady Holland.[120] In 1872, a prominent notice for Harper's Periodicals in the Boston monthly *The Literary World* stated that the firm had "secured the plates and advance sheets of 'London: A Pilgrimage,' by Gustave Doré and Blanchard Jerrold, a new and magnificent series of illustrations from the pencil of the great French artist."[121] In 1880, *The Literary News* announced that a "new novel by Rhoda Broughton, entitled 'Second Thoughts,' will be published by D. Appleton and Co. from advance sheets."[122] Publishers were at pains to stress that they paid their foreign authors, as in 1882 when J. B. Lippincott & Co. wrote the editors of *The Critic* that

> when what are known as the "trade courtesy rules" (still in force with all reputable publishers, but ignored by the "pirates") gave the authorized American publisher some protection in his ventures, we were enabled to pay large sums for the advance sheets of foreign books. For instance, we paid Ouida £300 for each of her novels, and we have paid as much for some of Geo. MacDonald's books, and of Bulwer's.[123]

Publishers in their advertisements and notices often emphasized the sum they had paid foreign authors. The mention of advance sheets or payment secured a publisher's courtesy title and signaled to other houses and to the public that the publisher was a reliable, rule-abiding firm.

Instead of paying up-front sums for advance sheets, publishing houses sometimes paid post hoc honoraria to authors whose books had made a success. Such after-the-fact gratuities were occasionally rejected, as when Lang rebuffed Mosher's suggestion of a "solatium." In other cases, authors welcomed honoraria as better than nothing. In 1836, the Carey firm of Philadelphia reprinted *Pickwick Papers* in an edition of fifteen hundred copies, sold at forty-five cents per volume. Two years later, the firm sent Dickens £50 in acknowledgment of the book's success.[124] George Haven Putnam observed, "[T]he author with no legal rights was thankful to get ten pounds when he could not get fifty and was very ready in receiving fifty to give a full quittance of any claim on the general proceeds."[125] Of course, the only so-called claim a foreign author might have was on the conscience and respectability of the reprinter. Legal claim there was none.

Later in the century, instead of honoraria for successful sales or initial payments for advance sheets, publishers began to offer foreign authors royalties on copies sold.[126] Sometimes authors would receive a smaller initial sum followed by a royalty on sales. If sales were insufficient to cover the publisher's costs, it was considered ethical to pay no royalty at all.[127] In 1867, the Boston publisher James T. Fields made Charles Dickens the unusual offer of a ten percent royalty on books and an arranged speaking tour if the celebrated author would make the firm his authorized American publisher.[128] Holt published numerous editions of Thomas Hardy's works in the 1870s and 1880s—several in the Leisure Hour Series—and paid ten percent royalties until widespread piracies made reprinting Hardy unprofitable.[129] In the 1870s, the Appleton firm arranged for royalty payments for the writings of the English novelist Charlotte M. Yonge. Again, courtesy imitated the formal copyright law: royalties were the usual form of payment to authors who controlled the exclusive rights conferred by copyright.

One of the benefits of association was that a firm could boast of being the authorized publisher of a foreign author. Such a relationship conferred respectability on the firm, lifting it up out of the mass of mere pirates and indicating to other publishers and to the purchasing public that the firm enjoyed the prestige of honorable dealings. Publishers frequently included letters or statements of authorization in their editions of foreign authors' works. A letter by Robert Browning appeared in Ticknor & Fields' edition of his *Dramatis Personae*, published in 1864. "I take advantage," he wrote, "of the opportunity of publication in the United States of my Poems, for printing which you have liberally remunerated me, to express my earnest desire that the power of publishing in America this and every subsequent work of mine may rest exclusively with your house."[130] In a single sentence, Browning assured readers that he had been paid by Ticknor & Fields and that he favored that house as the one with which he wished to be associated in the United States.

Ticknor & Fields' editions of Thomas De Quincey's writings reproduced a letter in which De Quincey authorized publication "exclusively" and acknowledged that the publisher had "made me a participator in the pecuniary profits of the American edition, without solicitation or the shadow of any expectation on my part, without any legal claim that I could plead, or equitable warrant in established usage, solely and merely upon your own spontaneous motion."[131] Similarly, in its 1891 edition of Rudyard Kipling's *Mine Own People*, the United States Book Co. included a facsimile letter in which the author affirmed that the edition "has my authority" and that he owed "to the courtesy of my American publishers that I have had the opportunity of myself preparing the present book."[132] The courtesy tradition of the authorization letter was a crucial component of Bennett Cerf's strategy for publishing James Joyce's *Ulysses* in America in the 1930s, as later chapters will show.

## Trade Courtesy: Punishments

Henry Holt, the most eloquent and persistent defender of trade courtesy, thought of it as a golden age of American publishing. The publishers who practiced courtesy, he averred, were inherently honest. For him, courtesy was less a system that publishers had forged for regulating their own cupidity than an expression of honor among better businessmen. None of the major publishers—Putnam, Appleton, Harper, Scribner—"would go for another's author any more than for his watch; or, if he had got entangled with another's author through some periodical or other outside right, would no more hold on to him than to the watch if the guard had got caught on a button."[133] With more ambivalence, Holt described nineteenth-century American publishing as "perhaps the greatest paradox in human experience.... At one end, its principal material was not protected by law, and the business lived to a large extent on what was morally, if not legally, thievery; while at the other end, there was honor among thieves, in the respect they paid each other's property."[134] Holt's paradox operated on several levels: American copyright law made pirates of honest men, so they banded together to act honorably according to voluntary norms of fairness that took the place of law. The "principal material" available to these businesses was a commons decreed by statute, yet it was a commons that publishers agreed to divide up and recognize as "each other's property." Here, thieves who were only acting as the law had bidden agreed to acknowledge property rights in a free resource. This unusual enclosure movement succeeded for much of the century in averting a crisis of the cultural commons.

Holt may have believed that courtesy was an embodiment of business virtue, but the courtesy system itself did not share the assumption that publishers, left to their own devices, would be good. Instead, along with rules for acquiring and maintaining exclusive rights, trade courtesy evolved a series of carefully calibrated penalties for transgressors. If informal exclusive rights to foreign titles were the carrots of the system, escalating sanctions were the sticks. These sanctions included, in order of increasing severity, mild remonstrance, angry protest, public shaming, refusal to deal, predatory pricing, and outright retaliation.

A gentlemanly rebuke, often expressed as a simple urbane inquiry, was the first step in enforcing exclusive courtesy rights. Holt and his associate Joseph Vogelius were quick to assert priority of claims. When the Harpers announced plans to reprint Hippolyte Taine's *On Intelligence* in 1870, Holt wrote the firm, "Doesn't the fact that we have published several of his books entitle us to that if we want it?"[135] The Harpers agreed to withdraw, acknowledging the rule of association whereby a publisher that had issued an author's earlier work was entitled to his or her later books. Four years later, Holt calmly objected when the Harpers planned to publish *The Return of the Native*, reminding Joseph Harper that Holt had been Hardy's authorized publisher in America. Harper again relented, and Holt later remarked that Harper had done "what the notions of honor then prevalent among publishers of standing required."[136]

Mild remonstrance became angry protest when a threat to courtesy persisted. A heated dispute arose between the Harper and Scribner firms in 1881 over James Anthony Froude's edition of Thomas Carlyle's *Reminiscences*. The Harpers claimed an arrangement with the late Carlyle himself; Scribner's insisted that Froude was its author and that, as Carlyle's executor, he had authorized the Scribner firm to publish the work. After bitter exchanges, the two houses issued their respective editions and then took to the trade journals.[137] The Harpers placed a full-page notice in *The Publishers' Weekly*, listing the works by Carlyle that they published and detailing the history of their dealings with Carlyle for *Reminiscences*. The Harpers reminded readers of the courtesy of the trade:

> The trade usage is familiar, and accepted by all the leading publishers of the country. It concedes to the house which has issued the works of an English author, either by agreement with him or with his English publishers, the option of republishing, upon mutually satisfactory terms, the subsequent works of the same author as they appear.[138]

The Scribner firm's reprinting of *Reminiscences*, charged the Harpers, "is a violation of our claim." Scribner's responded the following week with its own full-page notice in *The Publishers' Weekly*, pointing to arrangements with Froude and Carlyle's niece and noting that the firm had received advance sheets from Froude and had duly announced that the volume was in press. Invoking trade courtesy by name, Scribner's concluded, "The public will choose between this edition, put forth by the clearly expressed authority of Mr. Carlyle's executor, and a reprint from our sheets under a claim to which he has distinctly refused his acknowledgment."[139]

These public accusations were examples of a further courtesy sanction. Because private remonstrance had failed, the two houses resorted to the more severe punishment of public shaming, trading charges that their courtesy claims had been violated. The Boston firm of Roberts Brothers had used the same tactic a year earlier when John W. Lovell of New York brought out an edition of the poems of Jean Ingelow, an English writer who had been associated with Roberts Brothers for years. The Boston firm promptly took out advertisements to "Booksellers throughout the United States," reminding them that Roberts Brothers had been publishing Ingelow's poems ever since announcing the volume as in press in 1863 and that she had "received from us her copyright [that is, her royalty payment] semi-annually, precisely the same as though she were legally entitled to it." Not until now had anyone in "the entire fraternity of American Book Publishers" tried to "interfere." Roberts Brothers implored booksellers not to "sanction a moral wrong by vending this unauthorized version" but, rather, to "show their admiration for this beloved authoress by favoring only the Author's Editions, issued by her own publishers."[140] By broadcasting its disgust, Roberts Brothers had subjected the transgressor Lovell—whom they never needed to name in the notice—to public shaming.

A common form of shaming was to denounce an unauthorized publisher as a pirate. At the trial of a libel action brought by the publisher Isaac K. Funk against *The New York Evening Post* for having charged him with pirating the uncopyrighted *Encyclopedia Britannica*, Holt testified that "in the trade the words 'pirate' and 'thief' are freely applied to those who reprint books already equitably in the hands of other publishers, and that the effect of such reprinting by Dr. Funk was 'not favorable' to his reputation in the trade."[141] George Haven Putnam testified at the same proceeding that words like pirate had "been applied to appropriations of works of foreign authors, and were used by authors like Lowell and Stedman as well as publishers."[142] In charging the jury, the judge explained that if the *Post* had used "pirate" and "theft" in a "special sense"—that is, a sense current among practitioners of courtesy—then the jury could find that the *Post* had printed a "just criticism" and render a verdict for nominal damages.[143]

As the judge's instructions and the testimony of Holt and Putnam show, the word *pirate* had acquired a specialized meaning in the American publishing business. Instead of referring to a publisher who simply reprinted a foreign work without authorization, it signified deviancy from the norms of courtesy—specifically, the act of reprinting books "already equitably in the hands of other publishers." If the *Post* used "pirate" in this "special sense," then the newspaper was doing nothing more than joining publishers of good standing in publicly shaming a violator of the courtesy rules. Scholars of social norms refer to this kind of communal reprimand as "coordinated punishment" or "multilateral costly sanctions."[144] Ellickson calls it "negative gossip" and observes that, within close-knit communities bound by informal rules, shaming of this kind "usually works because only the extreme deviants are immune from the general obsession with neighborliness."[145] Practitioners of trade courtesy in the nineteenth century used negative gossip and public shaming to expose deviant pirates and to compel reform, thus contributing a specialized professional sense of "piracy" to the rhetoric of aggrieved authorship in the nineteenth-century. If the offenders would not mend their ways, then communal shaming might at least have the effect of encouraging others—publishers, booksellers, and purchasers—to engage in a further type of sanction: refusal to deal.[146] Multilateral refusal to carry on business with the transgressing firm would force it to conform or to take its chances as a pariah outside the publishing comity. As later chapters will show, the courtesy traditions of negative gossip and public shaming were seized upon by Joyce, T. S. Eliot, and other modernist figures to address the problem of transatlantic piracy.

Harsher than private protest or public shaming was the sanction of predatory pricing. If a firm "printed on" a publisher with a claim to priority, the latter would sometimes reissue the disputed title at a reduced price in an effort to undersell the pirate. Predatory pricing became common during the cheap book wars of the 1830s and 1840s and again in the 1870s and 1880s. In declining to interfere with C. S. Francis & Co.'s courtesy rights in Elizabeth Barrett Browning's works, Ticknor & Fields ruefully explained to Robert Browning in 1855 that such interference would cause Francis to "print at any rate, and at a cheaper rate, and perhaps set on our other books full chase, & try to injure us in every way."[147] The established houses would sometimes go to great expense to beat the prices of piratical reprinters. To combat the cheap paper-book libraries of the 1870s, Harper & Brothers launched its Franklin Square Library, offering reprints of backlist novels for ten cents a copy.[148] In 1879, Holt wrote that the Harpers "are, at considerable immediate cost to themselves we fear, fighting the pirates with their own weapons."[149] The Harpers and other firms would sometimes intentionally price their books so low that they could not recover their own costs, believing it would serve as a punishment to pirates to learn that their depredations had created a climate in which no one could profit.[150] "We determined," wrote the Harper firm in 1879, "that [the cheap reprinters] should not share our profits, because we intended that there should be no profit for a division. We began to print on ourselves."[151]

The severest punishment of all was reserved for the worst outrages against courtesy. This was the sanction of retaliation, occasionally employed even by publishers of the first rank when their rights were threatened by another house. Retaliation meant printing on a transgressor by issuing one or more of its foreign titles at a competitive price. The aggressive Harper firm often resorted to this form of reprisal, or threats of it. "If a publisher declined to comply with the requirements of trade courtesy," wrote Joseph Henry Harper, "some method would be adopted to discipline the offender—generally by the printing of lower-priced editions of his foreign reprints by his aggrieved competitor."[152] In 1871, the Harpers wrote to W. E. Tunis of Detroit that the courtesy right to George Eliot's *Middlemarch* "belongs to us alike for Canada and the U.S.—the right of both countries having been purchased by us," and that any interference would occasion "severe retaliation."[153] Retaliation could be devastating. In 1870, Harper & Brothers responded to a breach of courtesy on the part of Fields, Osgood & Co. by issuing an illustrated edition of Tennyson's works. When other publishers piled on by printing rival editions, a thirty-year relationship between Tennyson and the Fields firm was severely eroded.[154] The Harpers' reprisal triggered the very behavior that trade courtesy had been created to avoid.

Lisa Bernstein, in her work on the social norms employed in the American cotton industry, characterizes informal retaliations of this kind as "tit-for-tat strategies" that can often be "costly for the defected-against transactor to impose."[155] The punishment of printing on an offender was often the last resort for respectable houses because it could be so costly. Many firms of good standing avoided it as both distasteful and destructive of business relationships. Courtesy had been evolved to rid the industry of piratical behavior; resurrecting lawless conduct, even to make a point, threatened reputational harm and a return to anarchy. In 1881, despite his quarrel with the Harper firm over Carlyle's *Reminiscences*, Charles Scribner chose not to strike back by reprinting any Harper titles, hoping that "by not descending to blatant piracy he could establish the ethical superiority of his own firm in the minds of British writers."[156]

When a publisher proved to be a hopeless deviant from courtesy, utterly indifferent to the gentlemanly code, the sanctions of negative gossip, predatory pricing, and even retaliation had no effect. During the feverish cheap book competition of the 1870s and 1880s, such renegades became increasingly common, less interested in acquiring respectability and maintaining author associations than in free riding on the successful experiments of other firms. These pirates rarely offered royalties or honoraria to authors, printed in the cheapest formats, and exploited the publicity for which the first publisher had paid.[157] Such firms were often new entrants that had nothing immediately to gain by adhering to courtesy and little to lose by flouting it. The close-knit community of gentlemanly publishers unraveled at the edges when new or opportunistic firms saw a chance to build a list quickly at little cost to themselves.

## Trade Courtesy: Settlement and Arbitration

Although courtesy permitted aggrieved publishers to engage in retaliation and other unilateral and multilateral punishments, publishers often resolved their disputes amicably through informal settlements called adjustments.[158] Adjustments usually took the form of payments of compensation. For example, in 1860, the firm of Rudd & Carleton arranged to publish an English translation of Alexander von Humboldt's correspondence, only to learn that the Appletons had purchased advance sheets of the English edition and were about to issue the book. The Appletons agreed to cede the volume to Rudd & Carleton upon payment of £40—the sum the Appletons had already invested. With monetary adjustments, practitioners of trade courtesy improvised a type of remedy familiar to the law: compensation for a party's justifiable reliance on an apparently available resource or uncontested opportunity.

Adjustments could also be made in kind. Quarrelling publishers sometimes sank their differences by agreeing that one house would issue a regular cloth edition of a disputed title while the other would bring out the same work in an inexpensive paperbound format. If the contested book was one of a series, "the right to the title in question could be balanced against the right to succeeding volumes."[159] Ticknor & Fields and the Harper firm resolved their dispute over Dickens's *The Mystery of Edwin Drood* in kind rather than through monetary compensation: Ticknor & Fields issued the novel in book form, while the Harpers brought it out serially in *Harper's Weekly*.[160] Like monetary adjustments, adjustments in kind imitated formal legal dealings; they were the courtesy equivalent of copyright sublicensing. A copyright owner might grant one sublicense for serial rights, another for hardbound rights, and still another for paperback rights. American publishing houses accomplished this by informally divvying up the market for a disputed foreign title. The extant correspondence of Charles Scribner's Sons from the 1870s contains many references to such amicable adjustments.[161]

The modes of informal dispute-resolution employed by nineteenth-century American publishers resemble the extralegal ways in which sophisticated businesspersons in other industries sometimes agree to solutions that are not required by law. Bernstein has shown that American grain and feed merchants frequently resort to informal mechanisms that permit them to vary the terms of written contracts, sometimes out of "concern for relationships, trust, honor and decency, or fear of nonlegal sanctions such as reputational damage or termination of a beneficial relationship."[162] These practices have strong parallels in the norms-based behavior of nineteenth-century American publishers. The difference is that Bernstein's merchants choose to sidestep existing contract law in favor of informal terms and commitments, whereas nineteenth-century American publishers were faced with a choice between informal rules and no rules at all.

Finally, when publishers could not resolve disputes on their own, they would sometimes submit them to informal arbitration, "the contention being commonly left to a fellow-publisher for arbitrament."[163] Thus, trade courtesy provided for the resolution of disputes in an arbitral forum presided over by a neutral publisher who would apply courtesy rules or other equitable principles to bring peace to the disputants. In this respect as well, courtesy resembles the forms of private ordering among members of trade associations that Bernstein has studied.

To sum up, the punishments meted out under trade courtesy ranged from private protest to public shaming to predatory pricing to outright retaliation. Each of these sanctions involved a kind of organized self-help, a means of seeking redress within the limits of an informal set of prescriptions. Although courtesy existed to stamp out aggressive, piratical behavior, ultimately an aggrieved publisher could turn pirate, within the rules, when it had no choice but to retaliate on a stubborn house or a confirmed deviant. Settlements—informal rightings of the balance through adjustments in coin or in kind—were the preferred mode of resolving disputes. But when two houses failed to make peace, a third publisher could step in and serve as an arbitrator. This ingenious and elaborate system of rights and remedies ultimately rested on a legal void—the legislated absence of copyrights for foreign authors—and served to mitigate, though not wholly to avert, a public goods problem that threatened to destroy incentives to invest in the dissemination of uncopyrighted works by foreign authors.

## The Persistence of Pirates: First-Mover Advantages and the Second Public Domain

At the edges of trade courtesy there were always eager opportunists. Sometimes they were extremely aggressive and numerous, especially during the publishing wars of the 1830s–40s and 1870s–80s when cheap books and inexpensive modes of distribution made the reprinting of unprotected foreign works irresistibly attractive to many firms. Publishers who operated outside of courtesy were frankly referred to as pirates, and their activities occasioned many colorful epithets during the latter part of the century. Courtesy, or what one commentator called the "gentility of this modified piracy," could "not obscure the lucrative character of the business"; as a result, new houses sprang up, operated by "these cheap Ishmaelites of the trade" who defied the courtesy system.[164] Ishmael, renegade, outlaw—the pirate was a thing apart, an "outside barbarian" whom Henry Holt contrasted with those "men of exceptional character" who reared and dwelled in the respectable house of courtesy.[165] Holt referred to the outsiders as "unscrupulous reprinters of all successful stories, who pay authors nothing and publish in cheap pamphlets without covers."[166] Years earlier, Ticknor & Fields had dubbed pirates "keen-scented rascals, our friends in the *Craft*."[167]

The major houses took considerable financial risks in publishing uncopyrighted foreign works. The inner circle of genteel publishers could be relied upon to observe the principles of courtesy, but the "outside barbarians" had no honor to uphold, no trading partners to impress, and no incentive to accept a code that could bring few immediate, tangible benefits. The major publishers had an additional strength, however; they enjoyed what economists call first-mover advantage. Because of their size and resources, the large houses were able to obtain advance sheets or early proofs of foreign books just ahead of publication abroad. Profits lay in being first to the American market with new titles, and a head start of only a few days could mean the difference between success and failure.[168] While publishers could rely on courtesy to restrain their respectable competitors, first-mover advantage was necessary to steal a march on the cheap Ishmaelites. The combination of courtesy and first-mover advantage was the key to profits.

As early as the 1820s, the Carey firm of Philadelphia was glad to obtain a head start of just two days over piratical competitors. The firm wrote Sir Walter Scott's Edinburgh publisher in 1823,

> We have rec'd *Quentin Durward* most handsomely and have Game completely in our hands this time. In 28 hours after receiving it, we had 1500 copies off or ready to go, and the whole Edition is now nearly distributed. In two days we shall publish it here and in New York, and the Pirates may print it as soon as they please. The opposition Edition will be out in about 48 hours after they have one of our Copies but we shall have complete and entire possession of every market in the Country for a short time.[169]

The "Game" was all about being first to the market. In 1855, Ticknor & Fields urged Robert Browning to send advance copies of a new work "just as early as it is possible to do so that we may have a full months start before our brethren of the trade smell the English copies across the sea."[170] In the 1880s, an authorized publisher's need for precious lead time still generated anxious discussion in the trade journals:

> A publisher who reprints in this country a popular English book, which he secures by paying the author for the sheets, has now, we believe, only about a week's sales from which to derive his profit. At the end of that time the pirate has caught up with him, published the book in a cheap form, and made the authorized edition unprofitable.[171]

An advantage of days or even hours was critical to these ventures. In this respect, nineteenth-century American publishers ran risks similar to those faced today by fashion designers, who likewise lack copyright protection in their creations and are menaced by rapid free riding. Discussing first-mover advantages in the fashion industry, Kal Raustiala and Christopher Sprigman note that in the short interval between the appearance of new fashion designs and the activities of copyists, design originators can "gain the the lion's share of revenues from their designs and will continue to engage in innovation."[172] Similarly, it was the brief period between authorized publication and piracy, supplemented by the protections of courtesy, that allowed Putnam, Holt, Appleton, and other major houses to earn their profits. The large sums paid to such authors as Dickens, Thackeray, Trollope, and George Eliot were "for the privilege of a few days' priority."[173]

Courtesy was a thin barrier against the work of determined pirates. A publisher might enjoy a courtesy-based relationship with a popular foreign author for years, only to lose the association overnight after some incident—a competitor's retaliation, perhaps—triggered a feeding frenzy among the cheap reprint firms. Houses that observed courtesy regarded their foreign titles nervously, as if they were protected by the most fragile of copyrights.[174] As previously noted, the young firm of Grosset & Dunlap justified reprinting Kipling's works without permission on the ground that his books had already appeared in so many unauthorized American editions that they had lost the aura of courtesy protection. The firm regarded itself as "honorable pirates, because to our credit be it said that in no case did we ever reprint anything that had not become public property by having been reprinted indiscriminately by about everyone else in the business."[175]

It might strike modern legal sensibilities as bizarre for an uncopyrighted work to be described as having become "public property," but it is a redundancy explained by the institution of trade courtesy. Courtesy raised a work up out of the public domain, gave it the status of private property, and caused the market to treat it as a public good clothed with the privileges of legal monopoly. The quasi-copyright enjoyed by such a work exerted a civilizing influence on participating houses and redounded to the benefit of otherwise helpless foreign authors and publishers. Supported by informal courtesy norms, publishers put on respectability, foreign authors expected and received honoraria or royalties, and market failure was averted for the sale of foreign titles. The magic of this informal system might continue undisturbed for years until one day an outside barbarian decided to seize upon some courtesy-protected work and to issue it in a cheap, flimsy edition. The spell broken, other reprint houses would leap in and try their luck with the same title. Suddenly, the artificial order of courtesy was temporarily wrecked by the anarchy of an unregulated commons. The trade now regarded the foreign work as having returned to its fallen condition among the heterogeneous mass of materials in the commons. For adherents of courtesy, this loss of recognized exclusivity was a lapse into a renewed public domain, a second death of protection.

Yet, as Grosset & Dunlap's experience suggests, the free availability of a popular work could benefit new entrants in the publishing trade, even as it injured the vested interests of older houses. Young firms could develop book lists free of costly overhead and the risks of experimenting with new or unknown authors. The public, too, could benefit from aggressive competition for cheap, popular books. The Harpers acknowledged in 1877 that occasional breakdowns in courtesy resulted in advantages to book buyers:

The American expedient of the "Law of Trade Courtesy" answers very well in most cases, for while it generally respects the arrangements made by a British author with his American publisher, it leaves open a way for reprisals on unfair houses, and the people are benefited occasionally by a free fight, in the course of which, while rival publishers are fighting over some tempting morsel, the reading public devours it.[176]

Here, the Harpers hinted at another way in which courtesy mirrored copyright law: in its creation of monopolies in public goods. The familiar costs of monopoly—increased prices and an artificial scarcity of goods—were experienced under trade courtesy, just as they are in markets controlled by formal laws. These effects did not go unnoticed, and the courtesy of the trade had many detractors.

## The Decline of Courtesy: Trusts, Literary Agents, and International Copyright

During the 1870s and 1880s, intense competition among American reprinters of cheap, poorly made foreign books threatened many firms with economic ruin. These pirate houses largely ignored the principles of courtesy and reprinted indiscriminately. During 1886 alone, twenty-six cheap libraries issued more than fifteen hundred different volumes. A large number of these were dime novels; many others were foreign reprints published without regard to courtesy.[177] The next year, paper-covered foreign titles were selling at prices from ten to fifty cents, and profit margins were vanishing. The manufacturing trade needed to be sustained, however, and new high-speed cylinder presses, folding machines, inexpensive paper materials, and low postage rates contributed to the frenzy.[178] "The law of evolution applies to the reprinting business as to everything else," remarked a writer for the *New York Herald* in 1889. "The fittest will survive. And the fittest should survive whether he be a 'pirate' or a 'courtesy of the trade publisher.'"[179] The market was soon glutted with cheap foreign books, and publishers of all stripes began to turn to the prospect of international copyright as a possible solution. At the same time, unrestricted piracy destabilized trade courtesy.[180] Even as the major firms tried to uphold its principles, the courtesy system was repeatedly pulled under by the riptide of competition. The respectable houses roundly blamed the pirate reprinters for the loss of dignity and profits in publishing.

For their part, the cheap reprinters indignantly denied that they were pirates and proclaimed themselves reformers seeking to abolish the privileges enjoyed by the clubby firms that had selfishly adopted the courtesy of the trade. George Munro, an industrious publisher of dime novels and founder of the Seaside Library of inexpensive books, argued that the "cheap libraries have broken down the Chinese or rather American wall of trade courtesy and privilege" that had been erected solely for the "monopoly of publishers in this country." These haughty book barons, Munro asserted, "dictated terms, and precious low ones too, to the [foreign] authors, on a basis of non-interference among themselves." Munro was claiming, in essence, that courtesy operated horizontally to benefit publishers by artificially maintaining monopoly prices, but did not work vertically to help foreign authors or to make books more affordable for the masses. Munro even hailed the possibility of "international copyright"—that is, American copyright protection for foreign authors—as an impending defeat for the courtesy cabal. "From this time forth," he declared, "we shall have a free field and no favor, and the longest finger takes the largest plum."[181]

Munro and others in the cheap reprint business assailed the gentlemanly club of publishers as a collusive trust or monopoly. The established houses responded by portraying themselves as honorable and decent, in contrast to the lesser breeds without the law of courtesy. Holt named himself, along with "Willie Appleton, Harry Harper, Haven Putnam, [and] Charles Scribner, Jr.," as among the core of courtesy-abiding houses. "[S]ome publishers," he sneered,

> more or less of specialties and sometimes of piracies, who did not know the leading group very well, supposed it to be a sort of trust, protecting each other and sharing all good things among themselves; and that the only way to get into the publishing business was to reprint books already published by these leaders.[182]

Holt always denied the charge that the large publishing houses were a bullying trust and that courtesy was the glue that held it together. There was "no close corporation about it," he once testified in court. "[A]nybody is welcome who will behave himself."[183] But the cheap reprint firms and the new startups disagreed. They spurned a welcome mat that bid them recognize the courtesy claims of the veteran houses even as it withheld the prestige and leverage necessary to enjoy the benefits such a system conferred. These pirates were indiscreet enough to remind the major firms of their own raffish beginnings, and they justified their freebooting methods in the same way that Mosher did his: foreign works were lawfully in the American public domain and were freely available to all; any attempt to claim such works and call it courtesy was simply a game played by the haves, to the detriment of the have-nots. Unrestrained competition would break down courtesy and benefit the book-reading public by placing "good cheap" editions of important works "within the reach of students, schoolteachers, and others of moderate means."[184] These claims echoed the republican rhetoric that proponents of reprint culture had used to defeat advocates of international copyright in the antebellum period.[185]

Like Munro, John W. Lovell—"Book-A-Day Lovell"—defied the publishing establishment and attacked trade courtesy as a monopoly posing as a piety. He argued that aggressive competition among American publishers for foreign works was the key to keeping prices down and sales brisk. Everything he did, he claimed, was for the masses.[186] Lovell was a master of a populist, anticorporate rhetoric aimed directly at his genteel competitors. With bold sarcasm, he urged the "younger and smaller houses" to "Go in heartily for the 'courtesy of the trade' and—starve. You will find that everything is expected of you and very little given you."[187] The publisher Isaac K. Funk, who was frequently charged with rank piracy, attacked courtesy as a "law" that had not been "framed in the interest of authors or of the public."

> It is a "right of possession" based primarily on the principle, or lack of principle, of first grab. It has proved itself inefficient to protect even the clique of publishers who framed it.... The "law" has proved itself an injustice to authors, a calamity to the public, a miserably clumsy and weak substitute for that law which right and public morality demand—the international copyright law.[188]

Funk painted courtesy as no better than an aggressive grab at the resources of the public domain, a raw claim of first occupancy undignified by the entitlements of Lockean labor in the commons. Genuine copyright protection for foreign authors—though undeniably a legal monopoly—now seemed superior, in the minds of Funk and other agitators for reform, to the cliquish, hidebound monopoly artificially maintained by the prestige houses. Funk, Lovell, and Munro carried the attack to the established firms with an evangelical and egalitarian fervor.

The perception that courtesy was an anticompetitive trust operated by a chosen few undoubtedly contributed to the decline of the informal, norms-based system. Authors themselves sometimes rebelled against the principle of association that required them to cleave to a single publisher as if "choosing a wife," a simile suggested by Holt to describe "the normal relation of author and publisher [of] mutual confidence and helpfulness."[189] Dickens moved opportunistically from one American publisher to another and in one instance, at least, obtained two contracts for the same book.[190] Holt had been William James's publisher for years, but when Scribner's made an offer for his new volume of essays, *The Will to Believe*, James invited Holt to make a competing offer, saying he would give the book to the highest bidder. Holt remonstrated, whereupon James, shocked to find himself a shuttlecock in the courtesy game, accused Holt of trying to undermine his negotiations with Scribner's.[191] James wound up publishing the book with Longmans, Green & Co., after Houghton refused it. Holt's attempt to preserve the "normal relation" of author and publisher had infuriated James; he recognized the anticompetitive nature of courtesy as an assault on his pocketbook.

Congress enacted the Sherman Antitrust Act in 1890, one year before passage of the Chace International Copyright Act. The Sherman Act prohibited "[e]very contract, combination in the form of trust or otherwise, or conspiracy, in restraint of trade or commerce" and criminalized the acts of "[e]very person who shall monopolize, or attempt to monopolize, or combine or conspire with any other person or persons, to monopolize any part of the trade or commerce."[192] The law was aimed at monopolies, combinations, and cartels that harmed competition in the marketplace. Horizontal restraints of trade were thought to be especially pernicious and often were deemed violations of the Sherman Act. In 1898, six manufacturers of cast-iron pipe who had conspired to allocate among themselves the right to serve particular customers in certain regions were held to have violated the act.[193] The U.S. Court of Appeals for the Sixth Circuit arrived at this conclusion even though the conspiracy was only a partial restraint of trade and other cast-iron manufacturers had remained outside the cartel. The participating manufacturers had divided up the market and insulated themselves from competition in ways that tended toward monopoly and potentially deprived the public of the advantages flowing from free competition.

The publishing houses that practiced trade courtesy were plainly combining in a horizontal restraint of trade. Instead of splitting the market up into exclusive territories and customers, as the cast-iron cartel did, publishers divided the free cultural commons into exclusively assigned books and authors, each publisher tacitly honoring every other publisher's courtesy title to a public domain work. This agreement to refrain from poaching on other houses potentially injured foreign authors because there was no competition to better the offer of the first publisher to claim courtesy.[194] This was what economists today call oligopsony, control of the market by a few buyers—in this case, the publishers who purchased foreign authors' permission to publish. "When two publishers are seeking an author," wrote George Haven Putnam, "the proportion of the proceeds offered to the author, goes up."[195] Although Charles Scribner asserted that he knew of "no recognized courtesy rights among publishers which restrict an author from changing his publishers if he desires to do so,"[196] the concerted alignment of publishers against authors' mobility, and the many attested refusals of publishers to treat with any author belonging to another house, suggest that authors were harmed financially by the courtesy cartel.[197] The publishers would have retorted that foreign authors should have been delighted to receive anything for books that were free for the taking in the United States.

There was also a form of oligopoly here, control of the market by a few sellers. Publishers adhering to courtesy effectively agreed to allow fellow publishers to fix the price of public domain works at levels artificially heightened by courteous treatment of authors and also to reduce the supply of copies. Constraints on price and supply occur as a result of ordinary copyright protection, of course, but copyrights are legal monopolies granted by Congress under the authority of the U.S. Constitution; trade courtesy, in contrast, created extralegal monopoly effects, fabricated through publishers' mutual forbearance to compete in free, public goods. Courtesy resembled in certain respects the combination that in the 1930s acted through the Fashion Originators' Guild, an American fashion-design cartel, to limit "style piracy" within the ranks of American garment and textile manufacturers. Like foreign works in the nineteenth century, fashion designs were not protected by copyrights, but the Guild, determined to stamp out piracy, refused to sell garments to retailers who sold pirated fashions, and compelled retailers to sign agreements pledging to forswear the sale of such copies. The Guild registered American designers and their creations and fined members who violated the rules. The U.S. Supreme Court in 1941 held that the Guild's program violated the Sherman Act because it narrowed the outlets for buying and selling textiles and garments, took away the freedom of members, and suppressed competition in the sale of unregistered textiles and copied designs—all tending to deprive the public of the benefits of free competition.[198]

There are obvious differences between courtesy and the fashion-design cartel, not least in that American publishers did not regularly organize boycotts of booksellers that handled the stock of pirate reprinters, or force booksellers to sign pledges to carry only courtesy-protected books. Yet the horizontal agreement to control competition in uncopyrighted garments, which the Supreme Court deemed illegal per se under the Sherman Act, shares broad features with the tacit agreement of the dozen powerful publishers to eliminate competition among themselves for a foreign author's book and to allow one of their number to dictate the price and supply of copies. The tendency of courtesy to deprive authors and book buyers of the benefits of real competition is clear and after 1890 might have been challenged by the U.S. government or an injured private party. When publishers and booksellers combined, at the turn of the century, to combat massive price-cutting by forming associations to maintain a uniform level for book prices, the New York department store R. H. Macy &Co. sued the American Publishers' Association for antitrust violations. After years of litigation, the U.S. Supreme Court unanimously held in 1913 that the association's net-pricing system violated the Sherman Act. By agreeing to prohibit the sale of books—copyrighted and uncopyrighted—to price-cutting retailers, the publishers and booksellers had colluded to act in restraint of trade.[199]

The nineteenth-century courtesy publishers, like the members of the American Publishers' Association and the Fashion Originators' Guild, conspired to suppress competition in uncopyrighted works. Although trade courtesy was not challenged in the courts, the legal climate at the turn of the century disfavored the kind of horizontal restraint of trade that the major publishing houses pursued as a matter of honor. The openly anticompetitive nature of their arrangements most likely contributed to the decline and seeming disappearance of courtesy in the early years of the twentieth century. The cheap reprint houses had mercilessly assailed the genteel publishers as a trust or monopoly; the antitrust laws condemned horizontal restraints as illegal per se. Trade courtesy withered in this inhospitable climate.

Also contributing to the erosion of courtesy was the rise of the literary agent in the 1870s and 1880s. Agents helped authors to grasp the complexities of copyright and contract law and to exploit increasingly valuable markets for such subsidiary rights as magazine serialization, translation, and dramatization.[200] These savvy middlemen became especially valuable to British authors who had to deal "with hustling Americans so many miles away" and who often feared that "Blank & Company [were] not paying all they might be made to pay, and that some other house might come down with a better advance."[201] Literary agency was, by definition, inimical to courtesy. British-based agents like A. P. Watt and, later, Albert Curtis Brown and J. B. Pinker, along with their American counterparts, saw it as their duty to foster economically adversarial relationships between authors and publishers and to obtain bids from multiple houses so as to maximize authors' remuneration (and their own percentages). As Mary Ann Gillies has noted, many publishers viewed the agent as "an unwelcome, opportunistic interloper."[202] William Heinemann, President of the Publishers' Association of Great Britain and Ireland, called the agent "a parasite living on our vital forces."[203]

Equally disgusted, Henry Holt described the agent as "a very serious detriment to literature and a leech on the author, sucking blood entirely out of proportion to his later services."[204] Holt complained that agents struck at the heart of the courtesy relationship between authors and publishers, undermining its continuity by their "fine work."[205] American publishers, accustomed to playing an avuncular role with their authors, felt that agents threatened the integrity and stability of this time-honored relationship. In particular, literary agents interfered with the principle of association, whereby foreign authors voluntarily remained with the American publishers that had first claimed them, and made it more difficult for publishers to justify the uncontested honorarium or royalty for which authors without copyrights were expected to be grateful. Agents introduced the friction of market competition into the hermetic paternalism of courtesy.

In addition to the pressures of ruinous competition, antitrust law, and literary agency, dramatic changes in American copyright law had a direct impact on courtesy. In 1891, Congress passed the Chace International Copyright Act, at last granting formal legal protection to foreign authors. The struggle for that reform had gone on for decades. Efforts to establish a reciprocal Anglo-American copyright law had repeatedly met with obstacles. British law made copyright protection available to foreign authors, including Americans, but a comparable privilege did not exist for British authors in the United States.[206] In response to a petition presented by British authors, Senator Henry Clay introduced a bill in Congress in 1837 that would have recognized British copyrights in the United States. The bill encountered strong opposition from the American book trade, however, and never became law. In 1854, President Franklin Pierce signed an Anglo-American copyright treaty providing for reciprocal recognition of the rights of authors and publishers in the two countries. Once again, stubborn resistance from publishers and booksellers caused the treaty to fall short of ratification by the Senate.[207] Writing in 1880, British poet and essayist Matthew Arnold remarked that the United States had repeatedly "refused to entertain the question of international copyright."[208] A series of Anglo-American copyright bills introduced in Congress between 1886 and 1890 met with the same fate.

When Congress finally granted rights to foreign authors in the Chace Act of 1891, protection came at the price of large concessions to American typesetters and platemakers. Chief among these was the express condition that a foreign (or domestic) book in any language could acquire copyright protection in the United States only if the book was "printed from type set within the limits of the United States, or from plates made therefrom, or from negatives, or drawings on stone made within the limits of the United States, or from transfers made therefrom" and if two copies of the book were deposited in the Copyright Office on or before the date of first publication anywhere else.[209] These provisions were known collectively as the manufacturing clause. Along with the stringent deposit requirement, the clause effectively made first or simultaneous manufacture and publication in the United States a condition of American copyright for any book published abroad.[210] Although resourceful or well-connected foreign authors might be able to satisfy these onerous requirements, many others could not. In place of an absence of copyright protection, Congress had granted foreign authors a form of protection that was openly and avowedly protectionist—conditioned upon compliance with inflexible rules that benefited American typesetters, platemakers, printers, and bookbinders.

The Chace Act was a compromise between advocates of international copyright and the manufacturing trades that feared loss of work if foreign authors were allowed to secure American copyrights unconditionally. If foreign books suddenly received automatic protection, these industries would be forced to compete against copyrighted imports and editions printed from type set overseas and thus would lose the benefits they had enjoyed when foreign works lacked copyright protection altogether. A manufacturing clause had long seemed expedient to legislators and lobbyists. When in 1837 the manufacturing interests protested that international copyright "would jeopardize an industry employing an estimated 200,000 persons with a capital investment of between $30 and $40 million," Henry Clay introduced a bill that conditioned copyright for British and French authors on American manufacture of their books.[211] In 1884, the Harper firm argued for manufacturing provisions that would require protected foreign books to be printed in the United States, "chiefly in order that they may not be made inconvenient and unobtainable, which would be the case if the base of supplies were so remote as London." The Harpers denied that they were taking a protectionist position: "we would not prohibit the importation of stereotype or electrotype plates."[212] Some publishing houses that had their own printing plants benefited directly from the Chace Act's manufacturing clause; others were hopeful that it "represented a part of a design to bring the manufacture of books for the entire English-speaking world under the control of American firms."[213]

The manufacturing clause was especially hard on foreign authors writing in languages other than English. The difficulty of producing an English translation of a work prior to its publication abroad was insuperable for most authors. George Haven Putnam observed,

> The condition of American manufacture, added to the requirement of simultaneous publication, made it almost impossible to secure American copyright for the books for which it was necessary to produce an English version before the manufacturing could be begun. We had given copyright to Germany, France, and Italy in form, but in fact, the authors of these countries could secure but a trifling possibility of advantage from their American market.[214]

Putnam also complained that the manufacturing clause was unnecessarily doing the protectionist work of a tariff on books. He contrasted American and European approaches to copyright legislation, pointing out that in England, France, and Germany the book manufacturing interests were not heard on the question of copyright but, rather, that these interests "were properly to be considered in the rooms of the tariff committees." Congress, Putnam lamented, had shown itself more ready to listen to the typographical unions and papermakers than to "authors, artists, or composers."[215] As

I show in chapter 3, Ezra Pound recognized that the manufacturing clause and book tariffs were twin protectionist devices that harmed the interests of creators.

\* \* \*

By the dawn of the twentieth century, trade courtesy had become difficult to practice openly. The climate of trust-busting, punctuated by antitrust lawsuits and the clamor of politicians, made the proud collusiveness of the genteel publishers an antiquated and suspect chivalry. Changes in the book trade, moreover, had eroded the basic purpose of courtesy. The vigorous ministrations of literary agents revealed the faithful monogamy of author and publisher to be dispensable in many cases; real competition, commensurate with an expanding literary marketplace, awakened an entrepreneurial spirit in authors. The experience of uncontrolled competition and piracy in the 1880s made courtesy seem fusty and ineffective.

More visibly, the Chace Act, with its new protections for foreign authors, created the perception that the courtesy code was superfluous. Gentlemanly honoraria gave way to up-front sums and backend royalties, paid not ex gratia but as a matter of law. No longer were advance sheets rushed across the ocean in order to steal a few days' march on competitors; such first-to-market strategies belonged to a world in which the cultural commons was augmented daily by unprotected materials from abroad, and the race and the profits were to the swift. Copyright protection for foreign authors now required domestic typesetting and, as a practical matter, domestic printing; simply binding sheets that had been set and printed abroad would not satisfy the manufacturing clause. The pressures generated by the law's manufacturing requirements ensured that authors and publishers would still be racing against time, but the compulsions were now legal ones, not fueled by contests with pirates or subject to a code of honor among statute-created thieves.

Did the statutory commands of the Chace Act improve on the norms-based informality of trade courtesy? Were copyrights for foreigners superior to courtesy relationships? Both gains and losses resulted from passage of the Chace Act. Foreign authors could now look to uniform federal law for protection against piracy instead of to an informal system of self-regulation adhered to by a dozen major publishers, a system subject to occasional breakdowns and always menaced at the edges by pirates. But copyright law was complex and technical; its machinery was operated by lawyers, its coercions administered by courts. Under the law's frigid rules, a dispute between publishers, or between publisher and author, was no longer adjusted by honorable concessions; deviants were not punished with public shaming or swashbuckling retaliations. The Chace Act was a bureaucratization of honor. Now, complaints were filed and served, motions made, infringements adjudicated, and injunctions and damages ordered. Although American publishers continued to preserve an ideal of fairness in their dealings with foreign authors, the old paternalistic spirit had been diminished and, with it, some of the sense of professional camaraderie and joint pursuit of honorable ends.

Foreign authors may have benefited in still other ways from the former lack of copyright protection in the United States. According to B. Zorina Khan, it can be argued that piracy allowed foreign authors "to reap higher total returns from the expansion of the market" and to enjoy the benefits of network effects and bundled products, such as best sellers and lecture tours.[216] During the 1880s, the cheap reprinter John B. Alden told foreign authors that they should be pleased with unremunerated circulation of their books in the United States because the widespread exposure would help their sales when international copyright finally did come.[217] The chief drawback to the Chace Act, however, was its manufacturing clause. Many foreign authors simply could not comply with its strict requirements. Protectionist and discriminatory, the manufacturing clause, together with other copyright formalities, prevented the United States from joining the Berne Convention for a century after other major nations had signed it in the late 1880s.[218]

But the manufacturing clause did more than create obstacles for foreign authors and opprobrium for American lawmakers in world opinion. It perpetuated, to a significant degree, the commons problem that international copyright had been enacted to solve. For the many foreign authors and publishers who could not satisfy its rigors, the clause played the same role that the affirmative withholding of copyrights had played in earlier statutes. Failure to accomplish book manufacture on U.S. soil deprived these authors of protection, feeding the American public domain with fresh materials that were freely and lawfully available to any publisher, just as all foreign works had been prior to 1891. Legalized piracy had not been banished by the Chace Act; it had merely been limited in scope. Nor did trade courtesy vanish altogether; it still existed, albeit in less vigorous and exacting forms, as a publishing ethic, a pattern of behavior, and an occasional tool for resolving disputes in the book trade. No longer openly practiced by publishing houses, it nevertheless quietly governed reputable publishers' relations with each other and with foreign authors.

To sum up, when historians ask whether the Chace Act successfully addressed the copyright problems faced by foreign authors, they should not measure its success in a conceptual vacuum. They should not assess the protections and incentives created by the Chace Act against some general notion of market failure, treating foreign copyright protection as the sole, stark alternative to piracy and the public goods problem. Rather, the Chace Act should be measured, at least in part, against the successes (and failures) of trade courtesy, the preexisting system of extralegal norms that had sought to bridge the copyright gap for American publishers and foreign authors. As Dotan Oliar and Christopher Sprigman note, "Intellectual property laws come with costs as well as benefits, and these must be assessed relative to those of non-legal regulation. In some cases social norms may do a reasonably good job of controlling appropriation, but perhaps not in others." They add that "the case for legal intervention is greater if we see significant dissatisfaction with such non-legal background incentives."[219] There was dissatisfaction with trade courtesy, but much satisfaction with it as well. Whether the uniformity costs and compliance burdens that the Chace Act and its statutory successors imposed were offset by the benefits they conferred on publishers and foreign authors is a question that is addressed implicitly throughout this study.

The following chapters tell the story of transatlantic modernism's encounter with U.S. copyright law, lawful piracy, and the American public domain. They also show that courtesy survived well into the twentieth century and that elements of that informal, norms-based system were deftly repurposed by James Joyce, T. S. Eliot, Bennett Cerf, and other modernist figures to combat piracy, to protect and consolidate American markets, and to lay the groundwork for authorial celebrity. The tradition of courtesy, with its shaming sanctions, authorized editions, and ex gratia payments, played a critical role in the production and consumption of modernism in the United States.

# TRANSATLANTIC MODERNISM IN THE AMERICAN PUBLIC DOMAIN

*Rep. Frank D. Currier: "I hope, Mr. Sullivan, that [you will work to]
have the law so modified that not only must [a book claiming copyright]
be from type set within the United States, but the book must be
printed in the United States."
J. J. Sullivan, representing the International Typographical Union: "Yes;
every part of the manufacturing."
—Senate and House Hearings on Amending the Copyright Act (1906)[1]*

*American publishers ... and copyright laws are not in my world.
—W. B. Yeats (ca. 1902)[2]*

I begin this chapter with a small but luminous detail from the history of
modernism to which I will return in later chapters. In 1921, the New York
Court of Special Sessions found the editors of *The Little Review* guilty of
obscenity under the state's penal code for publishing the portion of *Ulysses*

in which one of the characters, Leopold Bloom, masturbates in public.[3] The criminal conviction frightened even the most sympathetic publishers. With English-speaking markets effectively foreclosed, James Joyce grew so desperate for a means of publishing his masterpiece in unexpurgated book form that he agreed to have Sylvia Beach, an American expatriate with no previous experience as a publisher, issue it under the imprint of her Paris bookshop, Shakespeare and Company. It is one measure of Joyce's anxiety to publish *Ulysses* free of fig leaves that he enlisted Beach, knowing that publishing first in France would place the work's American copyright in jeopardy. He had been mulling the idea of publication in Paris for some time. In the fall of 1920, several months before the *Little Review* trial ended and more than a year before Beach's edition appeared, the New York publisher B. W. Huebsch met with Joyce in Paris to urge him to bring *Ulysses* out first in the United States. But Huebsch added a deal breaker: because no legitimate American publisher could risk handling a book chargeable with obscenity, certain strong passages would have to be deleted or revised. Joyce flatly refused to discuss the question of alterations.

Huebsch explained that publishing the book first in France, though it would spare Joyce the pain of expurgating his text, would cost him his American copyright. Huebsch described the meeting for John Quinn:

> My conversation with Joyce related to the manner in which the book might be published without sacrificing his American rights and as these depend upon manufacturing the book in the U.S., I wanted him to understand that he was jeopardizing the thing that he holds most dear, namely, the publication of the book intact, by printing it in Paris, because that would leave the book free for a pirate after sixty days, and the pirate, in order to overcome the objections that now lie against it, would eliminate the offensive passages. Thus Joyce would lose not only his property but that which as an artist I presume he cherishes even more.[4]

With the canny prescience of a publisher who had to know the laws of obscenity and copyright in order to navigate their intricate courses, Huebsch foresaw the activities of American pirates six years before Samuel Roth began appropriating Joyce's novel in the pages of his magazine *Two Worlds Monthly*.

Huebsch's argument to Joyce was a flawless piece of legal prediction, lucid and arrestingly simple: Joyce could publish first in the United States, but, to avoid running afoul of the obscenity law, he would have to expurgate.

Alternatively, Joyce could publish first in France and keep his work intact there, but in doing so he would risk not securing a copyright in the United States and inviting the depredations of pirates. And the pirates, to avoid running afoul of the obscenity law, would expurgate. Thus, whether Joyce published first in the United States or in France, he would have to live with a sanitized American *Ulysses*. The difference was that if he chose the former course, he could control the alterations to the text, and his work would enjoy copyright protection in the United States. Joyce, with an obstinacy born of earlier encounters with censors, refused to compromise his creative integrity by changing a word.

Huebsch's account of the meeting left one point unclear: why should publishing *Ulysses* initially in France threaten the American copyright? The publisher actually hinted at the answer but so telegraphically as to be intelligible only to a lawyer acquainted, as Quinn was, with the world of authors and literary rights. Huebsch's fleeting mention of "manufacturing the book in the U.S." and his cryptic prophecy about pirates getting to work "after sixty days" alluded to two statutory challenges that awaited authors like Joyce: the manufacturing and ad interim provisions of the 1909 U.S. Copyright Act.

## The Persistence of the Manufacturing Clause

Beginning in 1891, authors, foreign and domestic, could obtain U.S. copyright only by having their books manufactured from type set within the United States or from plates made from such type. Congress retained these requirements when it enacted, in 1909, the first significant revision of the copyright law since 1891. Section 15 of the new law provided that, in the case of printed books or periodicals,

> except the original text of a book of foreign origin in a language or languages other than English, the text of all copies accorded protection under this Act ... shall be printed from type set within the limits of the United States, either by hand or by the aid of any kind of typesetting machine, or from plates made within the limits of the United States from type set therein, or, if the text be produced by lithographic process, or photo-engraving process, then by a process wholly performed within the limits of the United States, and the printing of the text and binding of the said book shall be performed within the limits of the United States.[5]

The exception for foreign-language books of foreign origin was an innovation of the 1909 act. Unlike previous law, the 1909 act allowed foreign works in foreign languages to gain copyright protection without being manufactured in America. Because foreign-language books would have only a limited readership in the United States, it was reasoned, book artisans would suffer no appreciable loss. Works with broad appeal would almost certainly be translated into English and "become subject to the manufacturing clause and thus give American labor its due."[6]

The clause continued, however, to govern an important class of works produced abroad: foreign books and periodicals written in English. For these works, the clause was even more stringent than its 1891 predecessor. Whereas the Chace Act had mandated only domestic typesetting or plate making, the 1909 act increased the burden by expressly requiring that printing and binding also be performed within the United States—a further concession to American book manufacturers. Henceforth, books and periodicals would have to be typeset, printed, and bound on American soil in order to enjoy a U.S. copyright. The clear legislative purpose was protection of American labor from the effects of foreign importation. "Manufactured in the United States" became a familiar recitation on the copyright pages of books claiming protection under U.S. law.

## Strait Is the Gate: Ad Interim Copyright Protection

To mitigate the harshness of the manufacturing requirements, the 1909 act carved out an exception for "books published abroad in the English language seeking ad interim protection under this Act." Ad interim protection was defined in a separate section of the statute:

> [I]n the case of a book first published abroad in the English language, … the deposit in the copyright office, not later than sixty days after its publication abroad, of one complete copy of the foreign edition, with a request for the reservation of the copyright and a statement of the name and nationality of the author and of the copyright proprietor and of the date of publication of the said book, shall secure to the author or proprietor an ad interim copyright, which shall have all the force and effect given to copyright by this Act, and shall endure until the expiration of four months after such deposit in the copyright office.[7]

Once a copy of the foreign edition reached the Copyright Office for deposit within sixty days of publication abroad, ad interim protection began from the date of receipt and endured for four months. Then, as further provided by Section 22 of the 1909 act,

> whenever within the period of such ad interim protection an authorized edition of such book shall be published within the United States, in accordance with the manufacturing provisions ... and whenever the provisions of this Act as to deposit of copies, registration, filing of affidavit, and the printing of the copyright notice shall have been duly complied with, the copyright shall be extended to endure in such book for the full term elsewhere provided in this Act.[8]

Thus, by satisfying the requirements of several linked provisions, the author of an English-language book or periodical produced abroad could acquire statutory copyright protection in the United States for the full initial twenty-eight-year term, starting from the date of foreign publication. Ad interim protection was, when it worked, a stepping-stone to full protection.

But it did not always work. A false step at any point along the tortuous path leading from publication abroad to reprinting in the States might spell doom for the American copyright. Failure to mail the foreign edition for deposit in the Copyright Office, or mailing it too late for receipt within the sixty-day window, would result in loss of the ad interim opportunity. Even if ad interim protection were secured, failure to reprint in the United States in accordance with the manufacturing clause would result in termination of copyright protection once the narrow four-month gate slammed shut.

## Codified Protectionism: The Manufacturing Clause and Modernism

The manufacturing clause was viewed by many as a hindrance to transatlantic authorship. As late as 1946, Roger Burlingame wrote, "Our curious copyright law, even since it has been called 'international,' allows protection only when a book is printed in America. As importations are printed abroad and brought over in sheets to be bound here with the importer's imprint, they become legally free here to anyone who cares to 'pirate' them."[9] Many other nations protected an author's copyright from the moment he or she created the work and extended to foreign authors the same protections enjoyed by citizens. This principle of national treatment was required of all signatories to the Berne Convention, an international agreement that the United States, as long as it insisted on the manufacturing clause and other copyright formalities, could not join.[10] American citizens could claim protection under the British copyright act for works first published in British territory (including Canada) or simultaneously published in such territory and the United States.[11] Publication could be satisfied under British law by the importation of copies typeset and printed elsewhere; unlike the United States, Britain did not require domestic manufacture as a condition of copyright.[12]

Economic protection for American book manufacturers was the openly avowed legislative motive behind the 1909 act's manufacturing clause. Frederic G. Melcher, editor of The Publishers' Weekly, described the clause to Ezra Pound in 1927 as "the handicap of our present attitude on copyright" for writers living abroad.[13] John Quinn had written Pound some years earlier that the "objectionable thing" about the manufacturing provisions was "that they require the books to be printed from plates made or type set here in order to get copyrights, and that printing is a little more expensive here than it is on the other side."[14]

Combined with the tariff on imported books and the elevated costs of printing in the United States, the manufacturing clause provided American printers and other book artisans with extraordinary protection from foreign competition. As a federal court explained in 1945,

> the copyright law, which was enacted in 1909 prior to the passage of the Tariff Act of 1922, and the [Tariff Act of 1930] ... have a common purpose—which is tersely stated in the title of the Tariff Act of 1922, "to encourage the industries of the United States," and in the title of the Tariff Act of 1930, "to encourage the industries of the United States" and "to protect American labor."[15]

Many American publishers opposed the 1909 act's manufacturing clause, but not all did. Magazine publishers, who were responsible for generating massive amounts of printed material, felt they benefited from the clause.[16] As late as 1954, the printers' unions and book manufacturers strongly opposed modification of the clause by legislation or international agreement.[17] Pound assailed the law's unvarnished protectionism as "iniquitous and stupid in principle."[18] In numerous articles and letters, he linked the tariff and the manufacturing clause as evils besetting international authorship and impeding the free, borderless circulation of books.[19]

Pound saw in the American copyright and tariff laws a triumph of capitalism over culture, materialism over mind. The U.S. copyright law, he complained, had shown a tendency to favor

> the printer at the expense of the author. It is the inheritance of our mob that any, absolutely any, material gain to no matter whom is of more importance than clarity of thought, enlightenment, or any possible property of the mind. So the "word of order has gone forth" in America: rob the author unless he submits to our exaggerated American printing charge.[20]

The gift of enlightenment that authors made to the world entitled them, in Pound's view, to a "property of the mind" that should be protected by the law, not subordinated to the interests of printers, typesetters, and bookbinders. The copyright law perverted the order of things, ranking articles of manufacture above authors' creations; treating paper, lead, ink, and buckram as if these mere physical media were of greater importance than the ideas they embodied. To use current copyright terminology, the law elevated "tangible media of expression" above creative expression itself, making the medium not only the message but the reward as well.[21] Pound's contempt for the manufacturing clause matched his hatred of American obscenity laws that "lump[ed] literature and instruments for abortion into one clause"[22] and confused "Catullus with smutty postcards."[23] Such laws inverted the Dantescan journey from the grossness of sin to the heaven of knowledge; they cast a Circean spell that brutalized the things of the mind.

With book manufacture capable of making or marring copyrights, foreign authors writing in English viewed the United States as an obstacle course of legal technicalities that, if not expertly negotiated, could lead to a nightmare of unauthorized exploitation. Popular authors with proven markets could satisfy the manufacturing requirements much more easily than authors who were new or unfamiliar to American readers. Arnold Bennett's popularity did not take hold in the United States until 1909, when the American publisher E. P. Dutton offered him an attractive advance and royalty on his next three novels. "A year ago," he confided to his journal, "no American publisher would publish my work on any terms, and the copyright of *The Old Wives' Tale* was lost there from this cause."[24] Robert Frost's early volumes of poetry, *A Boy's Will* and *North of Boston*, were first published in London by David Nutt in 1913 and 1914, respectively. Because Henry Holt did not reprint them in the United States until 1915, after the period of ad interim copyright had expired, these collections lacked U.S. copyright protection.[25] Even works published abroad by Americans could be swept into the American public domain.

Pound acknowledged in 1916 that his collections of poems—*Canzoni* (1911) and *Riposte* (1912), first published and printed in England—were probably unprotected in the United States, though he hoped that the appearance of individual poems in putatively copyrighted American magazines might strengthen his position (a hope that was nurtured by Quinn).[26] Without established American readerships, the early writings of Pound, Bennett, Frost, and others were vulnerable to unauthorized though entirely lawful reprinting.

The early modernists suffered under U.S. copyright law in part because the reading public had not yet learned the language in which they wrote. Their styles were unfamiliar or rebarbative, and their messages, when decoded, were often objectionable, running counter to approved morality and literary convention. American copyright law penalized transgressive writers by making the path to legal protection run through the predilections and prejudices of American publishers and readers. The law, Pound wrote in 1915, was "all against the author, and more and more against him just in proportion as he is before or against his time."[27] In this, Pound echoed William Wordsworth, who eighty years earlier had contended that inadequate copyright protection harmed "the production of works, the authors of which look beyond the passing day, and are desirous of pleasing and instructing future generations."[28] In 1927, Pound warned that the small window for reprinting foreign-origin works under the 1909 act posed a "danger to the really good authors, whose stuff is likely to lose copyright if we print here [in Europe]."[29] As late as 1951 he was scheming for ways to publish "early stuff" by Wyndham Lewis that was "NOT covered by cawpyright in this kuntry."[30] Particularly when a work was regarded as obscene or indecent, the manufacturing clause could be an insuperable barrier. As Sylvia Beach noted, "To secure the copyright, a book had to be set up and printed in our country, an impossibility for a banned work."[31] The manufacturing clause was a crude sorting device that rewarded the proven, the safe, and the popular.

In 1920, Maurice S. Revnes, writing to D. H. Lawrence from New York about film rights, stressed that "many English novels are not protected in this country by copyright."[32] The English writer Richard Aldington was startled to learn in 1927 that he had paid for "illusory rights" to translate Remy de Gourmont's *Une Nuit au Luxembourg* for an American edition; de Gourmont's prose fantasy had never enjoyed copyright protection in the United States.[33] Foreign authors were not always unfamiliar with the complexities of the law, however. Wyndham Lewis showed himself well acquainted with the effects of the manufacturing clause when he observed of his polemical work, *The Art of Being Ruled*, that "6 months after publication in England it has to be setup in or arranged for in America, else I lose the american copyright."[34] He had the ad interim and manufacturing provisions in mind.

The effects of the manufacturing clause were felt well into the twentieth century. Vladimir Nabokov became anxious over the American copyright in *Lolita*, first published in 1955 by the Olympia Press in France, when the press was slow to provide information he needed to comply with U.S. copyright formalities.[35] The doubtful copyright status of J. R. R. Tolkien's *The Lord of the Rings*—due in part to questionable compliance with the manufacturing clause—led to unauthorized American publication of the trilogy in the 1960s.[36] As late as the 1970s and 1980s, James Laughlin, founder of New Directions Publishing Corp. in New York, worried that copyrights in Pound's works would be impaired by the importation of foreign editions that had not been printed in the United States. "[T]he old manufacturing clause still persists," he warned in 1981.[37] The clause's legal effects were mitigated to the point of harmlessness in later years, but it was not finally repealed until July 1, 1986.[38] A memory of its rigors continues to haunt publishing houses. Some form of "Manufactured in the United States"—an avowal no longer compelled by law—can still be found on the copyright pages of books produced in this country.

## "I mean copyright plus printer": The Case of *The Exile*

One of the factors that made the manufacturing clause an obstacle for foreign-domiciled authors was the comparatively high cost of printing in the United States. Some authors would willingly have paid for American manufacture if they could have afforded it. Pound's short-lived magazine,

*The Exile*, illustrates the dilemma these writers faced. In 1926, Pound, living in Italy, hit upon the idea of founding a little magazine that would enable him to combine "that highly special sort of writing" that he admired with his increasing political restiveness and antibureaucratic polemics.[39] As he conceived it, *The Exile* would merge the rebellious spirit of the *BLAST* of 1914 with the uncompromising aesthetics of *The Little Review* of 1918. In addition to himself, contributors would include John Rodker, William Carlos Williams, W. B. Yeats, and Robert McAlmon as well as lesser known authors. Pound's plan was to hurl the feisty booklet in the face of his countrymen three times a year. The problem was that an ocean separated him from his target.

At first, Pound assumed he would have the magazine printed in Europe and shipped to America, but then he began to consider the advantages of printing in the United States, which would ensure copyright protection and avoid the interference of customs officials.[40] Yet he knew that printing costs could be prohibitive in his native country. As early as 1915, he had remarked, "The printing is supposed to be so costly that it is impossible to publish in America, especially periodicals."[41] Pound resolved that "in view of copyright," he should, if at all possible, have *The Exile* manufactured in the United States, and he asked John M. Price, a young New York newspaperman who had declared his willingness to act as Pound's agent, to obtain estimates from American printers.[42]

In December 1926, Price reported that his initial contacts with New York printers had been discouraging. Of those who had replied, one had written that producing 500 copies of Pound's magazine would cost $250; another guessed that the cost would be between $300 and $350; a third gave a detailed estimate of $262 for 500 copies and $282 for 750 copies.[43] Each of these estimates exceeded the anticipated total revenue from the first number of *The Exile*; with copies selling for fifty cents, even a sellout of the first number would not repay printing and mailing costs and other overhead. Pound's reaction to the printers' estimates was to set up a visceral howl at the plight of foreign authors at the mercy of the manufacturing clause: "The American printing price is out of the question. Excellent example of American laws framed AGAINST the mind and in favour of material. Printer favoured above the author. I mean copyright plus printer."[44] Again, Pound was assailing American law as inimical to culture and pointing to the maddening predicament that the law had created for impecunious foreign authors who lacked a regular American publisher: if they wished to print their work in the United States and secure copyright there, they would have to pay the high costs of American manufacture; if they wanted to produce their works affordably, they could do so by printing in Europe, but then they would forfeit copyright protection in the United States. Many authors were forced to surrender American copyrights in exchange for being printed at all.

Pound finally gave in and had the first number of *The Exile* printed, at a fraction of American manufacturing costs, by Maurice Darantiere of Dijon. (The job could be done in Europe, Pound reckoned, for seventy-five to a hundred dollars.)[45] But this left the problem of the American copyright. Pound's agent, Price, tried to circumvent the 1909 act's manufacturing requirements through a scheme that Pound had concocted for having short extracts from *The Exile* printed and copyrighted in the United States. The U.S. Copyright Office would have none of it and explained to Price that "copyright protection for this magazine could not be secured here without printing it entirely in the United States." When Price complained of the prohibitive costs of printing a small, unfunded magazine in America, the assistant register of copyrights coolly informed him of the protectionist purpose behind the manufacturing clause: "No doubt it is more expensive to print books in the United States than in Europe, but this is one of the principal reasons why Congress passed the law requiring them to be printed in this country."[46] The manufacturing clause had been enacted to shield American printers, typesetters, and bookbinders from cheap foreign competition. Pound, who despised all legal and bureaucratic obstacles to the free circulation of authors' writings, was reduced to an impotent wail: "GOD DAMN ALL BUREAUCRATS."[47] He had the final three issues of *The Exile* produced in the United States under the imprint of the Chicago (later, New York) publisher Pascal Covici, who agreed to bear some of the costs of bringing out the magazine.

## The Other Dreaded Formalities: Copyright Notice and Renewal

The manufacturing clause was not the only legal formality that jeopardized authors' American copyrights and set U.S. law apart from the laws of other countries. The requirements of copyright notice and copyright renewal were also conditions of protection and could easily be bungled by an unwary author or copyright proprietor. Unlike current American law, which recognizes a valid copyright from the moment a work is created, the 1909 act required a work to be published with a proper copyright notice before federal protection could commence. "[A]ny person entitled thereto by this Act," the statute provided, "may secure copyright for his work by publication thereof with the notice of copyright required by this Act; and such notice shall be affixed to each copy thereof published or offered for sale in the United States by authority of the copyright proprietor."[48] Approved forms were "Copyright," "Copr.," and in some cases "©," together with the date of publication and the owner's name.[49] Notice was necessary, said lawyers and lawmakers, for alerting the public to the existence of claimed rights. If an author or publisher neglected to include a notice, or included an improper one, the work would be cast into the public domain as soon as copies were distributed to the public. The law distinguished between "divestive" and "investive" publication: the act of publishing a work divested it of any common law protection it had enjoyed prior to publication; if copies did not bear a proper copyright notice, the act of publishing was deemed not to have invested the work with federal protection.[50] In such a case, the work had put off state law protection without having put on federal protection and, as a result, was free to all comers.

Even minor errors in the form or placement of a copyright notice could result in forfeiture of protection. In 1929, a federal trial court denied relief for a flagrant infringement where the plaintiff had affixed the notice to the last page of all copies of a booklet instead of to the title page or the page immediately following, as required by the statute. The plaintiff had lost its copyright by failing to observe "strict compliance with the provisions as to notice under the Copyright Act."[51] In an earlier case, Judge Learned Hand had dismissed a claim for infringement of the copyright in a popular song where the plaintiff had included in the copyright notice a business name that was unlawful under New York law. "The vice," explained Judge Hand, "goes to the notice itself and the statute forbids a suit where notice has not been given."[52] Failure to include a proper copyright notice was tantamount to omitting the notice altogether. In later years, courts found ways to avoid the loss of rights for such technical lapses, but many works continued to enter the public domain because of an author's venial sin of omission.

John Quinn had a keen eye for copyright formalities. When Margaret Anderson and Jane Heap, the editors of *The Little Review*, changed the format of volume six of the magazine by printing the table of contents and the copyright notice ("copyrighted, 1919, by Margaret C. Anderson") on the first page of text instead of on the inside cover as formerly, Quinn worried that they might have forfeited copyright protection.[53] "Can it be possible," he asked Anderson, "that you have been using this thing without copyrighting it? I mean copyrighting the number as a whole. That is a very serious oversight, if that be true."[54]

This peccadillo alone probably would not have impaired the copyright, but Anderson and Heap occasionally blundered more dangerously. For example, the May 1917 number of *The Little Review*, in which Pound introduced himself as foreign editor, lacked any form of copyright notice.[55] A court in this period would have deemed the omission a forfeiture of copyright in the entire contents of the *Little Review* number, which included the first part of T. S. Eliot's witty prose dialogue "Eeldrop and Appleplex."[56] Although no court had occasion to rule on this point for *The Little Review*, the error had its consequences. In 1926, Samuel Roth, a pragmatic student of the copyright law and a hawkeyed examiner of the copyright pages of books and magazines, reprinted "Eeldrop and Appleplex" in the second number of his new magazine, *Two Worlds Monthly: Devoted to the Increase of the Gaiety of Nations*.[57] Roth had not asked for permission, nor need he have.[58] He shrewdly subtitled the selection "A Fragment" because he had no intention of reprinting the concluding portion of Eliot's dialogue, which had appeared in the September 1917 number of *The Little Review*. That issue bore the notice "Copyright, 1917, by Margaret Anderson." Having bagged the public domain half of Eliot's piece, Roth left the potentially copyrighted moiety alone and then twisted the knife by placing his own notice, "Copyright, 1926, by Samuel Roth," on the title page of the *Two Worlds Monthly* issue containing the Eliotic spoils.

The other formality that worried authors was copyright renewal. Under the 1909 act, federal copyrights could last for a total of fifty-six years from the date of first publication, but protection came in two parts. Publishing copies of a work with a proper notice gave the work an initial twenty-eight years of protection. If the copyright proprietor desired an additional twenty-eight-year term, he or she was required to submit a renewal application and fee to the Copyright Office "within one year prior to the expiration of the original term of copyright." If the renewal application was not filed within the prescribed period, the copyright in the work would "determine," that is, terminate, "at the expiration of twenty-eight years from first publication."[59]

The renewal formalities were not onerous, but they could be a trap for the unwary or the lazy. Sometimes, a copyright owner would confuse the paperwork or miss a deadline and be forced to pay the penalty of relinquishing the work to the public domain. The legal landscape is strewn with prematurely expired copyrights, including the films *Pygmalion* (1938)[60] and *It's a Wonderful Life* (1946)[61] and the Twentieth Century Fox television series *Crusade in Europe* (1949), based on Dwight D. Eisenhower's book about World War II.[62] But for every failure to renew that resulted from a clerical error, many more can be traced to the indifference of copyright owners. The act of renewing a copyright meant that its owner cared enough about the property right to observe the modest formalities required by the law. It is surprising how few copyright owners ever took the trouble. Several decades ago, the U.S. Copyright Office conducted a study of original registrations of copyrights made during the fiscal year 1927, matching those registrations with their corresponding renewals filed twenty-seven years later, during the fiscal year 1954.[63] Original registrations for all classes of works totaled 180,864; renewals totaled 17,304. Owners of statutory copyrights that had been acquired in 1927 renewed a scant 9.5 percent of their copyrights during 1954.

While some small percentage of those nonrenewals no doubt resulted from inadvertent technical lapses, a very large number of copyright owners simply did not find it worth their while to renew copyright claims for works that held no economic or other significance for them. When it is added that the highest percentage of renewals in 1954 were in the categories of published music (45 percent) and motion picture photoplays (43.7 percent), it becomes clear that the vast majority of traditional literary and dramatic works—books, stories, plays, and the like—were simply allowed to enter the public domain at the end of twenty-eight years. The renewal requirement thus served as a valuable clearinghouse for unwanted copyrights, sweeping into the cultural commons vast quantities of works that no longer needed the protections of a legal monopoly. Essentially a mechanism for allocating resources to their highest and best use, the renewal formality permitted the diverse, undisciplined creativity of the public to operate on works whose transformative potential their owners had failed to recognize or exploit.

Once stripped of copyright protection through inadvertence or indifference, unrenewed works were a valuable resource for the reprint trade. During the 1950s and 1960s, Roth frequently wrote to the U.S. Copyright Office on behalf of his publishing company, Seven Sirens Press, to check on the copyright status of works first published in the 1920s and 1930s. Like other reprint publishers, Roth was dependent on a steady flow of works falling into the American public domain; he repackaged and reissued such works under his own imprint without the overhead of permissions fees and royalties. One of his requests revealed that for D. H. Lawrence's *Sons and Lovers*, originally registered for copyright by the New York publisher Mitchell Kennerley in 1913, no renewal registration could be found. Similarly, no renewal registration was recorded for Lawrence's novella *The Virgin and the Gypsy*, which had been registered for ad interim protection by Frieda Lawrence in 1930 and again later that year by Alfred A. Knopf, Inc., for the full initial copyright term.[64]

Copyrights in most of the works that Roth inquired about had not been renewed. For example, in 1966 he sought information about the copyright status of issues of *The Smart Set* published from 1919 to 1923. Under the editorship of H. L. Mencken and George Jean Nathan, the magazine in that period had published work by F. Scott Fitzgerald, Theodore Dreiser, Willa Cather, Dashiell Hammett, and others. The Copyright Office answered Roth's query by stating that all sixty-one issues from those years had been initially registered for copyright but that a "[s]earch in the Renewal Indexes … failed to disclose any renewal registrations relating to these works."[65] For a dedicated reprinter like Roth, research in the Copyright Office could lead to pay dirt. Throughout his career, he found ways of excavating uncopyrighted material and repurposing it for American readers in search of titillating entertainment. He specialized in reframing the experimental energies of modernism as a libidinous art of sophisticated "gaiety." Copyright law and the American public domain were his collaborators in this enterprise.

## "Piracy (if it is piracy)": The Manufacturing Clause and Its Discontents

In the fall of 1925, Roth began publishing a new magazine, *Two Worlds: A Literary Quarterly Devoted to the Increase of the Gaiety of Nations*, which contained, among other assorted writings, a "New Unnamed Work" by James Joyce. Joyce was predictably upset to learn that Roth was reprinting extracts from his "Work in Progress" (later gathered and revised by Joyce as *Finnegans Wake*) that had appeared initially in European magazines. In November 1925, Herbert Gorman, Joyce's biographer, reported a conversation he had had with Huebsch, who took a characteristically clear-eyed view of Joyce's predicament. Huebsch had remarked, "[T]here is no redress on such piracy (if it is piracy) [because] there is only a six months period directly after publication when the contents of foreign magazines are protected in this country."[66] Although as reported by Gorman these remarks blurred some fine points of the law, their import was clear: without a reservation of rights under the ad interim provision of the 1909 act, Joyce could not invoke an American copyright against Roth's activities.

Because of the difficulties and hardships imposed by the manufacturing provisions, the 1909 act helped create the conditions for much unauthorized though lawful reprinting of foreign-origin works in the United States. To call such reprinting piracy was to take an ethical, not a legal, position on the question, and the tension between moralistic condemnation and agnostic legalism implied in the phrase "piracy (if it is piracy)" recalls directly the heated debates over the unauthorized reprinting of foreign works prior to the Chace Act of 1891. The moralized sense of piracy, so often used in the nineteenth century to disapprove of publishers who took advantage of foreign authors' predicament, continued well into the twentieth century. What Reverend Henry Van Dyke in 1888 had called, with quasi-abolitionist passion, "the national sin of literary piracy" could still arouse indignation in 1925. In that year, Grant Overton, tracing the history of the Appleton publishing house, wrote, "In publishing, honesty—a moral honesty, a scrupulous fairness—invariably pays."[67] Honor still lay, for many publishers, in resisting the temptation to take what was freely and lawfully available to everyone.

Van Dyke had urged in his sermon that the ultimate question was not "what is actual, nor what is expedient, but what is right."[68] For him, piracy was piracy; it could not be varnished over with arguments about the permissive letter of the copyright law. Carl Sandburg registered the same indignation in 1926 when he learned that Roth, with the assistance of the manufacturing clause, had lifted several of his poems from *This Quarter*, an English-language journal published in Europe: "If Roth is not a swindler, at least he operates by a dirty code."[69] Sandburg's distinction between a criminal and a cad, and thus between legal prescription and ethical propriety, echoed the longstanding piracy debate. The English literary agent A. D. Peters was frankly uninterested in such fine distinctions when he responded to an editorial concerning Roth in *The New Statesman* in 1927: "This man is correctly described by you as a 'pirate.' People like myself ... would not hesitate to call him something worse."[70]

*Pirate* was a term often used to denigrate the new breed of American publishers, such as Albert Boni, Horace Liveright, Huebsch, and Thomas Seltzer, who emerged in the 1910s and 1920s to challenge the dominance of the older houses. Like many newcomers to the publishing field—indeed, like many of the established houses when they were just beginning—these young firms occasionally swelled their catalogues with the casualties of American copyright formalities. Quinn wrote Huebsch in 1917 that he had noticed that "this concern, Boni and Company, or Boni and someone, are pirating books for which the copyright has expired, or on which there never was a copyright, one of the last being a book of Chesterton's, or a compilation of his uncopyrighted things into a book."[71]

Quinn frequently voiced his suspicion of "[p]irates like [Thomas Bird] Mosher and pirates like Boni & Liveright" who were "very keen" to exploit works that had passed into the American public domain for failure to comply with copyright formalities.[72] In 1918, he wrote Pound about a rumor that Albert Boni was planning an unauthorized edition of T. S. Eliot's poems. Pound replied with blustering suggestions about what might be done if "that shister [sic] Boni tries to pirate 'Prufrock,'" but the rumor had evidently been unfounded.[73] In any case, Quinn's use of "pirate" was loose and bilious rather than legally exact. Years later, Huebsch remarked that a work "can't be pirated if it never had a copyright, except from the moral point of view, which I don't think that Quinn recognized anyway."[74] If a basis in law was lacking, Quinn the lawyer was not reluctant to feign moral indignation.

As late as 1927, Pound, writing to his father for help in finding an American publisher for his prose writings, warned him to avoid "new wildcat or dishonest firms, Selzer [sic], Boni and Boni. Selzer dishonest, and Boni hardly sound."[75] *Pirate* was a term that could expand and contract with the nature of the perceived outrage. Bennett Cerf, who early in his publishing career had worked with Horace Liveright and admired him, later conceded that Liveright was distrusted by some publishers. "They believed the minute they'd give him a good book, Horace would establish contact with the author and steal him for himself."[76] As late as the 1960s, Cerf complained that some of the best known American publishers were "veritable pirates."[77]

His lively disapprobation was a direct descendant of the nineteenth-century rhetoric of trade courtesy. For Cerf, as for Henry Holt in the 1880s, imputing piracy was a way of condemning deviation from the unwritten norms of fair dealing—in this case, the informal rule that protected the association of an author with a publishing house. The spirit of courtesy continued well into the twentieth century and came to serve as a quiet but crucial extralegal remedy for transatlantic modernists disadvantaged by American copyright law.

The disgust shown in the early twentieth century for lawful piracy was in part a continuation of the nineteenth-century evangelism against the exploitation of unprotected foreign authors. But additional factors now fueled this feeling. The 1891 and 1909 U.S. copyright acts, in making copyright protection conditionally available to foreign authors, had altered the moral climate of publishing and rendered piracy even less acceptable than it had been in the past.[78] The existence of new legal constraints on the exploitation of foreign authors, however imperfect or limited in practice, made technically lawful forms of piracy seem more unjust than they had seemed prior to 1891. In contrast to the nineteenth century, when the absence of an international copyright law had stimulated militant support for foreign authors' rights, now the protections that Congress had finally vouchsafed were whetting the public's appetite for justice. On learning that a Boston firm planned to issue an unauthorized edition of Joyce's uncopyrighted volume of poems, *Chamber Music*, Quinn remarked, "I thought that sort of literary piracy was largely out of date."[79]

The slowly expanding protections for foreign authors were not wholly altruistic. In part, legislators were responding to the fact that the United States, long a net importer of culture, was becoming increasingly competitive in the international market for literary and artistic works.[80] As long as American publishers and readers were dependent on British novels and stories, legislative policies favored a copyright law that maintained foreign works as a free, continually replenished resource; the copyright vacuum for non-U.S. authors was justified by pious reference to an impecunious public seeking to boost its literacy and to the jobs that would be created in the book-manufacturing trade. But by the first decades of the twentieth century, the direction of cultural exports was changing. Huebsch wrote in 1942, "Not only the British but the Continentals read American books; indeed, the liking for our product has increased markedly, especially in England in the past few decades, so that today we probably export as many titles to England as we import from it."[81] With foreign markets opening up to American works, it seemed expedient in 1891 and 1909 to extend some protections to foreign authors in America. As the U.S. copyright law changed to accommodate greater cultural and economic reciprocity with other nations, the moral climate in the United States grew less tolerant of the lawful pirate. Casual piracy was becoming a disfavored thing.

Despite the change in ethical sensitivities, unauthorized exploitation of foreign authors continued throughout the late nineteenth and early twentieth centuries. George Bernard Shaw's early novels *An Unsocial Socialist* (1884) and *Cashel Byron's Profession* (1885–86) were reprinted without his permission in the United States, though he quipped that American publishers were only claiming "their national inheritance ... at the rate of a dollar and a half per copy, free of all royalty to the flattered author."[82] Yeats was reprinted without authorization, or at least without remuneration, by Mosher and other American publishers well into the 1920s.

Long before Roth began reissuing extracts from "Work in Progress" and *Ulysses* in his magazines, Joyce's early volume *Chamber Music* had been reprinted without his permission by a Boston firm called the Cornhill Co. Reprinting Joyce's poems was a way for a small press to enhance its list and its coffers, now that the Irish author was gaining a name in the United States. Huebsch, who was Joyce's authorized American publisher, complained that the Cornhill Co. had taken advantage of the 1909 act's manufacturing clause, which had claimed Joyce's poems for the American public domain shortly after their appearance in London in 1907.[83] Quinn wrote Joyce in 1919 that *Chamber Music* "has been pirated here ... by Cornhill Company ... at $1. a volume."[84] Sylvia Beach observed that the Boston volume was the first she had heard of "pirates boarding Joyce's craft."[85]

Beach published Joyce's second collection of poems, *Pomes Penyeach*, in Paris in 1927. The slim volume of thirteen poems was also reprinted without permission in the United States, this time in Cleveland by two university students, Alexander Buchman and Edwin Johnson, who produced a private edition of one hundred numbered copies on a hand-operated press.[86] This was in 1931, nearly four years after the appearance of Beach's edition, which she had not deposited for ad interim protection or reprinted in America within the period mandated by the law. When Buchman wrote to Beach to inform her of his tribute to Joyce, Beach enlisted her father to have a small edition hastily printed by the Princeton University Press and registered for copyright in Washington, DC.[87] She believed that this belated action might save the U.S. copyright for *Pomes Penyeach*, but she was mistaken. Once an English-language edition had been published abroad and not reprinted according to the prescriptions of the 1909 act, it was not possible to rescue that same edition by printing a later edition within the United States, as Beach and Bennett Cerf learned with respect to the Paris edition of *Ulysses*.[88] That many of the poems in *Pomes Penyeach* had originally been published in American magazines might have helped to bolster a copyright claim for the volume, but magazine publication was a precarious device for securing protection for individual contributors' writings.

Beach never fully understood the complexities of American copyright law. In an unpublished version of her memoirs, she observed that "pirators" of Joyce's writings seemed to make a little game of their unauthorized activities. The game involved looking about for something by Joyce that lacked copyright protection and then rushing it into print "before he could stop you, [thus dispensing] with the nuisance of a contract with the author."[89] The legal contradictions contained in this statement highlight Beach's copyright naïveté. If a work was not protected by copyright in America, there was nothing that Joyce or anyone else could do to "stop" an intending publisher, and there was no way to impose contractual obligations on such a person. Joyce was outraged by what he called "picking his pocket,"[90] but his image of a stolen wallet or pocket watch—a commonplace among antipiracy campaigners of the nineteenth century—failed to capture the true legal status of a public good freely available in the American public domain, however much this argument from chattel may have aroused righteous indignation. The only thing that could modify the rules of the pirate's game was another set of extralegal rules—those of trade courtesy, which American publishers quietly observed well into the twentieth century.

By the 1920s, Joyce was a controversial, banned author whose uncopyrighted works were a temptation to American reprinters. So was D. H. Lawrence. His first novel, *Sons and Lovers*, was reprinted without permission by Boni & Liveright in their Modern Library series in 1922. The novel had originally been issued in London by Duckworth on May 29, 1913. Lawrence's authorized American publisher, Mitchell Kennerley, published it on September 17, 1913, nearly four months later.[91] By operation of the manufacturing clause, which at the time required reprinting in the United

States within thirty days of an ad interim deposit, *Sons and Lovers* entered the American public domain no later than the end of July 1913. Kennerley registered a copyright claim for his edition—possibly because he had had the text reset from corrected page proofs and believed that variants constituted a freshly copyrightable version[92]—but the Duckworth first edition was free for the taking. Lawrence knew he had no legal remedy against Boni & Liveright. His solution, a sanction reminiscent of trade courtesy, was to strike back at the pirates through predatory pricing. "[W]e have to beat that Boni brute," he declared, "issue a standard size book for the same price as his cheap edition and while the fight lasts I cut down my royalty to a minimum."[93] Lawrence's willingness to sacrifice earnings for moral victory recalls the self-inflicted losses that Holt and other American publishers had been prepared to sustain in order to teach a lesson to deviants from courtesy norms.

*Lady Chatterley's Lover* was notoriously and frequently reissued without Lawrence's knowledge or permission in the United States (and in Europe). After he published the volume privately in Florence in 1928, it became fair game in America within a few months' time. In December of that year, he complained that there had "come out two pirated editions of *Lady C.* in America: they are being sold in London at £3 and one I heard at 30/—but usually £3. I believe they are being sold in Paris too."[94] "I'm done in the eye!" he groaned.[95] The "pirated lot" was harming sales of his expensive Florence edition, and by April 1929, he was worrying over "three, perhaps even four pirated editions produced in U.S.A."[96] "[I]t would be a service to literature," he remarked, "if this unabashed piracy were stopped, or even checked."[97] But there was no legal redress in the United States. Unauthorized American reprints of *Lady Chatterley's Lover* continued to appear after Lawrence's death. During the early 1930s, Roth issued an expurgated version under his William Faro imprint, listing it as number one of the "modern amatory classics"; he also published his own dramatization of the novel.[98] He claimed to have tried to obtain reprint permission before Lawrence's death, and in 1931 he offered a bemused Frieda Lawrence five thousand dollars if she would authorize his plans. But she would have nothing to do with this "awful man" and his "terrible" play. Undaunted, Roth went ahead anyway.[99] Then, in 1931 and 1932, he added to his Faro list two unauthorized, anonymous sequels, *Lady Chatterley's Husbands* and *Lady Chatterley's Friends*.[100]

The immediate cause of the loss of American copyright in the foreign editions of *Sons and Lovers* and *Lady Chatterley's Lover* was not that these works were regarded as immoral. Scholars have erred in stating that a work deemed indecent could not receive copyright protection in the United States.[101] Although in a few recorded instances courts ruled or suggested that copyrights in obscene works were not valid or enforceable,[102] the true proximate cause of Lawrence's and Joyce's copyright woes was that they had not complied with the 1909 act's manufacturing clause. It is true that the controversial nature of their works made it difficult or impossible to have them reprinted in America within the requisite time period, but the rigors of the copyright law caused the loss of protection in the first instance; obscenity laws and strict moral standards formed the disabling background.

Under its "rule of doubt," the U.S. Copyright Office registered many works of questionable morality.[103] During the early 1930s, Roth succeeded in registering copyright claims for various titles that had appeared under his Faro imprint, including Ralph Cheyney's *Pregnant Woman in a Lean Age* (1931); Ralcy Husted Bell's *Memoirs and Mistresses: Colors and Odors of Love* (1931); Clement Wood's *Loose Shoulder Straps* (1932) (published under the pseudonym Alan Dubois); *Anecdota Americana: Five Hundred Stories for the Amusement of the Five Hundred Nations That Comprise America* (1933); and *Woman's Doctor: A Story of the Abortion of Human Life* (1933) by one Dr. Walter Lennox. These works ranged from sex pulps and gallantiana to lurid medical exposés; some merely bore titillating titles or offered suggestive themes and spicy passages designed to catch pennies.[104] The Copyright Office carried on a technical correspondence with Roth about all these books but never suggested that registration might be withheld for reasons of salaciousness.[105] Roth obtained registrations for other racy Faro titles as well: *Lady Chatterley's Husbands* (1930), *Lady Chatterley's Lover: A Dramatization* (1931), Daniel Quilter's *Body: A New Study, in Narrative, of the Anatomy of Society* (1931), and a translation of Octave Mirbeau's *Celestine, Being the Diary of a Chambermaid* (1930).[106]

The manufacturing clause was the cheap reprinter's best friend, and Roth took ingenious advantage of it, filling his magazines of the 1920s with serialized novels, memoirs, stories, translations, and poems that had been published abroad and not reprinted in the United States in accordance with the statutory formalities. He used the law's defects to build a marbled modernism in his magazines, a hybrid of verbal experiment, free expression, and entertainment for men. I discuss his reprinting of Joyce, Pound, Eliot, and other authors in later chapters. Here, it is enough to offer examples of his keen and relentless eye for foreign works that had fallen afoul of U.S. copyright formalities and so rested reliably in the American public domain.

One such work was Gertrude Beasley's controversial memoir of her West Texas upbringing, *My First Thirty Years*, published in Paris in 1925 by Contact Editions. Barred by New York customs, Beasley's unsentimental picture of ignorance, poverty, and incest was ideal for Roth's blend of literary seriousness and prude-baiting frankness. Calling it "probably the first honest book ever written by a woman,"[107] he serialized it in his "privately printed" magazine *Casanova Jr's Tales: A Quarterly Book for Subscribers*, edited by himself under the pseudonym Francis Page.[108] Published for a thousand subscribers by Roth's Two Worlds Publishing Co., *Casanova Jr's Tales* sold for $5 a copy or $15 for a year. The hefty price, the limited subscription base, and the label "privately printed" were intended to keep vice crusaders and prosecutors from descending on the publication.[109]

By April 1926, when Roth issued the first installment of Beasley's memoir, any copyright in the work had been lost to the American public domain for months. In December 1926 she was still hoping for payment from Roth and wondering whether he made "an assignment of copyright for each instalment or for the whole work when the serial is completed." She had spotted a general copyright notice in the issues of *Casanova Jr's Tales* and was "anxious to get the copyright in my name."[110] Like Sylvia Beach, she vainly hoped that republication in the United States might secure copyright for her there. The manufacturing clause was not so forgiving, however. What the law took away, it could not restore, despite later efforts to reprint and give American book manufacturers their due. Roth's copyright notice, whatever value it may have had for the issue as a whole, could not resuscitate Beasley's lost rights.

The *Contact Collection of Contemporary Writers*, published in 1925 by Robert McAlmon's Contact Editions and printed in Dijon by Maurice Darantiere, was one of Roth's favorite quarries for reprint material. The volume, published in Paris, contained a veritable roll call of established and emerging writers and transgressive voices, and McAlmon's preference for scraps, fragments, and works in progress was just right for redeployment in Roth's voracious periodicals. His first raid on this resource yielded a four-page extract from Joyce's "Work in Progress," which he printed in the December 1925 number of *Two Worlds*.[111] From the *Contact Collection* Roth also culled, for the September 1926 number of his companion newsstand magazine *Two Worlds Monthly*, a story by Djuna Barnes entitled "A Little Girl Tells a Story to a Lady."[112] In the very next number of *Two Worlds Monthly* Roth reprinted, also from McAlmon's volume, Norman Douglas's "A Fragment," a lighthearted account of the Syrian goddess Derceto and her quest to abort her child, Semiramis, conceived with a mortal.[113]

T. S. Eliot's London-based literary magazine *The Criterion* also was a frequent source for Roth. From it he reprinted a ten-page extract from Joyce's "Work in Progress," D. H. Lawrence's story "Jimmy and the Desperate Woman," and poems by Eliot that later formed sections of his unfinished verse drama, *Sweeney Agonistes*.[114] Other material that Roth mined for his *Two Worlds* magazines included poems by John Synge taken from Dublin editions first published by the Cuala Press and by Maunsel; "Mr. Handy's Wife," a story by Theodore Francis Powys, snatched from *The Calendar*, a London quarterly; poems by W. H. Davies drawn from volumes issued in England; and John Galsworthy's autobiographical piece, "Memorable Days," which previously had appeared as a privately printed pamphlet in London.[115]

**Figure 2.1** Samuel Roth, *Vanity Fair*, 1932.

Roth's timing was usually impeccable. He waited just long enough to be sure that his sources had not been reprinted in the United States in accordance with the manufacturing clause. He built his eroticized modernism from borrowed materials that were often only a few months old, recent enough to have the appearance of literary discoveries but not so new as to risk liability in case a foreign author or publisher had actually managed to secure ad interim protection. Roth's was a slightly delayed, oblique modernism, an evening edition of the morning news, a bringing together of "two worlds," Europe and America, in magazines that promised an increase of "gaiety," a more vivid living in the moment, an experience of candor, sophistication, and entertainment, in equal parts. Like Thomas Bird Mosher before him, Roth claimed to be providing a service to American readers who lacked the funds to purchase European writing in expensive formats. Whereas Mosher purveyed fine editions of out-of-the-way poetry and prose at affordable prices, Roth purported to give his readers bold modern writing at a cost much lower than that demanded by the "genial booklegger." He guaranteed "a certain freedom of speech … that would have been frowned upon in the Victorian nineteenth century." *Two Worlds Monthly* would "speak freely without overstepping the bounds of good taste."[116]

Roth's tasteful freedom of speech and his unique contribution to the gaiety of nations would scarcely have been possible without the American public domain. The 1909 act's formal requirements—American manufacture of books, affixation of copyright notices, and timely renewal of copyrights—played a distinct role in the production and dissemination of modern writing, foreign and domestic, in the United States. At the expense of authorial compensation and control, the law aggressively eliminated or truncated the monopoly protecting many works, giving to those works their full, unbounded character of public goods. The result was an unauthorized modernism, freed from copyright, often disapproved by moral-rights purists, sometimes condemned as indecent, but undeniably there, available in the marketplace. Although Roth's free speech was beset by burdens—notably, obscenity laws and vice crusaders' raids—the copyright law was one of the means by which he and other unauthorized reprinters repackaged and distributed transatlantic modernism to American readers. These two faces of the American public domain—destroyer of copyrights and preserver of access—contributed significantly to cultural experience in the twentieth century, just as in the nineteenth.

## Combating the American Public Domain: Attempted Remedies

Foreign-domiciled authors and publishers were not always passive in the face of the American public domain. There were strategies for seeking copyright protection in the United States. Most of these were not guaranteed to succeed; they were methods of the second best, consolations for the ravages of the manufacturing clause. Four distinct approaches can be discerned from the dealings of authors, publishers, and magazine editors in the early decades of the twentieth century. First, foreign authors who were well-established, well-connected, or simply fortunate were able to arrange for simultaneous or near-simultaneous printing in the United States and abroad, thus satisfying the copyright law's manufacturing requirements. This was the preferred way, the one fully complying with the dictates of the law. Second, American publishers often insisted, as a condition of reprinting a work previously issued abroad, that the author revise or expand the text so as to include new matter that might qualify for a U.S. copyright. This approach did not resurrect copyright for the foreign edition, which remained a free resource in the American public domain, but by printing a revised work in compliance with the manufacturing clause, a publisher could stake a colorable claim to protection that might make pirates blink before entering into competition with the authorized American edition.

Third, foreign authors sometimes published their writings initially in an American magazine, hoping that the copyright claimed for the entire issue might secure protection for their individual contributions. Pound and Quinn were true believers in this strategy for "holding down" copyrights in the United States, but there were potential pitfalls, and courts were divided on the efficacy of this approach. Finally, authors occasionally sought to print portions or fragments of larger works on American soil within the window allowed by the manufacturing clause. The results were sometimes doubtful, as with Joyce's efforts to print and copyright portions of "Work in Progress," and sometimes ludicrous, as with Pound's scheme to gain protection for fragments of works that he had printed as "broadsides" in the United States. I discuss each of these methods below.

### Coordinating Transatlantic Publication

The surest way for a foreign-domiciled author to obtain a copyright under the 1909 U.S. Copyright Act was to coordinate simultaneous or near-simultaneous printing on both sides of the Atlantic. Though writers with an established reputation were often able to accomplish this, new, unknown, or controversial authors were at a disadvantage. The 1891 Chace Act had posed often insuperable difficulties because it required works to be typeset in America and copies to be deposited in the Copyright Office on or before the date of publication abroad. Leonard Smithers, Oscar Wilde's London publisher, tried to effect simultaneous publication of *The Ballad of Reading Gaol* in England and the United States, urging Wilde's American agent to "fix the day on which you wish to publish, and I will publish on the same day here."[117] February 13, 1898, a Sunday, was the day on which the poem was to be printed in *The New York Journal*, but the plan fell through, possibly due to extensive reportage that the *Journal* devoted that day to the sinking of a transatlantic steamship.[118] Wilde's American copyright in the *Ballad* was cast into doubt.[119]

After helplessly watching some of his unprotected collections of fairy tales and folklore appear without permission in the United States, Yeats managed to have a few of his early works, such as *The Wind among the Reeds* (1899) and *The Shadowy Waters* (1900), typeset in accordance with the manufacturing clause. At the urging of the English publisher John Lane, *The Wind among the Reeds* was printed in Cambridge, Massachusetts; sheets were then dispatched to Elkin Mathews in London to be bound for an English edition. In later years, the Macmillan Co. of New York, Yeats's authorized American publisher, studiously protected his copyrights by making sure that his works were printed in a timely fashion in the United States. Moreover, with the help of Quinn and the British literary agent A. P. Watt, Yeats developed the regular practice of publishing the same poem in British and American books and magazines within the period required by the law.[120] The necessity of resetting American texts from English proofs often resulted in variants between editions of his writings.[121]

Though he was not a copyright specialist, Quinn possessed a serviceable knowledge of American copyright law and dispensed it freely for the benefit of his literary protégés. Shortly after he met Yeats in 1902, Quinn began to attend to his copyrights. In his first letter to the Irish writer he enclosed a legal memorandum, specially prepared by his office, setting forth the steps necessary for securing copyright in the United States; he counseled Yeats to obtain protection for all his works that there was "a fair business reason for copyrighting."[122] Quinn took it upon himself to produce, at his own expense, small editions of Yeats's works that satisfied the manufacturing clause and other formalities. He had printed and registered for U.S. copyright Yeats's plays *Where There Is Nothing* (1902), *The King's Threshold* (1904), and *The Golden Helmet* (1908).[123] He performed the same service for J. M. Synge and Lady Gregory and even collected copyright royalties from sometimes uncooperative acting troupes. Shrewdly, he negotiated a contract with the theater manager Phillip Bayard Veiller that guaranteed Yeats a royalty on American performances of his plays, copyrighted or not. Quietly informing Yeats that *The Countess Cathleen* was "not copyrighted" in the United States, Quinn boasted that "the fun of the thing is that Veiller, being bound by a contract, happens to be the only one who could not give [the play] without permission."[124] In this aggressive twist on trade courtesy, Quinn bundled copyrighted and uncopyrighted works together in a contract that secured economic benefits for his friend. It is not too much to say that Quinn, unostentatiously and pro bono publico, built a substantial part of the legal infrastructure for the American reception of the Irish literary revival.

Quinn became a legal adviser to Pound as well. In July 1916 he asked Pound whether *Canzoni & Ripostes of Ezra Pound*, published in London by

**Figure 2.2** The lawyer John Quinn, seated far right, with two of his pro bono clients, James Joyce and Ezra Pound, far left, and Ford Madox Ford, Paris, 1923. (*Harry Ransom Center, University of Texas at Austin*)

Elkin Mathews in May 1913, was "copyrighted here in this country." "You know," he explained, "that in order [for it to be] copyrighted here it must have been printed from plates made or type set here."[125] Pound replied that "'Canzoni-Ripostes' is not copyright in U.S.A.," but he believed that separate magazine publication of some of the poems would "make it damd uncomfortable for anyone who tries to pirate it."[126] Pound added that his "books copyright in America" were two volumes published by Small, Maynard of Boston: *Provença* (1910), which contained a selection of poems from his earlier collections, and *Sonnets and Ballate of Guido Cavalcanti*. The latter work, issued in April 1912 shortly before its appearance in an English edition, satisfied the requirement of timely manufacture in the United States.

Several of Pound's earlier books had missed the narrow statutory window. *A Lume Spento* (1908), *A Quinzaine for This Yule* (1908), *Personae* (1909), and *Exultations* (1909) had all been published first in Europe and had not been reprinted in the United States within the timeframe mandated by U.S. law. But, rather remarkably for a writer as disliked as he was in some quarters, Pound managed to achieve prompt publication in America of a number of other early works, including the volumes *Pavannes and Divisions* (1918) and *Instigations* (1920). The prompt manufacture of these works gave them a fighting chance for U.S. copyright. As often in this period, Pound benefited from the legal and practical ministrations of Quinn, to whom he dedicated *Pavannes and Divisions*.

Under Quinn's tutelage, Pound learned to keep a close watch on his copyrights. In 1923, Pound complained that the rejection of some of his poems by the American magazine *The Dial* meant that they would not appear simultaneously in Britain and the United States. Writing to the magazine's principal stockholder James Sibley Watson, Pound pointed to the economic impact of failed copyright protection: "I trust you enjoy inflicting this financial loss (admittedly problematical) mais tout de même."[127] A few years later, he urged *The Dial* to coordinate publication of some of his cantos with their planned appearance in England in a deluxe edition entitled *A Draft of the Cantos 17–27*. "[O]ne wants to do all one can," he explained, "to protect the cantos from the thieves which our dastardly (and for the nonce lemonfaced) govt encourages."[128] Characteristically, Pound trained his anger on the U.S. copyright law as much as on the "thieves" who used it to exploit foreign-domiciled authors. These two villains—the law and those who sheltered within it—had been targets of antipiracy campaigns since the

nineteenth century. Pound took up and extended the double-barreled rhetoric of outrage.

Pound's anxiety over his American copyrights played a significant role in
his decisions to publish and formed an integral part of the "socialization" of
*The Cantos*.[129] In 1934 he wrote to T. S. Eliot of his efforts to orchestrate initial publication in the United States of portions of his long poem: "My hurry
to print [*Eleven New Cantos XXXI–XLI*] was for the American edtn and I
spose fer copyright reasons the Brit edtn shd not precede."[130] As it turned
out, Farrar & Rinehart published the volume in New York in October 1934;
Faber & Faber, of which Eliot was a director, issued the volume in London
five months later. Eliot kept an anxious eye on his own American copyrights. In 1936, in preparation for a volume of his poems to be published by
Harcourt, Brace in New York, he listed the poems that might and might not
have been protected in the United States, underscoring the "difficult case"
of *Sweeney Agonistes*, which Roth had issued without permission some years
before.[131]

## "The more alterations the better—because of copyright"

Once a foreign-domiciled author failed to comply with the 1909 act's manufacturing clause, there was no way to revive protection for the particular
edition that had been issued abroad. Simply resetting the foreign edition ver-
batim or binding imported sheets gave an American publisher no assurance
that other houses would not lawfully free ride by reprinting the work and
exploiting whatever market the publisher had managed to create. Publishers
responded to this incentives gap and the market failure it threatened by urging or requiring that foreign editions be altered or expanded so as to create
"new" works that, once typeset, printed, and bound in the United States,
could plausibly claim copyright as revised American editions. The texts of
many modernist authors were altered or recast to bolster publishers' copyright claims.

In November 1919, with her reputation rising in Britain, Virginia Woolf
was approached by George H. Doran about reissuing her first two novels,
*The Voyage Out* and *Night and Day*, in the United States. The English edition of *The Voyage Out* had lost any chance of American copyright several
years before; *Night and Day*, published in England in October 1919, had
narrowly missed the thirty-day window for securing ad interim protection
under the 1909 act.[132] Doran wanted her to revise the texts for publication in

the United States. "[W]ould you be so angelic," she wrote Lytton Strachey, "as to tell me if any special misprints, obscurities or vulgarities in either occur to you. I have to send the books off on Monday and they say the more alterations the better—because of copyright."[133] Although Woolf would later adopt a conscious policy of providing variant texts for her American publishers and of issuing creatively different versions on either side of the Atlantic,[134] in 1919 legal compulsions drove the revision process as much as aesthetic preferences. Scholars have noted the large number of deletions and changes that Woolf made for the American edition of *The Voyage Out*.[135] Her apprenticeship in designing around the American public domain in order to comply with the copyright law helped her to evolve, for her later works, a playful craft of transatlantic differences.

The strategy of copyright-by-revision was not new; the practice was well established among American publishers of the previous century. Henry Holt had urged the British publisher George Bentley to have his books reviewed "by some judicious American" who could make changes, subject to authors' approval, to "secure us copyright and choke off opposition."[136] Often, authors were encouraged to prepare a revised text even before the English edition appeared in order to prevent any time lag during which the latter might be vulnerable to unauthorized reprinting in the United States. In 1879, when Holt published *Probation* by the English writer Jessie Fothergill, he wondered if the novel "could be doctored enough to secure an American copyright, or could wait until we have international copyright protection."[137] For Holt as for other American publishers hoping to circumvent the statute's rigors, the choice lay between coming to the law through some strategy such as revision or waiting for the law to come to him through legislative action. But despite decades of debate, Congress had not yet acted, and publishers were loath to hold their deadlines for the ever-receding prospect of change. During Wilde's visit to America in 1882, his manager arranged for a revised edition of his play *Vera; or, The Nihilists* to be privately printed and registered for copyright. The London edition, which had appeared in 1880, enjoyed no protection in the United States. Wilde added a prologue and inserted numerous variations for the American printing. The resulting text was registered in pamphlet form with the Library of Congress, and the copyright claimed for the version proved useful when a dispute arose over rights to the play and its title.[138]

Holt's dream of an international law that would eliminate the need for second-best forms of protection was imperfectly realized with the passage of the 1909 act. Congress's retention of the manufacturing clause meant that many foreign-domiciled authors would continue to lose their copyrights and American publishers would still have to rely on makeshifts. When he learned in 1917 that the Cornhill Co. of Boston planned to bring out an unauthorized reprint of Joyce's uncopyrighted *Chamber Music*, Quinn urged Huebsch to issue an authorized edition augmented by several new poems that might give the volume a margin of protection and make it more difficult for "pirates" to compete.[139] Joyce acknowledged the problems created by the Boston reprint but characteristically refused to allow any supplementing of the volume, prepared as always to sacrifice legal considerations to his passion for aesthetic integrity.[140]

In 1919 Huebsch wrote to D. H. Lawrence about bringing out a revised American edition of his *New Poems*, which had been published by Martin Secker in London in October 1918. Troubled by Huebsch's remark that the work was "unprotected by copyright [in the United States] and may be reprinted by anyone who wishes to do so,"[141] Lawrence appealed to Secker, "Is that so?"[142] But Huebsch, who had an impressive knowledge of U.S. copyright law, was rarely wrong about such matters. With characteristic thoroughness, he explained to Lawrence his reason for wanting to issue a revised volume:

> I suggest that some slight change, substitution or addition be made; or you might include a short foreword if you can appropriately do so. This will make it possible to copyright the book because technically it becomes a different book than the one already published in England, though actually it will not interfere with anyone's right to reproduce the English volume.[143]

Just as when he informed Joyce of the copyright consequences of publishing *Ulysses* in France, Huebsch here candidly described the inexorableness of the American public domain: publishing a revised edition of *New Poems* might have some deterrent effect on unauthorized reprinting in the United States, but the London edition would remain fair game for anyone minded to issue it. Eschewing the emotional rhetoric of piracy in which Quinn and Pound frequently indulged, Huebsch dispassionately acknowledged "anyone's right to reproduce the English volume." For Huebsch, the law was the law. Though he himself would not take advantage of the legal right to publish *New Poems* without Lawrence's permission, others were free to do so.

In late August 1919, Lawrence provided Huebsch with a preface to be added to the American edition of *New Poems*. A critical document of modernism and a sustained exposition of Lawrence's poetic vitalism, the preface ran to ten pages in the edition that Huebsch issued in June 1920 with the notice "Copyright, 1920, by B. W. Huebsch Inc." The preface was not new, however; it had appeared the previous year under the title "Poetry of the Present" in two issues of the "radically modern" magazine *Playboy*, edited and published in New York by Egmont Arens.[144] This earlier appearance would not necessarily have impaired Huebsch's claim to a copyright in his edition of *New Poems*. Arens had been diligent about placing copyright notices in issues of his short-lived magazine, and he registered some of these issues with the U.S. Copyright Office. *Playboy*'s collective-work copyright notices may have salvaged some protected matter for Huebsch to bind into his edition.

Lawrence's preface was not the only item in Huebsch's edition of *New Poems* that had appeared earlier in an American periodical. At Lawrence's request, Huebsch included a note on the flyleaf: "Thanks are due to *Poetry* for permission to reprint some of these poems." Publication in magazines was an opportunity for foreign authors to gain exposure to American readers, but it was also a method for seeking a kind of piecemeal legal protection. By placing their poems, short stories, or serialized longer works in magazines that were printed in accordance with the manufacturing clause, authors hoped to secure a patchwork of copyrights that might add up to the protection afforded a complete work duly manufactured in the United States. Copyright-by-magazine-publication was another strategy of the second best, however, because it rested on the assumption that contributors' works always shared in the blanket copyright claimed for the issue as a whole. That assumption was not firmly grounded in the law but rather remained an unsettled question in U.S. courts throughout the first half of the twentieth century. Once again, American copyright formalities were at the heart of the problem.

## "Holding down American copyrights": Magazine Publication

Publishing in an American magazine was one way for a foreign-domiciled author to attempt to satisfy the manufacturing clause. Because magazine issues were typeset and printed in the United States and carried a general or blanket copyright notice, it was reasoned that anything contained in such issues must likewise be protected on behalf of the contributors. Yeats regularly relied on American magazine publication, noting in 1926 that his relationship with *The Dial* had enabled him to "synchronize publication on both sides of the Atlantic [so as to avoid] loss of my American copyright."[145] Pound, too, remarked that most of the legal protection he enjoyed in the United States was "that of the magazines."[146] When he was told the rumor that Boni & Liveright was planning an unauthorized reprint of Eliot's *Prufrock and Other Observations* (London, 1917), Pound retorted that many of Eliot's poems had previously appeared in *Poetry*: "That is enough to hold up Boni's little game."[147] Pound's faith in this method had been kindled by Quinn, who had urged him to arrange for magazine publication of his versions of Japanese Noh plays. "That would save the copyright," Quinn assured him. "Then no pirate could pirate the whole book."[148]

Quinn was convinced of this approach. Writing to Huebsch in 1917 about alternatives for obtaining a U.S. copyright for Joyce's play *Exiles*, he stated, "Of course if a magazine publishes the play, the magazine would copyright the play."[149] Quinn had in mind Section 3 of the 1909 copyright act, which provided that "copyright upon ... periodicals shall give to the proprietor thereof all the rights in respect thereto which he would have if each part were individually copyrighted under this Act."[150] The language seems plain enough, yet a problem lurked just beneath the surface: who owned the copyright in a contribution to a magazine, the author of the contribution or the proprietor of the magazine? And what consequences might this have for the validity and enforceability of any copyright claimed for the separate contribution? These questions, to which I will return in chapter 4, are crucial for testing Quinn's faith in magazine copyrights and for understanding, among other things, the copyright status of the version of Joyce's *Ulysses* that was serialized in *The Little Review* between 1918 and 1920.

The use of American magazines for securing elusive copyright protection for authors living abroad is a largely unexamined aspect of transatlantic modernism. It is well known that Pound became the foreign editor or correspondent for *Poetry*, *The Little Review*, and *The Dial* in order to set up an overseas command post for progressive arts and letters and to provide a regular outlet for the writers he admired. His editorial roles gave him access to the country he most wanted to educate and allowed him to serve as a conduit and spokesman for developments in European writing. From the start of his relationship with *The Little Review*, Pound insisted on the freedom to select contributors and to use the magazine as a mouthpiece for his opinions, including his views on copyright reform. "The American copyright regulations, the tariff on books imported into America are both scandals," he wrote Margaret Anderson in early 1917. "I should want to feel free to say so. Not more than half a page per issue."[151]

But even as Pound insisted on writing *about* copyright abuses in American magazines, he saw his editorial role as including the far more practical ability to help transatlantic authors obtain U.S. copyrights for their contributions. As he explained to Quinn in 1918, his plan was to use *The Little Review* "to hold down American copyrights, and for general convenience."[152] He boasted that he had "placed a lot of [Yeats's] stuff and saved him a certain amount of trouble during the past years ... with the convenience of holding down his copyrights etc."[153] Two years later, discussing the appearance of some of Yeats's work in *The Dial*, Pound wrote that the Irish poet "wd. want to know when it was to start and finish so as to protect, or have the pleasure of thinking he was protecting, his Eng. Copyright."[154] This faintly ironic note of doubt about American magazines as a source of copyright protection for foreign authors is sounded as well in Pound's persistent remark about "holding down" copyrights. He used the same metaphor in 1927 to stress that he intended his own little magazine, *The Exile*, to be financially self-sufficient, "with AMERICAN PRINTING to hold down copyright."[155] Pound's agonistic image suggests that he saw himself as locked in an ongoing and possibly futile struggle to subdue legal uncertainty and to stabilize a volatile property right, as if the law were a protean shape-shifter that must be pinned to the ground before it would yield its benefits.

Part of the uncertainty lay in the transitional nature of American copyright law and its dependence on technical formalities and abstruse doctrines. By the early twentieth century, courts had evolved the doctrine of copyright indivisibility, which held that a copyright was an unbreakable whole that could not be divided into multiple pieces and owned by different persons or entities. If an author assigned one exclusive right—say, the right of North American book publication—then all other exclusive rights under the copyright were deemed to have been assigned along with it. Any attempt to transfer something less than the totality of a copyright resulted not in the assignment of an ownership right, but in the granting of a license. In contrast to an assignment of the whole copyright, which rendered its recipient a "proprietor," a "mere license," as courts often called it, conferred nothing more than permission to make a particular use of the work.[156] A licensee could never be a proprietor. Although Congress later recognized the shortcomings of many of these rules and drafted the 1976 copyright act to ensure that copyrights could be successfully subdivided into many exclusive rights, the doctrine of copyright indivisibility flourished under the 1891 and 1909 acts and remained a troublesome piece of the U.S. copyright puzzle for decades.

That puzzle was further complicated by the rigid rule that a statutory copyright could exist only if a proper copyright notice had been placed on copies of the published work. Not just anyone was entitled to be identified in the copyright notice. Because ownership of a copyright was indivisible, only the "proprietor" of the copyright could properly be named in the notice. If any other name appeared—such as the name of a mere licensee—the notice was defective and the copyright was at risk of being deemed forfeited. These inflexible rules held special danger for authors who published in magazines and other periodicals. Such authors initially owned the copyrights in their contributions, but when they agreed to allow a magazine to print their work, they granted rights to the magazine. Because of the doctrine of indivisibility, this grant of rights could be only one of two things: either a transfer of the entire copyright in the contribution, whereupon the magazine became the copyright proprietor, or a giving of a mere license, in which case the author retained ownership of the copyright. If, as often happened, the magazine, as a licensee, affixed a single blanket copyright notice in its own name to all copies of the magazine, the copyright in the author's contribution might be destroyed. Such a copyright notice, though properly naming the magazine as proprietor of the *collective* work, omitted the name of the true owner of the copyright in the *individual* contribution—the author. An erroneous notice was the same as no notice at all. The doctrine of indivisibility, meant to preserve copyrights from deleterious fragmentation, often led to their unintended destruction.[157]

The 1903 case of *Mifflin v. R. H. White Co.* illustrates these copyright dangers for magazine contributors. In 1859, Oliver Wendell Holmes authorized the serialization of his volume of witty table talk, *The Professor at the Breakfast-Table*, in *The Atlantic Monthly*. Although the magazine proprietor failed to secure copyrights for the first ten issues containing installments of Holmes's work, the proprietor satisfied the statutory procedures for the final two issues. But the proprietor, not having received an assignment from Holmes initially, was only a licensee with respect to the installments, and the blanket copyright notices citing *The Atlantic Monthly* failed to name the true owner of rights in the installments—Holmes. The U.S. Supreme Court explained that not just "any form of notice is good"; rather, the purpose of notice was "to warn the public against republication of a certain book by a certain author or proprietor."[158] Lacking copyright notices naming Holmes, the issues of *The Atlantic Monthly*, though copyrighted as collective works, afforded no protection to Holmes's separate contributions. Those contributions were in the American public domain, freely available for anyone to reprint singly or collectively. The doctrine of indivisibility and the requirement of proper notice combined to frustrate magazine contributors well into the twentieth century.[159]

Not without compassion for authors whose copyrights were jeopardized through no fault of their own, courts sometimes resorted to the maxim that the law abhors a forfeiture. There were chiefly two judicial theories for salvaging protection for magazine contributors. The first and most direct could be invoked when a magazine had placed a separate copyright notice naming the author at the foot of his or her contribution.[160] Such a notice correctly cited the actual owner of the copyright (unless the author had assigned it to the magazine), and the issue's blanket notice would not be deemed to have vitiated the author's copyright. But this practice was inconsistent; many magazine owners, if they thought about it at all, simply assumed that they held rights to the entire contents of issues, and contributing authors frequently lacked the bargaining power or the legal knowledge to demand a personal copyright notice.

The second judicial approach was the "trust" theory of copyright ownership, an elaborate legal fiction that involved a creative application of law to the facts of publication. Here, courts resourcefully concluded that a magazine or other publisher, even though it seemed to have received only a license from the author, had nevertheless managed to secure copyright for the author's benefit. This doctrine required the court to treat an irregular copyright notice not as a forfeiture of protection, but rather as evidence of a trust undertaken by the publisher on behalf of the author. On this theory, the publisher became a trustee, holding legal title to the copyright for the purpose of protecting the author, who was deemed the equitable or true copyright owner.[161] As the true holder, the author could exercise all rights of ownership, including the right to sue for infringement. Courts were careful to state that the existence of such a copyright trust was a factual question "dependent on the circumstances of the case."[162] Chief among those circumstances were the intentions of the author and the publisher; in particular, courts required evidence that the author had had "no intention to donate his work to the public."[163] If the facts suggested that the author had been indifferent to his rights or that the publisher had regarded itself as the true owner of the copyright, the trust theory was more difficult to apply. But when circumstances did not preclude it, the trust theory offered courts a plausible basis for avoiding a judgment that would "deprive the [author] of the fruits of his creative effort."[164]

Although unacquainted with the intricacies of the trust theory, Pound, inspired by Quinn, essentially viewed magazines as if they were trustees of their contributors' copyrights. He remarked to Quinn in 1916, "'Poetry' [magazine] etc. hold the copyrights of scattered poems for me and could therefore stop a pirated edition."[165] In addition to signaling his struggle to obtain protection for foreign authors, Pound's persistent characterization of magazines as "holding" or "holding down" authors' copyrights sketched an intuitive trust theory of copyright and transatlantic authorship. Magazines safeguarded the rights of their foreign authors until such time as those authors, the true owners, might need to sue a trespasser.

The more direct strategy of including authors' names in separate copyright notices was also discussed by Pound and Quinn. In 1916, Quinn remarked that an American magazine could "save" the copyright in Pound's volume of Noh plays by "publishing parts of the book [and copyrighting] those parts in [Pound's] name."[166] Pound had recourse to the same idea when, in 1927, he urged *The Dial* to "have the copyright of the cantos ... registered separately in my name."[167] *The Dial* partly obliged by printing special notices ("Copyright 1928 by Ezra Pound") on the opening pages of "Part of Canto XXVII" and "Canto XXII" in the January and February 1928 issues, respectively. But despite Pound's and Quinn's awareness of the value of a separate notice, the magazines with which they were involved, like many magazines, rarely used this approach. The notices in Pound's name were almost *The Dial*'s sole concession to authorial copyright during 1928.[168] Contributions by Yeats, Eliot, William Carlos Williams, Conrad Aiken, and others carried no individual notices. Pound himself seems to have confined his requests for separate protection to his poetry contributions. His prose essay "Dr. Williams' Position" in the November 1928 issue bore no special notice.[169]

*The Little Review* was similarly sparing of separate notices. One exception was the January 1919 issue, which contained Yeats's play *The Dreaming of the Bones.* In addition to a general copyright notice in Margaret Anderson's name on the inside front cover, the first page of Yeats's drama carried the notice "Copyright, 1918, by William Butler Yeats."[170] No doubt this scrupulous touch owed to Quinn, who regularly cared for Yeats's copyrights and wrote a short essay on the play for the same number. None of the other contributions to the issue, including the section of the "Lestrygonians" episode from Joyce's *Ulysses*, bore a separate notice.

## Copyrighting Special Editions and Fragments of Works

In 1897, Oscar Wilde wrote to his London publisher that he was concerned about "plagiarism" of his forthcoming poem, *The Ballad of Reading Gaol*, by American newspapers. He wondered whether "copyrighting *portions* of the poem [in the United States] will prevent the piracy of quotation in the papers," but he decided against this strategy, observing with resignation that "the moment you publish in England, the American papers, under pretence of criticism, will publish the whole affair. That is certain."[171] The costs of printing, the challenges of simultaneous publication, and other legal and practical obstacles often drove European authors to contrive ingenious schemes for obtaining at least partial copyright protection in the United States—just enough to give color to a claim of exclusive rights.

In the 1880s, Gilbert and Sullivan devised an elaborate plan for obtaining an American copyright in *The Mikado* without having to publish the orchestral score and run the risk of piracy. To this end, they hired one George L. Tracey, an American citizen, to come to London and prepare a piano arrangement of the full operatic score. Tracey then registered the copyright in this arrangement with the Library of Congress and assigned the rights to Richard D'Oyly Carte, the theatrical impresario and partner of Gilbert and Sullivan. With an American copyright apparently secured, the team felt it was safe to publish the libretto, the vocal score, and the piano arrangement in England. But the enormous popularity of Gilbert and Sullivan inspired audacity in American entrepreneurs. When an unauthorized production of the opera was announced in New York, Carte sued for an injunction, claiming that the rival orchestration, which had been painstakingly recreated from the piano arrangement, would infringe the American copyright in the latter work. A federal court rejected Carte's claim, however, holding that U.S. copyright law did not grant a right of public performance for musical compositions and that Gilbert and Sullivan had forfeited American rights in the libretto and the vocal score by publishing those works initially abroad. The defendant was free to stage his version of *The Mikado*, "however unfair commercially or reprehensible in ethics his conduct may be."[172] The celebrated team's efforts to enjoy protection for the whole opera by copyrighting a part of it had run aground on the technical distinctions and protectionist policies of U.S. copyright law. Yet it was a strategy that would appeal to many transatlantic authors in later years.

When ordinary publication was unavailable, it helped to have a patron or a benevolent lawyer who could arrange for a special private edition to be printed in accordance with copyright requirements. Quinn played such a role for several Irish writers, ensuring legal protection, for example, for limited editions of Synge's *In the Shadow of the Glen* and act 2 of *The Playboy of the Western World*.[173] The New York attorney kept an eye out for publishers who might issue and copyright small editions of Yeats's plays, but if no publisher could be found, Quinn himself stood ready to "have them printed from lynotype [*sic*] and ... do it for the fun of it, or else that part of it may be considered my part in the [Irish] Theatre work on this side."[174] In 1908, he secured a U.S. copyright for *The Golden Helmet* by paying for a special printing of fifty numbered copies of the play.[175] He sent two of the copies to the Copyright Office for deposit and "put one or two on sale in a bookshop in order to comply with the law [requiring publication]," although he confided to Yeats that the latter copies would "probably be purchased back on my behalf."[176] Other copies he distributed as gifts or review copies.

Particularly attractive to some authors was the device of securing copyright for a portion of a work, especially when obtaining protection for the entire work was difficult or impossible. As with piecemeal rights in magazine contributions, securing de jure protection for part of a text gave hope of enjoying de facto protection in the whole. Stung by Samuel Roth's unauthorized publication of his writings in the United States, Joyce instructed his lawyers to arrange for the reprinting and copyrighting of extracts from his "Work in Progress." Between 1928 and 1930, the New York law firm of Chadbourne, Stanchfield & Levy took steps to secure U.S. copyrights for four separate gatherings of fragments—none more than sixty pages—that had appeared in the Paris journal *transition*. Because prior publication abroad threatened to cast these extracts into the American public domain, in each case the attorneys first satisfied the 1909 act's requirements for ad interim copyright by depositing with the Copyright Office, within sixty days of publication in Paris, one copy of each extract as it had appeared in *transition*. This secured a temporary U.S. copyright that lasted for four months from the date of deposit.[177]

Next, Joyce's lawyers instructed the Paul Maisel Co., job printers at 355 Broadway, to produce exactly five copies of the extract using the *transition* text as setting copy. The five copies, which Joyce referred to as "copyright dummies,"[178] were bound and stapled in orange, yellow, or tan covers, with the front cover serving as the title page. Once manufacture had been performed on American soil, two of the copies were deposited with the Copyright Office, as required by Section 22 of the 1909 act for extending ad interim copyright to the regular term of protection. The remaining copies were mailed to Joyce or retained by the law firm. Joyce's lawyers performed these tasks for Parts 11 and 12, 13, 15, and 18 of "Work in Progress."[179] At first, Joyce was relieved that portions of his evolving work seemed to be safeguarded from Roth and other American exploiters, but his anxiety returned when he saw that the pamphlets lacked the requisite copyright notices. Joyce's lawyers scrambled to have notices added to remaining copies of Part 18 and submitted these to the Copyright Office as substitutes, but Joyce was not placated and later refused to pay most of his lawyers' fees and costs. In December 1931, he complained that the specially printed volumes did "not contain any printer's mark or anything else to show that American copyright law has been complied with and [are] therefore quite worthless for the protection of my rights in this work."[180] The unpaid legal costs included some three hundred and fifty dollars that the law firm had advanced for printing fees.[181]

As with other stopgap measures for obtaining copyright protection, the scheme carried out by Joyce's attorneys foundered on the strict formalities of U.S. copyright law. But the failure to attach copyright notices to the volumes was not the only flaw in the plan. The other statutory requirement for acquiring copyright in this period was publication of the work in copies. It is hard to see how an edition of five copies could constitute the necessary general publication when two of those copies were sent to the Copyright Office and the others were mailed to Joyce or kept in the law firm's files. A deposit of copies in Washington, DC, was a dubious basis for establishing publication,[182] and there is no evidence that Joyce or his attorneys offered any of the remaining copies for sale or other distribution to the public. Had Joyce's scheme ever been tested in court, it is likely that the defendant would have escaped liability by demonstrating that the "Work in Progress" extracts resided in the American public domain.

The irony of Joyce's plan is that in focusing so intently on the requirements of the feared manufacturing clause, his representatives lost sight of other crucial formalities mandated by the 1909 act. Ezra Pound was afflicted with the same copyright myopia. Having decided that printing his magazine *The Exile* in the United States would be too costly, he directed his American agent John M. Price to secure a copyright for selected portions of the magazine's contents. In January 1927 he sent Price twenty dollars with instructions to have twenty copies of an extract of his Canto XX printed as a "broad side, or CHEAPEST POSSIBLE slop printing, but on strong paper," and then to have the extract registered in Washington, DC, so that it would be "COPYRIGHT, iron bound, (That'll hold up Mr. Roth, and his like.)." Next, Price was to contact Pound's father and "tell him he is to buy a copy, i.e., he is to send you six cents in stamps, and you mail him the extract. That ought to constitute legal publication and sale. If it don't, take somebody out into Madison Sq. Garden and sell 'em a copy for two cents, or five cents."[183] Like Joyce, Pound hoped that by securing federal protection for a fragment of a larger work he could technically comply with the requirements of the manufacturing clause and at the same time fire a shot across the bow of any pirate who might take a fancy to *The Exile*.

Price found a printer to do the job for fifteen dollars ("damn high at that") and promptly sent Pound fifteen copies of a three-column broadside containing "Part of Canto XX" and the opening paragraphs of John Rodker's novella "Adolphe 1920," also planned for *The Exile*.[184] Pound's poem had been crudely printed as unindented text, with the first letter of each line capitalized.[185] Price posted copies of the broadside to the Copyright Office, explaining that Pound could not pay to have the entire magazine printed in the United States but wished to print and copyright the broadside, which was "as much as he could afford," as a kind of "American edition."[186] The Copyright Office balked. William L. Brown, assistant register of copyrights, pointed to Pound's admitted plan to print *The Exile* abroad and informed Price that "copyright protection for this magazine could not be secured here without printing it entirely in the United States, and the procedure you have suggested for printing a brief extract of it in this country would not seem to meet the difficulty."[187] Pound erupted. If the Copyright Office was fixated on the definition of "periodical," then Price should "go ahead and copyright the broadside as something" and "[w]orry their god damnd hides off" while he was at it.[188]

Price indeed worried Brown, but the assistant register worried back. Price tried to persuade him to accept the broadside as a "book," but the bureaucrat rejected the reclassification. When Price persisted in seeking "partial protection" and tried to justify the plan as involving "the bona fide sale of two copies,"[189] Brown patiently explained that the Copyright Office could not accept an incomplete deposit copy of a larger published work and that in any case the sale of two copies would be insufficient "to constitute publication in the meaning of the copyright law." Brown did not mince words. What Pound and Price were proposing was "a mere pro forma publication in an attempt to avoid the manufacturing provisions of the copyright law."[190]

Once again, the manufacturing clause stood in the way of legal protection for transatlantic writers. Trapped between the prohibitive cost of American printing and the penalty of copyright forfeiture for publishing abroad, Pound had attempted a middle way by paying American book manufacturing its due for portions of *The Exile*. Pound's naive plan had a kind of deep logic consistent with his sense of economic justice: if the policy of the law was to protect the interests of book manufacturers, it should be possible for an author to pay an American printer for just so much work as the author could reasonably afford and then to have the remainder of the work published more cheaply abroad. But legal formalities have a life of their own, independent of the policies they reflect. As a controversial expatriate author of limited means, Pound was in no position to bend U.S. copyright law to his will. If Joyce's lawyers could be tripped up by copyright formalities, what chance had Pound? The first issue of *The Exile*, though printed in Dijon, claimed, by virtue of "local printings," a U.S. copyright in the entire issue as well as in Pound's and Rodker's contributions.[191] But Pound had learned his lesson; the remaining three issues of *The Exile* were printed and copyrighted in the United States.

## The Persistence of Trade Courtesy

The various schemes for satisfying or circumventing statutory formalities show just how difficult it was for foreign-domiciled authors to secure copyright in the United States. Many writers never even tried; they simply resigned themselves to the potential loss of income and creative control. Just as in the previous century, the American public domain was an aggressive acquirer of new foreign works. Yet vulnerable authors were not always or routinely exploited, because a sense of honor and propriety still underlay the practices of American publishers. The old informal equities of trade courtesy continued to shape respectable publishing, more quietly and less systematically than in the previous century but with perhaps a keener sensitivity for foreign authors' rights in the wake of the partial concessions to international copyright that Congress had made in the 1891 and 1909 acts. The "ghost of trade courtesy," as Jeffrey Groves has called it, persisted well into the twentieth century.[192]

Older firms such as Henry Holt kept the flame of courtesy alive in the early twentieth century. Even after passage of the 1891 Chace Act, Holt championed the principle of association between authors and publishers and shunned what he viewed as unseemly bidding for writers and aggressive advertising of their books. He refused, for example, to pursue Henry James, even though James had expressed interest in publishing with his firm, because the expatriate author had been associated with another house, and Holt wished to avoid even the appearance of alienating an author's affections.[193] Holt maintained the etiquette of announcing forthcoming titles long after other publishers had retired the practice. His squabble with the Boston publisher D. C. Heath over courtesy claims to certain uncopyrighted titles became so bitter that he resorted to the retaliatory measure of "printing on" some of Heath's titles.[194]

A critical feature of trade courtesy in the twentieth century was that it was not confined to the old, established houses but was picked up and carried on by many of the newcomers to the business. In 1925, the enterprising publishers Bennett Cerf and Donald Klopfer paid $200,000 to acquire the Modern Library, a reprint series that had proved a valuable property for the firm of Boni & Liveright.[195] Shortly after the purchase, Cerf and Klopfer visited Alfred Knopf, who told the young men that he had always regarded Horace Liveright as a "crook" for having included in the Modern Library the exotic romance novel *Green Mansions* (1904) by the British author W. H. Hudson. Cerf recalled the reasons Knopf gave for his resentment:

There was no United States copyright on [*Green Mansions*], but Alfred Knopf considered it his property because he had met the author, W. H.

Hudson, and introduced the book in America. Furthermore, it was at the time the biggest-selling book in the whole Modern Library.

I said, "I didn't know about this, Mr. Knopf."

He said, "Well, what are you going to do about it?"

I proposed then that we pay him a royalty on *Green Mansions* of six cents a copy. He acknowledged that he thought it was very fair, since legally he had no case. I left him with my admiration unimpaired and I think he decided we were pretty decent kids.[196]

The chief elements of courtesy as practiced in the previous century are on display here. Knopf confidently declares his "property" right in a public domain work, on the basis of an earlier association between his firm and the author. Cerf, discovering that he is a trespasser, does not dispute Knopf's asserted title but instead quickly initiates settlement negotiations that result in an adjustment: Cerf will pay Knopf a fair royalty on every copy of *Green Mansions* that his firm sells. All of this is accomplished well beyond the shadow of the copyright law, with full knowledge that neither publisher has any legal rights in Hudson's bestseller, and as part of a ritual performance of good faith and fair dealing in which a young publisher sacrifices immediate gain for the good opinion of his elder in the trade. The drama might be entitled *Order without Law*, and the villain would be Horace Liveright, who emerges as an outside barbarian, a transgressor of courtesy. Singled out by Knopf for negative gossip, Liveright is punished by means of the time-tested sanction of reputational harm.[197]

What is particularly striking about this scene is that it was played by three of the new breed of American publisher, the very group that was being stigmatized as "pirates" and "dishonest" by established publishers who feared the upstarts' competition and disdained their lists and tastes. Yet this purported generation of vipers quietly adopted courtesy practices as if it had been bred to them, treating uncopyrighted titles as exclusive property to be respected by competitors and as a source of revenue for authors. Even the "crook" Liveright observed the unwritten laws. When in 1922 he offered Yeats twenty-five dollars for certain reprint rights, the poet urged his agent to accept the fee, "as [Liveright's] term 'courtesy fee' suggests that he has found out that those very early poems of mine are not copyright in U.S.A."[198]

Another vivid example is Huebsch's negotiations for rights to Joyce's *Chamber Music*, a work that had lain in the American public domain since its publication in London by Elkin Mathews in 1907. Beginning in 1915, Huebsch bargained with Joyce and Quinn to issue the volume in New York. His eagerness was fueled in part by his desire to be the authorized American publisher of other, copyrighted works by Joyce. (He issued *A Portrait of the Artist as a Young Man* in 1916 and *Exiles* in 1918.) Everyone involved treated the book as if it were fully protected in the United States. Mathews and Harriet Shaw Weaver wrote Huebsch about terms on which Mathews would be "willing to dispose of the American copyright."[199] The copyright was nonexistent, of course, as Huebsch and Quinn knew, but no one broke character.

Huebsch published the volume on September 30, 1918, but not before the Cornhill Co. of Boston had issued its unauthorized version. Huebsch's efforts to persuade these "pirates" to withdraw from the field had been pure trade courtesy. Refusing Quinn's help (courtesy and lawyers did not mix), Huebsch had written Cornhill in November 1917, "I am confident that you will not violate the moral right of the author to his property, and that you will withdraw the volumes that you've announced."[200] This mild "plea of [a] fellow publisher" was preferable to threats, Huebsch reasoned, because, "the book being without legal protection, honey may prove more efficacious than vinegar."[201] Like other new firms with a list to build and scant allegiance to the trade, Cornhill was deaf to Huebsch's plea. Everyone else, however, continued to play the courtesy game. Huebsch even put some negative gossip on record by writing *The Nation* that his was "the only authorized American edition of the book" and that Cornhill had taken advantage of the inadequate protection of Joyce's rights under U.S. law.[202]

Like Holt in the previous generation, Huebsch prided himself on treating foreign authors fairly, as his negotiations for D. H. Lawrence's unprotected *New Poems* amply show. Other American publishers also dealt courteously with Lawrence or his estate. Although *Lady Chatterley's Lover* was plainly in the American public domain after Lawrence published it privately in Italy, Knopf issued an "authorized" expurgated edition in September 1932 at $2.50 a copy.[203] *Sons and Lovers*—unprotected in the United States since 1913—commanded similar deference among publishers. Boni & Liveright had begun by publishing an unauthorized edition of the novel in 1922, but the firm thereafter issued authorized printings until the early 1930s.[204] As previously noted, even Samuel Roth attempted to pay for various proposed exploitations of *Lady Chatterley's Lover*, until Frieda Lawrence's intransigence allowed him to return to buccaneering form.

Huebsch's willingness to pay Joyce for permission to be the authorized publisher of at least two early works unprotected by U.S. copyright—*Chamber Music* and *Dubliners*—points up an unusual feature of trade courtesy in this period. Because the 1891 and 1909 acts made possible, but did not guarantee, copyright for foreign-origin works, a given author's writings might be unevenly protected in the United States, some enjoying copyright, others residing in the public domain. Typically, a foreign writer's early works were unprotected simply because they had not interested an American publisher. But an author's later works might also have failed to secure copyright because they embodied controversial matter or aesthetic experimentation to such an unusual degree that otherwise willing publishers balked. Joyce's output reveals both patterns. His first books, *Chamber Music* and *Dubliners*, lost any chance of enjoying U.S. copyright when he published them in England without having an American publisher standing ready to issue them in time to satisfy the manufacturing clause. By 1916, Joyce's reputation among knowledgeable persons was strong enough to justify Huebsch in publishing *A Portrait of the Artist as a Young Man* in December 1916, two months before the first English edition appeared. Huebsch published *Exiles* on May 25, 1918, the same day as Grant Richards issued it in London.[205] These works therefore qualified for U.S. copyright. Yet, despite having established a reputation that commanded transatlantic synchronicity, Joyce found no American publisher willing to issue an unexpurgated book version of *Ulysses*, which consequently entered the American public domain shortly after its publication in Paris in 1922. Joyce's oeuvre markedly exhibits the checkerboard effect that U.S. copyright law inflicted on many modernist authors.

Publishers adapted trade courtesy to meet this checkerboard effect by introducing the principle of bundling. If an author's output contained both protected and unprotected works, a publisher might agree to treat all of them as protected and worthy of remuneration. This is precisely what Huebsch did in becoming the authorized American publisher of Joyce's copyrighted and uncopyrighted works. In contrast to the Cornhill Co., which seized a discrete chance to exploit the poetry of a rising author, Huebsch invested in his own future as Joyce's preferred American publisher by bundling all of Joyce's writings into a contractual relationship in which Joyce was courteously treated the same as a fully protected author. Quinn had also employed contractual bundling when he required the theater manager Veiller to pay Yeats royalties for performances of both copyrighted and uncopyrighted plays.

Bundling also benefited Edgar Wallace, the English crime writer. Realizing that stories that Wallace had previously published in England might be in the American public domain, Street & Smith, the New York publisher of *Detective Story Magazine,* agreed to pay him $500 or more for original stories and $350 for stories already published abroad. This differential-pricing system allowed Street & Smith to discount for the risk of competitive piracies by bundling protected and unprotected works together in a courtesy relationship that resulted in scores of Wallace's works appearing in the magazine over the years.[206] Bundling was essentially a clever variation on the traditional courtesy principle of associating an author's various works in a single publisher's list. Through bundling, the whole of an author's output became more valuable than any of its protected or unprotected parts.

Publishers during the 1920s and 1930s carried on the practice of trade courtesy quietly and unostentatiously, in contrast to the clubby self-congratulation and moral peacocking of their counterparts of the previous century. Frederic Melcher observed in 1942, "Only those in the center of trade activity can realize how many points of trade dispute are settled by reference to unwritten but effective codes of fair practice."[207] Yet observers on both sides of the Atlantic did notice the good behavior of American publishers. Writing Sylvia Beach in March 1927 to inform her that *The Publishers' Weekly* was following closely Joyce's dispute with Samuel Roth, Melcher added some reflections on courtesy. "On the whole," he wrote,

> I have been rather proud of American publishers in recent years and their attitude toward non-copyright but current material. I know several English books that lack copyright here, but no American house has thought of infringing on the American house which first brought the book to the public's attention. For instance, Robert Frost's best book, "North of Boston," is not copyrighted over here, having been first published in London, and yet I know that no single poem from it even has been printed without permission. It may be just good sense to be careful, but we may as well give people credit for their standards, also.[208]

Melcher was not denying that publishers were *homines economici*, rationally motivated to be cautious and self-interested, yet he felt they should be given credit for a certain internalized morality, a generous impulse to do the right thing irrespective of material or legal promptings.

The furor over Roth's unauthorized activities called forth numerous tributes to American trade courtesy. Arnold Bennett went on record to say how "rare" Roth's conduct was. "The great mass of American publishers and editors behave far better than their copyright law would allow them to. They continually ask for and obtain the permission of British authors to reprint work which they might reprint without permission and without payment."[209] The *Saturday Review of Literature* commented that, though Roth was "legally entitled to publish such a work as 'Ulysses' without the permission of the author, without recompense, and with, if he desires, changes in the text," his actions did "not follow the best precedent of the editorial profession in the United States" and were "subject to moral reprobation."[210] Roth was an outlier, a deviant from the honored tradition of courtesy. There was a difference, Roger Burlingame wrote, between "the better publishers" and the "occasional freebooter on the high seas of the book business."[211] By 1927, Roth had been indelibly marked as a moral pariah among businessmen.

As long as U.S. copyright law remained wedded to formalities, however, Roth and his marginalized brethren would continue to ply their trade. In 1965, the American publishing house Ace Books seized the opportunity to exploit the rising popularity of J. R. R. Tolkien's *The Lord of the Rings*, which, published initially in Britain, enjoyed questionable copyright protection in the United States. Selling at seventy-five cents a copy, the Ace paperback edition quickly eroded the market for the six-dollar authorized Houghton Mifflin hardback. Realizing that he must shore up his American sales, Tolkien permitted Ballantine Books to issue an authorized paperback, selling at ninety-five cents per copy and heavily promoted for the college market.

Trade courtesy was the key to Tolkien's recovery of the American market. He spread negative gossip by launching a letter campaign that branded Ace Books as unauthorized and unscrupulous, and the press took up his cause with articles on the flaws of American copyright law, the plight of foreign authors, and the ethical implications of Ace's conduct. Tolkien added revisions and new prefaces to the Ballantine edition; the back cover carried his stamp of approval and his direct appeal to the morals of the common reader:

"This paperback edition, and no other, has been published with my consent and co-operation. Those who approve of courtesy (at least) to living authors will purchase it, and no other."[212] In the end, Tolkien benefited enormously from the controversy. "I am getting such an advt. from the rumpus," he wrote, "that I expect my 'authorized' paper-back will in fact sell more copies than it would, if there had been no trouble or competition."[213] This aggressive, war room approach to courtesy helped raise Tolkien and his stories of Middle-earth to iconic status in the United States.

\* \* \*

As later chapters will show, James Joyce made similarly muscular use of trade courtesy to combat the unauthorized publication of *Ulysses* in the United States. Forty years before Tolkien, Joyce ingeniously placed the author at the center of courtesy and expanded the reach of its principles beyond the publishing trade to include the relationship between the author and rest of the literary economy: book dealers, advertisers, the media, the consuming public itself. By that deft maneuver, Joyce transformed courtesy from a tool for regulating competition among businessmen into a machine for manufacturing authorial celebrity. As with the larger history of transatlantic modernism, the story of *Ulysses* in America cannot be fully understood apart from the institutions of copyright law, legalized piracy, and courtesy.

Joyce and Tolkien mastered the art of public grievance and honed to perfection the rhetoric of creative entitlement. Their American copyrights were often nonexistent or questionable, so they taught the world to respect an inherent moral right of authors that transcended the fallen world of copyrights, statutes, and courts. Yet trade courtesy was only partly a virtuous fiction about exclusive rights, just as legalized piracy was only partly a villainous exploitation of authors. In the early decades of the twentieth century, piracy and courtesy each in its way embodied a disseminative impulse as well, a desire to spread disapproved books, controversial subjects, and modernist experiments in a society burdened by the everlasting nays of Prohibition, motion picture production codes, vice societies, postal regulations, and customs seizures—the culture of repression that Ezra Pound in 1927 referred to as "official America" and likened to "the inside of a mad house."[214] Pound thought longer and more deeply about copyright law than did most of his literary contemporaries; he saw in it a valuable tool for protecting authors' rights but he also worried that it could become a vehicle for thwarting the diffusion of books and ideas among nations. While the law could ensure dignity and remuneration for writers, it could also be used to intensify the demoralizing effects of official America. It is to Pound's systematic ambivalence about copyright law that I now turn.

# EZRA POUND'S COPYRIGHT STATUTE

## Perpetual Rights and Unfair

## Competition with the Dead

*Perhaps you are familiar with Pound's ejaculations whenever he thinks*
*or talks of American copyright law.*
—John Quinn to Sylvia Beach (1922)[1]

*[A publisher] has got to do what they make people do here in Italy*
*when they give concerts, even if they play dead men's music,*
*i.e. pay in a small percentage for the upkeep of the living.*
—Ezra Pound to his father (1927)[2]

In the midst of copyright we are in death. Copyrights—those legal monopolies that confer, for limited times, the power to control the use of creative works—are mortal creatures of statute.[3] Their terms are tightly bound to the lives and deaths of authors. In many countries today, copyrights endure for fifty or seventy years *post mortem auctoris*, persisting as a sort of after image of the author, a prolongation of legal and economic consequences after the incandescence of living creativity has been quenched. The very thought of these time-bound monopolies calls forth a lugubrious poetry of last things. We speak of copyrights expiring, of works lapsing or falling into the public domain. Copyright maximalists clamor for perpetual rights or for protection that will last "forever less 1 day."[4] Public domain advocates retort that legislators are already granting "perpetual copyright on the installment plan."[5] Unlike most forms of property, but like the religious doctrines of death and resurrection, copyrights inspire rhetorical and conceptual extremism, a vivid eschatology of property talk.[6]

Ezra Pound was a passionate copyright polemicist who believed that intellectual property played an important role in culture. For Pound, an indispensable condition of creativity was the artist's ability to move about freely in time and space. Writing to the English poet F. S. Flint in 1912, he defended his preoccupation with medieval poetry by explaining that "I have not been penned up within the borders of one country and I am not minded to be penned into any set period of years."[7] Just as he had "escaped the limitations of place" through a restless expatriate wanderlust, so he resisted "the limitations of time" by making the works of long-dead poets—Dante, Guido Cavalcanti, the twelfth-century troubadours—central to his evolving métier.[8] But travel in time and space could occur only to the extent permitted by law. Pound denounced passport regulations, book tariffs, obscenity laws, and customs seizures as meddlesome interferences with the ability of writers and their works to gain free passage across national borders and exposure to new readers. Throughout the 1920s he inveighed against "passport and visa stupidities, arbitrary injustice from customs officials; ... Article 211 of the Penal Code [banning obscene materials from the mails], and all such muddle-headedness in any laws whatsoever."[9] Prominent on his list of legal abuses was the U.S. copyright law.[10]

Pound recognized the power of copyright law to police the borders of geography and history. Backed by the state, a rights holder could permit distribution of a copyrighted work in some countries and deny it in others. As with book tariffs, the supracompetitive pricing that copyrights allowed could discourage importation and sale of new works. Throughout much of the twentieth century, protectionist features of U.S. law empowered customs officials to seize certain classes of imported books that had not been printed on American soil in accordance with manufacturing requirements.[11] As noted in the previous two chapters, these statutory requirements, if not complied with, also withheld American copyright protection from certain foreign-origin works, thus encouraging legalized piracy within the United States. What was banned at the docks could thus reappear, sometimes in distorted or mutilated forms, as knockoff copies issued from the shops of "bookleggers."[12]

Copyright law also plays a role in controlling access to the past. A copyright holder's failure or refusal to keep a work in print or to authorize translations slams shut one window on history. The length and scope of copyrights ensure that many letters, diaries, and other unpublished writings will not soon become part of the historical record and that so-called orphan works— out-of-print texts whose copyright owners cannot be located—will play only a limited role in our understanding of the past.[13] A misused or neglected copyright can, Cerberus-like, bar the way to dialogue with the dead, denying living creators a valid passport for time travel. Pound was aware of both the power of copyrights and the fallibility of copyright holders, and his attitudes toward intellectual property were accordingly more complex and rigorously reflective than his tirades against literary piracy and wrongheaded laws would sometimes suggest.

Nowhere are Pound's views more fully revealed than in a copyright proposal he advanced toward the end of World War I. Ever since the United States had entered the war in the spring of 1917, Pound, domiciled in London, had been looking for ways to contribute to the effort. In August 1918, on the recommendation of the American embassy, he went to the office of the U.S. Committee on Public Information—recently established for disseminating pro-American propaganda—and was informed by John Russell, son of the head commissioner, that English magazines "wont touch us" and that the committee "wanted America's higher ideals put about."[14] If America did not get to know its allies better, Pound was told, "'this war is a *failure.*'"[15] Pound, who thought these words the "finest … spoken by any American official since the death of Abraham Lincoln," promptly flaunted his connection with the British weekly magazine *The New Age* and offered to write some articles that would further Anglo-American relations. He would advocate "two perfectly simple moves": "get rid of the silly tariff on books" and "get a decent copyright law, without so much flummydiddle."[16] With additional encouragement from Paul Perry, Russell's successor as head of the committee, Pound threw himself into the task. He even recruited H. G. Wells, who at an "amiable lunch" in

September 1918 promised that he would do "exactly" what Pound told him concerning "English reciprocal action re/ copyright."[17]

But just as Pound was immersing himself in copyrights and tariffs, the American war effort began to make its own propaganda on the battlefield. In mid-September, an independent American army under the command of General John J. Pershing struck a swift and decisive blow against German positions at the St. Mihiel salient in northeastern France. Catching the Germans in the act of abandoning the salient, Pershing's forces, assisted by French colonial troops and strong aircraft cover, quickly overran the enemy and recaptured the fortified area, which had been in German hands for four years. The success of the Americans, who had been regarded as inexperienced latecomers to the European conflagration, boosted Allied morale and persuaded Pershing and Allied Commander Marshal Foch that American doughboys had the fighting ability to make a difference in the war.[18]

Pound was among those who welcomed the news of the victory. He had never made a secret of his detestation of the Great War, which he frequently referred to as Armageddon.[19] Several of his friends and fellow artists had gone to the conflict, and some had not returned. In his long poem *Hugh Selwyn Mauberley*, published not long after the war, Pound lamented the "young blood and high blood, / fair cheeks, and fine bodies" that had been sacrificed "[f]or a botched civilization."[20] His sense of the waste and futility of war, combined with a growing belief that wars were created for profit by powerful international banking interests, fed a bitterness that eventually caused him to lose faith in the efficacy of liberal democracies.

But in September 1918, with Pershing's brilliant stroke at St. Mihiel fresh in the news, Pound could not conceal his patriotic pride. Writing in *The New Age*, he hailed the battle as a "magnificent and epic incident" that might smooth the way for warmer relations and better understanding between Britain and the United States.[21] Such an entente was critical now, he felt, because significant legal and bureaucratic obstacles still stood in the way of full and free interaction between the two nations. Chief among these obstacles, he believed, were the copyright policies of the two countries, especially America's legislative giveaway to the book manufacturers. In his *New Age* article, entitled "Copyright and Tariff," he declared,

> The present American copyright regulations tend to keep all English and Continental authors in a state of irritation with *something* American—they

don't quite know what, but there is a reason for irritation. There is a continuous and needless bother about the prevention of literary piracy, a need for agents, and agents' vigilance, and the whole matter produces annoyance, and ultimately tends to fester public opinion.[22]

Insisting that even American success on the Western Front was no lasting remedy for the strained relations between Britain and his native country, Pound called for a "cure" that only a new law of "reciprocal copyright" could bring about. "The cure must be effected *now*," he declared, "now while the two countries are feeling amiable."[23]

Pound envisioned an international copyright law that would provide authors fair remuneration for their intellectual labor but would not stand in the way of wide dissemination of their works at affordable prices. He believed that, with America's entry into Armageddon in 1917, the need for cross-cultural communication among writers and thinkers was more urgent than ever, and he sought to eliminate the barriers raised by "the red tape and insecurity of the copyright regulations" and high American book tariffs.[24] Such "hindrance[s] to international communication [are] serious at any time," he wrote, "and doubly serious now when we are trying to understand France and England more intimately."[25]

Pound believed that now and again a gifted author emerges as an unofficial communicator among nations, a sort of literary ambassador–interpreter with the ability to translate the meaning of one culture for the benefit of other cultures. A month or so before his copyright proposal appeared in *The New Age*, Pound edited a special issue of *The Little Review* devoted to Henry James. James's recurrent theme in *The American*, *The Portrait of a Lady*, *The Ambassadors*, and other works of fiction had been the moral and cultural implications of the encounter between Americans and Europeans, and the differences between the New World and the Old. Like Pound, James had lived as an American expatriate in England and had deplored the coming of the Great War.[26] In *The Little Review*, Pound wrote that James—who had died in 1916—had spent a "life-time ... in trying to make two continents understand each other, in trying ... to make three nations [Britain, France, and the United States] intelligible one to another."[27] James, Pound observed, was a "hater of tyranny" whose entire career had been a "labour of translation, of making America intelligible, of making it possible for individuals to meet across national borders."[28]

As Pound saw it, James had been a literary laborer for world peace. "Peace comes of communication," he observed in one of his essays on the expatriate novelist. "The whole of great art is a struggle for communication. All things set against this are evil whether they be silly scoffing or obstructive tariffs."[29] Pound viewed his own efforts to reform copyright laws and book tariffs as consistent with James's attempts to remove cultural barriers through the creation of fictional worlds.[30] A reformed copyright law would serve as a legal counterpart to James's efforts to get nations to understand each other, even as it furthered Pound's vision of modern writing as the abolition of geographical and historical borders. As he put it in his *New Age* article, forging an international copyright law would require "reciprocal intelligence and reciprocal action between England and America."[31]

Pound was profoundly dissatisfied with the copyright law of the United States as it stood in the early years of the twentieth century. He considered its inflexible technicalities to be hindrances to authorship ("flummydiddle") and its provisions mandating the domestic manufacture of books to be an open and cynical invitation to literary piracy[32] or what earlier critics had called "bookaneering."[33] No true cultural bond could exist between Britain and the United States, Pound believed, until American copyright law was amended to provide better protection for foreign authors. A "decent simple copyright regulation" was what was needed, he told John Quinn.[34] Convinced that he could do a better job than the legislators, Pound used the pages of *The New Age* to "set down a sketch of what the copyright law ought to be, and what dangers should be guarded against."[35] So proud was he of his copyright "brief" that he half-jokingly predicted for himself "a great jurisprudential career" and quipped that the lawyer Quinn would soon ask him "to come over and take on [his] more difficult cases."[36]

Pound's "brief" was more than a poet's florid wish for a better world; it was a set of detailed prescriptions expressed in a statutory idiom, with separate provisions for entitlements, exceptions, and remedies. Although Pound did not specify a mechanism for giving his plan the force of law, he seems to have imagined it as a kind of self-executing treaty or a statute to be implemented by the United States and Britain on the basis of a bilateral protocol. Like William Wordsworth and Samuel Clemens,[37] Pound's views on literary property were shaped by a particular conception of authorship and the role of art in society. Drafted at a critical moment in the development of modernism, his copyright statute reflected the complex legal and economic conditions that underlay literary production in the early twentieth century.

Ambitiously, Pound sought in his statute to reform intellectual-property laws that had created transatlantic asymmetries in the protection and circulation of works and that hobbled American authors by giving a competitive advantage within the U.S. market to European writers, living and dead. These inequities, Pound believed, only increased the burden of the past with which modern authors generally and American authors in particular already struggled. Torn between a desire for enhanced legal protection for authors and a commitment to a wide circulation of affordable books, Pound sought in his copyright statute to reconcile, on the one hand, his ideal of borderless access to past and present cultural achievements and, on the other hand, the rigorous control over those achievements that strong intellectual-property rights confer. This careful balancing of authors' entitlements with users' needs required a candid assessment of the costs and benefits of copyrights. Pound, the self-elected expatriate lawmaker, took on that task.

## American Book Piracy and the Manufacturing Clause

Pound made it clear that one of the chief purposes of his proposed statute was to render it "easier for an author to retain the rights to the work of his brain than for some scoundrel to steal them." The particular source of Pound's irritation was the "continuous and needless bother about the prevention of literary piracy."[38] Legalized book piracy was a theme he returned to again and again over the next decade. The "infamous state of the American law," he wrote James Joyce in 1926, "not only tolerates robbery but encourages unscrupulous adventurers to rob authors living outside of the American borders."[39] At every opportunity, Pound heaped colorful invective on the U.S. copyright law: "dishonest[]," "rascally," "barbarous ... obstructory," a "clot."[40]

As noted in chapter 2, the 1909 U.S. Copyright Act—the law in force when Pound proposed his statute in 1918—had modified the manufacturing requirements of the 1891 Chace International Copyright Act but had not abolished them. When Pound assailed the U.S. copyright law as elevating materialism and capitalism above "the mental life of the country," he had in mind a history of codified protectionism for domestic book manufacturers that, as one American observer put it in 1879, "has been the occasion of more bitter feelings between [Britain and the United States] than many a war has engendered."[41] The law, Pound insisted, had been "framed in the interest of a few local mechanics" and as "an obstacle to the free circulation of thought."[42] Although there were other, more public-minded reasons for legislators to withhold automatic copyright from British works—such as the fear that inexpensive American reprints, which served a large and increasingly literate population, would be replaced by small, pricey British import editions[43]—this unabashed protectionism rendered the United States an outcast from the international copyright community. Pound deplored his country's determined resistance to worldwide norms for protecting authors' rights.

Pound had been complaining about the U.S. copyright law and the tariff on foreign books since at least 1915. Like other critics of America's protectionist policies, he recognized that the manufacturing clause and the book tariff combined to raise a double barrier to the circulation of affordable, authorized foreign works in the United States.[44] At first, the book tariff, which in 1915 stood at fifteen percent, seemed to Pound the greater evil. "The Tariff on books is an INFAMY," he declared to Margaret Anderson in early 1917.[45] The previous year he had written that the "iniquity" of the book tariff led to "insularity, stupidity, backing the printer against literature, commerce and

**Figure 3.1** Ezra Pound, photographed by E. O. Hoppé, 1918. (© 2012 Curatorial Assistance, Inc./E. O. Hoppé Estate Collection)

obstruction against intelligence." The tariff allowed "dishonest booksellers [to] shelter themselves behind it and treble the price of foreign books."[46] But by the fall of 1918, the book tariff and the copyright law had acquired parity in his rogues' gallery of misguided laws and policies. Both were hindrances to the "free circulation of thought," which he regarded as "the very core and pulse" of civilization.[47]

At the time Pound drafted his proposal in 1918, American copyright exceptionalism distorted the international publishing scene and encouraged legalized book piracy. A few years later, these distortions would result in Joyce's *Ulysses* being reprinted in the United States in expurgated forms without his authorization, as discussed in the next chapter. Although Pound knew well that piracy was one source of cheap books in the United States—and he did not deny this benefit—he was outraged by a law that protected some foreign-origin works but not others and that, by discouraging legitimate publication of the latter, abetted their dissemination at the hands of bookleggers. Because U.S. copyright law failed to protect numerous English-language works of foreign origin, those were the works that opportunistic publishers could produce most cheaply for the American market, adding new materials to an already vast public domain that, in Pound's view, unfairly competed with living authors whose copyrighted works were sold at higher prices.

## "Plugging for decent copyright law": The Text of Pound's Statute

In his *New Age* article, after explaining the urgent need for an Anglo-American copyright law to cure American book piracy and the ill will it fostered, Pound settled down to the details of his proposed statute. He began by declaring that the "copyright of any book printed anywhere should be and remain automatically the author's" and that "[c]opyright from present date should be perpetual."[48] Thus, under Pound's statute, copyright in a work printed anywhere in the world would vest automatically and exclusively in the author and would last forever.[49] The statute's indifference to the country of manufacture and publication would have tacitly repealed the manufacturing clause of the 1909 copyright act and brought U.S. law closer to the principles of the Berne Convention, which protected the rights of authors as long as their works were first published in any member country.[50]

Two things are immediately striking about this first provision of Pound's statute. First, as might be expected of a poet and freelance journalist, Pound thought of authorship in traditional, individualistic terms, apart from any rights that an employer might acquire through work-made-for-hire principles. He therefore made no provision for employer- or corporate-owned copyrights and did not address basic issues of joint authorship and copyright transfer. More startlingly, he blithely legislated a "perpetual" copyright despite the fact that such an enactment would have been unconstitutional in the United States, where the supreme law of the land empowers Congress to grant copyrights for "limited Times" only. Pound was not the first or the last prominent American to argue that authors' rights should last for eternity, but his unconstitutional prescription is especially curious in light of his originalist insistence, later in his career, on the plain meaning of the textually proximate clause empowering Congress "[t]o coin Money [and] regulate the Value thereof."[51] Pound believed that the latter clause by its clear terms gave the power to regulate the value of money exclusively to the federal government, effectively prohibiting banks and other private interests from fixing usurious lending rates or otherwise "arrogat[ing] to themselves unwarranted responsibilities."[52] Yet the plain meaning of the adjacent Copyright Clause either eluded or did not concern him in 1918.

In exchange for exclusive, perpetual rights, Pound's statute required the author to "place on file copies of his book at the National Library, Washington, and in the municipal libraries of the four largest American cities."[53] This requirement reflected Pound's commitment to the preservation and accessibility of cultural products. The 1909 act already required that domestic authors deposit two copies of the best edition of a copyrighted work in the U.S. Copyright Office and that foreign authors deposit one copy of the foreign edition in order to obtain an ad interim copyright.[54] Pound expanded the requirement to include libraries in the four largest American cities at the time—New York, Chicago, Philadelphia, and either St. Louis or Detroit[55]—apparently in emulation of the 1911 British copyright act's provision for deposit of copies in the British Museum and, upon demand, libraries in Oxford, Cambridge, Edinburgh, Dublin, and Wales.[56]

The deposit requirement was the only copyright formality that Pound retained. All other formalities mandated by the 1909 act—domestic manufacture, affixation of copyright notice, renewal of the copyright after the first term—were silently repealed by his statute. The 1909 act made compliance with these formalities a condition of copyright protection; failure to comply meant that the work was automatically injected into the public domain. As long as American law made copyright protection for foreign authors turn on such technicalities, the United States could not hope to join the Berne Convention. Pound's statute was pointedly pro-Berne in this respect.

No sooner had Pound settled on his perpetual copyright, however, than he dramatically qualified it: "BUT the heirs of an author should be powerless to prevent the publication of his works or to extract any excessive royalties."[57] He went on: "If the heirs neglect to keep a man's work in print and at a price not greater than the price of his books during his life, then unauthorised publishers should be at liberty to reprint said works, paying to heirs a royalty not more than 20 per cent. and not less than 10 per cent."[58] This provision—effectively creating what the law calls a compulsory license— stripped heirs of the power to prevent reprinting of authors' works or to raise book prices above those that existed during the authors' lifetimes and substituted a royalty entitlement fixed by statute. This clause was, in effect, a rule that required heirs "to give a license to use the property to anyone who [met] governmentally-set criteria, ... at governmentally-set rates of compensation."[59]

Pound's compulsory license, however, was triggered not so much by aspiring publishers who satisfied certain statutory criteria as by the inaction or greed of heirs who failed to keep authors' works in print at affordable prices. Pound's statute effectively made heirs the stewards of their ancestors' works and gave them an opportunity to profit modestly by their own diligence in keeping those works in print. If heirs did not act as faithful stewards, their exclusive property right would vanish and they could no longer seek injunctive relief against unauthorized uses. Their only protection would then be found in a liability rule that gave them a legal right to damages in the form of fixed royalties withheld by the state-licensed publisher.[60]

Pound's daring blend of property rules and liability rules did not end there. Declaring that "the protection of an author should not enable him to play dog in the manger," Pound added a second, even more aggressive, compulsory license:

IF, having failed to have his works printed in America, or imported into America, or translated into American, an American publisher or translator apply to said author for permission to publish or translate a given work or works, and receive no answer within reasonable time, say six months, and if said author do not give notice of intending other American publication (quite definitely stating where and when) within reasonable time or designate some other translator, then, the first publisher shall have the right to publish or translate any work, paying to the original author a royalty of not more than 20 per cent. and not less than 10 per cent. in the case of a foreign work translated. The original author shall have right at law to the minimum of these royalties.[61]

This complicated limitation on the author's perpetual monopoly is even more startling than the first one. According to this rule, a foreign author would retain the exclusive right to control reproduction, distribution, and translation of a work in the United States unless the author failed to have it printed in or imported into the country or did not grant translation rights for an American edition. If the author slumbered on these rights or refused to exercise them, an American publisher or translator could step forward and apply to the author for permission to make use of the work. If the author did not reply within a reasonable time and gave no notice of specific plans for authorized American uses, the publisher or translator could proceed with the proposed use, with the sole duty, enforceable at law, of paying a royalty of at least ten percent.[62] Once again, Pound had fashioned a penalty for a copyright owner's failure to make works available to the public: the author would lose the protection of a strong property rule, at least within the United States, and have to be content with a liability rule in the form of a fixed royalty. Thus, Pound's statute allowed authors to maintain exclusive literary rights in America only if they actively fostered the circulation of their writings. If they did not do so, publishing rights might be involuntarily transferred to others who, in effect, would assume control of distributing the neglected writings within the United States.

Pound then added an exception to the exception: "But no unauthorised translation should inhibit the later publication of an authorised translation. Nevertheless, an authorised translation appearing later should not in any way interfere with preceding translations save by fair and open competition in the market."[63] Thus, once a translation had entered the marketplace pursuant to the compulsory license provision, the author (or the author's heirs) could grant permission for a new translation to compete with the unauthorized one, and the only limitations on competition between the negotiated

license edition and the compulsory license edition would be those arising from supply and demand, the quality of the translations, the tastes of
the public, and other non-legal factors. Pound's demand-side logic plainly
favored a multinational marketplace abundantly supplied with statutorily
compelled original works and translations.

Finally, Pound included a special exception for extremely successful
works: "After a man's works have sold a certain number of copies, let us say
100,000, there should be no means of indefinitely preventing a very cheap
reissue of his work. Let us say a shilling a volume. Royalty on same payable at rate of 20 per cent. to author or heirs."[64] According to this additional
copyright limitation, even if an author complied fully with Pound's statute
by supplying the American market with copies of a work and authorizing a
translation, and even if the author's heirs were diligent in keeping the work
in print at a fair price, once the work had sold one hundred thousand copies, any publisher would be free to bring out a shilling edition, with royalty
payments fixed at twenty percent.[65] As a British shilling was worth approximately twenty-five American cents (in unadjusted 1918 dollars) at the time
Pound was writing,[66] a compulsory license edition would have been regarded
as inexpensive. (In a related article written in 1918, Pound complained of
having to pay three dollars for a reprint of an old book.)[67]

Pound's compulsory license for cheap editions of successful works was an
especially radical innovation, representing a significant impairment of the
author's copyright. Instead of allowing a best-selling author to control the
market for cheap editions and to choose, if the author wished, to continue
to extract profits from exclusive, pricey editions, Pound treated the author's
copyright as if its incentivizing purpose had run its course and supply-side
rewards must now yield to demand-side realities. The ex ante incentives of
the property right, having served to induce creation and generate profits,
were retired in favor of the public's need for inexpensive reprints. Pound
had thus found a way to mitigate the unconstitutionality of his perpetual
copyright. Rather than imposing an external time limitation on copyrights, he rendered them self-limiting—in a sense, self-consuming—by
making a work's popularity serve as a proxy for the essentially legislative
task of determining the appropriate duration of the property right. When
sales of a work reached one hundred thousand, the copyright with respect
to inexpensive editions would no longer be enforced by a strong property
rule and the author would have to be content with set royalties on cheap

editions. Pound's self-consuming copyrights were fully consistent with his decades-long crusade for "cheap books."[68] His call for a compulsory license for inexpensive editions suggests the depth of his commitment to free trade in cultural works.

In sum, Pound's unusual statute began by granting a perpetual monopoly to authors and ended by carving out extremely broad compulsory licenses that would permit any qualifying person to issue reprints or translations of works that authors or their heirs had failed or refused to keep in circulation. The statute thus eclectically combined property rules and liability rules to create an international system for keeping books and translations in print upon pain of loss or impairment of the exclusive property right. As long as the foreign author did not delay in authorizing American publications and translations, he or she would retain a strong property right to engage in supracompetitive monopoly pricing and to sue for injunctive and monetary relief in the event of infringement.[69] Likewise, heirs could maintain the author's original monopoly pricing and sue for injunctive and monetary relief, but only if they kept the work in print and did not raise the price. If any of these conditions was not met, the property rule favoring authors and heirs would turn into a liability rule favoring the public: the perpetual copyright would become a mere right to damages in the form of a fixed royalty.

Pound's conditioning of exclusive rights on compliance with statutory directives strangely recalls the 1891 and 1909 U.S. copyright acts, under which foreign authors could obtain copyright protection only by complying with the manufacturing clause and other formalities—requirements that Pound vehemently opposed. The difference is that the primary intended beneficiaries of the protectionist manufacturing requirements were American typesetters, printers, and bookbinders, whereas Pound meant the reading public to benefit from statutory compliance by authors and heirs. Moreover, by quietly repealing the manufacturing clause and granting perpetual and exclusive copyright protection, his statute sought to restore legal symmetry and reciprocity to the transatlantic publishing scene, effectively elevating all foreign-origin works to copyright equality with works manufactured on U.S. soil.

What is perhaps most intriguing about Pound's scheme is that it set up elaborate machinery to arrive at essentially the same result that American publishers of the nineteenth century had brought about through the courtesy of the trade: a wide dissemination of inexpensive books with a fair payment to authors. What, then, was the practical difference between Pound's statute and trade courtesy? The chief difference was that in the latter system, once an American publisher had been the first to announce and pay for a British work, other competitors in the book trade voluntarily respected the publisher's courtesy title to the work. Under Pound's statute, once the compulsory license provision had been triggered by the neglect or obstinacy of authors or their heirs, any and all qualifying publishers could issue the work, nonexclusively and simultaneously (unless publishers began to observe something like courtesy again). Of course, under Pound's proposal, foreign authors and their heirs would initially have much more control over publication than they had when American copyright law afforded foreign-origin works little or no protection. But that control was fragile; it would be lost or impaired if authors or heirs failed to meet Pound's criteria. His scheme was radically free trade and committed to the robust diffusion of works as a way of promoting international understanding and a borderless culture.

A striking consequence of Pound's statute is its implicit redefinition of authorship. By compelling authors to keep their works in circulation, the statute deposed them from their privileged position of creative control and recast them as participants within the larger collective process of dissemination. Possessive authorial selfhood, with its sovereign right to withhold the products of genius, would have to yield to the imperatives of communication, even if authors abdicated their Jamesian responsibility to spread understanding among nations. At the same time, Pound's compulsory licenses imitated features of the public domain by encouraging the finders of neglected works to publish or translate them without fear of injunctive relief and high damage awards as penalties for their unauthorized acts. Pound's scheme effectively canceled a critical prerogative of modern authorship: the power to say no.

The tension in Pound's statute between authorial control and public access, between monopoly and multeity, is enigmatically captured in his Canto IV, first published in 1919, a year or so after his *New Age* article. In the midst of the poem's celebration of the sensuous freedoms of nature, Pound introduces the flattering words of an ancient Chinese poet to his king: "This wind, sire, is the king's wind, / This wind is the wind of the palace."[70] The rebuke that the king is said to have made to this assertion of royal monopoly is reported by the poem's disembodied voice-over: "No wind is the king's wind. / Let every cow keep her calf."[71] A public good like the wind, these lines suggest, cannot be annexed to the king's dominions—just as the tide could not be made to halt by command of Canute the Great, the eleventh-century

Viking king of England.[72] The Chinese ruler had not authored the wind and could claim no natural right in it.

Yet the reference to cows and calves complicates the antimonopoly mood here. Pound privately glossed the line "Let every cow keep her calf" as a reference to "copyright."[73] Indeed, the line recalls the words of the sixth-century Irish king Diarmid, who, the story goes, was asked to determine whether the monk Columba was justified in copying, without permission, the manuscript of a psalter belonging to the abbot Finnian. In a ruling that led to the bloody Battle of the Book, King Diarmid drew upon Brehon law concerning vagrant livestock to declare, "To every cow her calf, so to every book its copy."[74] Pound thus juxtaposes contrasting images of the possessive self: a monarch who is humbled by nature's ability to defeat eminent domain; another who draws upon nature and natural law to give judgment in favor of monopoly. Although Pound evinces here some of the solicitude for authors' natural rights that he manifested in his *New Age* piece—the lines intimate a distinction between legitimate authorial claims and overweening state claims—once again he appears to stress the virtues of uncontrolled dissemination, concluding the passage with an ode to the uncolonized wind: "'This wind is held in gauze curtains … ' / No wind is the king's … "[75] Some years later he would reprise this morality play of ownership in one of his polemical prose tracts: "The two extremes: superstitious sacrosanctity of 'property' *versus* Jefferson's 'The earth belongs to the living', which was part dogma, and part observation of a fact so obvious that it took a man of genius to perceive it."[76]

Pound's copyright statute was also consistent with his later theories of money, which likewise were grounded in principles of utility and free circulation. Notably, he championed the system of "stamp scrip" advanced by the German monetary reformer Silvio Gesell in which paper money would require "the affixation of a monthly stamp to maintain its par value." Instead of rewarding individuals for saving or investing, this system "accelerated the circulation of … money"—that is, encouraged spending—because the monthly stamp imposed a mounting cost for hoarding.[77] Pound's copyright statute was similarly designed to discourage the sterile accumulation of property. The threat of compulsory licenses would promote the circulation of works and translations and impose a penalty on copyright misers: the loss of exclusive control over their texts.

It is not hard to see that what Pound initially characterized in his *New Age* article as perpetual protection for authors' intellectual labor was essentially a scheme for maximizing the availability of works and translations. On balance, Pound seems to have been more interested in supplying the market with affordable books than with increasing protections for authors. His was a rare kind of copyright proposal: a consumer-side scheme couched in a plea for creators' rights. Through the mechanism of easily triggered compulsory licenses, he managed to preserve authorial rewards while sustaining his vision of literary production as a solvent of the limitations of time and place. His statute required publishers to pay authors a just price whenever their books were sold but at the same time limited the power of copyright law to patrol the borders of geography and history in the form of customs officials, lawyers, court injunctions, and high damage awards.

## Historical and Philosophical Backgrounds of Pound's Statute

Pound recognized that his efforts at American copyright reform were part of a tradition of advocacy that stretched back to the early nineteenth century. "Old Putnam," he wrote Quinn, "began on this ... strain in 1830, but it aint been brought off yet."[78] Pound was referring to the American publisher George Palmer Putnam (1814–72) or perhaps to his son George Haven Putnam (1844–1930), both of whom were ardent champions of "international copyright." Like Pound, the elder Putnam believed that a just copyright law would enhance relations among nations; he cherished, his son recalled, an "ideal of a world-wide republic of literature which should be unhampered by political divisions or restrictions."[79] Pound went so far as to hint that his reformist zeal was a family trait: "Old *Putnam* has been fighting for this all his life / also he must be a distant relation of mine."[80] Quinn, who had little patience for amateur legislating while there was a war to be won, was irritated by Pound's noisy enthusiasm: "There are liver and bigger issues. Copyright and tariff on books are all right for Mark Twain and old Putnam and Henry Van Dyke and others, the old academicians' business, but it is not for creative artists. Drop it, my boy, drop it."[81] In 1918, copyright reform struck Quinn as a pedantic survival of the former century, a quixotic undertaking at odds with the active creativity of artists and the ongoing struggle for world peace.

Quinn's estimate of copyright heroics was hardly new. In 1899, the English politician and law professor Augustine Birrell had written, "Perpetual copyright is dead. Nobody cares about it any longer."[82] Recent scholarship has echoed his assessment: "[P]erpetual copyright was a dead issue by the end of the nineteenth century. So ... was the notion of an alternative to fixed-term monopoly copyright" in a broad-based royalty or compulsory license scheme.[83] But in his 1918 *New Age* article, Pound sought to resurrect both lost causes—everlasting copyright and comprehensive compulsory licensing—and, even more ambitiously, to fit them together in a workable scheme. "Old Putnam" had never attempted anything so daring.

As idiosyncratic and eclectic as his effort was, Pound's statute was a product of identifiable legal traditions and copyright discourses that he had inherited from the nineteenth century and his own time. One of those traditions, of course, was the practice of trade courtesy among American publishers. Others include the Lockean theory of labor as the source of natural rights in property, the Romantic ideology of unique personality, and, most important, nineteenth-century efforts to reform British and American copyright laws by introducing a royalty system to replace what seemed to some observers to be a dangerously bloated monopoly. The latter movement, with its daring proposals for compulsory licenses and liability rules, was probably the most powerful influence on Pound's idea of a perpetual monopoly that could quickly turn into a bare entitlement to royalties if the conduct of authors or their descendants threatened to deprive the public of a plentiful supply of inexpensive literature.

## Genius, Intellectual Labor, and Oil Stock

In his *New Age* article, Pound justified his proposal for a perpetual copyright by invoking two related traditions of copyright discourse. First, he observed, "It ought to be easier for an author to retain the rights to the work of his brain than for some scoundrel to steal them."[84] (In another version of the same article, Pound made the allusion to authorial labor even more emphatic: "It should be easier for a man to keep or keep the right to the work of his hands, or of his brain, than for another to steal it.")[85] Second, he likened copyrights to more familiar forms of property. "In my own case," he wrote, "I wish to leave my royalties as a literary endowment. I should be able to do this with as much security as if I had acquired oil stock, or government bonds, instead of producing literature."[86] These two remarks—one appealing to a notion of natural rights grounded in authorial labor, the other to the no-nonsense intuition that "property is property"—derived from related areas of copyright discourse, or property talk, and help illuminate Pound's willingness to legislate a perpetual right for the products of authorship.

The idea that intellectual property has its genesis in the mental exertions of authors is often traced to John Locke's labor theory of the origins of property.[87] Locke conceived of property as something appropriated from the spontaneous common state of nature by one who, having "a *Property* in his own *Person*" and in the "*Labour* of his Body, and the *Work* of his Hands," "mixe[s] his *Labour* with [what he has removed from the state of nature], and joyn[s] to it something that is his own, and thereby makes it his *Property*."[88] Having removed a portion of the commons and "annexed" his labor to it, the laborer is entitled to "exclude[] the common right of other Men."[89] For Locke, property was therefore a natural right that resulted from a merger of private labor and public domain in something that could be demarcated and owned. Locke viewed this "original Law of Nature, for the beginning of property" as antecedent to the "positive laws" that were enacted "to determine Property."[90] Natural property rights, arising from human interaction with the unowned environment, preceded and justified the rules of ownership as codified by legislatures and interpreted by courts.

Although Locke was not writing of intellectual property, in later years scholars, courts, and polemicists came to apply his theory to copyrights, patents, and other intangibles.[91] In 1776, the British Protestant minister William Enfield wrote, "Labour gives a man a natural right of property in that which he produces: literary compositions are the effect of labour; authors have therefore a natural right of property in their works."[92] Throughout the nineteenth century, proponents of strong copyright protection employed a loose, neo-Lockean rhetoric to assert that authors had special "abstract rights ... in what is called 'brain production.'"[93] Often, these proponents suggested that authorial labor justified the belief that "literary property exists by common law,"[94] even though it had long been settled in the courts, at least with respect to published works, that copyright was a limited creature of statute rather than a perpetual common law entitlement.[95] This did not stop polemicists from contending that copyright "should be perpetual, like other kinds of property" and from arguing that it was "a strange perversion of justice to limit an author's right in the creations of his mind, and a time may come when this anomaly shall cease to be a stain on our statute-books."[96]

The nineteenth-century British philosopher Herbert Spencer, an ardent defender of authors' rights, elaborately invoked the Lockean theory to make this point:

> [The author] has simply combined with certain components of [the common stock] something exclusively his own—his thoughts, his conclusions, his sentiments, his technical skill: things which more truly belong to him than do any visible or tangible things to their owners; since all of these contain raw material which has been removed from the potential use of others. So that in fact a production of mental labour may be regarded as property in a fuller sense than may a product of bodily labour; since that which constitutes its value is exclusively created by the worker. And if so, there seems no reason why the duration of the possession in this case should not be at least as great as the duration of possession in other cases.[97]

Spencer's chain of reasoning traces a familiar argumentative crescendo: an author's mental labor is more intimately bound up with his or her unique emotion and intellect than is manual labor. It follows that an author's intellectual property is more truly property than other kinds of property. If mere chattel or other common forms of property can be owned and transferred forever, then intellectual property a fortiori should, at a minimum, be entitled to such benefits.[98]

Pound's reference to "the work of [an author's hands], or of his brain" came directly out of this tradition of applied Lockean labor theory, trailing with it implications of natural authorial rights. But, as Spencer's hymn to intellectual labor also hints, this discourse drew as well upon a conception of the author as someone possessing unique personality and genius. Spencer's reference to the author's "sentiments" glances at the Romantic underpinnings of copyright law as it developed in the eighteenth and nineteenth centuries. Scholars have examined this aesthetic and ideological dimension of copyright extensively, noting that "the originality of the work, and consequently its value, [became] dependent on the individuality of the author" and also that the notion of authorial personality dovetailed with "Locke's primary axiom" that property arises from the mixing of the laborer's "person" with the elements of the commons.[99]

Given the growing ideological connection between originality and literary property, it should be no surprise that William Wordsworth, the dominant British Romantic poet of the first half of the nineteenth century, was a passionate advocate of strong copyright protection for works of genius. He believed that lengthy copyright terms were necessary for original writings because, unlike popular books, their innovations were slow to find a receptive audience and so yielded monetary returns late, if ever, in their authors' lifetimes.[100] Long copyrights would also help ensure that authors' descendants received financial benefits when innovative works finally came into their own.[101]

Wordsworth famously recorded his disdain for opponents of strong copyright protection in his sonnet "A Plea for Authors, May 1838," in which he warned that "social Justice" would become "a mockery and a shame" if it did not show reverence for "natural rights."[102] Combining Lockean natural rights with a salute to Romantic "Genius," Wordsworth declared that only a longer copyright term—a "lengthened privilege"—could properly incentivize and protect the "streams of truth" that flowed from their source in original authorship.[103] The sonnet goes on to assert that the "Law" would be but a "servile dupe of false pretense" if it "guard[ed] grossest things from common claim / Now and forever" but begrudged a "short-lived fence" to "works that came / From mind and spirit."[104] This is the a fortiori argument that was advanced some decades later by Herbert Spencer: if chattel and other common forms of property ("grossest things") are protected forever from theft and trespass, how can legislators withhold a similar right from the lofty creations of the intellect?

Wordsworth's blending of labor theory and the argument from chattel was present as well in Pound's justification for a perpetual copyright. Pound combined the Locke-like reference to "the work of [an author's] hands, or of his brain" with the assertion that he should be able to bequeath his copyright royalties "with as much security as if [he] had acquired oil stock, or government bonds, instead of producing literature."[105] As with Wordsworth and Spencer, but even more emphatically, Pound argued that the law's recognition of perpetual rights in common forms of property rendered anomalous its failure to offer the same protection to literary property.

While overt references to authorial genius are absent from Pound's *New Age* article, the Romantic justification for authorial property is nevertheless tacitly present. In another essay published only a month earlier, Pound announced that "[a]rtists are the antennae of the race" and that "it is the business of the artist to make humanity aware of itself."[106] In Pound's view, artists—by which he meant authors as well as other kinds of creators—had a superior awareness of reality and a responsibility to enhance others' awareness by communicating across the borders of time and space. This definition of artists is not unlike the famous assertion of Percy Bysshe Shelley that "poets are the unacknowledged legislators of the world."[107] In his *New Age* article, Pound sought to be both the sensitive, prescient "antenna[]" of Anglo-American cultural relations and, literally, a legislator of world copyright.

## Nineteenth-Century Royalty Schemes and Antimonopoly Reform

Pound's statute was Janus-faced. One aspect gazed off into the realm of perpetual copyright; the other more mundanely scrutinized the practical needs of the immediate public. The latter imperative he addressed by proposing a compulsory license or royalty system[108] that would be activated by the sloth or greed of copyright owners. Although Pound's broad compulsory license scheme may have struck readers as unusual in 1918, it had distinct nineteenth-century antecedents in Britain, the United States, and other countries.

Proposals to adopt royalty schemes or compulsory licenses for solving the problems of international copyright were not unknown in nineteenth-century America. In 1838, the Philadelphia scholar and bookseller Philip H. Nicklin entered the debate over international copyright with a polemical tract entitled *Remarks on Literary Property*. He opposed the extension of copyright to foreign authors chiefly on the ground that monopoly would make English books dearer and scarcer in the United States. But he seized the opportunity to set forth what he believed to be a fair copyright regime. First, contrary to the "unjust and defective statutes" then existing in Britain and the United States, an author "ought to have [a perpetual right] in the product of his own labour." A perpetual right, argued Nicklin, would incentivize better writing, allow the "fruit of [authors' labors to] descend to their children," and, because "a great circulation is much to be desired for works that will last for ages," lead to cheaper and more plentiful books.[109] Nicklin invoked the a fortiori argument based on Locke: just as "it is admitted that a person shall have a perpetual property in the work of his hands," so a person who "labours day and night with his head and pen" should receive nothing less.[110]

But Nicklin was not finished. Although he himself inclined "to the belief that authors should have a *full property in perpetuity* [and] that they, their heirs, and assigns, should possess the entire control over their works for ever," he conceded that it was unlikely that "public opinion will yet sustain such a law."[111] Therefore, drawing extensively on a proposal made two years earlier by the French bookseller Hector Bossange, Nicklin suggested a pragmatic middle way, "a full property for a limited term, succeeded by a limited property in perpetuity."[112] This "limited property" would be ensured by broad compulsory licenses not unlike those proposed by Pound: "Abolish then the author's exclusive privilege, and allow every body to print any books they choose, on condition of paying a small allowance to the author on every edition."[113] Nicklin's middle way was a method for reconciling authors' natural rights with the fixed habits of American publishers who reprinted foreign works freely and, with a consistency grounded in strong professional norms, offered their authors advances and honoraria based on courtesy.

Resistance to strong authorial rights, whether the product of a republican ideology that viewed private ownership of texts as a temporary alienation of public property or the result of a utilitarian concern with disseminating knowledge to an increasingly literate populace, was keen in nineteenth-century America.[114] In 1872, Congress considered two bills containing compulsory license schemes. The first proposal, advanced by the Louisville publisher John P. Morton, would have permitted widespread reprinting of foreign works upon payment of no more than a ten percent royalty to authors. The second, favored by the journalist John Elderkin, would have set the royalty at five percent.[115] In 1887, the Philadelphia author and revivalist preacher Robert Pearsall Smith advocated a system by which any American publisher would be free to reprint any foreign book upon payment to the author of ten percent of the retail price. This fixed royalty was to be paid, prior to publication, by purchasing from the author a quantity of "stamps" equal to the number of copies to be printed. Only books bearing authentic stamps would be regarded as genuine articles, and there would be penalties for issuing unstamped books.[116] Although it met with the "quasi approval" of some noted British authors, Smith's idea was assailed as a "crude and visionary scheme[]"[117] on various grounds: authors and publishers knew better than the government how to fix proper compensation for authors; such a proposal would invade the "trust" (or courtesy) relationship between authors and publishers and limit their freedom of contract; authors would lose control over the quality and accuracy of their texts; and publishers would be wary of investing in the production of a successful book if other publishers could come along and compete cheaply.[118]

Royalty schemes and compulsory licenses were introduced or proposed in other countries as well. The British Copyright Act of 1842 contained a provision permitting a complaint to be filed with the Judicial Committee of the Privy Council if a copyright proprietor refused to allow the reprinting of a book after the death of its author; the statute empowered the Privy Council to grant a printing license to the complainant.[119] In 1841, the French poet Alfred de Vigny proposed a scheme for abolishing literary property on the death of authors and replacing it with a compulsory right to stage their plays and print their books, provided that appropriate payment was made to their heirs or transferees.[120] According to a system in vogue in Italy around 1900, works that had entered their second forty years of copyright protection could be issued by any publisher upon payment of a fixed royalty.[121] In Canada, a bill permitting Canadian publishers to reprint copyrighted English texts upon payment of a royalty to the copyright owners was passed in 1872 but failed to receive the consent of the Crown.[122] Three years later, a modified Canadian bill containing only a remnant of the original fixed-payment provisions was ratified by the British Parliament.[123] Moreover, Article 5 of the Berne Convention of 1886 provided that an author's exclusive translation right would cease to exist "when the author shall not have made use of it within a period of ten years from the time of the first publication of the work."[124] Pound's statute likewise encouraged the prompt translation of works.

The most concerted effort to introduce a full-fledged royalty system was made in Britain by members of the Royal Commission on Copyright of 1876–78. The commission was established to make a thorough review of British copyright law and to recommend reforms. The membership was divided between those who supported traditional monopoly copyright and those who advocated a royalty system for fostering free trade and the diffusion of cheap books. As Paul K. Saint-Amour has noted, the Royal Commission was "a serious attempt *from within the government* to abolish copyright law or at the very least to rethink its immanent ideology and economics from a standpoint of free trade, and, at least putatively, in the name of the public interest."[125] Chief proponents of the so-called royalty copyright were Sir Louis Mallet, undersecretary of state for India, formerly at the

Board of Trade; T. H. Farrer, permanent secretary to the Board of Trade; and Robert Andrew Macfie, a former Liberal member of Parliament.[126]

Farrer, acting as an adviser after resigning as a commissioner, testified before the commission that he believed a royalty system to be preferable to monopoly copyright as a means of protecting British authors' interests and distributing their works in Britain, the United States, and Canada:

> The ideal of a copyright system is that it should be co-extensive with the English language, giving the author the benefit of an enormous market, and the reader the benefit of a price proportionately reduced. But in order to effect this, monopoly must be in some way restricted. And I have heard of no means of doing this which sounds practicable except that of a right of republication with a royalty.[127]

Despite the vigorous efforts of Farrer and the other free trade members, the commission voted to retain monopoly copyright, and the commission's report so reflected: "We have arrived at the conclusion that copyright should continue to be treated by law as a proprietary right, and that it is not expedient to substitute a right to a royalty defined by statute, or any other right of a similar kind."[128] So ended the last comprehensive attempt in Britain to substitute royalties and compulsory licenses for the system of monopoly copyright essentially as we know it today.

Compulsory licenses would eventually enter copyright law in more limited forms. By the time Pound came to draft his statute, both British and U.S. copyright laws had "mechanical license" provisions that allowed anyone to reproduce copyrighted musical works on records, piano rolls, and other devices without permission as long as the copyright owner had authorized at least one earlier mechanical reproduction of the work and the user paid a fixed royalty per copy.[129] The 1911 British copyright act also retained a version of the old Privy Council license for post mortem reprints in certain circumstances and included another compulsory license permitting anyone to reprint the published work of an author who had been dead for twenty-five years, upon notice and payment of a ten percent retail royalty to the copyright proprietor.[130]

The compulsory license provisions in the 1909 U.S. act and the 1911 British act reflected a legislative awareness of situations in which arm's-length bargaining between copyright owners and aspiring users would be difficult or undesirable.[131] But none of these provisions was as sweeping and aggressive as the royalty reforms urged by the antimonopoly members of the 1876–78 Royal Commission on Copyright. Pound's compulsory license proposals, in their expansiveness and public-mindedness, hearkened back to the free trade spirit of the minority commissioners. Moreover, the stark contrast within Pound's proposal between a perpetual copyright and royalty provisions echoed the sharp philosophical and ideological divisions within the commission between advocacy of a strong monopoly right and calls for antimonopoly mechanisms for making cheap books available to a wide readership. Pound was an inheritor of both traditions, and the tensions are evident in his copyright statute. In the final analysis, however, he was more an antimonopoly free trader than a perpetual-rights diehard.

## The Public Domain: Competing with the Dead

If dissemination of works and robust competition among publishers and translators were the primary goals of Pound's statute, why did he grant a perpetual copyright in the first place? Why didn't he propose to abolish copyright altogether and rely on an unstinted public domain to achieve these ends? Part of the answer is that, in addition to believing that authors were entitled to royalties that could be enforced through some kind of legal right, Pound felt a measure of distrust for the literary commons, believing that it gave earlier, uncopyrighted works an unfair competitive advantage over contemporary, copyrighted works in the economic and intellectual marketplace.

Like many of his fellow modernists, Pound viewed contemporary writers as locked in a struggle with literary predecessors who, because they were established and familiar, more readily commanded the attention and respect of ordinary readers. Modernist authors' relationships to their predecessors were intensely competitive and often fraught with anxiety. According to Harold Bloom, T. S. Eliot's "true and always unnamed precursor was ... an uneasy composite of Whitman and Tennyson."[132] Modernists frequently registered their rivalry with earlier authors in the form of ridicule or dismissiveness. Eliot once wrote that Tennyson had "a large dull brain like a farmhouse clock."[133] Pound wickedly mocked Tennyson's status as poet laureate by pointing to "the edifying spectacle of ... Tennyson in Buckingham

Palace."[134] "Wordsworth is a dull sheep," Pound wrote in 1916, and "Byron's technique is rotten."[135] Matthew Arnold was limited by his "mind's frigidity."[136] In her famous essay "Mr. Bennett and Mrs. Brown," Virginia Woolf took to task precursor novelists such as H. G. Wells and Arnold Bennett for failing to treat "life" and "human nature."[137] These novelists "have made tools and established conventions which do their business," Woolf wrote. "But those tools are not our tools, and that business is not our business. For us those conventions are ruin, those tools are death."[138] The sense of a gulf between the present generation and previous ones, between staid incompetence and candid experimentation, between us and them, pervades the writings of modernist authors.

For Pound, however, rivalry with the past was more than aesthetic competition; it had a distinct economic dimension as well. If books were too expensive, they would fail to make their mark on culture, no matter how important their contents. "Only cheap good books can compete with cheap bad books," he noted in his discussion of the costs imposed by the U.S. book tariff.[139] Copyright played an important role in this contest between present and past authors. Among the reasons Pound gave in his 1918 *New Age* article for advocating a perpetual copyright was that "the present law by which copyright expires permits dead authors to compete on unjust terms with living authors. Unscrupulous, but well-meaning publishers, well serving the public, print dead authors more cheaply than living ones BECAUSE *they do not have to pay royalties*."[140] Thus, in addition to the first-mover advantage they held by having shaped the tastes of present readers and ingratiated themselves through passage of time, "dead authors" could undersell contemporary authors because their works had shed copyright protection and were free for the taking. "This is to the disadvantage of contemporary literature, to the disadvantage of literary production," Pound declared.[141] Publishers could reprint Tennyson's or Arnold's public domain texts without the overhead of copyright royalties. In this respect, modernist authors were handicapped even when copyright law did succeed in protecting them.[142]

Thus, for Pound, the international asymmetries created by copyright law's selective policing of territorial boundaries were mirrored in the same law's unequal treatment of the living and the dead. In addition to inhibiting their movement along the modernist axes of space and time, copyright law was simply unfair to contemporary writers as a matter of economics. American writers in particular had to "struggle against the dead-hand of the past generation composed of clerks and parasites," Pound complained.[143] In his draft statute, he offered a radical corrective by making copyrights perpetual "from present date."[144] Because the public domain, regularly augmented by expiring copyrights, would always contain a ready supply of works of high quality, eliminating this free resource was one sure way to redress the competitive imbalance.

But there are questions that Pound did not answer. Would only future works come within his statute, or would existing copyrights be extended for eternity as well? Would the statute retroactively restore copyright to works that had previously entered the public domain when their statutory terms expired? Would it reach back further and grant protection to works that predated copyright regimes altogether, such as "The Seafarer" and Chaucer's *Canterbury Tales*? Would other classic texts be included, such as *The Odyssey*, *The Aeneid*, and *The Divine Comedy*—texts that Pound regularly drew upon for his own creative work? These questions are not irrelevant. According to Pound's logic, only a complete abolition of the public domain could place all authors—past, present, and future—on a level economic playing field. Anything less would give some portion of the dead an unfair advantage over the living.

The imbalance was more keenly felt in the United States, Pound believed, where the law's double standard had created the extremely anomalous situation in which American authors, already at a disadvantage as comparative newcomers to world literature, saw their books marketed at monopoly prices while pirated British works could be sold at bargain rates. In 1819, the American author Washington Irving had written that "the public complains of the price of my work—this is the disadvantage of coming in competition with those republished English works for which the Booksellers have not to pay anything to the authors."[145] "Who will give two dollars a volume for Prescott," asked the American historian William Prescott in 1857, "when one can buy Macaulay for seventy-five cents?"[146] Edward Eggleston, the Hoosier novelist, chafed under the necessity of competing "with stolen wares. The wonder is that we have any literature. A reader must pay a dollar and a half for a novel by an American, while he can buy *Middlemarch* and *Daniel Deronda*—incomparable offsprings of genius—for twenty cents."[147] One historian of publishing has gone so far as to suggest that "[a]uthorship as a profession, in fact, did not really become possible in America until after 1891," the date of the Chace International Copyright Act.[148]

Nearly one hundred years later, Pound echoed Irving's frustration, with a twist: "As America has less past literature than other countries it is particularly to American disadvantage that the living author should not fare as well as the dead one."[149] Pound meant that contemporary American authors had to vie not only with pirated contemporary European authors, but also with centuries of unprotected Old World matter. The burden of the past weighed even more heavily when economic advantages were added to historical and cultural ones.

## Taxing the Publishers of Dead Authors

Pound's statute lacked one critical piece: what to do about the tilted playing field for copyrighted and uncopyrighted authors. Eliminating the public domain by legislating eternal protection was not the answer; retroactive copyright protection for every work created since *Gilgamesh* would be impracticable. Pound hit on a solution, but he decided not to include it in his *New Age* proposal. About two weeks after the proposal appeared, he wrote John Quinn, "A point I have not made in my tariff copyright articles … is the huge sum earned by good dead authors which does not go to the living author but to the living J. M. Dent, the living SmakSmelling, the living Cassell."[150] Pound was still brooding on the economic imbalance between living and dead authors, but now he turned his frustration on publishers that trafficked in the uncopyrighted dead. The successful British firms of J. M. Dent, Macmillan, and Cassell had issued the works of defunct authors. Dent was already famous for the Everyman's Library series and had sworn to stock it with one thousand classic titles. How were "decent" living authors to compete with "good dead authors" when the latter could fill a capacious list like Dent's for the cost of basic overhead and when, as commodities that had already proven their appeal, the dead posed less commercial risk than writers whose works and reputations were still developing?

Pound's solution was to tax the income derived from dead authors' works: "The trade profits on Shakespeare, etc. which go OUT of literature into commerce, and on which a tax could be levied for living authors with perfect fairness." Profits on deceased authors were tainted; they enriched "commerce" rather than "literature" because those profits did not directly support living, creating writers. Then, an even better idea occurred to Pound. So that free trade and fair competition could operate to the fullest extent, he suggested that, instead of having the state impose a tax, "publishers of dead authors might be compelled to spend [their profits from such sales] on living authors, thus getting the competition of individual taste instead of the probable badness of government taste."[151] According to this scheme, publishers, required by the state to part with at least some of their tombstone profits, would have to choose, on the basis of competitive merit, which living authors to support either by direct subvention or by publishing such of their works as might not otherwise see the light of day. Pound's preference for nourishing living creators was a logical step for a copyright free trader who a few years later would adopt the Jeffersonian mantra: "The earth belongs to the living."[152]

With his taxation scheme in place, the machinery of Pound's copyright law was complete. Copyrights were to be perpetual and exclusively held by authors in the first instance. To ensure a wide distribution of works, once an author or an author's heirs neglected or refused to reprint a work or to authorize a translation, any publisher could issue the work or translation without permission and with the sole duty of paying a reasonable fixed royalty. Any subsequent authorized translation could compete freely with the compulsory license translation, and vice versa. Since expiration of copyrights created a competitive imbalance that unfairly favored the work of dead authors, living writers would receive a subsidy from publishers' profits on older works. This subsidy would be provided either through a state-levied tax or by a legal requirement that, in the interests of free and intelligent competition, publishers choose which authors they would support and the manner in which that support would be provided. Instead of abolishing the public domain, Pound's tax plan would simply have re-fenced it, establishing a price of admission to the cultural commons, a levy on the past to be paid to the present.

## Blindness and Insight in Pound's Statute

By including compulsory license provisions in his copyright statute, Pound ensured that the public would not be deprived of reprints and translations. But his statute did not address other copyright-related rights and activities. For example, apart from translations, Pound offered no discussion of derivative works, such as dramatic or cinematic adaptations, or of performance rights, though by 1918 copyright laws addressed these issues in one way or another.[153] Nor did Pound show any concern about fair use or fair dealing, a doctrine that had recently been codified in Britain.[154] Yet adaptation rights and fair use are vital to the creative process, as Pound the poet surely knew. If Pound the legislator felt the need to include statutory provisions preventing authors and their heirs from blocking reprints and translations, why did he not incorporate comparable safeguards for other reasonable uses of copyrighted works?

Most likely, Pound included in his statute only those matters that he believed needed urgent attention on an international level—perpetual copyright and rules for reprints and translations—leaving other matters to be dealt with by domestic legislation. After all, duration of copyright, piracy, cheap reprints, timely translations—these were the issues that had dominated discussions of international copyright for the past century, and Pound, as a self-appointed successor to "Old Putnam," was consciously entering that conversation and proposing a unified theory for the needs of authors and readers. Moreover, the focus of Pound's statute was less on the creative process than on the diffusion of affordable works with fair compensation to authors. That was the pragmatic challenge he chose to address: putting in place statutory machinery that would facilitate the kind of cross-cultural communication that Henry James had made the focus of his fiction writing.

Yet Pound's omission of any discussion of fair use and derivative works (other than translations) is puzzling, because the freedom to create adaptations of, and to borrow extensively from, the work of others was a hallmark of modernist writing. Pound's own major poetic sequence, *The Cantos*, was modeled on Homer's *Odyssey* and Dante's *Divine Comedy*, among other literary sources. James Joyce composed and promoted *Ulysses* as a modern-day epic based on *The Odyssey* and, to a lesser extent, on *Hamlet* and other works. Both *The Cantos* and *Ulysses* quote freely from texts that were copyrighted at the time, and there is no indication that Pound or Joyce ever sought licenses for their allusive borrowings.[155] T. S. Eliot likewise perfected a craft of original verse assembled from fragments of previous authorship, both ancient and modern.[156] Poems by Marianne Moore contain precise and sometimes lengthy quotations from contemporaneous sources, such as books and magazines.[157]

It is hard to imagine literary modernism without its extensive and overt use of texts by others, yet that aspect of the writer's craft does not seem to have concerned Pound in 1918 when he proposed his copyright statute. Although some of the most celebrated achievements of modernism, such as *Ulysses* and *The Waste Land*, were not completed when Pound wrote his *New Age* article, the use of quotation, allusion, and textual collage was already well established in Pound's own literary practice and that of his contemporaries. That Pound saw no need to address issues of adaptation rights and fair use in any of his discussions of copyright suggests that he did not regard these kinds of literary borrowing as unlawful, unethical, or otherwise controversial. Moreover, there is no record of Pound, Eliot, Joyce, or other high modernist *bricoleurs* being challenged by copyright owners, either informally or by means of legal process.

Had Pound and his fellow modernists produced their writings under today's regime of intellectual-property laws, it is likely that they would have met with legal obstacles or that they would have found it necessary to alter their literary practice to conform to a climate more jealously protective of authors' rights and the potential for capitalizing on them than was the case in 1918. As Saint-Amour has noted of Joyce's signature use of quotation and parody, "[i]t is difficult to imagine that *Ulysses*, had it been written and published under [the current copyright] regime, would have made nearly as extensive use of its protected source texts or of the unpublished writings … of others." Many other works of modernism likewise would have been different had they been created under "a standard that recognizes the smallest reuse of material as a potential infringement and reduces fair use to the quotation of brief passages for review."[158]

The more permissive and less propertized climate in which Pound and other modernists produced their richly allusive and collagist experiments was an enabling condition that those writers were able to take for granted. Nor did they directly record any gratitude for copyright laws that left intact a public domain brimming with raw materials that the individual talent could use without cost to situate itself in relation to tradition. Although Pound in his *New Age* article complained about the impact on contemporary writers of unequal competition with public domain authors, he does not seem to have considered the real cost savings that he and his fellow writers enjoyed by being able to borrow freely from those same authors.[159] It could be argued that any competitive disadvantage that modernist writers suffered with respect to earlier literary periods was at least mitigated by modernists' ability to mine those periods for literary material without having to contend with permissions fees, transaction costs, and threats of litigation. The cost savings that allowed publishers to issue Shakespeare more cheaply than T. S. Eliot arose from the same free public resource that allowed Eliot in *The Waste Land* to quote from and adapt Shakespeare without having to acquire a license[160]—though this does not alter the fact that in 1922 a publisher of Shakespeare's sonnets could presumably have undersold a publisher of *The Waste Land*. In drafting his copyright statute, Pound was concerned with inequities in the marketplace, not with the economics of the creative process.

Except in his poetic practice, Pound did not overtly acknowledge modernism's dependence on fair use and the literary public domain.[161] Problems of distribution and compensation, not the scene of writing, captured his imagination as a volunteer legislator. Unlike Wordsworth, who contended that ever stronger rights were needed to spur authors to creation, Pound did not treat authorial labor as something that needed to be incentivized by enhanced copyright protection. True creativity, his statute suggested, would manifest itself through the stress of internal compulsions, what he called "inherent activity,"[162] once the doors of space and time had been thrown open by a sensible legal regime. Perpetual copyright could provide an income stream and make for a fairer marketplace, but Pound did not offer his eternal monopoly as an ex ante stimulus to literary production. By requiring state-licensed publishers to make royalty payments, he simply acknowledged the right of authors and their heirs to ex post remuneration. Pound's legislative energies were stirred by the prospect of unchecked dissemination of books and art, not by economic stimulus packages for creators. His philosophy of copyright was therefore essentially a consumer- or demand-side philosophy.

## "Go to it. Pirate him. Read him": Pound and Disseminative Piracy

Pound's genuine distaste for literary piracy was balanced by his attraction to schemes for dissemination: compulsory licenses, cheap books, purchasing power made possible through stamp scrip or state-supplied dividends. The literary public domain was a potent engine for distribution, but Pound did not openly celebrate it; he even thought of taxing it and turning the revenues over to living authors. He did, however, acknowledge the importance of what he called the "cultural heritage," a concept he derived from the writings of the British economic reformer Clifford Hugh Douglas. Douglas, whose work Pound first encountered in 1919 or 1920, was a pioneer of the movement known as Social Credit. Douglas appealed to Pound in the years after the war by articulating a humane alternative to the reigning orthodoxies of capitalism, finance, and economic value. Douglas believed that the received idea that wealth consisted in land, labor, or capital, or some combination of these, was incomplete to the extent that it ignored the dependence of society on the cultural heritage, which he defined as "the legacy of countless numbers of men and women, many of whose names are forgotten and the majority of whom are dead."[163] The "proper legatees" of the innumerable forgotten or uncredited inventions, processes, and ideas that undergirded modern life were not capitalists or industrialists who captured that value for themselves, but rather "the general community, as a whole."[164] An economic system that failed to recognize universal ownership of the cultural heritage would fail to achieve a just distribution of the wealth produced by that system.

In later years, Pound came more and more to honor this legacy of the nameless dead. He hailed the cultural heritage in 1935 as "the whole aggregate of human inventions, ameliorations of seed, of agricultural and mechanical process belonging to no one man, and to no group, escaping the possibilities of any definition of patents under any possible system of patent rights." Like Douglas, he thought of this heritage as the antithesis of monopoly and saw in it a historical successor to such "ancient moderations" as "the establishment of common land, held simultaneous with fief and with freehold."[165] The cultural heritage was a vast commons underpinning and nourishing modern industrial society and its systems of value and exchange. It was also a source and warrant for a just distribution of purchasing power to the public.

According to his daughter, Pound was "dead against all forms of monopoly."[166] Although in 1918 he flirted with the idea of stinting the literary commons through a perpetual copyright and a tax on profits from older texts, he never lost sight of the need to place limits on the powerful copyright monopoly. He ultimately recognized that cohabitation rather than competition with the dead was compelled by the logic of the cultural heritage and the ethics of distribution—a hospitable stance that required a certain tolerance for what the monopoly-minded called piracy. As early as 1916, excited

by the prospect of editing a literary magazine with Quinn's financial backing, Pound had suggested that the high costs of American printing might
justify having the magazine printed in England, "copyright or no copyright.
Infringements at the start might advertise & help us."[167] Even if the manufacturing clause claimed the early numbers for the American public domain,
such legal piracies might serve as a loss leader to stimulate demand for future
issues.

In September 1918, while drafting his copyright statute, Pound summed
up for Quinn his commitment to international communication: "The sort
of internationalism that I have always held is simply the belief that distant
or foreign people are bound to be hostile through conflicting interests: war,
commerce etc, it is only through the arts that they can meet in friendship or
at least with a sort of mutual curiosity and desire to learn from each other
rather than a bull-headed wish to annihilate the dissimilar."[168] Twenty-two
years later, eager to communicate the insights of the American historian
Brooks Adams to other nations, Pound urged the Japanese, "Go to it. Pirate
him. Read him. Perhaps men who read him in 1897 and 1903 found him less
lively than you will, reading him now."[169] This lawless cheerleading reflected
a deep-seated desire to foster Jamesian communication among nations. The
need to limit the copyright monopoly and to tolerate or even encourage
disseminative piracy when necessary was remarkably consistent in Pound's
thinking. As I show in chapters 4 and 5, he could never wholly despise Samuel
Roth—much as James Joyce wanted him to—because he saw in Roth both
a symptom of the defective American copyright law and a disseminator of
literary works that the public might not be allowed to encounter in more
legitimate forms.

*　*　*

Pound did something that few advocates of a perpetual copyright would
dream of doing: he candidly faced and articulated some of the dangers to
which such a strong property right could give rise. Wordsworth, who also
believed that copyrights should be everlasting, never conceded the harm
that concentrating such potent rights in a single owner might inflict on the
public interest. Pound was a man whose *idées fixes* about politics and economics ultimately led him into foolish and tragic errors, yet on the question of copyright he was open-minded and flexible enough to see beyond his

own interests as an author and property owner. That flexibility was so great that in proposing an international copyright law he combined a powerful monopoly right with extremely broad exceptions to that right.

Although he did not pursue the details of his copyright proposal in later years, Pound avidly followed the efforts of others to reform the law along similar lines. In particular, he admired the attempts of Congressman Albert Henry Vestal (1875–1932) in the 1920s and early 1930s to conform American copyright law to international standards. Pound first learned of Vestal's efforts during his failed attempt in 1927 to obtain U.S. copyright registration for portions of his magazine, *The Exile*. In a letter informing Pound that the 1909 U.S. Copyright Act required, as a condition of protection, compliance with all statutory formalities, including manufacture of the entire magazine on American soil, Thorvald Solberg, register of copyrights, offered the consolation that two bills pending before Congress provided for the partial or complete abrogation of the manufacturing provisions.[170] Solberg mailed Pound copies of these bills, one of which was sponsored by Vestal.[171] By late April 1927, Pound was writing to his American agent John M. Price of Vestal's "clean and decent copyright bill," adding that future issues of *The Exile* "will be printed after ~~the fall of the american bureaucracy~~ the passing of Mr Vestal's COPYRIGHT BILL, if the surprise of an honest measure having been introduced into the American congress has not by that time completely disorganized conditions of American trade."[172] Pound, who a decade earlier had referred to his own copyright proposal as "decent," now equated Vestal's crusade with cataclysm for American trade and bureaucracy. This was only partly comic exaggeration. More soberly, he wrote H. L. Mencken two days later that Vestal's "decent bill ... wd. stop Rothism."[173]

In the third issue of *The Exile*, which Pound published despite Congress's failure to astonish American commerce by passing Vestal's proposals, he testily declared that "those impeding Vestal's reform of copyright dishonesty ought to be suspended in chains."[174] Pound still hoped for a cure along the lines he had urged in 1918, but Vestal died before any of his sweeping reforms could be pushed through. Had they been enacted, his proposals would, among other things, have extended the copyright term to the author's life plus fifty years, eliminated formalities as conditions of copyright protection, reduced the impact of the manufacturing clause on foreign authors, and permitted the United States to join the Berne Convention.[175] Indeed, Vestal's draft legislation anticipated many features of the 1976 U.S. Copyright Act, a law that would not come into force until January 1978, more than five years after Pound's death.

Pound passionately believed that communication should not be hampered by the monopoly power that copyrights confer. He was a copyright free trader at heart. Yet he did not feel that the work of dissemination could be left to an unfettered public domain because he believed that authors and their heirs were entitled to remuneration for as long as works remained of interest to the public, and he worried that the expiration of copyrights created unequal competition between past and present writers. Pound sought a *via media*. In proposing special safeguards against the abuse of copyrights by authors' heirs, he showed himself to be presciently alert to the dangers posed by lengthy copyright terms unaccompanied by limitations that adequately protect the public interest. In recent years, the estates of Joyce, Eliot, Samuel Beckett, and other authors (though not Pound's) have used extended copyrights to discourage or control use of those authors' works by scholars, critics, and others. Pound's perpetual, royalty-based copyright would, at least in principle, have removed or reduced such obstacles to the study and enjoyment of modernism. His statute reminds us that the law cannot safely continue on a course of unqualified maximalist protection for copyright owners. If the labor of translation among generations and cultures is to continue, if the modernist dream of unregulated travel in space and time is to be realized, the law must find a better balance between authorial entitlements and the public weal.

# *ULYSSES* UNAUTHORIZED

## Protectionism, Piracy, and Protest

*The protest is all poppycock: nobody that the pirate cares
about will blame him for taking advantage of the law.*
—G. B. Shaw to Sylvia Beach (1926)[1]

*As my ancestor Saul brought gold to the Witch of Endor, I brought
gold to the witch of Paris.*
—Samuel Roth (1930)[2]

In 1927, Ezra Pound, living in Italy, dispatched to the editor of *The Nation* a pugnacious letter containing what must have seemed an unusual declaration:

For next President I want no man who is not lucidly and clearly and with no trace or shadow of ambiguity against the following abuses: (1) Bureaucratic encroachment on the individual, as [in] the asinine Eighteenth Amendment, passport and visa stupidities, arbitrary injustice from customs officials; (2) Article 211 of the Penal Code [the federal statute criminalizing the knowing use of the mails for disseminating obscene matter], and all such muddle-headedness in any laws whatsoever; (3) the thieving copyright law.[3]

Three years later, in an article in *The Hound and Horn*, Pound returned to his list of official abuses, now describing them as "[c]ertain specific laws and regulations [that] are contrary to the welfare of letters in America in 1930" and placing special emphasis on "our copyright law, originally designed to favour the printing trade at the expense of the mental life of the country."[4] As early as 1918, he had regularly expressed his exasperation, as an American author living abroad, with the trinity of legal forces that he believed was crippling the progress of literature and enlightenment in the United States: obscenity statutes, the discretionary powers of customs and postal officials, and the copyright law.

Pound perceived that literary modernism, if it was to thrive in the international context, required the freedom to cross borders. Quite simply, manuscripts and books by foreign-domiciled authors had to pass through customs and the mails before they could come to rest in the hands of American publishers, sellers, and readers. Less literally, modernist border crossing involved the transgressing of moral and ideological boundaries: such authors as Radclyffe Hall, D. H. Lawrence, and James Joyce sought to disturb social, sexual, and aesthetic complacencies. Yet such transgressions could scarcely occur in the absence of the first kind of border crossing. The artistic and ideological ambitions of authors were dependent on the socio-material means of producing and disseminating texts. Transformation could not take place without transmission.

These prerequisites of the modernist project met their greatest challenge during the first half of the twentieth century in the American legal forces that Pound so colorfully identified. While obscenity statutes sought to neutralize the transgressive power of modernist works, those same statutes—in concert with the discretionary acts of customs and postal officials and a copyright law that required works seeking protection to be typeset, printed, and bound in the United States—prevented many foreign-produced works in English from crossing American borders and taking their place in the cultural scene. When controversial books did manage to reach readers in the United States, they often did so without an American copyright, through underground channels of piracy or booklegging, disseminative practices that deprived authors of financial rewards and the power to control the quality and placement of their texts.

This chapter traces the copyright history of James Joyce's *Ulysses* in the United States and shows that Pound's trio of legal abuses combined to destroy Joyce's chance of obtaining an American copyright within months of the book's initial publication in France in 1922. As a consequence of its early notoriety and subsequent fame, *Ulysses* today enjoys an iconic status that gives its less familiar identity as intellectual property and its encounter with the American public domain an intrinsic interest. Yet the legal career of *Ulysses*, though unique in many ways, is a representative one in that it was shaped by a protectionist regime that sacrificed the copyrights of many foreign authors to the interests of American book manufacturers in the years before Congress enacted more cosmopolitan intellectual property laws. The failure of U.S. copyright law to protect *Ulysses* engendered a complicated history that witnessed, among other things, the lawful pirating and distributing of the work by Samuel Roth and the retaliatory stigmatizing of Roth in a campaign that featured a highly publicized protest signed by writers and intellectuals from many countries.

In launching the international protest and stirring outrage against Roth, Joyce and his supporters drew upon the tradition of trade courtesy, with its sanctions for publishers who refused to participate in the communal fiction that recognized informal, synthetic rights in uncopyrighted works. Raising the cry of piracy, Joyce repurposed courtesy practices to brand Roth as a deviant from norms of professional fairness and to promote his own celebrity as a deserving artist victimized by an isolationist copyright law and an unscrupulous brigand. By presenting himself as a sufferer under American law, Joyce rewrote a narrative that had cast him as the law's subverter; he deflected the cataract of adjectives that had poured upon his work—obscene, lewd, lascivious, filthy—by introducing a new legal lexicon: literary property, moral rights, unauthorized publication, textual mutilation. In the wake of Joyce's revisionary campaign, *Ulysses* came to seem more sinned against than sinning, less a corrupter of morals than a scene of trespass. Fashioning himself as an aggrieved rights holder and his book as a vandalized temple, Joyce laid the groundwork for the eventual authorized edition of *Ulysses* in the United States. Roth's exploitation of *Ulysses* and Joyce's exploitation of Roth represent a critical moment in the history of transatlantic modernism and the American public domain.

## The Uneasy Case for Magazine Copyright: *Ulysses* in *The Little Review*

Joyce first conceived *Ulysses* as a short story while living in Rome in 1906, but he did not begin serious composition for nearly a decade, by which time the work had grown in conception from a short story to a novel-length book.[5] By late 1917, Joyce had completed the first three episodes. He mailed typescripts of these portions to the editors of *The Little Review* in New York, who, with Ezra Pound's encouragement, had agreed to print episodes of the novel-in-progress as Joyce produced them. When installments began to appear in *The Little Review* in March 1918, *Ulysses* was launched on its American copyright adventure.

Current U.S. copyright law grants protection to a work from the moment the work is created. Under the 1909 copyright act, in contrast, a work did not acquire federal protection until it had been manufactured in the United States and published with a proper copyright notice affixed to each copy. As noted in chapter 2, copyright protection for magazine contributors was precarious. Although the blanket copyright notice placed on copies of a magazine secured for the magazine proprietor a copyright in the selection and arrangement of the issue's contents—sometimes referred to as the collective-work copyright—a contributor to the issue might or might not enjoy copyright protection in his or her separate contribution. It all depended on whether the contributor had retained copyright or transferred it to the magazine. If the contributor had not assigned the copyright but had only granted a license for serial reproduction—a common circumstance—then the blanket copyright notice in each issue might be deemed by a court to be an improper notice with respect to the individual contribution because the notice named only the magazine proprietor, not the author who had retained the copyright in the contribution. Since courts often treated an improper notice as no notice at all, copyright in the individual contribution might be held to be nonexistent. Only if the contribution bore a separate copyright notice naming the author—a relatively rare practice among little magazines of the period—would the author be assured of protection in the United States.

None of the twenty-three segments of *Ulysses* that appeared in *The Little Review* bore a separate copyright notice in Joyce's name. Each of those issues contained the blanket notice "Copyright ... by Margaret Anderson."

Anderson had founded the magazine in 1914; from 1916 she had coedited it with her companion, Jane Heap. The validity of an American copyright in the *Ulysses* installments would turn on whether Anderson, the person named in the blanket notice, owned the copyright in *Ulysses* by assignment from Joyce. Heap believed that she and Anderson had received such a transfer.[6] The "'serial rights' transaction," she recalled some years later, was "carried out verbally" in John Quinn's law office.[7] A few months after Samuel Roth began issuing unauthorized installments of *Ulysses* in his magazine *Two Worlds Monthly* in July 1926, Heap contacted a New York law firm about preventing Roth from "infringing [her] copyright interest in James Joyce's 'Ulysses.'"[8] But Heap was assuming that the oral "'serial rights' transaction" had resulted in a transfer to her and Anderson of a full ownership right in *Ulysses* rather than a mere license to issue the novel in their magazine. Were the editors owners of *Ulysses*, or did they enjoy only a temporary tenancy?

When he learned that Heap was claiming that he had sold her the "American copyright" in *Ulysses*, Joyce was outraged and asked Pound, who had originally arranged for the serialization, to provide a clarifying statement that he could pass on to his New York lawyers.[9] Pound, too, was angry. "BUNK," he exclaimed. "Whatever [money] J[oyce]. recd was for magazine rights only. Hell. I paid him, not Jane."[10] Pound obliged Joyce in February 1927 by sending multiple statements reiterating the point that "[t]here was at no time any question WHATSOEVER of your surrendering your copyright. You permitted a serial publication; the copyright remained yours."[11] In 1918, Pound had paid Joyce £50 for the serial rights to *Ulysses* out of his own pocket, from a subsidy provided by Quinn for Pound's editorial work on *The Little Review*.[12] Pound felt that he had simply passed on a piece of Quinn's largesse, in acknowledgment of one-time magazine rights; he had not purchased Joyce's copyright for *The Little Review*. On balance, it appears that Joyce granted the magazine a mere license to serialize *Ulysses*, nothing more. Ironically, had he actually transferred the copyright to Anderson and Heap, the blanket copyright notices in issues of their magazine would have been legally correct and a copyright in the serialized *Ulysses* would not have been jeopardized (though it would have been owned by Anderson and Heap, not Joyce). But since Joyce retained ownership rights, the notices were technically flawed—and a technical flaw could spell doom for a copyright under the formalistic law of the period.

There was still a chance that a U.S. copyright in the serialized *Ulysses* had not been lost. Courts were divided over the legal consequences of faulty blanket copyright notices. Some courts ruled that an improper notice destroyed any copyright in the individual contribution; other courts, wishing to avoid a forfeiture of authorial rights, resorted to the legal fiction that the magazine proprietor held the copyright in "trust" for the contributor—the beneficial or equitable owner—and that the copyright notice in the proprietor's name was simply a handy device for evidencing the trust. Courts that accepted the trust theory stressed that a copyright trust was always a factual question, "dependent on the circumstances of the case."[13] Although the known facts of the transaction between Joyce and *The Little Review* suggest that he granted only a license, it is not at all clear that Anderson and Heap intended the blanket notice, "Copyright ... by Margaret Anderson," as a vehicle for holding a copyright in trust for Joyce. Heap probably would have testified that she owned the copyright free and clear, not as trustee for Joyce. In any case, Joyce's New York attorneys never tested the trust theory in court. Instead, they chose to sue Roth on a completely different theory of liability, as recounted in chapter 5. At best, Joyce's beneficial ownership of an American copyright in the serialized *Ulysses* was a debatable theory—an insecure basis for an aggressive lawsuit for copyright infringement.[14]

While publication with a proper copyright notice was sufficient to secure protection, the 1909 act also required that copies of the work be deposited in the U.S. Copyright Office and that a claim of copyright be registered there.[15] Margaret Anderson did not consistently comply with the deposit and registration requirements. The Copyright Office has a record of registration for only the first four of the twenty-three *Little Review* issues that contained *Ulysses*.[16] Although failure to deposit and register copyright claims for the remaining issues would not have destroyed copyrights in those issues, it would have impaired their enforceability, since registration and deposit were statutory prerequisites for bringing an infringement action.[17] Anderson's seeming carelessness is therefore puzzling.

The anomaly may be explained by events that overtook *The Little Review* soon after *Ulysses* began to appear in its pages. Between January 1919 and January 1920, post office authorities suppressed three different issues, each containing a portion of Joyce's novel, by revoking the magazine's second-class postage privileges.[18] An issue of *The Little Review* had been declared nonmailable once before, in October 1917, when the postmaster of the City of New

York decided that Wyndham Lewis's short story "Cantelman's Spring-Mate" was "obscene, lewd, or lascivious" within the meaning of Section 211 of the U.S. Criminal Code—the "Article 211" that Pound decried as one of the three American abuses.[19] The absence of copyright registration records for issues of *The Little Review* after the middle of 1918 may be the direct result of the post office's obscenity suppressions. Nonmailable issues could not readily have been deposited in the Copyright Office, of course. Once the magazine had acquired the stigma of obscenity, moreover, the register of copyrights had a plausible ground for refusing to register claims of copyright in its issues, though I have found no evidence that such discretion was ever exercised with respect to *The Little Review* or any of Joyce's writings. Perhaps Anderson and Heap simply stopped registering issues after the first few *Ulysses* installments.

Matters soon grew worse for *The Little Review* and for Joyce. In the autumn of 1920, John S. Sumner, secretary of the New York Society for the Suppression of Vice, swore out a complaint against Anderson and Heap for publishing the July–August issue, which contained the section of the "Nausicaa" episode in which Leopold Bloom masturbates while observing Gerty MacDowell on the seashore. In early 1921, the New York Court of Special Sessions found the editors guilty of publishing obscenity under the state's penal code and fined them fifty dollars each.[20] With this new setback, Joyce's still unfinished novel had gone from suffering the sporadic suppressions of postal officials to receiving the formal condemnation of a court of law.

Unsurprisingly, American publishers began to back away from the idea of publishing an unexpurgated book version of *Ulysses*. Shortly after the *Little Review* trial, B. W. Huebsch, the authorized American publisher of several of Joyce's earlier works, wrote John Quinn, who had served as the magazine editors' defense counsel, that he would not risk defying the judgment of the Court of Special Sessions by publishing *Ulysses* "unless some changes are made in the manuscript." He added, "In view of your statement that Joyce declines absolutely to make any alterations, I must decline to publish it."[21] Other publishers followed suit.[22] Thus, after the appearance of just over thirteen of its episodes in *The Little Review*, *Ulysses* had run aground on the shoals of the obscenity law. With his masterpiece far from complete, Joyce found his hopes for further American publication dashed. The copyright protection for those portions of the novel that had appeared serially was questionable, as Joyce himself suspected.[23] As bleak as the situation seemed in early 1921, however, his American copyright troubles were only beginning.

## Publication of *Ulysses* in France

Despairing of publication in the United States or Britain, Joyce gratefully accepted the offer of Sylvia Beach to act as publisher of *Ulysses* in France. Joyce and Beach agreed on a Dijon printer and a first edition of one thousand copies, whereupon Joyce set about finishing his book. After several delays, *Ulysses* was published in Paris on February 2, 1922.[24] The copyright page of Beach's Shakespeare and Company edition bore the notice "Copyright by James Joyce." The book version of *Ulysses* differed substantially from the version that had appeared serially in *The Little Review*. No longer under pressure to meet magazine deadlines, Joyce had found time to add four lengthy episodes to his novel. Other episodes he had amplified or recast to fit his changing conception of the work, sometimes altering them radically from their serial appearance. Only a handful of episodes remained relatively unchanged.[25] According to Joyce, of the published book's 732 pages, more than 300 had never appeared in any form in *The Little Review*.[26] This new *Ulysses*, in its quest for protection in the United States, could expect only limited assistance from any *Little Review* copyrights, even if they were found to be valid.

In chapter 2, I described the strict statutory formalities that foreign-domiciled authors writing in English had to satisfy in order to enjoy American copyright protection. In 1922, once a work in English was published abroad, the author had sixty days in which to deposit a copy of the foreign edition in the U.S. Copyright Office and to request what was called ad interim protection in the United States. An ad interim copyright lasted for four months from the date of deposit. If, within those four months, the author succeeded in having an edition of the work published with a proper copyright notice in the United States in accordance with the manufacturing clause, then ad interim protection would be extended to a full U.S. copyright term, running from the date of first publication abroad.[27]

James Joyce had everything a European writer needed to brave the complexities of U.S. copyright law—tenacity, legal counsel, growing fame, and an authorized publisher—but *Ulysses* proved a scarecrow to all birds. In 1922, despite some tentative interest from American publishers, no legitimate house was willing to take a risk on Joyce's acknowledged masterpiece. Although the work was duly deposited for copyright in France shortly after it appeared there, Joyce never attempted to obtain ad interim protection in the United States.[28] The U.S. Copyright Office contains no record of such an application, and Joyce admitted under oath that he had never "applied for a copyright of the book 'Ulysses' in the United States of America."[29] Hoping to salvage some measure of protection, Beach wrote Quinn a week before her edition of the book appeared in France to inquire if it was necessary to have "two sets of the proofs of Ulysses" deposited in the Library of Congress in order to "insure" an American copyright. Quinn testily replied,

> Joyce must have forgotten what I told him about this copyright question last summer when I saw him. A book, in order to be copyrighted here, must be printed from type set or plates made here.... I told him that those parts of the book that had been printed in the Little Review had been copyrighted, and that, in my opinion, would protect the copyright of the book as a whole.

Quinn added that the New York vice society was "sure to have instructed the customs authorities to confiscate all copies of 'Ulysses' that come by mail or any other way."[30] Thus, the advice of Joyce's American lawyer was that the manufacturing clause stood in the way of a U.S. copyright covering the full text of *Ulysses* and that Joyce would have to rely on the patchwork of putative *Little Review* copyrights to keep pirates from exploiting the complete Paris edition. But Quinn was no copyright expert, and it is unlikely that he was intimately acquainted with the doctrinal complexities of magazine copyrights. In any case, on his express recommendation, Joyce and Beach did not pursue ad interim protection in the United States.

As a result, the Paris edition of *Ulysses* lost any chance it might have had of gaining complete American copyright protection after April 2, 1922. Without an ad interim copyright, Joyce could not avail himself of the small four-month window for producing an American reprint and extending the temporary copyright to the full initial twenty-eight-year term. In the wake of the 1921 obscenity trial, Joyce and Quinn had despaired of getting the requisite deposit copy of *Ulysses* past a vigilant U.S. customs check, through the mails, and into the hands of the register of copyrights, who in any case might refuse to allow deposit and registration on the ground of immorality. With no chance of a legitimate American reprint, efforts to secure an ad interim copyright in *Ulysses* would have been virtually meaningless anyway.

## The Failure of American Copyright: *Ulysses* and *Candy*

Apart from typographical errors, unavoidable in circumstances that required French printers to set a difficult, extensively revised English text, the Paris edition of *Ulysses* was spared mutilations of the kind introduced to appease the censor. Joyce had his unexpurgated text. What he did not have was a secure American copyright in the entire book. For years, Beach clung to the hope that, one day, lawful publication of *Ulysses* in the United States might cure the failure of 1922 and establish belated protection there. In November 1931, smarting from American piracies, she wrote the U.S. Copyright Office to inquire if her hope had some basis in the law. She received a deflating reply from William L. Brown, acting register of copyrights:

> The copyright law contemplates that the necessary steps to secure copyright shall be taken at the time when the work is first published. The original English text of this book [*Ulysses*] appears to have been printed and published in France over a decade ago. It would not seem possible to secure copyright now, even though the ban were lifted and the book reprinted in the United States. For the law contains special provisions setting forth what steps must be taken to secure copyright for a book first published abroad in the English language. One copy of the foreign edition should be deposited for ad interim copyright "not later than sixty days after its publication abroad." The American edition is to be brought out within four months after such deposit. Aside from other considerations, the failure to take these steps prescribed by law would seem to bar the copyright privilege now after the lapse of so many years.[31]

Brown's discouraging analysis accorded with the prediction that Huebsch had made to Joyce in the fall of 1920: if Joyce chose to have the book printed in France so as to avoid an expurgated text, he would lose his American copyright and suffer mutilation of his work when pirates sanitized the text to avoid liability under the obscenity laws.

There is remarkably little published case law on the question of noncompliance with the ad interim and manufacturing provisions, but that little tends to support the Copyright Office's position that noncompliance resulted in irrevocable injection of the work into the American public domain.[32] Of the handful of pertinent court decisions, most addressed ad interim copyright only indirectly or by way of dictum. But almost all affirmed the inescapable condition of American manufacture for works falling within the ad interim provision.[33] One particularly well-documented case contains facts astonishingly similar to those of Joyce's predicament. In 1958, a novel by two Americans, Terry Southern and Mason Hoffenberg, appeared in France under the title *Candy*. The pseudonymous book was published in English and bore a notice of French copyright. Like Joyce, Southern and Hoffenberg neither sought ad interim copyright in the United States nor attempted publication there within five years of the French publication.

*Candy* was a mildly erotic satire and picaresque romp, loosely patterned after Voltaire's *Candide* and intended as a spoof of American female innocence. The wholesome heroine, Candy Christian, "Good Grief!"s her way through a series of bizarre adventures, repeatedly encountering the importunate desires of men and tripping over her own unsuspected libido. Sometime prior to 1964, copies of the book intended for importation into the United States were seized by customs authorities under the Tariff Act, "presumably on moral grounds."[34] Like *Ulysses* forty years before, *Candy* suffered the interdiction of two of Ezra Pound's American abuses: the obscenity law and customs officials.

Pound's third abuse entered the picture in 1964, when, following a determination by the Bureau of Customs that the book was admissible under the Tariff Act, Southern and Hoffenberg published a slightly revised version of *Candy* in the United States with G. P. Putnam's Sons. The authors deposited copies of the Putnam edition in the Copyright Office and, on the strength of evasive answers on their application, received a certificate of copyright registration for the revised book. The copyright notice cited a string of dates that included the French copyrights along with the newly claimed American one: "Copyright © 1958, 1959, 1962, 1964." Marketed in hardcover at $5 per copy, the book quickly became a bestseller in the United States.

In January 1965, Lancer Books, known mostly for publishing science fiction and fantasy, issued an unauthorized paperback edition of *Candy* retailing at seventy-five cents per copy. This unauthorized version, "copied word for word from the French edition," incorporated none of the revisions made to the American Putnam edition.[35] Putnam, together with Southern and Hoffenberg, sued Lancer for copyright infringement, seeking a preliminary injunction barring Lancer from publishing and distributing its pirated version of *Candy*. Unlike Joyce, who contented himself with suing Samuel Roth on a noncopyright theory, the authors of *Candy* decided to test the validity of their purported copyright in the United States.

The U.S. District Court for the Southern District of New York denied the authors' request for a preliminary injunction. Suspecting that the French edition of *Candy* was in the American public domain, the court noted that the language of the 1909 copyright act "gives rise to a permissible inference that if the book is not published in the United States until after the five-year period [as then provided for ad interim protection] has expired, no permanent copyright on it can be secured."[36] Confining itself, however, to the undisputed fact that "[p]laintiffs never applied for registration of copyright on the French edition and hence … never obtained one," the court held that "under Section 13 [the deposit and registration provision] they may not sue for infringement of something which they do not have."[37]

Southern and Hoffenberg took the hint and applied for registration of a claim to ad interim copyright in the French edition as well as for registration of an ordinary copyright in an American edition of substantially the same text. The Copyright Office refused to register either claim, noting that the authors had not complied in a timely manner with the ad interim and manufacturing provisions. When the action returned to the Southern District of New York for injunctive relief and damages, the court granted the defendants' motion to dismiss on the same basis as its earlier denial of a preliminary injunction. The court specifically refused to consider the authors' constitutional challenge to the ad interim requirement and their argument that their early failure to comply with that provision had been unavoidable since "the novel [had been] banned by the Customs Bureau until after the time limitations of [ad interim protection] had expired."[38]

The authors' sole remedy now lay in an action in the nature of mandamus seeking to compel the register of copyrights to register a copyright claim in the work he had lately rejected for failure to comply with the statutory provisions. In a brief per curiam opinion, the U.S. Court of Appeals for the District of Columbia ruled that "[s]ince the novel 'Candy' was first published and printed abroad in the English language and there is no ad interim registration of that edition, registration of the American edition was properly refused."[39] As for the authors' challenge to the validity of a Copyright Office regulation giving force to the ad interim provision, the court tersely remarked that the regulation "is not only not inconsistent with the pertinent sections of the Copyright Code, but in our judgment it accurately reflects the intention of Congress."[40]

The implications of the extended *Candy* litigation are unmistakable: the French edition of *Candy* was not protected by copyright in the United States. Equally unprotected was any version of the novel based on the French edition, with the exception of such revisions as had been printed in the United States in compliance with the manufacturing clause. The public domain had unceremoniously claimed *Candy*; for all practical purposes, the work was free for the taking.

Samuel Roth in 1926 had done no more and no less than Lancer Books did forty years later: he had taken advantage of an author's inability to comply with the strict protectionist requirements of the 1909 copyright act. As with *Candy*, so with *Ulysses*: the copyright code, the obscenity law, and customs officials—Pound's trio of abuses—had combined to strip Joyce of his literary property in America. Like other works in English first published abroad, *Ulysses* had entered the public domain—prematurely, but nonetheless surely.

## "That Abominable Samuel Roth" and Joyce's New Work

Roth had coveted a connection with Joyce from the first time he encountered *Ulysses* in the pages of *The Little Review*. Of all contemporary European writers, Joyce had "made the most intimate appeal" to him, as he confessed to the Irish author in February 1921. Although Joyce would later deny it, he replied a week later that he would be "very pleased" to meet Roth if his business brought him to Paris.[41] No such meeting occurred, however, and more than a year would pass before Roth found another occasion to write his idol. This time, he had a more substantive message. He was founding a literary magazine in New York, he wrote in May 1922, and wanted to begin with a "novel" or anything else Joyce might have on hand, "a play, a story or an essay."[42] The margins of Roth's letterhead explained in minute type that each issue of this new magazine, *Two Worlds: A Literary Quarterly*, would be privately printed in an edition of seven hundred copies priced at $1.50 each, with an additional fifty copies, signed by the leading contributors, offered for $3 each. (In 1921 $3 had the buying power of approximately $40 in 2012.)[43] Sold by private subscription in order to escape official condemnation, the magazine would contain "honest writing" and serve as a more sustained realization of the energies of *The Little Review*, which censors had so often threatened and suppressed. Had *Two Worlds* been in the field at the time, Roth's letterhead improbably boasted, it would "simply have included [*Ulysses*] in one issue."[44]

Roth's choice of "Two Worlds" as the name for a new intervention in contemporary letters acknowledged the inescapability of transatlantic influences on the American temperament. Americans lived, he thought, "not in one world, but in two, in Europe as well as in America, with American culture fruitful only as an extension of the European." He himself "belonged to both worlds" and so felt specially qualified to edit a magazine that would import daring and experimental literary products from abroad. Three noted writers agreed to be contributing editors, Arthur Symons, Ford Madox Ford (formerly Hueffer), and Ezra Pound.[45] Roth's selection of Pound and Ford signaled his determination to be on the cutting edge of developments in prose and poetry. His addition of Symons reflected a penchant for the decadence and aestheticism of the 1890s, a *Yellow Book* note that Roth consistently sounded in his magazines and in his own prose style. A fourth invitee, Aldous Huxley, declined, pleading a busy work schedule.[46]

But Roth did not launch *Two Worlds* in 1922. When he returned to the project three years later, he announced that the quarterly magazine would be printed in sets of 500 copies, 450 of which were to be numbered and sold to subscribers at three dollars each or ten dollars for a year. *Two Worlds* was subtitled "A Literary Quarterly Devoted to the Increase of the Gaiety of Nations," and its cover declared, next to the image of a medallion embossed with boisterous nude figures, that the magazine was published "at the sign of the Mocki-Grisball...where contributions, subscriptions, admonitions, and invitations to tea will be graciously received." The odd mixture of literary seriousness and cavalier preciosity, the hint of ribaldry in the nude figures, the promise of "gaiety"—a word that Roth regularly used to signify erotic entertainment—and the reference to Jewish and Italian immigrants in the slangy term "Mocki-Grisball," all set Roth's project apart from the kind of respectability that other Jewish newcomers were seeking in the American publishing profession.[47] Alfred Knopf had his elegant borzoi trademark, Bennett Cerf his torchbearer device, Huebsch his distinctive menorah colophon.[48] Roth adopted the Mocki-Grisball as if to declare in advance his refusal to play

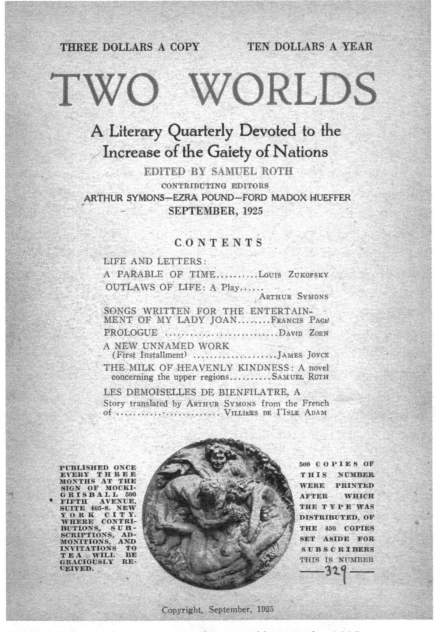

THREE DOLLARS A COPY        TEN DOLLARS A YEAR

# TWO WORLDS

A Literary Quarterly Devoted to the
Increase of the Gaiety of Nations

EDITED BY SAMUEL ROTH

CONTRIBUTING EDITORS

ARTHUR SYMONS—EZRA POUND—FORD MADOX HUEFFER

SEPTEMBER, 1925

CONTENTS

LIFE AND LETTERS:

A PARABLE OF TIME.........Louis Zukofsky

OUTLAWS OF LIFE: A Play......
                            Arthur Symons

SONGS WRITTEN FOR THE ENTERTAIN-
MENT OF MY LADY JOAN........Francis Page

PROLOGUE ........................David Zorn

A NEW UNNAMED WORK
(First Installment) ....................James Joyce

THE MILK OF HEAVENLY KINDNESS: A novel
concerning the upper regions..........Samuel Roth

LES DEMOISELLES DE BIENFILATRE, A
Story translated by Arthur Symons from the French
of ....................... Villiers de l'Isle Adam

PUBLISHED ONCE EVERY THREE MONTHS AT THE SIGN OF MOCKI-GRISBALL 500 FIFTH AVENUE, SUITE 405-8. NEW YORK CITY. WHERE CONTRIBUTIONS, SUBSCRIPTIONS, ADMONITIONS, AND INVITATIONS TO TEA WILL BE GRACIOUSLY RECEIVED.

500 COPIES OF THIS NUMBER WERE PRINTED AFTER WHICH THE TYPE WAS DISTRIBUTED, OF THE 450 COPIES SET ASIDE FOR SUBSCRIBERS THIS IS NUMBER

——329——

Copyright, September, 1925

**Figure 4.1** Cover of the first number of *Two Worlds*, September 1925.

the genteel game and as a confession of his inability to transcend the role of pariah capitalist and middleman erotica dealer.[49] Roth's aggressions as a literary pirate and his resistance to prevailing norms of trade courtesy were bound up with a compulsion, evident long before his dispute with Joyce sealed his ostracism, to remain a proud outsider among outsiders.

The phrase "Two Worlds" referred to more than transatlantic influences; it also pointed to the provocative heterogeneity of Roth's magazine, with its nervous oscillation between literary ambition and bawdy entertainment—the "fields of erotica" into which he was led, he claimed, by his desire to offer mature writing from "the pens of the great ... hidden from sight by a prudish editorial conventionality."[50] The first number of *Two Worlds*, appearing in September 1925, contained a poem by Louis Zukofsky, a play by Arthur Symons, a story by Villiers de l'Isle Adam, and an extract from James Joyce's new work, along with contributions by Roth under his own name and various pseudonyms. Apart from a somber black masthead adorned with the masks of tragedy and comedy, Roth's introduction, "Life and Letters," suggested anything but literary ideals. "Give the wench a chance, say I," the piece began. "Let her show what she's got, from the heels up and from the head down." Evidently the monologue of a high-spirited sailor (or pirate) haggling over a comely woman, the squib ended abruptly with the speaker, having learned the woman's price, growling incredulously, "Come off. Really? Tell her to go to the king of Spain. What does she think we are—a lot of damned millionaires?"[51] The bartered female was a quirky figure for *Two Worlds* itself, an organ offered in an expensive format for the entertainment of mature readers. Roth would later praise his magazine as a "damnably handsome" woman whose purpose, despite a "bit of gay dallying by the way," was "to free journalism in America from the clutch of the pale sisterhood."[52]

Roth's "Life and Letters" varied wildly in tone from issue to issue. In the second number, he adopted the wistful voice of a disenchanted immigrant as he recalled how his mother, nineteen years earlier in a Leipzig railway station, had spoken of the beauty and affluence that New York held for all comers. "Much gold has turned into iron since that time."[53] In the following issue, he affected an urbane, prolix ribaldry: "Man, wrote Carlyle, is a hole-filling animal [and] such a hole, once made, remains contented only as long as it is kept filled—to overflowing."[54] Roth wrote a cultured, slightly stilted prose, but under the courtly surface there often lurked a common leer: old men are cuckolded; young women are insatiable and unreliable;

the daring flapper is a prisoner of rigid codes; women, once introduced to passion, turn strumpets. Roth attempted no real stability of tone or persona. His fourth installment of "Life and Letters" contained a strange plea to his mother to come back from the grave and calm his anxieties. "You have said nothing since that day I stood by, and saw you boxed up, lowered into a yellow hole in the ground, and covered up with wet lime."[55] The same number was decorated throughout with illustrated initials showing nude women in various postures, some wrapped languorously around letters, some swinging on them in the manner of pole dancers.

When Roth resumed his plans for *Two Worlds* in 1925, he did not reapply to Pound, Symons, and Ford for permission to use their names but simply listed them on the cover as contributing editors. Nor did he seek Joyce's permission to include an extract from "Work in Progress" in his first issue: in a boldly unauthorized act, he lifted ten pages of Joyce's work from the July 1925 issue of T. S. Eliot's *Criterion*, retitling the extract "A New Unnamed Work (First Installment)."[56] By September, when Roth published his first issue, it had been exactly two months since Joyce's fragment had appeared in Eliot's London-based magazine—precisely the period mandated for seeking an ad interim copyright in the United States. Knowing that Eliot and Joyce would not obtain such protection, Roth alertly drew upon the American public domain for his first lawful piracy of Joyce. Fittingly for this initial incursion, Roth chose the section of "Work in Progress" that abounded in questions about the authenticity of an important document (the "untitled memorial to the All highest") and that ended with references to the "insufficiently malestimated notesnatcher, Shem the Penman," and Shem's reputation for plagiarism.[57]

Joyce was shocked by the appropriation and galled to learn that his name had been blazoned across full-page advertisements for *Two Worlds* in *The Nation*, *The New Republic*, and other American and English periodicals.[58] Reasoning from the size and apparent cost of the ads, Joyce and his friends assumed that Roth was running a large operation and raking in enormous profits, when in fact his usual practice was to create an initial splash and then to cut corners on the actual product. He took out (though he did not always pay for) lavish advertisements, but his magazines contained much material drawn gratis from the American public domain.[59] Although he paid some of the contributors to his magazines, his rates were comparatively low, and his checks were often slow to arrive; authors might have to send several reminders before they received payment or a contributor's copy.[60] Roth believed that his treatment of authors comported with economic justice; if they were to be paid at all, it should be after the fact, out of any profits he might realize.[61] In many cases, after all, he was simply reprinting uncopyrighted material—"scraps," as one of his antagonists remarked, "that could somehow be tacked onto the names of some fine writers"—and making controversial texts available to a puritanically starved public.[62] Compensation for such unprotected fragments should come as a matter of grace, or what Thomas Bird Mosher—one of Roth's piratical precursors—called a "solatium," a gentlemanly payment made "when the deed was done."[63] In this respect as in others, Roth was a throwback to the previous century, a vigorous exploiter of the American public domain and a descendant of those shrewd, sometimes disapproved practitioners of trade courtesy who held that material that the law made free to all comers should command at most a post hoc gratuity, paid when the pirate himself had been paid.

Each of the first five issues of *Two Worlds* contained a different extract from Joyce's new work, drawn from various European publications whose contents lay in the American public domain. Roth timed his appropriations expertly to ensure their lawfulness under the U.S. copyright law and to maximize their currency for his readers. His December 1925 number contained the "Humphrey Chimpden Earwicker" fragment that had appeared in May 1925 in Robert McAlmon's *Contact Collection of Contemporary Writers*. His March 1926 number offered the "Anna Livia Plurabelle" segment previously issued in October 1925 in *Le Navire d'Argent*. He ran Joyce's "Shem the Penman" extract, from the Autumn–Winter 1925–26 number of *This Quarter*, in the June 1926 issue of *Two Worlds*, and Joyce's "Mamalujo" segment, from a 1924 issue of *The Transatlantic Review*, in the September 1926 number.[64] Roth later claimed, dubiously, that he had received permission to publish Joyce's work from Ezra Pound in 1922.[65] Although it is possible that at some early point Pound encouraged a general proposal to print future work by Joyce, Joyce did not even begin to draft what came to be known as "Work in Progress" until 1923 and did not publish an extract until 1924.[66] Even if he had had the power, Pound in 1922 could not have given meaningful authorization to publish work that did not yet exist.

But Roth did enjoy a brief period of legitimacy during which he almost succeeded in building a relationship with Joyce. The entente began inauspiciously when Roth, shortly after reprinting the first unauthorized Joyce extract, wrote Joyce in late September 1925 to express his admiration and to request a "contribution, long or short," for which he would be willing to pay.[67] In early December, Sylvia Beach wrote Roth to express puzzlement over why he had proceeded by first reproducing Joyce's work without his permission and then asking him for new material.[68] On January 2, 1926, Roth responded by sending Beach a check for a hundred dollars, drawn upon his New York bank and made payable to Joyce, for the two extracts from "Work in Progress" that he had issued in the September and December numbers of *Two Worlds*, and reminded Beach that these segments had previously appeared in European publications (and so, he implied, were free for the taking in the United States). He would gladly pay more for "the exclusive right to use material from the new work" and assured Beach that of all living writers he "loved [Joyce] the most." With transparent puffery, he boasted that *Two Worlds* was "in greater demand than any other periodical in English" and urged Beach to help him establish his magazine as "the organ of the best writing in your colony."[69] He was making a bid to rise above his status as a parasitic reprinter and to become the sole authorized publisher of "Work in Progress." The one hundred dollar honorarium was an earnest of his intentions.

On January 21, Beach thanked Roth for the hundred dollars in a letter that was palpably warmer than her previous one. She promised to send him the forthcoming issue of *This Quarter* with Joyce's "Shem" extract (which Roth would reprint in June) and requested a copy of *Two Worlds* containing Joyce's work. Explaining that she was in charge of Joyce's business affairs, she formally inquired what Roth would pay Joyce "for the exclusive right to bring out the next four parts of his new book."[70] Joyce was taking bids on his latest material, the "Shaun the Post" chapters that eventually would become Book III of *Finnegans Wake*. Roth jumped at the chance. In early March, Joyce mentioned that he was trying to revise the Shaun material "for Mr Roth," who had offered three hundred dollars for it, and that Roth had also promised payment for the extracts from *Le Navire d'Argent* and *This Quarter* that he would shortly reprint in the March and June numbers of *Two Worlds*.[71] On March 18, Roth made good his promise by sending Beach another check for one hundred dollars to cover the March and June reprints and urged her to let him know what she wished to do about "Joyce's future work." He was "now negotiating for the works of James Joyce in this country" and hoped soon to be able to propose "an exceptionally good financial arrangement."[72] This was a remarkable development. Roth was no longer offering reactive post hoc honoraria for Joyce's work but was courteously paying for current and future reprint material, and even angling to become Joyce's legitimate publisher in the United States. No longer condemned to being a pariah publisher dabbling in uncopyrighted scraps and tendering belated payments, he seemed on the verge of realizing his old dream of forging a bond with the Irish writer.

But it was not to be. Roth had neither the temperament nor the funds to sustain his flirtation with legitimacy. In July 1926, Beach offered the Shaun chapters to *The Dial*, noting that a "certain review"—no doubt *Two Worlds*—had made an offer but that the price was too low and the magazine was not a "suitable place" for Joyce's work.[73] By July, Beach and Joyce had probably seen copies of *Two Worlds* and noticed the jejune ribaldry and rib-nudging erotica. Moreover, Hemingway told Joyce that he had met Roth in New York and heard him boast that he was only using Joyce's "name and pieces as a draw" to attract thousands of subscribers who in any case, Roth purportedly claimed, were tiring of Joyce's verbal experiments.[74] Joyce agreed to give the Shaun chapters to *The Dial* for six hundred dollars but later withdrew the manuscript when the editor asked for changes.[75] He did not try to revive Roth's offer, however, and Roth no doubt sensed the snub. He turned pirate with a vengeance and in the September 1926 number of *Two Worlds* reprinted Joyce's "Mamalujo" fragment from *The Transatlantic Review*, apparently without permission or payment.[76] More boldly and with great fanfare, he launched a new magazine in July 1926 called *Two Worlds Monthly*. Like *Two Worlds*, it was "Devoted to the Increase of the Gaiety of Nations." The centerpiece of gaiety was to be James Joyce's *Ulysses*.

## "He merely swipes everything that isn't copyright": Roth's Reprinting of *Ulysses*

For Roth, *Ulysses* had always been the great desideratum. In his first letter to Joyce in 1921, he had inquired when the work would be published as a book,[77] and the letterhead for his quarterly *Two Worlds*, during the abortive 1922 campaign and again in 1925, all but asserted that he had inherited from *The Little Review*, by a kind of privilege of destiny, the right to complete the serialization of *Ulysses* in America. It plainly was Roth's intention as early as

1922 to use *Two Worlds* as a vehicle for reprinting *Ulysses*; in June and July of that year he actively sought permission from Joyce. On June 6, Beach passed on to Harriet Shaw Weaver a letter from Roth proposing to publish *Ulysses* in a single issue of *Two Worlds*. Joyce was not interested. He asked Beach, his French publisher, to ask Weaver, his British publisher, to convey to Roth the brief message that he was "unable to accept [the] proposition."[78] Two days later, Weaver wrote Roth on letterhead of the Egoist Press that Joyce was "unable to fall in with [his] suggestion" and that in any case it would be impossible to print the whole book in one issue of a magazine.[79]

Roth was not to be put off so easily. He wrote again to Weaver, pressing the offer of two hundred and fifty dollars or whatever sum she thought appropriate for the right to print *Ulysses* in one issue of *Two Worlds*, the money to be paid thirty days after the number appeared (Roth's preferred practice of paying out of future profits). Weaver wondered aloud whether Roth planned to use type "the size of a needle's head" and doubted that "financial results" could flow from a limited-run magazine selling for $1.50 a copy.[80] Quinn, whom she had asked for information about Roth, reported that he had consulted Alfred Knopf and others and had been told that Roth was a "nut poet," full of "crazy ideas." He must be "either a fool or a wild man," Quinn felt, to think that he could publish *Ulysses* unexpurgated in the United States and not be arrested and prosecuted for obscenity. Roth should be renamed "Samuel Froth," he quipped, "the pseudo-peanut publisher—in his own mind." Quinn added that he would be surprised if Roth had "money enough in his pocket to pay for two weeks' board."[81] The lawyer's derision shows that even at this early date Roth was viewed as an eccentric outsider in the world of New York publishing, a would-be poet full of ungrounded ambitions, a tall talker and a "luftmensch, or chancy risk taker looking for a way into solvency and respect," as Jay Gertzman has aptly described him.[82] On the strength of Quinn's report, Weaver again wrote Roth in September 1922 "definitely declining on Mr Joyce's behalf" the proposal to print *Ulysses* in *Two Worlds*.[83]

Joyce had unequivocally refused permission to reprint *Ulysses*, but this did not stop Roth. In July 1922, after receiving Weaver's first letter, he was still trying to purchase space in the *New York Evening Post Literary Review* to advertise the appearance of Joyce's novel in *Two Worlds*. Only the refusal of the editor Henry Seidel Canby to allow advertising space for a work that he felt certain would attract John S. Sumner and his smuthounds slowed Roth down. It seems possible that, contrary to Joyce's express wishes, Roth would have gone ahead with *Ulysses* in 1922—just a few months after the Paris edition had entered the American public domain—had he then managed to launch his quarterly magazine.

As it turned out, he waited until the inaugural number of *Two Worlds Monthly* in July 1926 to fulfill his ambition. Joyce had never withdrawn his refusal, but Roth was not to be deterred. When challenged, he later claimed that Ezra Pound, as Joyce's "agent," had given him permission in the early 1920s to run *Ulysses* in a magazine. This claim generated controversy at the time and still fascinates scholars, though under the law of agency (to the extent that the law enters into questions of the public domain) Roth's position was untenable. The explicit refusal of Joyce, the known principal, would have terminated any apparent authority of Pound, the alleged agent, to grant permission.[84] But the facts and the law have been muddied, and a clarification of Pound's role is in order.

Roth was never precise about the circumstances of Pound's purported authorization. In essence, his claim was that Pound, who had acted as Joyce's agent in arranging for episodes of *Ulysses* to appear in *The Little Review*, had turned over to Roth "all the rights to whatever he had brought to the LITTLE REVIEW" sometime after the obscenity conviction of Anderson and Heap in February 1921. According to Roth, Pound had instructed him to go to the office of *The Little Review* and "rifl[e] its contents," though out of respect for the editors he never did so.[85] Pound had been "endowed by Mr. Joyce," Roth stated under oath, "with the right to make any disposition that he pleased of [the *Ulysses*] manuscript," and the poet–agent had chosen Roth to succeed to *The Little Review*'s rights and responsibilities.[86] An immediate difficulty with this claim is that Anderson and Heap had discontinued the serialization of *Ulysses* after the first few pages of the "Oxen of the Sun" episode and did not receive typescripts of Joyce's later episodes. Roth would not have been able to retrieve an entire manuscript of *Ulysses* even if he had had the audacity to storm the office of *The Little Review*.

Yet it is clear that Pound communicated some kind of approval, as he himself acknowledged in a 1928 letter to the Paris *Chicago Tribune*:

> *The Little Review* was barred from the United States mails and finger prints of its editors taken by the New York police because they had published the opening chapters of Mr. Joyce's *Ulysses*. Shortly after this a certain

Mr. Roth suggested a means of publishing the *unpublished* remainder of the book. As I consider the law under which *Ulysses* was suppressed, an outrage, the people who tolerate such a law little better than apes, I approved the suggestion. That is to say, I wrote as nearly as I can remember that I approved any legal means of nullifying the effect of article 211 of the United States penal code.[87]

Several things emerge from Pound's account. His exchange with Roth occurred by mail "shortly after" the *Little Review* editors had become embroiled in the criminal proceeding, and he approved Roth's suggestion of a "means" of publishing the "*unpublished* remainder" of *Ulysses*. This correspondence—which has not been located—could scarcely have taken place in mid-1922 when Roth was directly seeking Joyce's permission to print *Ulysses*. By then the work had been published in its entirety by Shakespeare and Company in Paris. Pound was proud of Joyce's sales and would not have undermined them by secretly authorizing a competing version.[88]

It is far more likely that Pound expressed some kind of approval in 1921, shortly after *The Little Review* discontinued the serialization of *Ulysses*, when it seemed that American readers would not gain access to the balance of the work by other means. Anderson and Heap's troubles made Pound yearn for "some publication for experimental work, not yet ripe enough for Dial … perhaps the country should be able to provide a new 'organ' for this."[89] Roth had been corresponding with Pound in the spring of 1921 about another proposed literary project, and it is probable that, with his passionate interest in *Ulysses*, Roth gallantly offered to complete the serialization in an expensive, privately printed, subscription-only magazine of the kind he tried to launch a year later.[90] Such a magazine, restricted to adults who could afford it, fits Pound's description of a "legal means of nullifying the effect of article 211 of the United States penal code," and it would have coincided with the view of Pound and Quinn in 1921 that only private publication of *Ulysses* could escape the law's strictures.[91] Committed as he was to the romance and ethics of dissemination, Pound would have warmed to such a proposal as an expedient means of circumventing the prohibitions of official America.[92]

It was not until a year later, in July 1922, that Roth wrote to Pound in greater detail about plans for his quarterly, *Two Worlds*. I believe that scholars have erred in concluding that this correspondence concerned *Ulysses*.[93] The only letter that has come to light is one by Pound, dated July 4, 1922, in which he suggested, as a contributing editor of *Two Worlds*, that Roth might coordinate with "a new Quarterly coming out in England this autumn" (he was referring to T. S. Eliot's *Criterion*) to "arrange simultaneous publication" of worthy authors.[94] As for potential content, Pound mentioned his own translations of Paul Morand's works and urged Roth to consider devoting separate issues to the art of Wyndham Lewis, Francis Picabia, Charles Demuth, and others. Pound's suggestion of art numbers was partly a way to stir up *The Little Review*, now a quarterly, which for some time he had been prodding to reproduce the work of Lewis and other artists. Shortly after he wrote Roth, he confided to Lewis that the *Little Review* editors might be "a little agitated at a note I wrote last week ... telling the two Worlds to take over all unpub. L.R. stuff and prepare a [Wyndham Lewis] number. An idea which ought to galvanize the L.R."[95] Pound was playing Roth against Anderson and Heap, hoping that a competition of egos might hasten the appearance of the artists he admired. At the same time, he was grooming *Two Worlds* to be the transatlantic twin of Eliot's *Criterion*—another chance for legitimacy that escaped the luftmensch Roth, who had set his cap for *Ulysses* in any case.[96]

To sum up, it seems that shortly after the conviction of Anderson and Heap in 1921, Pound expressed approval of a suggestion by Roth to issue unpublished future episodes of *Ulysses* in a privately printed subscription magazine, as a way of foiling the censors. But Roth missed this opportunity to conclude *The Little Review*'s serialization of the unpublished *Ulysses*. When he got around to the concrete planning of *Two Worlds* in the spring of 1922, he sought permission from Joyce to reprint the whole of *Ulysses*, a work that by then had been published in France and was furtively entering the United States. It would have made little sense for Roth to seek Pound's authorization then, when he was already corresponding with Weaver, who spoke directly for Joyce. The surviving correspondence suggests that Pound probably confined his advice in 1922 to strategies for gaining exposure for new material by artists and writers and for generating competition and collaboration among *Two Worlds*, *The Criterion*, and *The Little Review*. He saw *Two Worlds* as a goad and potential substitute for the slow-moving *Little Review*, but there is no evidence that he urged a new serialization of the recently published *Ulysses*.

Four years later, in the face of public accusations of piracy, Roth found it convenient to conflate these events, collapsing Pound's very different suggestions of 1921 and 1922 for the *Little Review* backlog into a single act of authorizing a reprint of *Ulysses*. But 1922 was not 1921, and both were very different from 1926. In the end, however, the scholarly debate over Pound's alleged permission is moot, for two reasons. First, Joyce had expressly refused to authorize Roth's plans for *Ulysses* in 1922 and did not change his mind. Second, Roth never needed permission anyway: by April 1922 the Paris edition of *Ulysses* lay squarely within the American public domain.

The wonder is that Roth sought permission at all. He generally took a pragmatic, demand-side view of U.S. copyright law, alert to opportunities for dissemination and keen to exploit the formalities that thrust so many works into the public domain. Testifying at a pretrial examination administered by Joyce's attorneys in 1927, Roth stated that he had chosen to reprint *Ulysses* because it "is not copyrighted in this country and the property of anyone wishing to use it for whatever purposes they wanted." "I merely took over all matter which came into my hands," he added, as if the tides of the public domain had simply washed *Ulysses* to his doorstep. Joyce's novel "was to be had by the mere matter of choice."[97] Like publishers in the previous century, he defended his practices by pointing to the laws that had created the American public domain. "[I]f that is piracy there is not a publisher living or dead who has not sinned more than [I] did," he once wrote.[98] In 1927, he responded to one of the European signers of Joyce's international protest by arguing that "art is more ancient than copyright laws, and the most beautiful things in the world were created long before copyright laws were thoght [*sic*] necessary." Turning the tables on those who condemned American laws as unjust, he asked his correspondent to consider "that your own copyright laws are not divine, that in at least one instance[,] my publishing of ULYSSES, they do not apply."[99] *Ars longa, lex brevis.*

Roth had an almost mystical belief that art and literature were gifts freely given so that the present generation might better understand itself. It was more than empty defensiveness when he wrote Sherwood Anderson, another protest signer, that "ULYSSES was given, without request for payment, by Mr. Joyce to America for serial publication in THE LITTLE REVIEW."[100] Roth claimed, not wholly disingenuously, that he did not publish magazines in order to earn profits but rather "to give artistic expression to the ideas and emotions of my time."[101] He was proud to have "added some color to the moral landscape of my generation,"[102] and he felt that he had been chosen to assist the zeitgeist by seeing its most vivid records into print. His belief in

aesthetic gifting linked him to Joyce as an instrument of generational understanding, yet when it came to the ideology of literary property he parted
ways with Joyce and aligned himself with Tolstoy, who, he said, "mocked all
copyrights and demanded to know if it is right to patent the creative word as
if it were a mousetrap."[103] Pound, too, believed in cultural gifting, the spread
of literature as a means to international understanding.

But if *Ulysses* was in the American public domain, why did Roth initially
seek Joyce's permission to reprint it in his magazine? The answer lies in Roth's
complex relationship to the tradition of trade courtesy. Permission from Joyce
would have established a cherished link to a beloved writer and enhanced
Roth's reputation within the publishing world. Like the established houses
of the nineteenth century, Knopf, Huebsch, Cerf, and other rising publishers
in the 1920s practiced courtesy among themselves and with their authors.
But Roth was conflicted. He both desired and distrusted legitimacy; he could
not really afford it, and an angry part of him rebelled against the genteel pre-
tensions of other publishers. He could bring himself to play the game up
to a point. He had sought Joyce's permission in 1922. In 1926, after he had
published six unauthorized segments of *Ulysses*, he tried to make amends by
offering Joyce a thousand dollars, though the sum was mostly made up of
promissory notes payable only if Roth realized sufficient future profits. Joyce
never responded, and Roth could hardly have expected him to be charmed
by such qualified courtesy. (I discuss this offer in chapter 5.) In the end, Roth
and trade courtesy were ill-matched; he preferred to be a lone wolf. When
in 1926 it became clear that Joyce was not going to make him the exclusive
American publisher of "Work in Progress," Roth turned with almost relieved
fury to pirating *Ulysses* in *Two Worlds Monthly*.

Roth described *Two Worlds Monthly* as an "auxiliary" to *Two Worlds*, but
it differed profoundly in that it was a monthly newsstand magazine offered
to bridge the "great gap" between a privately subscribed quarterly and "the
ordinary commercial magazine."[104] *Two Worlds Monthly*, Roth promised,
would be "gay" and "sophisticated," confined largely to "modern writers ...
whose interests are of our times and of our society." As the standard of "interest and entertainment," Joyce's *Ulysses* would be offered in twelve installments so that "millions of people" would no longer have to talk about a book
they had not read or pay "the genial booklegger" a high price to obtain a
copy.[105] Roth's philanthropic boasting was similar to that of Mosher three
decades earlier, but whereas Mosher had sought to supply American readers

with choice bits of prose and poetry previously locked up in rare and pricey volumes, Roth was declaring war on the scarcity created by prudery, vice societies, and obscenity laws. Pound offered a qualified defense of Roth as "a man desiring ... to rebel against and satirise something more vile [the obscenity laws] than any possible act of an individual." Roth was "far from being the first American pirate," Pound noted;[106] indeed, he was "a better Pirate, possibly than the late T.B. Mosher (but Mosher's blah was perhaps a nicer flavor)."[107] Pound recognized something of himself in Roth: a committed disseminator with a fixed and sometimes quixotic hatred of conventional authority.

Roth dedicated the first number of *Two Worlds Monthly* to "James Joyce who will probably plead the cause of our time at the bar of posterity."[108] This image of the Irish author as a skilled attorney pleading a generation's cause would come to seem bitterly ironic less than a year later when Joyce brought a cause of action against Roth in the New York courts for misappropriating his name for commercial and advertising purposes. Out of a mixture of admiration and ballyhoo, Roth placed the names of other noted avant-garde writers—Pound, Eliot, D. H. Lawrence, Arthur Schnitzler—on the dedication pages of later installments of his monthly magazine. His unauthorized dedications combined a desire to participate in the economy of generational gifting made possible by authorship with a keen awareness of the increasing dollar value of modernist celebrity.

*Two Worlds Monthly* was very different from the experimental little magazines; it was nothing like the uncompromising *Little Review* or the more polished *Dial*. It was, as the Paris *Chicago Tribune* noted, "a magazine of reprint material drawn from contemporary sources."[109] Roth offered fragments of modernism fixed in an amber of transatlantic decadence, mild eroticism, and international realism. Poems by John M. Synge, Carl Sandburg, Emanuel Carnevali, Lawrence, and Pound were offered together with *Yellow Book* verse by Richard Le Gallienne and racy translations of Arabic poems by E. Powys Mathers. Fiction and prose experiments by Joyce, Lawrence, Eliot, and Djuna Barnes appeared alongside work by Frank Harris, Catulle Mendes, Richard Middleton, and Caradoc Evans. A translation of Octave Mirbeau's *A Chambermaid's Diary*—a picaresque account of fetishism, sexual manipulation, and ruined innocence—appeared in the same issues as *Ulysses*; Roth advertised them together as "great suppressed novels."[110] Sprinkled among these offerings were tidbits of tart misogyny by Ambrose

**Figure 4.2** Cover of the first number of *Two Worlds Monthly*, July 1926.

Bierce and Charles G. Shaw and quaint seventeenth-century poems on cuckoldry drawn from collections of amatory verse. Added to the mélange were Roth's own "Life and Letters" and his theater review section, "Mr. Roth is Entertained," in which he combined witty, acerbic criticism with observations on the comparative charms of stage actresses.

The broad ribaldry of Roth's quarterly magazine was toned down in *Two Worlds Monthly* to a pervasive risqué note and a quietly dogmatic insistence on sexual freedom. But there was much that was not new or au courant. Roth drew a great deal of his material from back issues of magazines and dated collections of international fiction. In many ways, *Two Worlds Monthly* resembled such turn of the century American periodicals as *Transatlantic Tales* or *Tales of Town Topics*, which had offered, in the words of one 1896 advertisement, a "complete novel, by some well-known author, selections of short stories, burlesques, poems, witticisms, etc., from [previous issues] so far back as to make the republication fresh reading."[111] Roth filled his monthly with such content, adding a veneer of modernism and a parade of glittering names to give color to his boast of purveying new and daring experiments.

Roth's chief source was the American public domain. In addition to quarrying works that had lost their copyrights through noncompliance with notice and renewal requirements, he took his materials gratis from dozens of European sources that had not satisfied the ad interim and manufacturing formalities of the 1909 act: periodicals such as *This Quarter* (for works by Sandburg and Djuna Barnes), *Poetry Review* (Pound), *The Criterion* and *The New Criterion* (Eliot, Lawrence, Humbert Wolfe), *The English Review* (Francis Gribble), *The Calendar of Modern Letters* (T. F. Powys, Herbert L. Kahan), *The Adelphi* (M. L. Skinner, John W. Coulter, Mary Arden, William Gehardi), *The London Mercury* (Hermann Bahr), *The Bystander* (Leonard Merrick), *The Illustrated London News* (G. K. Chesterton), and *The Dublin Magazine* (George Manning-Sanders, Michael Scot); and such publishers as Hutchinson (J. A. Brendon), Unwin (Middleton), Oxford University Press (Jan Neruda), Eveleigh Nash (Merrick), the Golden Cockerel Press (A. E. Coppard, Martin Armstrong), Stephen Swift & Co. (Pound), Elkin Mathews (Pound), A. C. Fifield (W. H. Davies), Selwyn & Blount (Jules Lemaitre), C. W. Beaumont (Hugh de Selincourt, Philip Guedalla), Curwen Press (John Galsworthy), Cuala Press and Maunsel & Co. (Synge), Contact Editions and Three Mountains Press (Barnes, Norman Douglas), and, of course, Shakespeare and Company (Joyce).[112] *Two Worlds Monthly* was largely a copyright-free omnibus, of which the only legally protected portions—apart from occasional original material and the editor's own contributions—were the selection and arrangement of uncopyrighted pieces. Roth coolly inserted the blanket notice "Copyright ... by Samuel Roth" in every number.

## "Practically run out of town": The International Protest and Trade Courtesy

Roth ran an installment of *Ulysses* in each of the eleven published issues of *Two Worlds Monthly*. Although he had promised to complete the novel in twelve numbers, he got no further than the "Oxen of the Sun" episode, just over half of the book.[113] In all, he published only about twenty-five more pages of the novel than *The Little Review* had managed—a bitter finale for a man who believed himself chosen to carry on from where Anderson and Heap had been forced to leave off. Unlike them, he had not been charged with a crime for serializing *Ulysses*, nor did copyright law bring him to heel. Instead, the forces that wrecked his magazine business were primarily two: money and James Joyce. Roth was inexperienced and undercapitalized when he launched *Two Worlds Monthly* and his other newsstand offering, *Beau: The Man's Magazine*. He had impulsively overextended himself, and, despite some initial success, his revenues from these and other publications proved insufficient to recoup his losses.[114] He had moved too quickly from private subscription to mass marketing.

In addition to money problems, "the Joyce gang," as Roth called it, systematically worried him until he abandoned his efforts to increase the gaiety of nations.[115] The relentless campaign to isolate Roth succeeded so well because Joyce and his supporters used reliable methods that had been evolved over the previous century for punishing transgressors of the unwritten norms of publishing: the reputational sanctions of trade courtesy. Before Joyce was through with him, Roth, a reprinter of mostly uncopyrighted material, appeared to the world as a pirate, a scofflaw, and, worst of all, a sinner against genius. Hoping to use Joyce's name to market his magazines, Roth in the end was immolated on the altar of Joyce's aggrieved celebrity.

By mid-August 1926, Joyce had learned that Roth was publishing *Ulysses* in *Two Worlds Monthly*. John M. Price, Pound's American agent, had written Beach in late July to inquire whether an American copyright existed to protect *Ulysses* from the depredations of Roth, whom Price knew to be "a literary swindler."[116] Joyce was startled by Roth's boast that, due in part to the inclusion of *Ulysses*, the first number of *Two Worlds Monthly* had sold 50,000 copies and had required a second printing.[117] He worried that the unauthorized serialization would erode his American market by destroying demand for the Paris edition.[118]

Joyce was even more alarmed that Roth was "mutilating" the text. Gertzman has usefully shown that Roth's edits were often less aggressive than the pruning that had been done in *The Little Review*,[119] but Joyce's point of comparison was the imperfect but unexpurgated Shakespeare and Company text, not the earlier serialization. Roth omitted words, phrases, and sentences that might rouse the censor, sometimes inserting sanitized alliteration ("crater" for "cunt," for example).[120] He passed numerous printing errors; in one instance, an entire page of the Paris text had been dropped.[121] Although Roth later denied responsibility for the alterations, in August 1926 he had assured the advertising manager of *The Nation* that Joyce's text was being "carefully expurgated by us" so that "this great modern classic" could be popularized "without bringing us into any difficulties with either the post office or other authorities."[122]

The Joyce gang's retaliation was slow but sure. Long before Beach organized the international protest, Joyce's supporters had set about sleuthing, baiting, and mudslinging. In November 1925, just after Roth had begun reprinting extracts from "Work in Progress" in *Two Worlds*, the New York critic Lloyd Morris vowed to assist Joyce and Beach by confronting Roth and demanding an explanation. He tried six times without success to see "the offending Mr. Roth" at his office and finally telephoned him to challenge his right to publish Joyce's work. Roth retorted that "no 'authority' was needed to reprint writing in the public domain."[123] Working as Pound's unpaid agent in New York and hoping to expand his services to other modernists abroad, Price monitored Roth's advertising and denounced him to magazines that accepted it, wrote to the district attorney and authors' leagues, and published a caustic letter under the caption "1 Roth + 2 Worlds = How Many Suckers?," in which he accused Roth of shady practices and of misusing Pound's name in *Two Worlds*.[124] Joseph Kling, a Greenwich Village editor and bookseller, told Price that Roth was "the stinkingest Galician Jew swindler alive" and that he had boasted of starting a magazine that would "cost him nothing at all, and which would suck up a record price from all the damn fools in America."[125] Price participated in and overheard several conversations of this type. By late 1925, anti-Roth gossip was spreading among New York publishers and booksellers.

Roth sensed the demolition-in-progress. In December 1925 he pleaded with Pound to help protect him against "the malign tongue of the literary gossiper" and a week later appealed to Beach not to assist "a wave of slander whose mud-puddles are even now creeping up to my toes."[126] Neither relented. Pound, with Price's help, wrote stern letters to *Vanity Fair* and other magazines that had carried advertisements for *Two Worlds* in which his name was mentioned, and urged his father "to write promptly to any paper printing Roth's ads."[127] After Roth began running *Ulysses* in *Two Worlds Monthly*, Beach kept up a steady drumbeat of correspondence with newspapers and magazines, charging Roth with piracy, mutilation, and nonpayment, and parrying his attempts to defend himself in the *New York Evening Post* and other periodicals.[128] She urged the American journalist Kate Buss to make the matter public and help rescue Joyce from Roth's clutches, and she asked her father, a clergyman in New Jersey, to look into "legal and social pressures" that might be applied to the New York pirate.[129] She even sent a statement denouncing Roth to the editor of *Mexican Life* in Mexico City.[130] A "firmly abusive campaign in the press" was the only effective means of redress, Pound advised Joyce.[131]

The use of the press to spread negative gossip was a time-tested sanction derived from trade courtesy practices of the previous century. The aim of the gossipers was to multiply punishments exponentially by destroying Roth's credibility with publishers, advertising departments, booksellers, newsstand owners, and readers, who would in turn refuse to deal with him and his magazine business. The strategy was effective. Helen M. Gifford, a Haverford bookseller, regretted that she had been "taken in by Roth" and hoped he would "get what is due him."[132] Roth angrily wrote her that she was welcome to believe Beach's "libellous" attacks if she could square it with her conscience and her church.[133] Gifford simply passed Roth's letter on to Beach, noting that "you got a rise out of them anyway."[134] Readers across the United States, even when they admired his courage in publishing *Ulysses*, scolded him in terms reminiscent of the rhetoric of courtesy: "I realize that if this [piracy charge] be true, you have every legal write [*sic*] to [reprint *Ulysses*]. I also know that such a thing is, ethically, utterly damnable."[135] "Do you think that [publishing Joyce without permission] was justified and honorable?"[136] "No one really admires a crook."[137] Joyce's efforts had stirred up public sentiment for authors' moral rights.

Writers in particular turned against him, including friends and acquaintances like Maurice Samuel and Louis Untermeyer.[138] Shortly before sailing for New York, Lewis Galantière told Beach that he was willing to write to the newspapers about Roth's misdeeds as soon as he arrived in the city.[139] Carl Sandburg, stung by Roth's use of his uncopyrighted poems in *Two*

*Worlds Monthly*, tacitly acknowledged that there was no legal redress but felt that Roth was operating "by a dirty code."[140] Hemingway deplored the acceptance of Roth's advertising by reputable publications and wondered if a national organization existed that could "blacklist the advertising of crooks." "Life seems quite complicated today," he lamented.[141] Hemingway's nostalgia for a world in which publishers banded together to ostracize those who rebelled against the standards of fair dealing glanced at the fact that, formerly, publishers prided themselves openly on the extralegal practice of trade courtesy. But Hemingway need not have worried. Courtesy still existed in 1926, but for the reasons I noted in chapter 1 it had become more an internalized corporate ethic than a flaunted chivalric code. Joyce and his friends were quietly shaping the courtesy tradition to their purposes, and Roth was feeling the lash.

The idea of an international protest was not new when Beach began assembling the roster of signers in 1926. America's protectionist copyright laws had elicited many protests from foreign authors and publishers during the nineteenth century, most notably, perhaps, in 1837 when a petition for copyright reform was signed by fifty-six British authors and presented to Congress by Senator Henry Clay.[142] The document Beach was planning, however, would not be addressed to legislators but, rather, to publishers, booksellers, and readers; it would condemn the law and the lawful pirate equally and express worldwide sympathy for a particular author exploited

**Figure 4.3** Mug shot of Samuel Roth, Philadelphia, 1930. (*Courtesy Jay Gertzman*)

by a particular reprinter. Such a case-specific effort was not without recent precedent. Following the conviction of Anderson and Heap, the Autumn 1921 issue of *The Little Review* had contained a "PROTEST against the suppression of the Little Review containing various instalments of the 'Ulysses' of JAMES JOYCE," signed by Constantin Brancusi, Jean Cocteau, Jean Hugo, Guy-Charles Cros, Paul Morand, Francis Picabia, and Ezra Pound.[143]

It was precisely the hybrid nature of the international protest—its targeting of Roth and the legal regime which tolerated him—that brought it within the courtesy tradition. Nineteenth-century publishers had used a similar bifocal approach to discredit transgressors of courtesy, deploring the inadequacy of American copyright law and blaming the "pirates" for taking advantage of it. An early version of the Roth protest, drafted around the end of September 1926, was intended to arouse the indignation of "American men of letters and publishers."[144] Captioned "Draft letter to American literary newspapers and magazines," the document began by pointing to the failure of American copyright laws to protect works printed abroad but quickly settled into a bill of particulars aimed at Roth. After stressing his Jewishness, the letter charged him with listing Pound and Ford as contributing editors of *Two Worlds* without their permission and with pirating Gertrude Beasley's *My First Thirty Years*. Moving on to Joyce's case, the draft arraigned Roth as a "get-rich-quick promoter" who was endangering Joyce's livelihood by reprinting *Ulysses* without payment and benefiting from "the innocent connivance of American law." The letter captured the essence of courtesy when it labeled Roth "a menace to honourable publishing in the United States" and urged periodical publishers to decline to advertise his "stolen goods" and readers to refrain from purchasing them. The document ended by conceding that such a protest could have "only a moral effect." "The law does not protect Mr. Joyce; it protects the pirate of Mr. Joyce's work." In the tradition of courtesy, the letter reminded publishers and readers of their moral responsibility to fill the vacuum created by American law by treating foreign authors fairly and refusing to deal with the likes of the "bold-faced" Roth.

By November 23, 1926, when Ludwig Lewisohn produced a shorter draft, the protest was plainly meant to include international signatures. The new draft again sought to mobilize American publishers and readers, contending that the subject was "of the gravest import not only to all writers but to all honest men."[145] Emphasizing Joyce's "momentary helplessness" at the hands of a law that "expresses the conventional mind," the draft accused

Roth of having "the shamelessness of a highwayman but quite without the highwayman's courage, since the law grants him a temporary immunity." The protest appealed to the "good name of American publishing" and "common honor and honesty." What the draft gained in brevity it lost in its stridency and the haughty suggestion that American law was ill-equipped to accommodate Joyce's genius. By likening Roth to a criminal, the draft also invited a lawsuit for defamation. No American periodical would risk publishing the potentially libelous statement that Roth, by reprinting a work unprotected by U.S. copyright law, was acting in the manner of a cowardly highwayman. Thirty years earlier, the publisher Isaac K. Funk had brought a libel action against *The New York Evening Post* for having accused him of pirating the *Encyclopedia Britannica*, a work known to be in the American public domain. Although Funk ultimately lost the case, the litigation was bitter and expensive.

The final version of the international protest was close to Lewisohn's November 23 draft, but it eliminated the inflammatory language in favor of a neutral, almost legalistic style, probably on the advice of the American poet and lawyer Archibald MacLeish. The opening sentences acknowledged Joyce's American copyright problems:

> It is a matter of common knowledge that the ULYSSES of Mr. James Joyce is being republished in the United States, in a magazine edited by Samuel Roth, and that this republication is being made without authorization by Mr. Joyce; without payment to Mr. Joyce and with alterations which seriously corrupt the text. This appropriation and mutilation of Mr. Joyce's property is made under colour of legal protection in that the ULYSSES which is published in France and which has been excluded from the mails in the United States is not protected by copyright in the United States.[146]

Whether, under U.S. law, there could be an "appropriation" of an author's "property" when that property was "not protected by copyright" was a nice question that the protest did not address. The statement confined itself to pointing to the inequity of the situation and exhorting the "public (including the editors and publishers to whom his advertisements are offered)" to refuse to deal with Roth and to oppose to his enterprise "the full power of honorable and fair opinion." In contrast to the previous drafts, the chastened rhetoric of the final version placed less emphasis on the ethics of trade courtesy and more on reputational sanctions. The entire "public"—not just the publishing world—was urged to gossip about Roth, honorably and fairly. The protest blended courtesy sanctions with an implicit appeal to First Amendment rights.

Bearing the signatures of more than 160 international authors and intellectuals, the protest was cabled to hundreds of American newspapers and magazines in time for publication on Joyce's birthday, February 2, 1927.[147] Some papers, including the *New York Times*, printed the text of the protest. Many editors, fearing a lawsuit, ran selected quotations or simply summarized the controversy.[148] Henry Seidel Canby, now editor of *The Saturday Review of Literature*, informed Beach that he could not print the protest; his lawyer, who may have been recalling the Funk litigation, had advised him that the statement was "clearly libellous under american law."[149] Marianne Moore, editor of *The Dial*, was careful to assure Roth that she and her coeditors were not "among those who have accused you of injustice to Mr. Joyce."[150] At least one of the signers of the protest also worried about legal consequences. H. G. Wells appended to his signature the disclaimer "Protest made subject to the facts being as stated above and not in confirmation of the statements made," but this was dropped from the final text.[151]

Roth tried gamely to fight back, but Joyce had captured the news cycle. Roth wrote to the editor of *The Nation*, blandly approving "any attempt to rebuild the copyright laws" but adding the wicked thrust that "there is no more copyright on ULYSSES than there is on the work of a certain William Shakespeare whose name is on Miss Beach's stationery."[152] The public domain was a great equalizer, Roth implied, and if he was exploiting a noted author's name for commercial purposes, then Beach was no better. *The Nation* refused to print Roth's letter, and other periodicals followed suit. It was like "trying to make a recording in a vacuum," he later lamented.[153] He had more luck with *The New Statesman* of London, which ran a letter in which he denied making money by *Ulysses* and suggested that Beach had orchestrated the protest as a way of protecting her racket of selling *Ulysses* "for a high price to people who think they are buying a dirty book."[154] This, too, recalled the previous century's courtesy quarrels, in which accused pirates attempted to seize the high ground by pointing to the affordability of their reprints. Roth, the practiced marketer of a quaintly salacious modernism, was accusing Beach of doing the same thing but at prices that were prohibitive for ordinary readers. Roth was everyman's disseminator of "wit, beauty and gaiety," a Lower East Side Robin Hood.[155]

Roth's satirical sneering was not calculated to win sympathy. He was sinking by his levity as Joyce rose by his gravity. Unlike renegades from courtesy in the previous century who stuck firmly to the position that works in the public domain were fair game, Roth multiplied defenses endlessly—he was the victim of a literary vendetta; the international protest was a sham; he had offered Joyce a thousand dollars; Pound had granted permission; publishing *Ulysses* had ruined sales of *Two Worlds Monthly*. Boycotted by other outlets, Roth finally resorted to the pages of his own magazine to make a last stand. He lashed out furiously in *Two Worlds Monthly*, accusing Joyce of being a "schnorrer," a beggar of the Paris cafés. He assailed "Work in Progress" as the product of Joyce's "semi-conscious demoniacism" and the "ludicrous gullibility of his friends."[156] Beach was a "vicious virago" and Roth the victim of "the most contemptible conspiracy to which a writer has ever been subjected by a group of his contemporaries."[157] The Joyce gang was pursuing him for no better purpose than to engage in international "log-rolling."[158] The entire affair, he contended, was a self-congratulatory campaign to generate publicity for the pampered and self-obsessed Irish writer.

Despite his contemptuous bluff, Roth was crushed and humiliated. As Joyce began to win the publicity battle, the press increasingly characterized Roth as a deviant from trade courtesy, and periodicals refused his advertising.[159] The editors of *The New Statesman* conceded that his reprinting of *Ulysses* was "perfectly legal" but pointed to his "offense against the unwritten laws and the decencies of his profession."[160] Only "unprincipled 'pirates'" would so shamelessly take advantage of the "obvious defect in the laws of international copyright."[161] *The Saturday Review of Literature* compared Joyce's predicament to that of Charles Dickens and Sir Walter Scott and noted that lawful piracy, in the nineteenth as in the twentieth century, "was not in accord with the best ethics of the publishing profession." Roth was "subject to moral reprobation," the weekly charged.[162] The acting editor of the *New York Times Book Review* wrote privately to Beach that he hoped the international protest might advance "decency and fair play."[163] Invoking the old struggle between advocates of international copyright and proponents of cheap books, *The Nation* described the protest as "surely the most significant one of its kind since the copyright wars of the last century."[164] Many of the anti-Roth statements elicited by the 1927 protest might have been made in 1880. Joyce's grievance had stimulated a powerful sense of professional rectitude that transcended copyright laws and united publishers, booksellers, and readers in respect for the natural, inalienable rights of authors.

Joyce did more than simply employ the received principles of courtesy, however; he made of them a tool for transforming his image and fashioning himself as an embattled, violated artist. When Roth began reprinting fragments of his new work in 1925, Joyce was still regarded in the United States as the author of an unreadable book that had been condemned as obscene by a New York court and was being clandestinely imported from Paris. *Ulysses* lacked formal copyright protection in America and could have been reprinted there by anyone; the only thing that prevented this—apart from the uncertain *Little Review* copyrights—was the book's reputation for obscenity, which barred everyone, including Joyce, from issuing the work. Joyce's campaign against Roth deftly rewrote the reigning legal narrative. It transformed Joyce from victimizer into victim and recast *Ulysses*, widely regarded as an instrument of corruption, as an object of legitimate readerly desire and the subject of international praise and sympathy. Joyce and his supporters substituted a discourse of authors' rights for the previous focus on indecency, rendering *Ulysses* a wronged piece of literary property rather than an offending book. The campaign allowed Joyce to have the best of two worlds: on the one hand, he could watch as Roth publicized his name and whetted the public's appetite for an unexpurgated book version of *Ulysses*; on the other hand, he could treat Roth's serialization as legally and morally forbidden and in any case a mutilated and garbled shadow of the genuine article. Roth was Joyce's front man in America whom Joyce had the luxury of continually repudiating.

Roth knew he was part of Joyce's self-fashioning program, a "cinder" thrown into the public's eye to keep the Irish writer's name in the papers.[165] Joyce exploited the Roth controversy at a critical moment in the development of modernism, just as it was entering into mainstream culture as a marketable movement and mass product.[166] Joyce made ingenious use of trade courtesy. Formerly, the practice had served to regulate competition among publishers for an essentially free resource (uncopyrighted works) and to stabilize the relationship between publishers and authors. The tacit agreement of publishers to behave ethically was the chief element. With the international protest and the publicity surrounding it, Joyce recast courtesy by placing the author at the center as the celebrity owner of potent though undefined moral entitlements and as the cynosure of the literary economy, commanding allegiance from booksellers, advertisers, the press, and even the reading public. No longer a passive beneficiary of publishers' largesse, the author could now claim courtesy as a natural right and become an enforcer of the prerogatives of creativity and a punisher of trespassers.

\* \* \*

Ezra Pound was no friend of piracy, and he did his part to undermine Roth's credibility in the United States. But he refused to sign the international protest, telling Joyce it was "misdirected." Roth, he felt, was merely a symptom of a copyright regime that tolerated and encouraged his activities; his "peccadillo" was dwarfed by "the major infamy of the law."[167] Pound declared Roth more a "barrater" than a "py-rate," hinting that, like the condemned sinners in Canto 21 of Dante's *Inferno*, Roth had abused a public trust but had not actually stolen another's property.[168] By producing magazines that mixed modernism with near-beer erotica, Roth was blurring the distinction between art and "smutty post cards"—a distinction Pound believed was "already muddled enough by the jackass law 211 U.S. penal."[169] Roth was using the sacred office of publisher to libidinize the efforts of the avant-garde, a sin against civilization. But Pound's chief objection to the international protest was that it personalized the legal issues and scapegoated Roth for the inadequacy of American law. He sensed that Joyce was using Roth to promote a cult of victimized genius, and he would not allow his name to be associated with the effort. He offered to have his views appended to the protest as a "minority report,"[170] but Joyce had no interest in sharing the spotlight or mitigating Roth's punishment with the suggestion that he was the inevitable product of bad laws.

As a born disseminator himself, Pound sympathized with Roth. Roth was "really much better than his surroundings,"[171] wrote Pound, who felt he could "appreciate the difficulties (Mr Roth's) more than they deserve."[172] Roth was, after all, "giving his public a number of interesting items that they would not otherwise get."[173] Pound's view exhibited the same studied ambivalence with which he had infused his proposed copyright statute in 1918. There he had argued that authors should enjoy potentially perpetual copyright but that this right should be firmly bounded by compulsory licenses that would be activated if authors or their heirs failed to keep works in print or refused to allow translations. It was as if, in the spirit of Pound's proposal, Roth was unilaterally declaring his compulsory privilege to publish a work that no one else in America dared to print in 1926. His methods were crude, perhaps, but he was furthering international communication, the Jamesian project of helping cultures to understand each other. At a profound level, Pound was uncomfortable with the image of the possessive authorial self that the international protest projected. The protest argued for the security of authors' rights, but it ignored the imperatives of dissemination.[174]

Joyce disregarded these cavils and insisted that his motives were altruistic, that the international protest formed part of "a test case for the reform of U.S. law."[175] A "repeal of that law is what is ultimately aimed at," he said, "and the more comprehensive the protest is the firmer will be the basis for a vigorous international movement of writers in that direction."[176] A test case would require more than a single public statement, however, and even as the protest was being cabled to American newspapers, Joyce's attorneys in New York were preparing the second phase of the campaign. Part one of the plan had been to make a public record of the support of international authors. Part two would require the filing of a lawsuit to establish that an author in Joyce's position, placed at a disadvantage by protectionist laws, could still extract a measure of justice from the American courts. Joyce's next step was to sue Roth and his publishing company—but not for copyright infringement.

# JOYCE V. ROTH

## Authors' Names

## and Blue Valley Butter

*Cheap scraps of stuff snitched from wastebaskets, to which
famous names can be attached.*
—John M. Price describing the contents of Samuel Roth's
Two Worlds (1926)[1]

*I resented from the beginning the talk that I capitalized
[on] the name of Joyce.*
—Samuel Roth (1930)[2]

Samuel Roth built his magazines of the 1920s on two things: uncopyrighted works and authors' names. Both were free resources that had been gifted to the American public domain by protectionist laws and the growing marketability of modernism. Roth drew upon the nascent celebrity of avant-garde authors to boom his magazines and tout the multiple virtues of their contents: literary experiment, freedom of speech, and erotic appeal. He was not just making free with the names of controversial authors; he was also, in his mind, working with fellow intellectuals and artists to administer needful shocks to a society bound by prudery and prohibition. Structural tensions within the laws governing literary property and literary morality made Roth possible: the strictures of obscenity law lent his magazines a deliciously taboo quality while the hyper-formalistic rules of copyright law supplied him with ownerless raw materials for his provocations. In the midst of this forbidden abundance, Roth reveled for a time. Copyright-free materials swelled the pages of *Two Worlds* and *Two Worlds Monthly* and were promoted by Roth as daring and gay entertainment for mature readers. The bankable names of authors, with which he adorned his stationery, his advertising, and the covers of his magazines, gave his enterprise an aura of sophistication and intellectual purpose.

The first issue of *Two Worlds* appeared in September 1925, more than three years after Roth had announced plans to launch the subscription-only magazine. On its cover in neat black type, just below Roth's larger name printed in red, were the names of the three contributing editors: Arthur Symons, Ford Madox Hueffer (Ford), and Ezra Pound. Pound might not have objected to the use of his name if he had thought Roth was running a legitimate operation. But once James Joyce began to complain of Roth's unauthorized use of extracts from "Work in Progress," Pound wanted no part of a piratical enterprise. He wrote Roth around mid-November 1925 to demand the removal of his name as contributing editor.[3] Roth had offered to pay Pound fifty dollars per installment for verse or prose contributions to *Two Worlds* and was especially eager to get some of his cantos, "the only really important poetry written by an American in—but who in hell can time such things?"[4] But Pound's stinging letter frustrated his hopes of collaboration. Roth wrote to express puzzlement over the "quaint sermon in conduct" that Pound had read him and to ask why the mere "metaphysical" lapse of three years between the announcement and the publication of *Two Worlds* should make Pound dismiss him as "scoundrelly." Pound would not budge, however, and Roth agreed to remove his name from the cover and all stationery, though he hoped the poet might reconsider and come "back to us."[5]

Pound did not come back, but even in defeat Roth found a way to exact a spurned pirate's revenge. He wrote Pound's father in February 1926 to inform him that there would be "several pages of Ezra Pound's poetry in the

March number of Two Worlds."⁶ Ezra erupted, cabling his father, "ISSUE INJUNCTION IMMEDIATELY PREVENTING TWO WORLDS PRINTING ANYTHING OVER MY NAME."⁷ He saw clearly that the real point of Roth's threat to print his poems was to continue exploiting his name in the pages of Two Worlds. Homer Pound obliged his son by seeking out legal advice, but the attorney he found told him there was nothing to be done until Roth printed something that injured Ezra and created a basis for claiming damages. Ezra contented himself with railing against "that son of a jew bitch Roth" and vowing to "boil his damn liver in vinegar if I ever get within boot shot of him."⁸

Pound cast about for possible remedies: he thought of writing to the New York police commissioner or a district attorney; attacking Roth in the New York press; enlisting the help of authors' societies; even threatening legal action against magazines that printed advertisements linking his name with Two Worlds. Nothing promised effective relief. He fantasized about wringing Roth's "dirty neck,"⁹ but even here Roth was a step ahead of the fuming exile. Veering from servility to pugnacity, he threatened Pound with a personal "lesson in correspondence" that the poet would not soon forget. He had always been able to handle "half a dozen goyim at a time" and would have no trouble with "one masturbated pimp." He added that he had composed an "epitaph" for Pound's tombstone:

Here lies Ezra Pound,
Most woe-begot of men:
He wet his shirttails twice
Ere once he wet his pen.¹⁰

Roth's scabrous doggerel combined allusions to Leopold Bloom's furtive masturbation in Ulysses, the opening section of Pound's Hugh Selwyn Mauberley ("E.P. Ode pour l'élection de son sepulchre"), and an anonymous jingle called the "Virgin's Prayer" ("Ezra Pound / And Augustus John / Bless the bed / That I lie on"), among other sources.¹¹ A few months later, Roth published a revised version, "Proposed Inscription to be Placed on the Tombstone of E_ P_," in Two Worlds.¹² He was bent on retaliating for the poet's public defection from his magazine. He still hoped to make a legitimate mark in modern letters—his courtship of Joyce (discussed in the previous chapter) had not yet run its unlikely course—but propriety meant nothing to him once his volatile pride was hurt. Now that Pound was irrevocably against him, he was dispensable.

Roth turned to the American public domain for his revenge. Although he did not print anything by Pound in the March 1926 number of *Two Worlds*, he ran two of his poems—"An Immorality" and "Song," a translation from Heinrich Heine—in the August 1926 issue of *Two Worlds Monthly*.[13] Both poems had first appeared in the English magazine *Poetry Review* in 1912 and were reliably in the public domain. Pound's verses were now keeping company in Roth's pages with works by Joyce, T. S. Eliot, Carl Sandburg, and other writers who had failed to obtain U.S. copyrights. Roth struck again in the April 1927 issue of *Two Worlds Monthly*, printing three more of Pound's early poems and dedicating the issue to "Ezra Pound who is, for all that, the greatest poet of this age."[14] Although he had lost the controversial exile as a contributing editor, Roth regained him as an involuntary author and was extracting publicity value by spreading his name across the covers and contents pages of his magazine.

Eliot was another of Roth's trophies. After printing a portion of Eliot's uncopyrighted prose dialogue "Eeldrop and Appleplex" in the August 1926 number of *Two Worlds Monthly*, Roth ran Eliot's "Fragment of a Prologue" and "Wanna Go Home, Baby? (Fragment of an Agon)" in the January and May–June 1927 issues of the magazine.[15] These pieces, which formed parts of Eliot's unfinished poetic drama *Sweeney Agonistes*, had recently appeared in England in *The Criterion* and had been cast into the American public domain for failure to comply with the ad interim and manufacturing provisions of the 1909 U.S. Copyright Act. Eager to take full advantage of Eliot's growing celebrity, Roth dedicated the May–June issue to him as a writer who "has given us some excellent verses, several sound critical formulae, and one of the most charming literary personalities of our time."[16] The dedication combined exploitation of the name of the author of *The Waste Land* with the suggestion that he had "given" his writings and his personality to "our time"—an example of Roth's rhetoric of generational gifting, his belief that art became the spiritual property of everyone the moment it was released to the world.

Eliot was so annoyed that he wrote the *New York Evening Post* to complain that "Mr. Roth chooses to interpret any gift to the world as a gift to himself."[17] Roth retorted that Eliot had "perverted" the meaning of his dedication, which was that Eliot's poems "were given to our generation."[18] Eliot had construed the dedication as a pirate's credo rather than as the philosophy of a man for whom niceties of courtesy were less important than the dissemination of valuable public goods. A part of Roth believed that authors gave their writings to the world as spiritual donations and that the legal public domain was simply a pragmatic reflection of this economy of gifting. He was not above claiming his privileges under the mundane law when necessary, however. To Eliot's accusation that he had published "Wanna Go Home, Baby?" without "offer of payment or communication of any kind," Roth rejoined that he felt justified in reprinting the works of authors "not protected by copyright without first asking their consent, or sending any money first or last, because it was legal in this country, because his magazines were not making money, and because he would be only too glad to pay the authors if he did make a profit with his publications."[19] This was the self-righteous language of nineteenth-century reprinters who had been accused of operating outside the rules of trade courtesy. Roth knew precisely when to invoke the American public domain.

Humiliated by Eliot's public rejection of his dedication, Roth lashed out by telling the *Evening Post* that he had printed "Wanna Go Home, Baby?" as a specimen of "the sort of rubbish which is ladled out to us these days as poetry" and that he was mailing Eliot a check for twenty-five dollars, "as a mere formality."[20] Roth's gesture hearkened back to the courtesy payments that publishers had made to unprotected foreign authors during the previous century, except that Roth was twisting the tradition of the solatium to punish Eliot for having excluded him from the collaborative circle of modernism. Eliot would have no part of Roth's "game," however. He stiffly forwarded the check to the *Evening Post*, requesting that it be returned to the sender and stressing that he would not accept any form of "bribery or hush money" from the New York publisher.[21] A hectic choreography of dedications had thus taken the stage: Roth had initially dedicated an issue of *Two Worlds Monthly* to Eliot, in recognition of the latter's gift of creativity to the world. Eliot promptly rejected the proffered honor, whereupon Roth sneeringly presented him with a gift of twenty-five dollars for his poetic "rubbish"—a gratuity uncompelled by the U.S. copyright law which had already effected the dedication of Eliot's poem to the public domain. Eliot in turn repudiated the monetary gift so as to avoid the appearance of having bargained away his right to continue to denounce Roth as a thief operating under shelter of a shameful law.

In this ritual of gift giving and returning, one thing remained constant: Roth's determination to boost his magazine through the uncompensated use of a famous author's name. It was not the first or the last time he captured the growing dollar value of authorial celebrity to promote his projects. In the

December 1926 issue of *Two Worlds Monthly*, he included a full-page notice urging readers to invest in his "Powerful Magazine Group." Splashed across the top of the notice was the seeming endorsement: "H. L. Mencken Advises Rich Young Men To Invest In Magazines."[22] Mencken, Pound, Eliot, D. H. Lawrence—these and other notable names graced Roth's advertisements, magazine covers, and dedication pages. But no name—with the possible exception of Roth's own—appeared as consistently as that of James Joyce. Hemingway claimed that he had heard Roth boast that he was using Joyce's name as a "draw" to reel in subscribers.[23] One reader of *Two Worlds Monthly* wrote to praise Roth for "making an economic unit out of Literature," adding, "On the principle on which it has come to be known that Blue Valley Butter Is Good Butter, every intelligent reader in the United States has come to know that James Joyce is a good writer."[24] Ostensibly lauding Roth for his promotion of literary excellence, the reader astutely pinpointed his trademark-like use of authors' names to brand his magazines and stimulate consumer interest. Roth drew upon the signifying power of literary celebrity as a grocer might plaster his storefront with advertisements for high-quality dairy products. Like butter brands, modernist authors' names carried a monetary value. In 1927, Joyce decided to test that value by suing Roth and his publishing company for half a million dollars in damages for the commercial misappropriation of his name.

## An Author in Search of a Lawyer

When Roth began running *Ulysses* in *Two Worlds Monthly* in 1926, Joyce was without legal representation in the United States. A year earlier, Sylvia Beach, Joyce's Paris publisher, had engaged New York attorney Arthur Garfield Hays to put a stop to Roth's unauthorized use of extracts from "Work in Progress" in *Two Worlds*. Hays was a noted civil liberties lawyer who had recently been a member of the defense team at the Scopes "Monkey Trial" and would shortly assist Sacco and Vanzetti with the appeal of their murder convictions. Hays and his colleagues had considerable expertise in copyright matters,[25] but they had trouble making contact with Roth and did not pursue the matter vigorously.[26] In October 1926, several months after *Ulysses* had begun to appear in Roth's magazine, Archibald MacLeish helped Joyce draft a cable to be sent to another New York lawyer, Paul Kieffer, requesting his services in obtaining an injunction against Roth.[27] Kieffer seemed a natural choice. He had been John Quinn's law partner until the latter's death in 1924, and he continued to run Quinn's old firm, now Kieffer & Woodward, which presumably retained useful files relating to Joyce and *Ulysses*. Kieffer disappointed Joyce, however, by cabling a terse refusal on November 5, 1926: "REGRET UNABLE UNDERTAKE CASE."[28]

Beach turned next to the New York law firm of Chadbourne, Stanchfield & Levy, a talented and efficient team of lawyers who were well equipped to handle complex litigation. Chadbourne had its offices in the thirty-six-story Equitable Building at 120 Broadway; its letterhead boasted a dozen lawyers, and others were associated with the firm. There was also a Paris office, located at 20 Place Vendôme, staffed by a small group of attorneys led by Benjamin Howe Conner, a prominent figure in the American legal community in France. Born in Kentucky in 1878, Conner had received his bachelor of laws degree (L.L.B.) from Albany Law School in 1902, with honorable mention for his thesis. By the time he was heading up Chadbourne's Paris office in the late 1920s, he had become president of the American Chamber of Commerce at Paris and Department of France Commander of the American Legion. Later, he was appointed by the Egyptian king to the Mixed Court, an international tribunal at Cairo, on the recommendation of President Franklin D. Roosevelt.[29] Joyce described Conner in 1927 as "the most influential American in Paris except the ambassador."[30]

Beach had known Conner personally for several years and had gone to him for assistance in securing a French copyright for *Ulysses*.[31] She met with him in late November 1926 to discuss the "matter of pirating of 'Ulysses' by Samuel Roth," as Conner's billing statements show.[32] The decision to sue Roth was quickly arrived at; on November 23, the *Chicago Tribune* in Paris reported that Beach was "preparing to bring action against Mr. Roth through counsel in New York."[33] A few weeks later, Conner arranged for Beach and Joyce to meet Paul M. Hahn, a principal attorney in the New York Chadbourne firm, who was visiting Paris. Hahn had received his LL.B. from Columbia University in 1917 and the next year joined Chadbourne (then known as Stanchfield & Levy), becoming a partner in 1926. He devoted much of his time to one of Chadbourne's important clients, the American Tobacco Co., of which he later became president.[34] In Paris, Beach and Joyce repeated for Hahn the story of Roth's allegedly piratical activities, and Conner urged Joyce to seek half a million dollars in damages, an enormous sum in 1926 (more than $6.5 million in 2012 dollars).[35] Joyce paid

**Figure 5.1** Benjamin Howe Conner, Cairo, Egypt, ca. 1937. (*Courtesy Robert Cox*)

a retainer of $150, and in late January 1927 Hahn sailed for New York with instructions to prepare a lawsuit as soon as he arrived.[36]

Just as Hahn and his associates were getting to work, another lawsuit against Roth was brewing. In November 1926, Jane Heap, editor of *The Little Review*, had contacted Arthur Garfield Hays for help in preventing Roth's further "infringement of [her] copyright interest in James Joyce's 'Ulysses.'"[37] As noted in the previous chapter, Heap believed she owned the copyright, or at least exclusive American rights, in *Ulysses*. She claimed that the only reason she hadn't acted more quickly to sue Roth was that Joyce himself had infringed her copyright—evidently by distributing the Paris edition in the United States without her permission—and she "didn't want to get Joyce in trouble."[38] Joyce was furious about her assertions and obtained for his lawyers a signed declaration from Pound setting forth the facts surrounding the *Little Review* serialization. Eager though she was to sue Roth, she was hampered by her inability to locate evidence that Joyce had transferred his rights to *The Little Review*. In the meantime, Beach and Conner were desperately trying to learn what Heap was up to. Beach cabled her several times in November and December 1926, asking whether she was suing Roth in her own name or in Joyce's. If Heap was suing in her own name, Beach was content to have two lawsuits pending against the harried Roth, but if Heap was suing in Joyce's name, Beach wanted her to instruct Hays to turn the matter over to Joyce's Chadbourne attorneys.[39]

Hays was perplexed. Joyce, despite having engaged another law firm, had not definitely terminated his services, and he felt bound to try to bring closure to the Roth matter. In January 1927, he invited Roth to his office to discuss a settlement with Joyce. Roth told Hays that *Ulysses* was in the American public domain and assured him—probably falsely—that he had offered Joyce a thousand dollars for *Ulysses* prior to launching *Two Worlds Monthly*. As a civil libertarian and free speech advocate, Hays was impressed by Roth's apparently sincere desire to make Joyce's controversial work more widely known. He urged Roth to renew his thousand dollar offer and agreed to act as escrow in brokering a settlement. Roth deposited with Hays a check for $100 along with four promissory notes for $100 each and a fifth note for $500, payable to Joyce on the fourteenth of February, March, April, May, and June 1927. (Evidently, the offer was later sweetened to a check for $200 and $800 in notes.) In conveying the offer to Joyce, Hays explained that the promissory notes were conditioned "largely upon Mr. Roth's future prospects." He also enclosed a pre-drafted release stating that Roth had made the offer before serializing *Ulysses*, a release that Joyce, if he chose to accept the offer, would be expected to sign.[40]

The proposal was not calculated to appeal to Joyce. Conditional payments out of future profits were reminiscent of nineteenth-century trade courtesy. They might have seemed reasonable to Hays, who was persuaded that *Ulysses* lacked copyright protection in the United States, but Joyce had little interest in a new serialization of *Ulysses* and could neither depend on nor verify Roth's turning a sufficient profit to make good on his notes. Joyce was loath, moreover, to agree to the fiction that the man whom he and Beach had been publicly assailing as a pirate had made a thousand dollar offer more than six months before. Most of all, keeping the dispute before the public was worth much more to Joyce than settling. By the time he received Roth's offer, his attorneys were already preparing the much publicized lawsuit, and Beach was distributing the international protest against Roth to the American press. The value of playing the victimized author and excoriating Roth as a violator and mutilator of his literary property was incalculable. Joyce did not deign to reply directly to Hays.[41] When the lawyer learned through Heap that Joyce would "make no compromise with Mr. Roth," he informed Heap and Joyce that he could provide no further services to them.[42] He had been paid nothing for his efforts to date and had no interest in representing clients for whom mere "fighting" was more important than "adjustment."[43] Hays had attempted to broker a courtesy settlement, as arbitrators had informally done during the previous century. When the attempt failed, Hays and Heap dropped out of the picture, leaving the Chadbourne firm to contend with the resourceful Roth.

## The Lawsuit

As late as March 1927, the correspondence flowing between Chadbourne's New York and Paris offices was headed "Re: Joyce & Beach v. Roth," "In re. Beach and Joyce v. Roth," or "Re. Claim for Piracy of 'Ulysses.'"[44] But Beach's name soon disappeared from the captions, along with references to piracy and *Ulysses*. As the attorneys refined their theory of the case, they decided not to base it, ostensibly anyway, on Roth's reprinting of *Ulysses* or on a claim of copyright infringement. An action for copyright infringement would have had to be filed in federal court, and Beach, as Joyce's licensed publisher, would likely have been joined as an interested party. Instead, the Chadbourne attorneys framed the lawsuit with Joyce as the sole plaintiff, and they filed the action in the Supreme Court of the State of New York, in New York County. Despite its name, the Supreme Court was, and still is, the trial-level court in the New York State court system. The lawsuit, which was captioned "James Joyce against Samuel Roth and Two Worlds Publishing Company," made Roth and his company codefendants.

On March 14, 1927, Joyce's attorneys served a summons and a verified complaint on Roth, both personally and as president of his publishing company, at 17 John Street in Manhattan, the address of his lawyer. The complaint was remarkably plain and simple. It consisted of six brief paragraphs alleging that Roth's company, a corporation organized under the laws of New York, published magazines for profit; that the defendants had, at "sundry times," knowingly "made use of and are now making use of the name of the plaintiff ... without the plaintiff's consent in writing first had and obtained"; and that such use was being made "for advertising purposes and for the purposes of trade." The prayer for relief sought an injunction against further use of "the name of the plaintiff," half a million dollars in actual damages, and "such exemplary [that is, punitive] damages as shall be deemed proper under the statute." The complaint was signed and sworn to by Paul M. Hahn, the chief Chadbourne attorney in the case, who stated that the allegations were based mainly on "conversations had with the plaintiff."[45]

It was what the complaint did not say that was most striking. Apart from the caption, there was no reference to James Joyce or his famed authorship, no mention of his book *Ulysses*, no allusion to Roth's unauthorized reprinting of the novel in the pages of his magazine. Piracy, textual mutilation, nonpayment—the outrages that had been trumpeted in the international protest and Beach's statements in the press—were nowhere to be found. Instead, the complaint focused entirely on Joyce's name. His attorneys had chosen as the basis of the lawsuit a state statute, Section 51 of the New York Civil Rights Law, which forbade commercial misappropriation of certain common indicia of personality:

> Any person whose name, portrait or picture is used within this state for advertising purposes or for the purpose of trade without ... written consent first obtained ... may maintain an equitable action in the supreme court of this state against the person, firm, or corporation so using his name, portrait or picture, to prevent and restrain the use thereof; and may also sue and recover damages for any injuries sustained by reason of such use and if the defendant shall have knowingly used such person's name, portrait, or picture in such manner as is forbidden or declared to be unlawful ... the jury in its discretion may award exemplary damages.[46]

By proscribing the unauthorized commercial use of an individual's name, portrait, or picture, Section 51 created a statutory right of privacy. The New York legislature had enacted Section 51—along with Section 50, a criminal provision that made the same conduct a misdemeanor offense—in 1903, after the New York Court of Appeals, the state's highest court, denied relief to a young woman whose likeness had been placed, without her consent, on flyers advertising Franklin Mills Flour. The woman, Abigail Roberson, claimed that she had been humiliated by the unwanted posting of her likeness in stores, warehouses, and saloons, and she sued for an injunction and fifteen thousand dollars in damages. The Court of Appeals rejected her claim. The "so-called 'right of privacy,'" Chief Judge Parker wrote, "has not as yet found an abiding place in our jurisprudence," and courts were not the proper institutions to improvise a right to be let alone.[47] The New York legislature took the hint and enacted Sections 50 and 51 the following year.

Joyce's bare-bones complaint characterized him as an ordinary individual whose privacy had been invaded by the commercial theft of his name. The

Chadbourne attorneys chose to plead no more than the basic elements of the statute, so as to avoid introducing facts that might make the complaint vulnerable to dismissal or arm Roth with affirmative defenses. The attorneys no doubt felt that a claim based directly on copyright would be difficult to sustain. No U.S. copyright existed in the Paris edition of *Ulysses*. The *Little Review* serialization enjoyed questionable protection, and Margaret Anderson had registered only a few issues with the U.S. Copyright Office. There was also the problem of Heap, who was claiming to be the exclusive rights holder in the United States.

In addition to all this, Joyce's attorneys had reason to worry that their request for equitable injunctive relief might be denied if they based their prayer on Roth's unauthorized use of *Ulysses*. *Ulysses* was widely regarded as a scandalous and immoral book, and a court of equity might refuse to exercise its injunctive power for a suitor who had "unclean hands." "He who comes into equity must come with clean hands," runs the familiar maxim, or, as it is sometimes quaintly phrased, "he that hath committed iniquity shall not have equity."[48] Joyce's ink-stained hands might prove an obstacle if redress were requested for Roth's exploitation of the notorious *Ulysses*. But if Joyce was asking only that Roth be prevented from appropriating his name for profit, the court might not feel that it was being called upon to protect an iniquitous book. This, and the uncertain status of the *Little Review* copyrights, counseled in favor of attacking Roth in state court by means of Section 51 of the civil rights law.

Yet Joyce's attorneys were only waiting for the right moment to introduce *Ulysses*. Much of the actual day-to-day management of the case was conducted by a young Chadbourne associate named Eugene Frederick Roth. He was no more than twenty-two years old when he was assigned to the case, fresh from studying law at Columbia University. He was unrelated to Samuel Roth and could scarcely have been more different. Samuel was a volatile, risk-taking luftmensch hovering on the margins of respectability, yearning to be accepted as an author and publisher but ready to cast aside strict probity, when necessary, in favor of piratical methods, bold hucksterism, and bawdy content. He frequently wrote about Jewish experience and drew upon his memories of the Eastern European *shtetl* from which he had emigrated to America as a boy. In contrast, Eugene, who had come to America from Hungary at the age of nine, coveted the white-shoe world of law firms and corporate affluence. He married the wealthy daughter of one of the owners of the Phillips–Van Heusen shirt corporation, and later served as the company's

**Figure 5.2** Eugene Frederick Roth on his honeymoon, 1931. (Courtesy Anne Roiphe)

counsel and director. According to his daughter—the feminist author Anne Roiphe—Eugene Roth was a handsome, driven climber who married for money, practiced law for power and status, and erased all sentimental ties to the Old World.[49]

Hidden from sight at the start of the lawsuit, *Ulysses* might come in handy, later on, to bolster Joyce's somewhat shaky claim under Section 51. A troublesome legal precedent was *Ellis v. Hurst*, a 1910 case that concerned two volumes of historical fiction that had been authored by Edward S. Ellis under the pseudonym "Lieutenant R. H. Jayne." The books lacked U.S. copyright protection, and certain publishers issued them under Ellis's actual name, without permission. Unable to bring an action for copyright infringement, Ellis sued the publishers under Section 51 of the civil rights law for misappropriation of his name. The court rejected Ellis's attempt to stretch Section 51 so far, holding that the defendant publishers' right to issue the uncopyrighted novels "carried with it the right to state the true name of the author." In printing Ellis's name on the volumes, the court said, the publishers had made "a truthful statement, directly connected with the authorship of the books, which they had a right to print."[50]

Samuel Roth's attorneys naturally viewed *Ellis v. Hurst* as strong support for their client's right to serialize the uncopyrighted *Ulysses* in connection with the true name of the author. "The facts in [*Ellis*]," Roth's counsel urged, "are so similar to the case at Bar that it must necessarily govern the law of this case."[51] But the Chadbourne team might try to distinguish *Ellis* from the facts of Joyce's case. First, they might argue that *Ulysses* was at least partially protected by the *Little Review* copyrights and that therefore, unlike the publishers in *Ellis*, Roth was not exploiting the pure public domain in reprinting portions of *Ulysses*. Such an argument would not be without risk; it would tend to rewrite *Ellis* as a case about copyright and to introduce, through the backdoor of Section 51, a copyright infringement claim in the state court, which was not empowered to hear such a claim.[52] Second, the *Ellis* court's emphasis on the publishers' "truthful" use of the author's name in connection with his novels might allow a skillful attorney to argue that by expurgating *Ulysses* in *Two Worlds Monthly* Roth was publishing a version of the work that Joyce had never authored or authorized. Roth's use of "James Joyce" in connection with a bowdlerized text might therefore be viewed as an untruthful statement. Such an argument would echo Joyce's repeated cri de coeur about textual mutilation and might prove the tipping point for obtaining a favorable decision from the court.

Four days after Roth was served with the complaint, his attorney, Nathan Padgug, entered his appearance in the case.[53] Nathan Mordechai Padgug was of a different cut from the Chadbourne lawyers. He was a Lower East Side attorney who mostly worked solo or with a few associates. At the age of ten, he had come to the United States from Minsk and settled with his family on a chicken farm in New Jersey. At sixteen, he ran away to New York to escape his father, an orthodox Jew whom he viewed as a tyrant. After obtaining his high school diploma at a private preparatory school, he studied law at night at New York University and earned his LL.B. in 1915, graduating in the same class with the poet Charles Reznikoff. According to his son, Padgug was fluent in English and Yiddish, a magnetic speaker, conservative in religion, and an early and passionate Zionist. He often took on pro bono or low-paying legal cases and was active in the American Jewish Congress, the Jewish

Court of Arbitration, and other organizations. He got his start in New York politics by working as an inspector in the Bureau of Weights and Measures and later served as Deputy Attorney General of the State of New York.⁵⁴

Samuel Roth had known Padgug before he became a lawyer. Padgug represented him in several matters, including criminal cases, but evidently there was a falling out in the years following the Joyce litigation. In his notoriously anti-Semitic book *Jews Must Live* (1934), Roth offered "Nathan Maggog" as a type of the dishonest lawyer who cynically manipulates the court system and lives on political graft and his clients' ignorance and helplessness. Roth described Maggog as "[o]f medium height, distressingly stout, [and] habitually mopping his florid face with a handkerchief. He gathers his clientele in the home voting district in which he has successfully brought in a safe majority for his political organization for more than twenty years."⁵⁵ Roth's bitter portrait was no doubt colored by his intemperate thesis that Jews were anciently and essentially parasites, "a people of vultures living on the labor and the good nature of the rest of the world."⁵⁶ Padgug was undoubtedly a Tammany adept, but Roth's Maggog seems an unfair and vindictive caricature. Padgug was a plucky lawyer, canny and resourceful within his limitations. He lacked the staff and the funding to meet the Chadbourne firm head-on, but he knew his way around the New York courts.

Padgug's initial strategy was to employ delaying tactics. He promptly filed two motions with the court, one requesting that Joyce be required to make

**Figure 5.3** Nathan Mordechai Padgug, 1950s. (*Courtesy Jay Padgug*)

his allegations against Roth more definite and certain, the other asking that Joyce, as a nonresident of New York, be ordered to give security for costs that Roth might incur in successfully defending against the lawsuit. Joyce's attorneys attempted to moot both motions: on April 11, they served an amended complaint containing greater specificity about Roth's alleged acts. Around the same time, Eugene Roth called at Padgug's office and tendered a security bond, but Padgug rejected the offer, claiming that two bonds were necessary, one for Samuel Roth and one for his company.[57]

On April 18, Justice John M. Tierney of the New York Supreme Court denied Roth's motion for more certainty, noting that Joyce's amended complaint was sufficiently definite and that if Roth wanted greater specificity he could seek a bill of particulars. As for the other motion, the court ruled that a single security bond of $250 running to both defendants was all that Joyce would be required to post. Padgug did not seek a bill of particulars but instead, on April 27, filed and served verified answers to Joyce's amended complaint. The answers denied most of Joyce's allegations and contained no affirmative defenses. With the issue joined, the Chadbourne attorneys served notice that the trial would take place on June 6, 1927, but they privately informed Joyce that, as a result of the crowded court calendar, the case would probably not come on for trial until December 1927 or January 1928. As it turned out, even this prediction was optimistic.[58]

## Roth Testifies

Samuel Roth had a knack for making himself scarce. Joyce's attorneys engaged two different firms, the Fischer Service Bureau and Kramer's Process Serving Agency, to attempt to serve Roth with papers notifying him of the date fixed for his pretrial examination or deposition. A process server finally caught up with him on May 25, 1927, at Seventy-Second Street and Broadway, not far from the luxurious Ansonia Hotel where, flushed with the early success of his magazine ventures, Roth had installed his family in an eight-room apartment.[59] The notice and subpoena required him to appear for examination on May 31, but Nathan Padgug managed to postpone the deposition for a week. On the morning of June 7, Roth presented himself before Joyce's attorneys, Harold A. Callan and Eugene Roth, at the New York County Lawyers' Association. He was accompanied by Isadore Kupfer,

Padgug's clerk, but Padgug himself was not with them. He had been held up, he later explained, by client matters involving a health violation and a partnership agreement. The partnership was evidently one that Padgug himself was forming with two other attorneys.[60]

Pretrial examination without a court order—a familiar device for obtaining information from an opponent in today's litigation—was relatively novel in New York in 1927, having been authorized by statute only seven years before.[61] Padgug's absence did not deter Joyce's attorneys. Callan began by asking Roth if any of his magazines had carried an advertisement referring to the serialization of Joyce's *Ulysses* in *Two Worlds Monthly*. Callan knew that the use of Joyce's name in advertising was more likely to count as commercial misappropriation under Section 51 of the civil rights law than the mere inclusion of his name at the head of extracts from *Ulysses*. But Roth refused to answer any questions of this type, "on advice of counsel."[62] Unable to extract testimony, Joyce's attorneys walked Roth over to the New York County Courthouse and applied to Supreme Court Justice Phoenix Ingraham for an order requiring Roth to answer their questions. Justice Ingraham was a native New Yorker from a prominent family of lawyers and judges and an active patron of the arts and collector of rare books and manuscripts. He had come to the Supreme Court bench just three years earlier. After listening in turn to Callan and Padgug's clerk, the patrician judge ordered Roth to answer the attorneys' questions on pain of being held in contempt of court.[63]

Resuming, Callan began probing Roth on each of the allegations in Joyce's amended complaint. When he reached the charge that Roth had been running his magazine business for profit, the publisher denied ever having produced a periodical in order to make money: "I can think of much surer ways of making profit than publishing my magazines." If he ever did realize a profit, he averred, he would use the windfall "in furthering the artistic ends of my magazine."[64] Roth's altruistic pose—not wholly insincere—was consistent with his claimed willingness to pay his authors something once he had netted a profit on their uncopyrighted writings. The tradition of the post hoc honorarium went back to earlier courtesy practices, when some publishers responded to the abundance of the American public domain by treating foreign authors to paternalistic largesse rather than entering into strict business relationships with them. Roth tended to view the literary commons as an opportunity for generous gestures rather than a source of obligations. If he made no money, his involuntary contributors would at least have the honor of sharing in his project of cultural gifting.

Callan then confronted Roth with the complaint's central allegation, that he had been exploiting Joyce's name for commercial purposes. Roth denied this vehemently, stating that he had appended Joyce's name only so as "not to outrage [his] right as the author of story material." He had chosen Joyce, he insisted, not for his name, but rather for "his work, which is not copyrighted in this country and the property of anyone wishing to use it for whatever purposes they wanted."[65] Roth was both asserting his right to publish material that lay in the public domain and proclaiming his sensitivity to Joyce's moral right of attribution as an author. But Roth also had the deeper purpose—no doubt coached by Padgug—of placing on record certain facts that could support a complete defense under Section 51 of the civil rights law. The statute contained an express exception for the use of "the name, portrait or picture of any author, composer or artist in connection with his literary, musical or artistic productions which he has sold or disposed of with such name, portrait or picture used in connection therewith."[66] This language reflected common sense: people should have the right, even in commercial contexts, to name the author of a published book without becoming liable for misappropriation and invasion of privacy. Padgug viewed the exception as possibly a more powerful weapon for combating Joyce's claims than the *Ellis v. Hurst* case. *Ellis*, after all, could be read as Joyce's attorneys might read it, as excusing the use of an author's name only in connection with an uncopyrighted or authorized publication. The statutory exception, in contrast, seemed to place no limitation on the kinds of published works with which an author's name might lawfully be used.

Next, Callan turned to the issue of authorization, asking whether Roth had ever received written consent from Joyce to publish *Ulysses* or to use his name. Roth launched at once into his favorite defense, that Pound, as Joyce's "agent," had written Roth a letter authorizing him to publish *Ulysses* and that "the mention of Mr. Joyce's name positively appears in that connection; I cannot remember just what things he mentions, but that I remember."[67] Challenged to produce proof that Joyce had given Pound authority to act for him, Roth replied that "it has been completely understood in the United States and in all parts of the world where Mr. Joyce's writing is known that Mr. Ezra Pound was the agent by which the manuscript of Ulysses was being released anywhere" and that this fact had been established as "a matter of record" in *The Little Review*. Roth conceded that he could produce no authorization in

Joyce's hand for the use of his name, but "it is understood," he cagily added, "that Mr. Joyce does not write any of his own correspondence."[68]

At this point, Joyce's attorneys agreed to a recess but not before getting Roth to sign a stipulation that he would return for the rest of the examination at 2:30 p.m. that day at the office of a clerk of the Supreme Court.[69] Roth did reappear but this time with his lawyer. Padgug's presence changed the tone and pace of the deposition. He objected frequently on grounds of relevance and privilege, at one point accusing Callan of conducting "a fishing expedition."[70] Whenever Callan mentioned *Ulysses*, Padgug protested that the complaint was "only concerned with the use of the name of the plaintiff in these publications" and that his clients (Roth and Two Worlds Publishing Co.) had never made use of the name "James Joyce, as such individually."[71] Nettled by Padgug's nimble deflections, Callan burst out, "Let me conduct my examination in my way. If you have any objections to make, make them on the record and we will go before the Judge."[72] Padgug seemed to relent but soon was objecting again to questions about *Ulysses*. He acutely sensed that Joyce's attorneys were trying to work around the copyright problem by obtaining testimony that would show Roth in the character of an unscrupulous pirate. Padgug insisted that *Ulysses* was "not within the issues."[73]

To cut short the relentless questioning about *Ulysses*, and to frame his client's conduct squarely within the statutory author's-name exception, Padgug announced, "I will concede on the record that [Roth] had published certain writings of which the plaintiff was the author and stated under the title 'By James Joyce.'" Encouraged by this bit of movement, Eugene Roth, who had said little up to this point, jumped in and asked if the defendant would concede that Joyce's name had been "merely printed" in his magazines "[w]ithout regard to whether it was attached to a certain writing or not." Defendant Roth saw that the young attorney was angling for a piece of testimony that could be taken out of context, and he neatly sidestepped the question.[74]

Callan now turned to Joyce's monetary damages. Roth had incautiously boasted in *Two Worlds Monthly* that fifty thousand copies of the first number had sold and that *Ulysses* was "one of the causes for the selling out of the issue in many localities."[75] Joyce calculated that Roth had raked in "one million francs" from the first issue and worried that if Roth "completes his plan he will collect about 20,000,000 francs out of my work which he has mutilated and probably bring my sales in Paris to a standstill."[76] Hoping to establish the commercial value of Joyce's name and the profits it had attracted, Callan began by asking Roth whether sales of *Two Worlds Monthly* had increased after the appearance of *Ulysses* in its pages. Padgug swiftly objected on causation grounds: there was nothing to show that sales had increased as a result of *Ulysses*.[77]

While Roth's profits were of interest, the Chadbourne lawyers also hoped to establish that his serialization of *Ulysses* was cutting into Joyce's own profits. Yet the tactic of measuring Joyce's damages according to hypothetical lost profits from *Ulysses* was a risky one. If *Ulysses* enjoyed no or questionable copyright protection in the United States, how could Roth's serialization of the public domain novel have harmed Joyce in any way? And how could a reliable distinction be drawn between profits derived from the unlawful use of Joyce's name and those derived from the lawful use of his uncopyrighted book? More fundamentally, if an unexpurgated *Ulysses* could not legally be published in or imported into the United States, how could postulated lost profits on a banned novel be a meaningful measure of anything? Once again, Chadbourne's litigation strategy threatened to turn the lawsuit into one essentially for copyright infringement, an approach the New York court might not countenance. Section 51 had been enacted as a remedy for invasion of privacy; damages could be awarded for injured feelings, humiliation, and emotional distress, but recovery for harm to a property interest required that the interest be "inherent and inextricably interwoven in the individual's personality."[78] Joyce's attorneys no doubt sensed these potential obstacles to monetary recovery, but lost profits from *Ulysses* remained central to the litigation.

Always ready to flaunt his credentials as a martyr to modernism, Roth answered Callan's question about sales by stating that "the circulation of Two Worlds Monthly decreased very appreciably since the announcement of an article by Mr. Joyce." *Ulysses* had nearly ruined him, he claimed; his readers found the work "brutal."[79] At this point, Eugene Roth tried to get him to admit that *Ulysses* was a valuable piece of literature, but Roth would only concede, with a mixture of cunning and venom, that *Ulysses* "contains very interesting elements that belong to literature: as to whether it has any value time alone can prove that. I think that time is going to do a great deal more to Mr. Joyce than he thinks of." Roth thought the novel an interesting phenomenon, just as a "man who stands on this window sill would be interesting." "Interesting to the people, you think?" Eugene Roth interposed.

"Interesting to me," replied Roth with studied Wildean subjectivism. "That is the only standard on which I judge anything."[80]

Callan tried to steer the inquiry back to Roth's profits from *Ulysses*, but Padgug was ready with his ace of trumps. "I now serve you," he announced to the startled room, "with a stay and an order to show cause."[81] This gesture halted the examination. Padgug's order to show cause was in essence a motion asking the court to vacate and set aside Chadbourne's notice of examination and to vacate and impound the testimony already obtained from Roth. Padgug had intended to serve this motion before the examination began, but his busy schedule had prevented him from doing so. The motion set forth various reasons why the examination was improper: the information sought was immaterial to the cause of action; the purpose was to annoy Roth and engage in a "mere fishing expedition"; questions about Roth's profits from the alleged misuse of Joyce's name were inappropriate; and Roth had been forced to testify against his will.[82] In their papers opposing the motion, Joyce's attorneys argued that, having submitted to several hours of questioning already, Roth had waived any privilege against testifying and that the questions were entirely proper in any case. The examination had been sought "in absolute good faith"; Padgug was simply employing "dilatory tactics."[83]

On June 13, Supreme Court Justice George V. Mullan denied Padgug's motion. Most of the topics for examination, Justice Mullan concluded, were "proper," including the questions about Roth's profits, which were relevant to the issue of punitive damages, at least.[84] But Padgug was not deterred. He had no intention of allowing the litigation to get back on track quickly. On June 16 he filed a notice of appeal, seeking a reversal of Justice Mullan's decision. Whatever its merits, the appeal was sure to have the effect of putting the case on ice for months as the dispute over Roth's examination worked its way through the New York Appellate Division. When on July 15 the Appellate Division granted a stay of further examination pending the outcome of the appeal, Padgug had done everything that an underpaid, understaffed attorney could do to make the lawsuit more difficult and more costly for Joyce.[85]

In his appellate brief, Padgug repeated most of the arguments he had made, unsuccessfully, before Justice Mullan. In addition, he contended that, because Section 50 of the civil rights law made name misappropriation a misdemeanor, Joyce's attorneys were seeking answers from Roth that might expose him to criminal liability, in violation of his right against compelled self-incrimination under the New York Constitution.[86] Padgug devoted a large portion of the brief to informing the court of facts that he felt would lay bare the insufficiency of Joyce's complaint and render a pretrial examination unnecessary. "[*Ulysses*] has never been copyrighted in this country," Padgug pointed out, "so that the defendants who are publishers of magazines, if they so desired, had a perfect right to publish the book in this country." Installments of the novel had invariably appeared in *Two Worlds Monthly* with "the words, 'Ulysses, by James Joyce.'"[87] Padgug insisted that, under *Ellis v. Hurst* and the author's-name exception contained in Section 51, Roth and his company simply could not be held liable for truthfully stating that Joyce was the author of the unprotected *Ulysses*.

It did not help that Padgug's brief was filled with misspelled case names and sloppily cited legal authority. But the real weakness was that he made his potentially meritorious arguments at the wrong point in the litigation. An appeal of a discovery ruling was not the place to challenge the sufficiency of Joyce's complaint. Procedures for obtaining early summary adjudication in civil cases were extremely limited in New York in 1927.[88] Still, Padgug might have sought judgment on the pleadings after demanding that Joyce provide a bill of particulars stating the facts of his authorship of *Ulysses*. The chances of succeeding on such a motion were slim, however, and Padgug never made the attempt. Nevertheless, he possessed persuasive arguments, backed by strong legal authority. Had the case been litigated today, Roth might well have defeated Joyce's claims on summary judgment relatively early in the case. But in 1927 he had little choice but to wait until trial to put his defenses to the test.

This was precisely why Joyce's attorneys had drafted such an austere complaint. In their appellate brief, they argued that Padgug's attempt to introduce unpleaded facts about *Ulysses* and its copyright status was inappropriate at this stage of the litigation: "The complaint contains no reference to any book nor any statement that plaintiff is an author.... Appellants are attempting to try the facts of the case upon this motion by bringing in various facts which may or may not be true, none of which are proved in any of the papers before this Court."[89] Joyce, his attorneys urged, had alleged nothing more than that he was a private person whose name was being commercially exploited by Roth and his company. Those allegations were sufficient and proper, and it was premature to attempt to litigate any other purported facts or defenses.

Joyce's attorneys also argued in their appellate papers that Roth had waived any testimonial privilege by submitting to several hours of examination

without objecting or reserving his rights and by previously filing verified answers (the equivalent of sworn testimony) to Joyce's complaint.
Moreover, they contended, Roth had not asserted any such privilege before
Justice Mullan in the trial court; he was improperly raising the issue for the
first time on appeal.[90] Finally, Joyce's attorneys noted that the topics chosen
for Roth's examination were necessary and proper in that they concerned
information, such as Roth's knowledge of the unlawfulness of his conduct,
that was exclusively "within [his] possession and control."[91]

On December 2, 1927, five justices of the Appellate Division, with Justice
Victor J. Dowling presiding, heard oral argument on Roth's appeal. Padgug
or his associate David M. Berger spoke for the appellant, Roth; Eugene Roth
argued for the respondent, Joyce. Seven days later, the Appellate Division
issued a terse decision rejecting Roth's appeal and ordering that his examination be resumed. The court also required Roth to pay the costs and disbursements that Joyce had incurred in fighting the appeal—a sum of $53.50, on
which Roth promptly defaulted. A bill of costs in that amount was entered
against him by the New York County Clerk.[92]

On January 12, 1928, after further adjournments, Roth's examination was
resumed. Harold Callan returned at once to the question of name misappropriation, but Roth was ready with a defense based on respect for authors'
moral rights: "I publish articles only for the sake of the articles and append
the names of the authors both as a courtesy and as an acknowledgment that
the work is no one else's but the author's."[93] He then invoked his "constitutional privilege" and refused to answer further questions. The examination
came to a halt, only to be resumed once more, on January 16, with Roth
again standing on his privilege to remain silent. The deposition hopelessly
stalled, Roth was asked to sign his name to the official transcript. He did so
in green ink—the color Joyce often used in the latter part of his life.[94]

## Joyce Testifies

James Joyce's testimony was critical for sustaining his cause of action. The
problem was that he had made it clear that he could not come to the United
States to be examined before or during the trial.[95] His attorneys therefore
moved the court for a commission to take his deposition in Paris by means
of written interrogatories. This would entail a cumbersome procedure, laden

with formalities. A justice of the New York Supreme Court would have to grant the motion for the examination and then execute a commission authorizing the U.S. consul general in Paris to place Joyce under oath and administer questions that had been prepared by the attorneys for both sides. Joyce's oral responses would be transcribed, signed, notarized, sealed, and transmitted to the New York County Clerk for filing as part of the case.

Nathan Padgug opposed the motion; only oral questioning, he argued, would enable him to cross-examine Joyce freely and fully.[96] But Supreme Court Justice Francis B. Delehanty disagreed, and, on February 11, 1928, he executed a commission, headed "The People of the State of New York," to Alphonse Gaulin, Esq., U.S. consul general in Paris.[97] The commission, accompanied by twenty-six interrogatories drafted by Joyce's attorneys and forty-five cross-interrogatories prepared by Padgug, was dispatched to Paris. On March 8 at 10:45 a.m., Joyce appeared at the American Consulate on rue des Italiens to be sworn in by Gaulin.

The interrogatories prepared by Joyce's attorneys focused almost exclusively on matters of permission. Had Joyce ever authorized Roth to publish any of his works or to use his name in any way? Joyce answered in the negative: "Mr. Roth published, without my permission, extracts from the book which I am writing. After a protest from my publishers he sent me two hundred dollars."[98] This was not strictly true. In 1926 Roth had sent advance payment to Sylvia Beach for reprinting certain extracts from Joyce's "Work in Progress" and had made an offer, at her invitation, for the right to be the exclusive publisher of future extracts. But Joyce was in no mood to clutter his testimony with extenuating details. Roth was a villain and must remain so.

In response to other interrogatories, Joyce firmly denied that he had ever authorized Ezra Pound to give Roth permission to use his name or to publish his writings. The limit of Pound's agency had been to accept episodes of *Ulysses* for serialization in *The Little Review*. That magazine, Joyce added, had paid him nothing for the episodes; the only sum he had received was £50 from John Quinn, a patron's honorarium.[99] This testimony, Joyce hoped, would put an end to Jane Heap's claims that she had acquired exclusive American rights in *Ulysses*.

Joyce's final piece of direct testimony concerned a copy of the Paris edition of *Ulysses* that his attorneys wanted to authenticate. Their plan was to introduce this copy at trial as a basis for demonstrating that Roth's serialization in *Two Worlds Monthly* was a mutilation of Joyce's original text. The copy that lay before Joyce in the consulate bore the exhibit letter "A" with a raised surface, so that if his weak eyes could not make out the letter, he could identify the volume by touch. He duly confirmed that the exhibit was a "true and authentic copy" of *Ulysses* and that the signature placed at the end of the volume was his.[100]

Gaulin now proceeded to administer Padgug's cross-interrogatories. In an incisive line of questioning, Padgug challenged Joyce to state whether, to his knowledge, Samuel Roth or his publishing company had "ever used [Joyce's] name in any other way than to indicate [his] authorship of the book 'Ulysses' or any other of [his] works." Joyce's answer, Padgug knew, would be crucial for Roth's defense under the author's-name exception in Section 51 of the civil rights law. To every variation of this question Joyce responded with an unqualified "no."[101] When he also answered "no" to the question whether he had ever applied for a U.S. copyright for *Ulysses*, the groundwork was laid for Padgug to contend that Roth, like the publishers in *Ellis v. Hurst*, had done nothing more than truthfully append an author's name to his uncopyrighted novel.[102] Such an act could not have constituted name misappropriation under Section 51.

One critical point remained to be explored: Joyce's claim for half a million dollars in actual damages. Padgug's fortieth cross-interrogatory inquired how he had arrived at that figure. The various Paris printings of *Ulysses*, Joyce explained, had so far brought him royalties of fifty thousand dollars, and he expected his earnings in France to reach seventy-five thousand dollars. He continued:

> I calculate that the sales of the book in the United States, published at a minimum price of ten dollars a copy and with a royalty to me of fifteen or twenty per cent, with an English-reading population of a hundred and twenty millions as contrasted with the small English-reading public in France, would have brought me at least six or seven times as much, viz., five hundred thousand dollars.[103]

Joyce's arithmetic was optimistic. He assumed that at least two hundred and fifty thousand copies of *Ulysses* would sell for $10 apiece in the United States, with $2 per copy entering his pocket as royalties. In fact, it later took Random House five years and ten printings of *Ulysses*, priced at $3.50 per copy, before the first fifty thousand copies reached the American public.[104] Joyce was also double counting. Many copies of the Paris *Ulysses* had been

purchased by or for Americans; these sales would properly have to be reckoned as part of Joyce's U.S. market. Finally, Padgug's questioning brought
out the fact that Joyce had never attempted to obtain a U.S. copyright for
*Ulysses* and therefore had never sought to publish the book in America. How,
then, as a matter of causality—quite apart from the incoherency of claiming
hypothetical lost profits from a banned book—could Joyce show that Roth's
serialization had displaced potential sales?

On March 19, Joyce, accompanied by his Paris lawyer Benjamin Conner,
returned to the consulate to review and sign his testimony, which had been
prepared as a formal document. Joyce made a few corrections and appended
his signature. Consul general Gaulin attached a ribbon and seal certifying
the regularity of the procedure and the authenticity of the testimony and
the exhibit copy of *Ulysses*. Joyce paid Gaulin his commissioner's fee of
$16.50 and a stenographer's fee of $4.75, and Gaulin placed the testimony
in a large envelope tied with a cloth ribbon and stamped with three red wax
seals bearing the legend of the U.S. consulate general. The package was then
dispatched to the New York County Clerk.

Outside the consulate, Joyce was approached by a reporter. He seemed
"quite as nervous at being obliged to take action against a fellow human
citizen as his character, Stephen Dedalus, would have been," and he was
unwilling to discuss details of the lawsuit. The action had been instituted
for the purpose of "focusing attention on the present copyright laws of the
United States ... and bringing about their revision. As the law stands, Mr.
Joyce has no protection from piracy, because his work is technically not
copyrightable."[105] Joyce often claimed that he was suing Roth in order to
establish a legal precedent in favor of foreign authors who were placed at
a disadvantage by pitiless American laws. Roth's rhetoric of cultural gifting was matched by Joyce's rhetoric of legal benefaction. Both poses were
genuine, to an extent.

## Pound Does Not Testify

Joyce had felt from the start that Ezra Pound's testimony would be essen-
tial to the case, but his sense of urgency was even greater after Roth made
Pound's alleged permission to reprint *Ulysses* the centerpiece of his defense.
Shortly after the examination of Joyce was completed, Pound wrote his

father cryptically that Joyce "wants me to alfreddavid [affidavit] something or other";[106] a week later Joyce reported to Harriet Shaw Weaver that he thought he had "managed to get Pound to testify in the Roth case."[107] Pound was indeed ready to state under oath that he had never specifically authorized Roth to reprint *Ulysses* in *Two Worlds Monthly*. "I have no objection," he wrote Joyce in late March 1928, "to swearing—in seven languages and on the rump of al Koran that Mr Roth is the son of a son of all the galled bitches of Judea from the days of Caiphas [*sic*] till the date of yr. birth."[108] The difficulty would be arranging for a deposition at a U.S. consulate in Italy and the cost of traveling there. Joyce forwarded Pound some money, but there the matter remained for several weeks.

There was an additional problem. The truth was that Pound, as noted in chapter 4, had approved a plan by Roth to print unpublished portions of *Ulysses* in a magazine format, though this had probably occurred in 1921, shortly after the criminal prosecution of the *Little Review* editors for publishing the "Nausicaa" episode, when it seemed to Pound that no other publisher or editor in the United States would risk issuing the unpublished remainder of Joyce's novel. A searching cross-examination of Pound would expose this fact, and Pound was probably reluctant to have to explain, under interrogation, that what he had urged Roth to do in 1921, before *Ulysses* had appeared as a book, was very different from what Roth had taken it upon himself to do in 1926. Pound was capable of making this temporal discrimination in good conscience, but Roth's attorneys would no doubt characterize it as defensive rationalization. Joyce, moreover, would not be pleased to learn that Pound had treated with Roth in 1921, even from the best motives. Perhaps as a way of making a clean breast of it in advance of any examination, Pound in May 1928 published his letter in the Paris *Chicago Tribune* describing his communications with Roth in the period after the suppression of *Ulysses* in *The Little Review*.[109]

During April 1928, the attorneys for Joyce and Roth discussed plans to examine Pound, but they left the matter unresolved, and in late October Pound wrote Joyce from Rapallo, "Dont I owe you 20 or 30 simoleon dollars, for not having had my fingerprints taken vs. Roth?? wotter hell ... wot became of it ... gone to trial without my Alf. David.??"[110] Joyce instructed Conner to remind his New York colleagues of the importance of obtaining Pound's testimony, but on November 26 Conner received a cabled reply from the Chadbourne firm: "SETTLING JOYCE CASE DEFENDANT IN JAIL."[111]

## Settlement and Injunction

When the Chadbourne cable arrived, Samuel Roth had already served several weeks in the workhouse on New York's Welfare Island. His troubles with the criminal courts had kept pace with his setbacks in civil litigation. In March 1927, he had been served with a summons to appear in Jefferson Market Court to defend himself against a charge of publishing lewd and indecent matter in his magazines. The complaint, brought by the Clean Books Committee of the Federation of Hungarian Jews in America, took special aim at the serialized *Ulysses*.[112] Padgug represented Roth, and the case went away without a conviction, but not before Roth had announced a "Two Worlds Defence Fund" to carry the fight to "the oppressors of the living spirit of beauty" and wondered publicly whether the Clean Books Committee's attempt at "communal cleaning" was "the work of those astute friends of Mr. James Joyce ... who, since the appearance of Two Worlds Monthly, have pursued a policy of threatening me, through the newspapers and the mails, with an interesting variety of unpleasant extinctions."[113]

In January 1928, Roth was again charged, this time with mailing obscene circulars for Richard Burton's translation of *The Perfumed Garden*, the erotic classic by Sheik Nefzawi. After pleading guilty in federal court, Roth was fined and given a suspended sentence of six months in prison, with a probation period of two years.[114] Scarcely four months into his probation, he was arrested at the Book Auction (a business in his wife's name) for possessing obscene books and pictures. Instigated by John S. Sumner of the New York Society for the Suppression of Vice, the charges were heard by three justices of the Court of Special Sessions, who found Roth guilty and sentenced him to three months on Welfare Island.[115] Throughout November and December 1928, Roth produced a steady stream of correspondence from his prison cell, arranging for visits with his wife Pauline, chatting with his young children, seeking legal assistance from Padgug, requesting books and magazines, and recording his delight when one of his keepers mistook his large volume of Lord Byron for a bible.[116] Roth remained on Welfare Island until January 1929, Joyce's lawsuit a faint murmur in the background of his carceral routine.

The trial in *Joyce v. Roth* had been rescheduled for June 1928 and then postponed again to October.[117] Had it gone forward, the case would have been tried to a single justice, sitting without a jury. The Chadbourne lawyers were prepared to offer in evidence Joyce's and Roth's depositions, copies of *Two Worlds Monthly*, and four certified deposit copies of *The Little Review* obtained from the Copyright Office.[118] Testimony was to be given by David Moss, part owner of the Gotham Book Mart, who had probably witnessed over-the-counter sales of *Two Worlds Monthly*. Arthur Garfield Hays also was to be put on the stand. Having presided over the failed settlement negotiations, he could testify that Joyce had not accepted payment for Roth's use of *Ulysses*.[119] For his part, Padgug was eager to introduce a January 1926 letter from Sylvia Beach to Roth acknowledging his payment for reprinting extracts from Joyce's "Work in Progress."[120] The case was ready, but Roth's arrests, together with his lack of funds, convinced Joyce's attorneys that further litigation would be fruitless, and they began to look for a way out.

**Figure 5.4** Illustration from Samuel Roth, *Jews Must Live* (New York: Golden Hind, 1934), showing Roth, seated right, visited by a ghostly presence.

As early as June 1928, shortly after Roth's arrest at the Book Auction, Joyce's attorneys had approached Padgug to discuss a settlement.[121] Negotiations resumed in September, and the Chadbourne firm cabled Joyce to recommend that he withdraw his damages claim and agree to a "consent injunction" against Roth. Lacking the ability to sue for copyright infringement, and with a judgment-proof opponent mired in criminal proceedings, Joyce bowed to his lawyers' advice, asking only that they "press for some judgment, an injunction against further use of my name with nominal damages of one dollar or whatever is the American equivalent for the English farthing." Joyce felt that he held a certain "position of trust" as a European author fighting transatlantic piracy, and he hoped that if damages were unavailable, he might at least have the satisfaction of reforming American law by obtaining a "judgment ... which, when recorded, would establish a precedent in case law in favour of unprotected European writers whose cause in this matter was the same as my own."[122]

The attorneys for Joyce and Roth discussed settlement terms on and off from September through early December, and the Chadbourne firm produced a draft version of a consent decree that the parties could submit for the court's approval.[123] On December 19 Padgug obtained the signature of the incarcerated Roth on a stipulation of settlement, along with the signature of Pauline Roth, who, in the wake of her husband's criminal convictions, had become nominal president of Two Worlds Publishing Co. Attached to the stipulation was the consent decree to which Roth had agreed. The document enjoined him and his company from using Joyce's name

for advertising purposes or for purposes of trade ... in connection with any magazine, periodical or other publication published by defendants [or] any book, writing, manuscript or other work [by Joyce], including the book "ULYSSES," in any issue of Two Worlds Monthly, Two Worlds Quarterly, or any other magazine, periodical or other publication, heretofore or hereafter published by defendants.[124]

Justice Richard H. Mitchell of the New York Supreme Court signed the injunction on December 27, 1928. This concluded the case, a few days before Roth left Welfare Island to rejoin his family.[125]

A consent decree is a hybrid remedy, part contract of the parties, part order of the court. As with all compromises, Joyce and Roth each gave up something. Joyce sacrificed his claim for astronomical damages; even the "one dollar" he had hoped to receive as a nominal recovery would not be forthcoming. The decree enjoined Roth from further commercial use of Joyce's name, but there was little left to enjoin: Roth had ceased publishing *Ulysses* more than a year before, and *Two Worlds* and *Two Worlds Monthly* no longer existed. Two Worlds Publishing Co. was an insolvent husk.

And yet the consent decree gave Joyce more than he might have obtained after a full trial. The scope of the injunction was vast, barring Roth from using

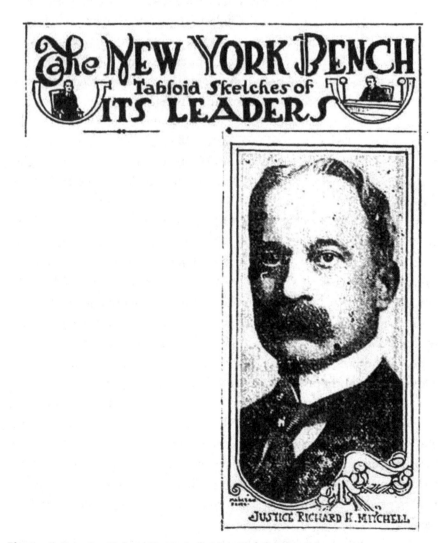

**Figure 5.5** Justice Richard H. Mitchell, *New York Evening Telegram*, January 3, 1917.

Joyce's name in connection with any magazine or other publication by Roth and any work or manuscript by Joyce, including *Ulysses*. This was more tangible relief than Joyce's skeletal complaint had prayed for, and it effectively deprived Roth of the ability to associate Joyce's name with the public domain *Ulysses*—something that *Ellis v. Hurst* and the author's-name exception in Section 51 of the civil rights law otherwise permitted him to do. The negotiated injunction was, in essence, a stint upon the American public domain, a shrinking of the cultural commons. In this respect, the Chadbourne attorneys had performed an impressive feat, and they did it without running the risk of encountering judicial refusal to give judgment in favor of an immoral book.

By agreeing to a consent decree, however, Joyce unwittingly relinquished his hopes for a legal precedent that might assist other foreign authors. A decree of the type Joyce obtained binds only the parties who agree to it and cannot be cited as precedent by other litigants in later cases.[126] Moreover, to be authoritative, a judicial decision must normally be published in an official volume, called a case reporter. Justice Mitchell's injunction was never printed in the New York reporters or any others; in the more than eighty years since he signed it, the decree has not been cited by a single court in a reported case.

Yet Joyce wanted to believe that the injunction was a legal milestone, and he was encouraged in this by Benjamin Conner. In late 1929, Joyce asked Conner to send a copy of the injunction to Hermon Ould, the London-based general secretary of the International P.E.N. Club. The consent decree had been published in *transition* earlier that year, and Joyce wanted the P.E.N. Club to draw attention to it as well.[127] Conner conceded to Ould that the injunction was "entered on the consent of [Roth]" but urged, grandiosely, that "this judgment of record will be a landmark in the protection of authors' rights in the United States against pirating, even in the case of uncopyrighted works."[128] Ould skeptically replied that, as the injunction was focused primarily on the protection of Joyce's name, clever pirates might safely reprint the uncopyrighted *Ulysses* by simply omitting the author's name from the cover and title page. Conner admitted this possibility but felt that Justice Mitchell's decree should not be read to permit "the anonymous pirating or plagiarizing of uncopyrighted works."[129]

Conner's outsized claims for the consent decree were echoed eight years later in an address that Joyce prepared for the Fifteenth International P.E.N.

Congress in Paris. After recounting the misfortunes of *Ulysses* in America, Joyce speculated that Justice Mitchell's injunction could be interpreted to suggest that, "though lacking protection under the copyright statute, and even if banned, a work belongs to its author by virtue of a natural right, and thus the courts may protect an author against the mutilation and publication of his work, just as he is protected against the misuse of his name."[130] Here, under the magnifying glass of Joyce's desire, the consent decree had grown to be a prophecy of unprecedented respect for authors' moral rights in the United States. Joyce was suggesting that the injunction, by acknowledging an author's right to control something as personal as his name, signaled a dawning judicial solicitude for the inherent natural rights of authorship— rights of attribution and textual integrity that preceded and survived the vicissitudes of legislative enactments.[131]

But what Joyce was describing was the European, not the American, attitude toward authors' rights. Far from reflecting a moral or natural rights view of authorship, U.S. copyright law in this period allowed authors' rights to be destroyed through mere technical blunders, such as the omission of copyright notices from books, the untimely filing of a copyright renewal application, or the failure to have a work printed and bound on American soil within the prescribed period. Moreover, the author's-name exception in Section 51 of the New York civil rights law explicitly acknowledged that even the unauthorized commercial use of an author's name was permissible if it occurred in connection with a work that the author had previously released to the public. American law, though it would later come to recognize creators' moral rights in limited ways,[132] has never embraced the comprehensive vision of natural authorial entitlements that Joyce wanted to read into Justice Mitchell's terse injunction.

## A Species of Mutant Copyright Law: Trade Courtesy and Trademark

There is an undeniable pathos in Joyce's dream of residual or incipient natural rights for foreign authors in the United States. He was helpless before the American copyright laws. Straitjacketed by the scandalous reputation of his masterpiece, he had been unable to comply with the rigid statutory prerequisites for obtaining a U.S. copyright and had found no reputable publisher to issue an unexpurgated *Ulysses*. So a disreputable publisher had found him, expurgated his book, and used his growing celebrity to build a magazine. Roth had exploited a famous name and novel, just as the Chadbourne attorneys contended, but his position was not without a certain pathos of its own: he genuinely loved Joyce's gift and had always wanted to be the American impresario of *Ulysses*. The public domain was as inescapable for him as it was for Joyce. With unprotected riches lying before him, and an intransigent author in Paris, Roth could not turn back; constituted as he was, he had no choice but to publish and be damned.

When he received Roth's offer of a thousand dollars for the serialization of *Ulysses*, Joyce found himself at a crossroads of copyright traditions. Had he accepted the money, the transaction would have linked him to the tradition of trade courtesy, with its private payments for public goods and its myriad little clearings of compromise within the wilderness of the American public domain. Joyce chose not to parley with the juggernaut commons but rather to find a way around it. Consciously reacting against the void of legal incertitude, he and his lawyers decided not to try to enforce a defunct or doubtful copyright in *Ulysses* or even to assert the abstract moral rights of aggrieved authorship. Instead, Joyce sued to protect the one thing of his that undeniably had value in jazzy, prudish, bibulous, Prohibition America: his controversial name.

Rejecting the path of courtesy, Joyce authorized his lawyers to place a half million dollar price tag on his name. Many plaintiffs who sued for misappropriation of their names or likenesses in this period alleged an invasion of their privacy, and they typically sought damages for humiliation and mortification.[133] Superficially, Joyce's claims under Section 51 were no different; he, too, was prepared to argue, formulaically, that he had suffered emotional harm as a result of intrusion upon his seclusion. Yet that was not what his lawsuit was really about. Instead, had the case gone to trial, Joyce's lawyers would probably have insisted that his valuable name had been exploited for profit and that sales of *Ulysses* had been displaced to the tune of half a million dollars. This was essentially a lawsuit about celebrity, not privacy. Unlike Abigail Roberson twenty-five years earlier, Joyce was not complaining that his cherished privacy had been shattered when Roth thrust his name noisily into the public sphere; he was asserting that Roth had found a way to cash in on his already famous name and had kept all the gains for himself.

What we glimpse in *Joyce v. Roth* is a right of publicity breaking from the husk of privacy rights, a de facto claim of economic harm emerging from lawyerly rhetoric about injured feelings.[134] Joyce was not the only noted figure in this period to advance a claim for publicity rights in the judicially acceptable form of a right of privacy. In 1922, Douglas Fairbanks had used Section 51 as a vehicle for suing a movie company that had reedited his motion pictures in ways he found objectionable.[135] Increasingly, however, celebrities were avoiding the fiction of privacy altogether and treating their public personas as legally enforceable property or arguing that unauthorized imitators were creating unfair competition and consumer confusion. Charlie Chaplin, for example, launched a series of actions that openly sought to enforce proprietary rights in his Little Tramp character.[136] But it was not until 1953 that a federal court expressly acknowledged that, "independent of [the] right of privacy..., a man has a right in the publicity value of his photograph."[137] Later in the century, a proliferation of lawsuits sought redress for the exploitation of the names, likenesses, or voices of celebrated persons: Bela Lugosi, Groucho Marx, Cher, Elvis Presley, Clint Eastwood, Johnny Carson, Bette Midler, Janis Joplin, Tom Waits, Vanna White, to name a few.[138] James Joyce was a precursor of these outraged personalities; like them, he had sought judicial approval for propertizing his public image.

It could even be said that Joyce and his lawyers were treating his name as if it were a kind of trademark—a signifier that, in addition to naming an individual who resided in Paris, had acquired a secondary meaning that designated a specific commercial source, distinguishing the Irish author from all other authors in the literary marketplace and assuring consumers that when they bought "James Joyce" they bought quality.[139] By associating Joyce's name with an unauthorized and mutilated text, Roth had sown confusion among consumers and engaged in a type of unfair competition. The analogy that the reader of *Two Worlds Monthly* suggested between the slogan "Blue Valley Butter Is Good Butter" and Roth's efforts to convince readers that "James Joyce is a good writer"[140] was more than merely fanciful. Joyce's name had acquired a range of increasingly stable secondary meanings among the reading public—modern, experimental, controversial, subversive, scandalous— all of which had contributed to his brand. Roth was a free rider on Joyce's accumulated goodwill; he threatened to reap where he had not sown or, worse, to dilute and destabilize the signifying power of Joyce's celebrity.[141]

The various legal theories, explicit and implicit, that Joyce's lawyers advanced—name misappropriation, unfair competition, trademark, moral rights—were strategies for grappling with the disabling lack of U.S. copyright protection for *Ulysses*. Today, it is common for litigants to multiply theories of recovery, especially when copyright claims are doubtful. In 1997, the Estate of James Joyce sought an injunction in the English High Court to prevent publication by British Macmillan/Picador of Danis Rose's Reader's Edition of *Ulysses*, in part because the estate regarded the edition as a mutilation of Joyce's text.[142] The estate's allegations included copyright infringement and the unfair competition tort of "passing off." The latter claim had been included to fortify a less than ironclad case for copyright infringement.

In November 2001, after a full trial, Justice Lloyd of the English High Court ruled that Rose's edition had infringed the copyrights in certain Joyce manuscripts, but he rejected the estate's other copyright claims. He then turned to the estate's alternative theory and carefully framed the question it raised: did Rose's edition constitute passing off—that is, was the edition so different from the "class of goods" that had come to be known to the reading public as "Ulysses by James Joyce" that the edition, as an instance of false labeling, substantially harmed the goodwill that the estate had acquired in the "trade name" of "Ulysses by James Joyce"?

Justice Lloyd answered this question in the negative. To be subject to passing off, he explained, *Ulysses* would have to constitute a class of goods sufficient to be identified in the public mind with certain characteristics conferring goodwill, or economic reputational value, on its present source, the estate. When challenged to describe the characteristics defining this class of goods, counsel for the estate had pointed to Joyce's use of unconventional word forms, interior monologue, and other distinctive literary techniques. But how, persisted Justice Lloyd, can we know when a product such as Rose's edition is or is not within the alleged class of goods? Counsel replied that any edition approved by James Joyce himself or subsequently by his estate was within that class. The court dismissed out of hand this circular and self-serving definition and rejected as well, for its "inherent uncertainty," the suggestion that "the general body of academic opinion at any given time" could serve to define what is and what is not within the class of goods known as *Ulysses*.

Justice Lloyd observed that, in contrast to the estate's strained effort to turn a literary text into a commodity, a more conventional instance of passing off would be "selling lemon juice in a plastic lemon-shaped container which customers associate with a different manufacturer."[143] A court observer wryly commented:

If someone went around selling copies of *Ulysses* that turned out to be John Grisham novels wrapped in the wrong dust-jacket, they might be liable [for passing off]. But while it could be argued (as many do) that Rose's isn't a good edition of *Ulysses*, you couldn't really say it wasn't *Ulysses* at all. And it is something, I suppose, to know that *Ulysses* doesn't fall into quite the same category as plastic lemons.[144]

In 2003, the U.S. Supreme Court registered a similar discomfort with attempts to stretch what are essentially trademark concepts to fit the traditional subject matter of copyright law. In *Dastar v. Twentieth Century Fox Film Corp.*,[145] a videotape producer, Dastar, had released its own adapted version of an earlier television series about the Second World War which had fallen into the public domain when Fox, the owner of the copyright in the earlier series, failed to renew the copyright. Despite the public domain status of the series, Fox sued Dastar for modifying and selling it without crediting Fox as the creator of the copied footage, alleging that in doing so, Dastar had passed the footage off as its own, in violation of federal trademark law. The Supreme Court rejected this theory, holding that the law's prohibition of passing off refers to unlawful uses of physical goods in commerce, not to expressive or communicative content, which is the province of copyright law. The opinion of the Court, authored by Justice Antonin Scalia, reflected a keen skepticism of efforts to use trademark as "a species of mutant copyright law that limits the public's federal right to copy and to use."[146]

Gazing into the abyss of the American public domain, Joyce's attorneys in 1927 skillfully worked around the copyright problem by basing the action not on Joyce's book but rather on Joyce's signifying persona, on the secondary meaning and reputational goodwill that "James Joyce" had acquired in the years since he had come to the attention of the American public. Just as the Joyce estate, seventy years later, attempted to persuade Justice Lloyd that "Ulysses by James Joyce" was a protectible trade name, so the Chadbourne attorneys constructed a theory based on a kind of mutant copyright law, a hybrid of trademark, unfair competition, and publicity rights that they used to bolster Joyce's precarious rights in his novel. Samuel Roth, a faithful product of the public domain, was in a sense simply the occasion for all this legal ingenuity. Yet the litigation took a human toll. Together with the international protest, Joyce's lawsuit did as much as anything to wreck

Roth's ambitions as a serious publisher and to ruin his bid for tenancy in the increasingly crowded house of modernism.

\* \* \*

No sooner had Joyce authorized his New York attorneys to settle the case than he began to dread the "bill of costs" that would "come rolling over the Atlantic."[147] Chadbourne's invoice for legal services, which included its efforts to obtain U.S. copyrights for extracts from "Work in Progress," came to roughly three thousand dollars, a third of which represented Benjamin Conner's fees and disbursements.[148] (Three thousand dollars in 1928 had roughly the same buying power as forty thousand dollars in 2012.)[149] Joyce arranged to pay most of Conner's portion from the proceeds of *Haveth Childers Everywhere*, published in 1930 by Henry Babou and Jack Kahane,[150] but he refused to pay his New York attorneys, who, he claimed, were guilty of "bungling the case, for they could have pressed for the injunction right away."[151] Joyce was displeased that the injunction had not taken precedential root in American law; Richard Aldington had advised him to pay nothing and simply treat his lawyers as having spent their time on a "public question."[152]

Feeling pressure to pay the balance of the invoice, Joyce contrived a childish scheme to wriggle out. In December 1930 he executed a "Memorandum of Agreement" by which he transferred to Sylvia Beach "the exclusive right of printing and selling throughout the world, the work entitled ULYSSES."[153] This formal document made Beach the owner of worldwide rights in *Ulysses*. When Conner again pressed him to pay the two thousand dollars still owing to the New York firm, Joyce sent him a copy of the "Memorandum," claiming that it was a "mere formalization" of an understanding with Beach that dated back to 1922. He had engaged the Chadbourne lawyers, he implausibly added, in the mistaken belief that he was "the owner of [the *Ulysses*] rights"; only recently had he learned that in fact Beach had been the rights holder from the start. He would not pay for legal work that concerned someone else's literary property.[154] Beach was shocked by Joyce's brazen "falsehood" and told him so.[155] They quarreled, but Joyce was adamant that she had always been the owner, though he was quick to reverse his position a year later when he needed a free hand to negotiate with publishers for an authorized American edition. Motivated by that new purpose, he and his friends hounded Beach into canceling the contract.[156]

Conner wrote Joyce again toward the end of 1932. He had ended his association with the New York lawyers and, on settling accounts, found that he had to pay them $811.63 for disbursements they had made on Joyce's behalf. With this fresh outlay, Conner was again in the hole, having reimbursed Chadbourne for more than he had ever received from Joyce. "Do you not think that, as an honorable gentleman," Conner urged, "you should pay something for Chadbourne, Stanchfield & Levy's services, and something for mine? These gentlemen have had nothing whatever; and I am out of pocket."[157] But Joyce was inflexible.

Three years later, Conner tried again. Acknowledging Joyce's dissatisfaction with the results in the Roth case, he reminded him of the limitations on what any American lawyer could have done for him in 1927. "Conditions were far more unfavorable in the United States at that time than they are today," he observed. *Ulysses* could now be legally published in America, but at the time of the litigation, "the attitude of the courts was far from friendly towards the type of literature in question, and I am convinced that Messrs Chadbourne, Stanchfield & Levy did their best for you."[158] The scandalous reputation of *Ulysses* had stood in the way of complete relief against Roth, Conner suggested, and the Chadbourne lawyers' skill in extracting at least a negotiated injunction should be regarded as a success in the circumstances.

There the matter lay for another four years. Then, in July 1939, Conner renewed his polite request for payment but this time added a menacing note: "if it is not forthcoming promptly, I shall take action to induce it."[159] One month later, he had a *sommation* served on Joyce with a demand for the unpaid $811.63 or its equivalent in French francs, upon pain of submission of the matter to the Tribunal civil de la Seine.[160] Nothing further came of the dispute. A few months later, the Joyces left Paris, and the German occupation of France soon swallowed up such minor quarrels as that between Conner and his now world-famous client.

Joyce never paid Chadbourne's invoice for $2,064.63 either. Lawyers sometimes forgive, but they never forget. In 1999, an article about Joyce in the newsletter of Chadbourne & Parke (the current name of the law firm) recalled the unpaid sum to the penny, then added, "If the check was ever received, it should have been framed and never cashed."[161] Joyce's growing fame had been worth its weight in publicity for Chadbourne. That value—the apparent subject of the lawsuit—proved fungible across various purposes. Just as Joyce's multivalent brand meant professional prestige for lawyers, so it generated cultural prestige for Roth's magazines, allowing him to market an eroticized modernism to an America struggling with prohibitions and inhibitions and attempting to come to grips with new and unfamiliar currents in transatlantic art and literature. Joyce's name was a dangerously potent talisman, however. It both made and marred Roth, who would henceforth always be branded a "pirate," even though he had taken much of his booty from the American public domain.

The lawsuit, like the international protest, was a vehicle for promoting Joyce's celebrity.[162] He was genuinely disappointed that the litigation had not brought him a treasure in damages and that it would not blaze a trail for legal reform in the United States, but the case kept his name in the newspapers and helped prepare the future market for a legalized *Ulysses*. Many years later, John J. Slocum told Roth that "the international protest and the publicity that went with it spread [Joyce's] name to the four corners of the civilized world."[163] Like Joyce's name, the lawsuit became a signifier that exceeded its original purpose. Officially an action to safeguard Joyce's privacy and restore his misappropriated name, the suit actually caused his name and fame to overflow any boundaries that could have been secured by legal process. Roth, who had positioned himself to exploit *Ulysses* just as its author was beginning to emerge into the mainstream from coterie appeal and literary scandal, and whose unauthorized disseminations greatly assisted that emergence, indelibly fixed Joyce's brand of martyred genius.

# *ULYSSES* AUTHORIZED

## Random House and Courtesy

*[S]ome of the best-known publishers in America are veritable pirates.*
*They'll have dinner with you one night and steal an author from*
*you the next day, and if that's their game, we'll play it.*
*—Bennett Cerf (1977)*[1]

*So far as the publishing world is concerned, you and Bennett Cerf have*
*performed a real service that is worth a gross of assorted codes.*
*—James Henle, president of Vanguard Press, to Donald Klopfer*
*following Judge Woolsey's* Ulysses *decision (1933)*[2]

"Joyce has genius and Roth is a fraud." So wrote Arthur Symons in January 1927 in a letter authorizing Sylvia Beach to add his name to the international protest.[3] Only six months earlier, Samuel Roth had included Symons's essay "James Joyce" as a preface to the first installment of *Ulysses* in *Two Worlds Monthly*. The essay combined a Paterian carpe diem aesthetic with a candid assessment of Joyce as a writer who dealt with "sexual instinct and its infinite manifestations and perversions, with the animal's natural functions, with the obscenity of sex itself at its utmost depth of turpitude."[4] In some respects, the essay foreshadowed the test for legally relevant realism that Judge John M. Woolsey would apply several years later in *United States v. One Book Entitled "Ulysses."*[5] Symons had been a frequent contributor to Roth's magazines, but by the time he received Beach's request, he had become exasperated with the New York publisher's repeated failure to send payments and author's copies. Symons's implied morality play, *The Genius and the Fraud*, was precisely the polarization that Joyce was hoping to fix in the public imagination by means of the protest against Roth.

Joyce's campaign ensured that the label "pirate" would always adhere to Roth, even though Roth had not been sued for copyright infringement in connection with any of his publishing activities during the 1920s.[6] The charge of piracy signified not legal infraction, but a potent sense that Roth had violated the unwritten norms of good behavior that governed the close-knit community of respectable publishers—the extralegal courtesy code that quietly persisted as a professional ethic well into the twentieth century and that underlay Joyce's public shaming of Roth and his rehabilitation of *Ulysses* as violated property. Even Joyce's lawsuit, short on legal results but long on publicity value, underscored Roth's pariah status and contributed to the martyrolatry that was gathering about Joyce's novel. Despite the fact that *Joyce v. Roth* was an action based on name misappropriation, many newspaper accounts treated the lawsuit as if it had been brought specifically to redress what Beach called "the rape of *Ulysses*."[7] The explicit mention of *Ulysses* in the injunction that Joyce's lawyers had extracted from the insolvent and incarcerated Roth reinforced this impression.

Roth's canny exploitation of the American public domain rendered him a deviant from communal publishing norms. His half-hearted attempts at courtesy—such as his after-the-fact offers of payment to Joyce and T. S. Eliot—served only to confirm his ostracism. The grudging tolerance of such renegades that had existed in the nineteenth century, before Congress extended conditional copyright protection to foreign authors, no longer existed in 1925. America's respect for foreign literary rights had increased in proportion to its growth as an exporter of culture, and a developing market for modernism had begun to legitimize avant-garde works and to confer monetizable celebrity on their authors. The compliment that George Meredith had paid to Thomas Bird Mosher in 1892—"a handsome pirate is always half pardoned [especially when] he has broken only the upper laws"—was withheld from Roth thirty-five years later.[8] The pirate of *Ulysses* would always be treated as a Caliban among publishers. Bennett Cerf, a proud practitioner of trade courtesy, condemned him as "a gutter rat of the worst type."[9]

Roth had suffered the full force of courtesy's shaming sanctions. By 1927 his reputation in the publishing business had been irreversibly damaged; periodicals were refusing to advertise his magazines, and many booksellers declined to carry them. The wrath of Joyce pursued Roth down the years. When he learned in 1932 that a short piece by Roth had appeared in a North Carolina little magazine called *Contempo*, Joyce wrote to Ezra Pound, a contributing editor of the review, to protest Pound's "immorality" in permitting himself to be associated with Roth in even a tangential way. "How can you possibly allow an honorable name like yours to be used as a shield for such a rascal?" Joyce asked. "I consider it monstrous that he should be offered the hospitality of any litterary [*sic*] paper."[10] Pound promptly urged *Contempo* to apologize to Joyce and promise not to print anything more by Roth.[11] A few months earlier, the harried Roth had written *Contempo*'s editor, "[Y]ou mustn't believe that people always wrote of me the terrible things they do now." There was a time, he reflected, when "the newspapers had only the very nicest things to say about me. You should see my scrapbooks of 1917, 1918 and 1919. Could I have been the same sinful Samuel Roth?"[12]

In his effort to bring Roth down, Joyce had made use of the punitive dimension of trade courtesy: the multilateral, indeed multinational, sanction of negative gossip. The next step was to apply once again to the American courts, this time for removal of the customs ban that shadowed *Ulysses* and clouded Joyce's title to literary fame.[13] Such a legal challenge was fraught with peril, however—and not just because it might not succeed. The one advantage to the novel's reputation for indecency was that it had reduced the temptation for American publishers to issue unauthorized reprints of what they knew to be a public domain work. Obscenity law, not copyright law, effectively protected *Ulysses* from copying but so completely that even its author could not issue the book in the United States. This was a deadweight loss that vastly exceeded the typical supply-reducing effects of the copyright monopoly. Morris L. Ernst, the New York lawyer who would shortly challenge the book's exclusion by U.S. customs, observed in 1931 that *Ulysses* "has no commercial value either to the author, Miss Beach or any publisher.

From a monetary point of view, it is now a valueless property in the United States except for a few isolated pirates."[14]

The problem was that if Ernst succeeded in lifting the customs ban, the last barrier to unrestrained piracy would be removed. It was a problem keenly felt by Bennett Cerf, cofounder of Random House, who desperately wanted to bring out the first authorized edition of *Ulysses* in America but was loath to spend money and time on a lawsuit that might open the flood-gates to lawful free riding. A solution lay, however, in the tradition of trade courtesy—partly in its shaming sanctions but chiefly in the tacit communal cohesiveness that had enabled participating publishers of the nineteenth century to enjoy synthetic rights in unprotected foreign works and to turn the American public domain into a paying commons. A great deal of schol-arship has been lavished on Random House's legal efforts to free *Ulysses* from the taint of obscenity. In this chapter, I examine the equally important extralegal strategies that Cerf, Ernst, and Joyce employed to secure courtesy protections for the book. If Joyce and Cerf hoped to capture the full benefits of a newly legalized, authorized *Ulysses*, they would have to find a way to inhibit the normal functioning of the public domain. Trade courtesy was the answer.

## "These Thieves": Bennett Cerf's Fears of Lawful Piracy

That *Ulysses* enjoyed no or questionable copyright protection in the United States was widely known and acknowledged during the 1920s and 1930s. Every draft of the international protest, including the final, published one, stressed the point.[15] Press accounts of Joyce's dispute with Roth regularly reminded readers of the novel's legal vulnerability: "'Ulysses' has not been and presumably cannot be copyrighted in the United States."[16] "It was barred from the United States mails, and therefore not copyrighted."[17] "'Ulysses,' ... under American law, is not copyright."[18] Joyce's literary agents entertained no illusions about the book's copyright status in America. Even Hollywood scented the possibilities of an unfenced *Ulysses*. When Warner Brothers briefly considered adapting the novel for the screen in 1932, the studio sim-ply assumed that "anybody could make a picture here" in the United States; permission to exhibit the film would be required only for countries where the book was legally protected.[19]

In the early 1930s, Joyce anguished over real and imagined piracies in the United States and elsewhere. His fears were sometimes wildly exaggerated. He issued a demand for "reparation" when the Ulysses Bookshop in London printed, without authorization, two of his early essays in limited editions.[20] Jacob Schwartz, proprietor of the bookshop, considered the demand "silly": the editions had not been offered for sale, he explained, and any copyrights in the essays had already expired, at least in the United States.[21] It seemed to Joyce that he was being subjected to Roth-like depredations everywhere he turned. When the Private Subscription Book Club of London offered to pay a modest fee for the right to print a few copies of *Ulysses*, Joyce ranted about obtaining an injunction and sought a barrister's opinion on the copyright status of the book in England.[22] He was furious as well that his short stories had been issued in unauthorized translation in Italy and that two Japanese editions of *Ulysses* had appeared in early 1932, reportedly running to thirteen thousand "pirated" copies by August. He was not mollified when he was told that copyrights in *Dubliners* and *Ulysses* had expired in Italy and Japan, respectively.[23] He even had to be talked out of suing over an innocent misattribution to "James Joyce" of a crime story authored by one Michael Joyce and published in the *Frankfurter Zeitung*.[24]

Rumored piracies of *Ulysses* also nagged at Cerf and kept him from taking full pleasure in the prospect of issuing an authorized American edition of the work. In October 1932, more than a year before Judge Woolsey's decision, Cerf learned from two different booksellers that a man named Joseph Meyers, doing business at One Hundred Fifth Avenue under the trade name Illustrated Editions, might be planning to bring out an unauthorized *Ulysses*. Cerf considered Meyers to be outside the communal orbit of trade courtesy, "a notorious pirate" for whom "any appeal on purely ethical grounds will fall on deaf ears." Cerf was anxious to protect his potential market for *Ulysses*: "obviously a cheap pirated edition will take all the cream off of our own."[25] Alexander Lindey, an associate attorney in Morris Ernst's office, advised Cerf to send Meyers a "decoy letter," whereupon the threat apparently subsided.[26]

The most tangible menace remained none other than Samuel Roth. Sometime after *Two Worlds Monthly* had ceased publication in the fall of 1927, he reissued the entire run of the magazine in two bound volumes in an edition of five hundred numbered copies, signed by himself. The edition contained a new "prelude" in which Roth related a colloquy he had had with

God when he was sitting one day in his study, sunk in despondency. The Lord wondered why His servant Roth, a good man in his generation, had allowed his name to be "constantly linked with the name of James Joyce." After listening to Roth lament his outcast status and rehearse his familiar defenses to the charge of pirating *Ulysses*, the Lord smiled and assured him that his insolent adversaries would eventually "all perish in their own filthy sweat."[27]

But Roth did more than simply reissue the serialized version of *Ulysses*. Despite having been enjoined by the New York Supreme Court in 1928, he produced, the following year, a bold forgery of the Shakespeare and Company *Ulysses*, printed by the Loewinger brothers of New York City. This fake edition, set from the ninth Paris printing but with a smaller type font on heavier paper and marred by numerous typographical errors, was not a photographic reproduction, as Joyce claimed, but rather an edition struck from new plates. Although copies were seized by the New York Society for the Suppression of Vice in October 1929, the forgery continued to circulate; some copies even reached Paris and were smuggled back into the United States as authentic imports.[28] Copies were sold to the book trade for five dollars, and dealers marked them up as they pleased. John J. Slocum purchased a Roth *Ulysses* for fifteen dollars in 1930. The next year, Sylvia Beach's father picked one up for $6.50.[29]

Joyce, always ready to believe the worst, complained that Roth had sold ten thousand copies of the lookalike *Ulysses*, a number that Cerf feared might be correct.[30] Joyce referred to Roth's simulation of the Dijon printer Darantiere's distinctive product as a *contrefaçon*, an offense in French law involving the counterfeiting of luxury goods. Joyce even entertained the hope that officials at the French Consulate General in New York might be persuaded to halt the trafficking in this knockoff *Ulysses*, which he likened to "a falsified French perfume."[31] He may have been recalling the Chadbourne lawyers' strategy of incorporating elements of unfair competition and trademark infringement into their theory of Roth's liability.

An obvious legal remedy lay to hand: the injunction that Joyce's lawyers had obtained, with Roth's consent, in December 1928. Justice Mitchell's decree had forbidden Roth and his "officers, assistants, agents and servants" from publishing or printing Joyce's name in connection with any "book" by Joyce, "including the book 'Ulysses', in any … publication, heretofore or hereafter published by defendants."[32] Surely, this expansive interdiction would have encompassed Roth's forgery, but Joyce had come to believe that the injunction was "a perfectly worthless piece of paper."[33] Morris Ernst also pronounced the injunction "not very impressive."[34] His associate Alexander Lindey went even further and told Cerf that, in his opinion, the legal position that the Chadbourne lawyers had advanced, based as it was on the New York Civil Rights Law, was "untenable." "[I]f a literary production has been dedicated to the public," Lindey explained, "anyone may publish the production under the name of the author and so advertise it, without incurring any liability under [Section 51 of] the Civil Rights Law."[35] He was partly referring to the author's-name exception contained in Section 51, which Roth's lawyer in 1927 had urged as a complete defense to Joyce's claims against his client. But Lindey also felt that once a work had entered the public domain, it was available for anyone to use. The commons should not be stinted by clever lawyering and exotic legal theories.

Despite its doubters, Joyce's lawsuit had produced a broad injunction, which remained the most direct means of attacking Roth's spurious edition. But Justice Mitchell's decree was not self-executing: Joyce would have had to take steps to enforce it, and he wanted nothing more to do with American lawyers and their invoices.[36] Moreover, copies of the forgery had already been dispersed through underground channels of booklegging and were being sold behind the counters of book marts in New York and other cities. The decree would have had no force against the shadowy operations of book dealers. As Lindey explained to Cerf, the injunction had been "granted by consent, and of course could have no binding force in any subsequent proceeding."[37] For Joyce, the threat of piracy had mostly worn the face of Roth, but the problem was actually much larger. Anyone could reprint *Ulysses* in the United States without running afoul of copyright or other intellectual-property laws. Only the threat of vice society raids and criminal prosecution secured a dubious and stultifying protection for the book.

Cerf knew that the Roth injunction would be ineffective against the full tide of lawful piracy, once loosed by a lifting of the customs ban. He faced this grim prospect with courageous lucidity in late 1931. "No copyright can possibly be obtained on the text of Ulysses," he wrote. If Random House were to wage a long, costly legal battle, he added, "there would be at least one, or possibly more than one, pirated edition of the book openly sold within a short time thereafter. In other words, the publisher who goes to all the expense necessary in this fight isn't going to get the full benefits."[38] Cerf's dilemma was uncomfortably clear. If, with the help of Ernst and Lindey, he managed to close the door on John Sumner and the U.S. attorney, he would be opening another door to Roth and his piratical brethren. Cerf was ready to take a calculated risk in challenging the customs ban, but he had no interest in paying for the privilege of becoming the patron saint of the American public domain. The problem was too big for mere lawyers and law courts, though the solution had to begin there.

## The Book's the Thing: *Ulysses* as Defendant

It is a common misconception that Cerf's lawyers defended *Ulysses* against criminal charges of obscenity.[39] In fact, the litigation that made it possible for the novel to be lawfully imported into the United States, and by extension to be published by Random House, did not involve the criminal courts at all. Ernst's strategy was to see that a copy of *Ulysses*, specially imported from Paris, was seized by U.S. customs and then made the centerpiece of a civil forfeiture proceeding authorized by the federal Tariff Act of 1930. Ernst knew the forfeiture procedure well; he had helped design it. In the late 1920s, he had interested Senator Bronson Cutting of New Mexico in reforming the harshness and irrationality of censorship by customs officials. Up to that time, when a book was seized by customs as obscene, the person to whom the book had been addressed could, if he or she wished, challenge the seizure in the U.S. Customs Court, but this was a weak safeguard. The addressee had the burden of proving that the book was not obscene; the collector of customs was not required to prove anything. The collector's subjective decision to exclude the book would not be overturned unless the customs court was persuaded that he had substantially abused his discretion. In most cases, the exclusion was upheld and the book was confiscated.[40] The unpredictable squeamishness of bureaucrats was practically immune from judicial review.

The Cutting amendment changed all that. Senator Cutting—who later showed himself receptive to Ezra Pound's ideas for reforming obscenity and copyright laws[41]—sought Ernst's help in revising the Tariff Act to set up barriers against capricious seizures.[42] The new statutory procedure, drafted by Ernst and codified in Section 305 of the Tariff Act of 1930, established a coherent mechanism for testing the validity of seizures: promptly after a seizure, customs was required to inform the U.S. attorney of the district in which the book had been taken; the U.S. attorney was in turn required to initiate proceedings in the federal district court (not the customs court) for the book's forfeiture. The government had to make a reasoned case for forfeiture, and the book's addressee was entitled to intervene as a claimant and demand a jury trial.[43] Under the Cutting amendment, the discretionary power of customs officials, which Pound considered one of the worst abuses tolerated by American law, was reined in and subjected to meaningful judicial oversight. Automatic confiscation was a thing of the past.

The Cutting amendment also prevented the government from directing its coercive power against the foreign sender or the domestic receiver of a seized book; those individuals were free from criminal prosecution under the revised Tariff Act.[44] Instead, the government was required to bring a civil forfeiture action directly against the allegedly obscene book, the legal *res*. The proceeding was referred to as one in rem, against the thing itself, rather than in personam, against an individual or a business entity. The government was obliged to initiate the action by filing a "libel" against the seized book—an old term used in admiralty law for the initiatory complaint or pleading in a lawsuit.[45] Under the Tariff Act, the book was, literally, the defendant in the case.

Such lawsuits, regularly filed against contaminated or contraband imports, were extremely common during Prohibition. The Admiralty section of the National Archives for the Northeast Region, located in New York City, contains the records of many such forfeiture proceedings. Turning the pages of these files, one can see why indecent books and bootleg hooch occupied the same imaginative space in the 1920s and 1930s, a linkage that gave rise to the playful term *bookleggers* for underground operators like Samuel Roth. In the same box that contains the files for *United States v. One Book Entitled "Ulysses,"* there are also records for *United States v. One Ford Truck*, a case dating from December 1932 and involving a vehicle caught transporting "intoxicating liquors" in violation of the Tariff Act and the Prohibition Reorganization Act. Other case files include *United States v. Approximately 126 Assorted Glasses, a quantity of intoxicating liquors, etc. found at Club La Lune on West 52nd Street*, and *United States v. One Cash Register, Remington #A-334, 163840, a quantity of intoxicating liquors, etc. found at premises at 584 Lennox Ave., Manhattan*. Each of these cases was a forfeiture action, or libel, brought against illicit articles by George Z. Medalie, the same U.S. attorney who in 1932 filed a libel against one book entitled *Ulysses*.

Ernst's initial task was to make sure that customs actually seized a copy of *Ulysses*. On Cerf's instructions, Joyce's friend and assistant Paul Léon carefully pasted into a copy of the Shakespeare and Company edition a number of documents—press extracts, critical assessments, copies of the international protest and the Roth injunction—that might serve as evidence of the book's literary importance.[46] In this period, American courts were often reluctant to admit evidence of critical praise for an allegedly obscene book, and judges worried that the testimony of literary experts would trespass on the fact-finding province of the jury.[47] If the seized copy actually embodied testimonial materials, however, those items would be harder to exclude.

After fortifying the volume with extracts, Léon dispatched it by registered mail for transport aboard the S S *Bremen*. The ship with its controversial cargo docked at the Port of New York in early May 1932. Prompted by Ernst's office, customs officials seized the volume and notified Lindey that it was being held as obscene, pursuant to the Tariff Act.[48] On May 24, as required by the Cutting amendment, customs transmitted the volume to the U.S. attorney for the Southern District of New York for initiating forfeiture proceedings.[49] After a long delay, on December 9, George Medalie, the U.S. attorney heading up the case, filed a libel that sought the forfeiture, confiscation, and destruction of the book. A week later, Ernst interposed a claim on behalf of Random House, the addressee of the volume, and answered the government's libel by denying that *Ulysses* violated the Tariff Act. With this exchange, the issue was formally joined.

The seized copy of *Ulysses* was now a defendant in a civil action. The law of forfeiture is unusual in making the inanimate instrumentality of alleged misconduct, rather than human actors, the target of the state's coercive power. Scholars trace forfeiture proceedings back to the early English law of deodands, under which a chattel, whether an animal or an inanimate object, was adjudged a deodand (*deo dandum*, "to be given to God") once a coroner's jury concluded that the chattel had caused the accidental or negligent death of a human being. Upon such a finding, the Crown was supposed to confiscate the chattel, sell it, and apply the proceeds to charitable purposes, but in practice the chattel's owner often paid a fine equal to the value of the deodand and the sum was turned over to a charity or the victim's family or simply added to the royal coffers.[50]

The law of deodands embodied a kind of animistic logic, a belief that if a thing caused harm to a person, the thing, rather than its human owner, was the culprit. "If an ox gore a man or a woman, that they die," the Mosaic code commanded, "then the ox shall be surely stoned, and his flesh shall not be eaten; but the owner of the ox shall be quit."[51] Vestiges of this logic have survived in the modern police practice of seizing the instrumentalities of crime, such as automobiles used to transport illegal liquor or drugs or vehicles operated by persons arrested for driving under the influence. Following such seizures, state and federal authorities routinely launch forfeiture proceedings against these passive conduits of alleged criminal activity.[52]

The lineaments of the law of deodands can be faintly glimpsed behind the libel filed against Random House's copy of *Ulysses*. Neither Cerf nor Joyce was the object of the law's wrath; it was the book itself, the immediate corrupter of morals, for which the U.S. attorney sought a decree of forfeiture and destruction, by way of just punishment. Yet the imported copy of *Ulysses*, as defendant, had no lawyer in the case; the book's defense was ventriloquized, as it were, through the arguments Ernst made on behalf of the intervening claimant, Random House. One of Ernst's briefs contended that the government should be required to prove its allegations beyond a reasonable doubt because the case was "something like a capital case. *Ulysses* stands before the Court as defendant. Charged with being a menace to public morals, it is fighting for its life. If condemned, it faces destruction by a means (i.e., confiscation) no less complete than that of hanging or electrocution."[53] This was no lawyerly flight of fancy. The retributive power of the state was being concentrated upon a public enemy, *Ulysses* by James Joyce.

The highly publicized lawsuit represented a further chapter in the martyrdom of *Ulysses*. Already the victim of pirates, Joyce's novel was now a federal prisoner as well. The caption of the case—*United States of America v. One Book Entitled "Ulysses"*—spoke eloquently of the forces ranged against the beleaguered book, a Goliath-against-David story in which philistine might asserted its right to confiscate and destroy an instrumentality of aesthetic and moral subversiveness. *Ulysses* was coveted in its character of tangible and intangible property: pirates plying their trade on the bounding public domain wanted to reproduce it in catchpenny copies; the government sought a decree for the annihilation of its physical embodiment, a latter-day deodand offered up to appease Victorian sensibilities. Yet, just as with the piracies of Roth, Joyce was able to benefit from this fresh spectacle of his victimized genius. The more *Ulysses* seemed the object of piratical desire or official condemnation, the more justified seemed its claims to literary greatness and lawful availability.

**Figure 6.1** Morris L. Ernst, center, book in hand, *New York Journal-American*, 1930s. (*Harry Ransom Center, University of Texas at Austin*)

A remarkable feature of the case was the spirit of collaboration in which the U.S. attorney's office and Ernst's team carried on their adversarial battle. This was not a collusive or friendly suit; the two sides genuinely contended for the court's judgment. But Medalie's office was frankly awed by *Ulysses*. Samuel Coleman, an assistant U.S. attorney who read the book with care, told Lindey that he considered it a "literary masterpiece," even though he felt that it was "obscene within the meaning of the federal law."[54] Medalie, too, thought the book "very important" and agreed with Ernst that the issues should be tested before Judge Woolsey, a literate and socially progressive judge who had recently dismissed Tariff Act libels filed by the government against two books by Marie Stopes, *Married Love* and *Contraception*, which openly discussed birth control, adult sexuality, and equality in marriage.[55] Medalie and Ernst had been opponents in those forfeiture cases as well.

These adversaries worked together to prepare the case for efficient adjudication by Judge Woolsey. They stipulated to a streamlined procedure whereby the book would be deemed incorporated in the pleadings and the parties would file cross-motions for judgment on the pleadings. Judge Woolsey would sit without a jury and, having read the book along with the parties' briefs, would rule on the motions, making determinations of fact and law.[56] The parties collaboratively shopped for the right judge, sometimes postponing court dates in order to avoid a judge known for his moral or religious rigor.[57] By August 1933 it appeared that Judge Woolsey would get the motions, but Ernst was not prepared to take chances. "Don't let it get away from Woolsey," he exhorted his team.[58] The judge himself seemed to be part of the benign conspiracy to get *Ulysses* as favorable a hearing as objectivity would permit. "Woolsey wants the case," Ernst remarked.[59] Coleman even promised to try to expedite the proceeding when Lindey told him that rumors of a new pirated edition of *Ulysses* were causing anxiety at Random House.[60]

There is an uncanny resemblance between this collaboration of adversaries and the institution of trade courtesy that encouraged competing publishers to unite in recognition of each other's informal rights in public domain works. The parallel is more than formal. Even as Ernst and Medalie were steering the case toward Judge Woolsey, Cerf was quietly laying the groundwork for courteous treatment of *Ulysses*, against the day when he would be free to issue the book legally under the Random House imprint. A feeding frenzy of piracy would ruin his efforts. He knew the courtesy tradition well and was determined to bring its norms-based resources—tacit cooperation among business rivals, legally uncompelled payment to authors, and shaming sanctions for outlaws—to bear on the challenge posed by a legal but uncopyrighted *Ulysses*.

## "Remarkable Probity": *Ulysses* and Trade Courtesy

In chapter 2, I painted a detailed picture of trade courtesy as it persisted into the twentieth century. Its survival was quiet, almost subterranean. The advent of antitrust laws, the passage of the Chace International Copyright Act, and the rise of the literary agent, all coming toward the end of the nineteenth century, transformed courtesy from an overt code of conduct into an implicit corporate ethic. Yet the practice retained its central feature: group recognition of a publisher's extralegal rights in a public domain work, especially when the publisher had contracted with or paid the author or could justify informal rights in some other way. Pound wrote in 1928 that he did not know whether American law had a "label" for Roth's unauthorized reprinting of uncopyrighted works but that "in the better Bohemia it can hardly be considered affable."[61] But courtesy was not limited to avant-garde publishing. The British literary agent A. D. Peters pointed to its widespread observance when he contrasted Roth's suspect "business morality" with "the remarkable probity of American publishers and editors in general; very often they put themselves to a very great deal of trouble to obtain permission for the publication of work which is legally non-copyright and to ensure that English authors shall receive the rewards which are their moral, though not their legal, due."[62]

Most publishers treated *Ulysses* with professional courtesy from the start. In April 1922, when the Paris edition had been in the American public domain for only a few days, Horace Liveright contacted John Quinn, Joyce's legal representative in New York, about obtaining rights to publish the novel, though at that time no American house could realistically hope to issue an unexpurgated version.[63] Six years later, in the midst of Joyce's troubles with Roth, the Covici–Friede firm made Joyce a handsome offer for rights to publish both *Ulysses* and "Work in Progress" in expensive, limited editions; for *Ulysses* alone the firm offered $1,500 upon publication, against a royalty of twenty percent.[64] The offer reflected the courtesy practice of bundling, whereby a publisher treated an author's copyrighted and uncopyrighted works as equally protected and, as a way of securing a formal association, offered payment for the whole. A few years earlier B. W. Huebsch had paid Joyce for the American rights to his early books, protected and unprotected, and thereby built a relationship that later helped him obtain rights to *Finnegans Wake* for the Viking Press. As it turned out, Joyce did not accept Covici–Friede's bundled proposal, but he boasted about the sum he'd been offered for writings that, a short time earlier, had been labeled by some as "gibberish."[65]

In 1931, Joyce asked his literary agent to invite offers for *Ulysses* from American publishers. He and Sylvia Beach were disappointed that most of the proposals came from firms specializing in erotica.[66] This suggests that *Ulysses* was still valued in some quarters for its scandalous allure, but it is also striking proof of the courteous treatment accorded the work even by marginal publishers with less to lose than the prestige houses or the rising firms by turning pirate. By 1932, several mainstream publishers, including

Harcourt, Brace and William Morrow, were pursuing a contract for *Ulysses*. Morrow offered generous terms but included a provision for decreasing Joyce's royalty from twenty to ten percent if Morrow faced competition from cheap piracies.[67] The clause, a descendant of royalty-chopping provisos in courtesy contracts of the previous century,[68] may have struck Joyce as punitive, requiring him to indemnify his publisher against the activities of faceless and ungovernable buccaneers.

As Joyce sorted through his suitors, it was increasingly apparent that Random House would emerge the victor. For a time, Huebsch had thought he could get the contract for Viking, and Cerf patiently waited his turn. But in late 1931, after negotiations with Beach broke down, Huebsch tendered Cerf a formal note of surrender: "You graciously stood aside for us, and naturally we cannot object if you should now determine to try to get the book."[69] Viking deemed it best to "retire, at least temporarily, from the field," Huebsch wrote Morris Ernst.[70] Cerf later recalled the delicacy of the moment: "Harold Guinzburg, the founder of Viking, was one of my best friends, and I didn't want to harm that relationship. There are some publishers who respect the rights of others. Viking and Random House would never dream of doing anything to hurt each other."[71] Preserving relationships with competitors by respecting their informal entitlements was just as important as grabbing a choice title for one's own list.

Here was trade courtesy in action, with a courtliness reminiscent of the previous century—one publisher bowing itself out of the picture so that another could take up the challenge of obtaining authorization for a work that, as far as U.S. copyright laws were concerned, was free for anyone to publish. Huebsch's use of the word "naturally" in ceding the project to Cerf hinted at the consensual inevitability of the courtesy regime and its strict allocation of rights and duties. Several months after Viking's withdrawal, just as Cerf was concluding his contract with Joyce, Vanguard Press of New York, a young firm with a reputation for publishing radical authors, declared its interest in *Ulysses*. Robert Kastor, the brother of Joyce's daughter-in-law, persuaded Vanguard not to compete with Cerf's firm, promising that if the contract with Random House fell through for any reason, Vanguard would get its chance.[72] According to the customary rules, Cerf had been the first publisher to communicate the news of an imminent contract with Joyce, thereby securing courtesy title to *Ulysses* that remained good as long as Cerf managed to deliver on his promise to publish.

Although reputable firms could be expected to cleave to courtesy, the *Ulysses* copyright vacuum remained an opportunity for deviants and upstarts in the trade. In late March 1932, Kastor, hoping to get Joyce to close with Random House, warned, "Every day's delay from now on is an invitation for someone to take the risk of publishing the book and making no agreement with Mr. Joyce, but trusting to luck to fight the legal battle and win it."[73] When Joyce urged a $5 price tag for the Random House edition (more than $80 in 2012 buying power),[74] Cerf countered with $2.50. An expensive edition, Kastor pointed out, would be "an open invitation to come in and pirate the book, which, as … Mr. Joyce knows, has no copyright over here."[75] Cerf felt that piracy was likely. "There are three or four firms in New York that are today boldly pirating anything that they possibly can without running afoul of the law."[76] As the lawsuit to free *Ulysses* from the customs ban progressed, Cerf grew increasingly worried that he would soon be facing competition from what Léon called a "plagiated edition."[77] Free or easy riding firms could simply photograph the Random House edition and sell *Ulysses* at a price that reflected few of the costs that Cerf had to bear.

In the end, Cerf priced the Random House *Ulysses* at $3.50, but he included a provision in the contract that permitted him to issue a cheap "popular edition," with a reduced royalty to Joyce, on the first appearance of "a pirated edition at a lower price than the authorized edition … in order to compete with this unfair competition."[78] This piracy clause resembled the one that the William Morrow firm had proposed, but it explicitly empowered Cerf to "fight [pirates] on their own grounds" by matching or underselling them.[79] Cerf's approach avoided a surrender of the market to renegades, promised to put more authorized copies of *Ulysses* into circulation, and gave Joyce a fighting chance to recover royalties that would otherwise be lost to nonpaying reprinters. This strategy derived directly from the courtesy sanction of predatory pricing. Like the Harper firm of the 1870s, Random House was prepared to sustain losses in a price-slashing war with outlaws. If "veritable pirates" threatened to board his ship, Cerf would not hesitate to play "their game."[80]

Joyce and Cerf also employed the courtesy practice of upbraiding potential pirates as a way of protecting the market for the authorized edition. In December 1933, just after Judge Woolsey handed down his *Ulysses* decision, the Albatross Press in Europe sought a piece of the newly liberated American market for itself. The Albatross Press was Joyce's authorized publisher of a Continental edition of *Ulysses*, which Albatross had issued in English under an imprint specially created for the occasion, the Odyssey Press.[81] Now, with the U.S. customs ban soon to be lifted, M. C. Wegner and John Holroyd-Reece, who ran Albatross, suggested a scheme for working with Cerf that they claimed would benefit both firms. Copies of the Odyssey Press edition, Holroyd-Reece explained, would inevitably enter the relaxed ports of the United States; though Cerf might regard these copies as "piracies," they would be the only piracies on which Joyce would be receiving royalties (from Albatross). Holroyd-Reece proposed to help "facilitate" Cerf's fight against real pirates by selling him sheets of the Continental edition that he could bind and use to "scare effectively ... any of the bright fellows in New York" who might try to compete "by underhand methods."[82] To Cerf, the proposal smacked of buccaneers who had spied an opportune plank.

Paul Léon was furious. He viewed the proposal as an "astounding" threat to exploit Joyce's copyright vulnerability as well as a potential breach of the contract between Joyce and the Albatross Press and an attempt to interfere with Joyce's contract with Random House. Léon insisted that Random House's contractual and courtesy rights were not to be tampered with. That *Ulysses* might not be copyrightable in the United States was a fact well known to Random House, Léon assured Wegner, when Cerf signed a contract to produce "the only authentic edition in the States."[83] If the Albatross Press went forward with its plans, Joyce and Random House would do everything in their power, "legally and morally," to suppress an influx of Odyssey Press copies into the United States. In addition to this courtesy rebuke, Léon threatened the sanction of negative gossip, warning Wegner that the plan that he and Holroyd-Reece were proposing would harm the name of anyone associated with it.[84] Indignant, Wegner protested that he had been misunderstood, but Joyce's bitter experience with unauthorized editions and inadequate laws rendered him deaf to nuances.

Cerf's reply to Holroyd-Reece was more diplomatic but no less menacing than Léon's under the surface. He was "not quite sure" that Random House could enforce a U.S. copyright in its authorized *Ulysses*, but he vowed, without directly naming the Albatross Press, to "proceed vigilantly if we can lay our hands on anybody who gets in our way." Implying the threat of severe shaming sanctions, he reminded Holroyd-Reece that when Roth reprinted *Ulysses* without authorization, "the wrath of all the critics and authors in

America descended upon his head."[85] Roth was now a measuring stick for unethical behavior among publishers—a byword for discourtesy—and the Albatross Press was on notice that worldwide ignominy awaited anyone who flouted the rights that Cerf had worked so hard to wrest from the American public domain.

Cerf added that his readiness to print a cheap *Ulysses* at the first sign of piratical activity rendered imported sheets from the Albatross Press unnecessary. Predatory pricing was a courtesy remedy that Random House was contractually empowered to employ, and no collaboration with foreign publishers could enhance that power. There were legal reasons, moreover, that counseled against importing sheets of *Ulysses*. Under the manufacturing provisions of the 1909 U.S. Copyright Act, any claim to a *Ulysses* copyright that Random House might be able to advance would depend on its having had the edition set and printed on U.S. soil. The 1909 act prohibited importation of copies not manufactured in the United States and provided for

**Figure 6.2** Bennett Cerf, photographed by Carl Van Vechten, 1932. (*Courtesy Van Vechten Trust*)

the seizure, forfeiture, and destruction of such copies.[86] If Random House acceded to the Albatross Press's plan, customs seizures of *Ulysses* might begin all over again, this time under the copyright law. Cerf wanted no part of such a scheme.

## "The Only Authentic One": Binding Courtesy into the Random House *Ulysses*

No aspect of Cerf's campaign was more carefully planned than the prefatory matter he selected for his authorized *Ulysses*. From the start, he had felt that two items were indispensable: a letter of authentication from Joyce and the text of any favorable judicial decision that might be issued in the federal forfeiture action. Inclusion of the judge's opinion would serve as a deterrent to future prosecutions and suppressions. After all, a judgment for Random House in the forfeiture proceeding would remove only one set of legal obstacles: customs seizures of *Ulysses* under the Tariff Act. The book and its publisher would still be vulnerable to attack from the postal authorities, state prosecutors, and vigilant vice societies; even customs officials outside of New York, Connecticut, and Vermont—the territory included within the jurisdiction of the U.S. Court of Appeals for the Second Circuit—might consider themselves free to seize the book.[87] Morris Ernst had found that inserting judicial opinions or similar matter in recently liberated volumes—Stopes's *Married Love*, Radclyffe Hall's *The Well of Loneliness*, and *The Decameron*—tended to "retard" the aggressions of law enforcement and to cause censorship groups to hesitate before commencing proceedings.[88] Cerf and Ernst considered it essential to include Judge Woolsey's opinion as a scarecrow to further official harassment of *Ulysses*.

The other crucial prefatory document was an authenticating letter from Joyce, by which Cerf could "give the public concrete evidence of our statement that ours was the only edition authorized by Mr. Joyce and Miss Beach."[89] At first, Cerf hoped that Joyce would write a lengthy introduction or preface, but he soon realized that a letter of "not less than 300 words" was all that could be extracted from this inscrutable man who refused to write critical essays and confined autobiography to the refractions of his art.[90] As it turned out, Joyce provided a letter of just over a thousand words, sketching the history of the publication, censorship, and piracy of *Ulysses*. Instead of writing about himself, he wrote a biography of his book, which had had, he noted, "a life of its own," just as all books have their own destiny ("*Habent sua fata libelli!*"). He approached the subject as if he were composing a saint's life, or that of a misunderstood heretic, complete with journeys, persecutions, and ritual sacrifices. Copies of *Ulysses* had been "seized and burnt" by customs officials in New York and Folkestone, Joyce wrote, and his inability to "acquire the copyright in the United States" had led to the abduction and unauthorized publication of the book by "unscrupulous persons."[91] If the rascality of Roth had begun to fade from the public's memory, Joyce's letter was there to remind everyone of the particulars of that scandal. Placed strategically just after the text of Judge Woolsey's opinion, the letter reinforced the perception of *Ulysses* as sufferer—victim of censorship, hostage of pirates, defendant in a forfeiture action, sacrificial deodand.

Of critical importance to Cerf was Joyce's endorsement: "I willingly certify hereby that not only will your edition be the only authentic one in the United States but also the only one there on which I will be receiving royalties."[92] With this gesture, Joyce joined Robert Browning, Thomas De Quincey, Rudyard Kipling, and other European authors whose letters testifying to their American publishers' courtesy had been bound into authorized though uncopyrighted editions of their works. Joyce's letter went on to declare that, through Random House, American readers would be able "to obtain the authenticated text of my book without running the risk of helping some unscrupulous person in his purpose of making profit for himself alone out of the work of another to which he can advance no claim of moral ownership."[93] With an eye for the legal mot juste, Joyce carefully avoided writing "legal ownership," for no law stood in the way of an unauthorized competitor's helping itself to the American public domain. Only the moral force of the arrangement between Cerf and Joyce, cleverly memorialized in the opening pages of the Random House edition, could dissuade challengers from entering the field.

There was also a copyright-related reason for including the forematter. Although Judge Woolsey's opinion, as a governmental work, enjoyed no protection, Cerf was eager to claim a copyright in Joyce's letter because the document would be printed in accordance with the 1909 act's manufacturing provisions. Fresh material by Joyce "could be copyrighted," Cerf noted early on in his planning.[94] So could a foreword by Ernst, which Cerf decided to include as the first piece in the volume. These two items would provide a basis for asserting at least a thin copyright for warding off pirates. Cerf's strategy was one that many American publishers before him had employed to justify a colorable claim for an otherwise unprotected work.[95]

Cerf also wanted to include a chart of Homeric correspondences and symbolic meanings that Joyce had prepared years earlier for select readers of *Ulysses*. The chart, Cerf thought, would enhance the marketability of Joyce's notoriously difficult book and, just as important, would add more potentially protectible material. "[W]e can copyright this chart," he wrote Léon, "and it will make one more feature of our own edition that cannot possibly be pirated."[96] He was absolutely convinced of the importance of having "as many copyrighted features in our own edition as possible."[97] But Joyce refused to allow the supplement on aesthetic grounds: *Ulysses* was a work of "pure literature" and should not contain self-exegesis.[98] Cerf pushed harder, stressing again the importance of having "as much copyrighted material in our edition as is humanly possible, in order to combat possible pirated editions which will undoubtedly come along to vex us all."[99] Joyce was adamant, however; he would allow Cerf to issue the chart separately, as publicity for the book, but not between its covers.[100] Just as he had been willing to sacrifice a U.S. copyright in order to publish *Ulysses* without expurgations in France, so now he was prepared to scant the copyrightable matter in the Random House edition so as to keep his text autonomous, uncontaminated by critical apparatus. Despite his dread of pirates, he still valued his artistic pride above legal protection.

Joyce had long entertained the hope that a lawfully published American edition of *Ulysses* might qualify for belated copyright protection, even though the window for complying with the manufacturing requirements had long since closed on the 1922 Paris edition. Sylvia Beach had made an inquiry along these lines with the U.S. Copyright Office in 1931 but had received a discouraging reply.[101] Paul Léon renewed the question with Joyce's literary agent in February 1932, a few weeks before Joyce signed the Random House contract:

If it is proved that the clause of the copyright Law providing for an American publication within six months of the publication of the book in Europe could not be complied with owing to the ban raised by the Customs Authorities, would not the legalization of the book and the immediate issue of an American edition automatically give the right to the editor fighting the case to acquire the copyright? Otherwise if the book is legalized it would seem that the American market is free for any publication.[102]

Léon, who had been trained as a lawyer, was asking a lawyer's question: since the book's reputation for indecency had been the cause of Joyce's inability to comply with the manufacturing clause, should not the removal of the customs ban enable Joyce, in equity at least, to claim the previously withheld copyright for a new and lawful edition? The answer, almost certainly, was no. The strict formalities of the 1909 act admitted of few equitable exceptions. The rigors of the law's technical requirements were as inflexible as Joyce's artistic principles.

The copyright notice in the 1934 Random House *Ulysses* confessed sotto voce to these difficulties: "Copyright, 1918, 1919, 1920, by Margaret Caroline Anderson. Copyright, 1934, by the Modern Library, Inc." The first string of dates referred to the serial installments of *Ulysses* that had appeared in *The Little Review*, and implied the theory—cherished by Quinn and Pound—that the magazine's collective-work copyrights were adequate to protect Joyce's separate contributions. The final date, "1934," indicated the Random House edition with its prefatory amplifications. Delicately omitted was "1922," the date of the first Paris edition—the only date relevant, in light of the ad interim and manufacturing provisions, for the protection of the entire work within the United States. Cerf confessed that he was unsure about the strategy of citing the *Little Review* copyrights, but he felt that Random House would at least have "a case" against unauthorized reprinters.[103] The copyright notice in the 1934 edition was a kind of *in terrorem* red flag to would-be pirates, a preliminary shot across the bow—one that a determined competitor or a deviant from courtesy might have chosen to ignore.

Within minutes of the announcement of Judge Woolsey's favorable decision, typesetters were at work on the legitimate, and now legal, American edition of Joyce's novel. The first copies of the Random House *Ulysses* reached Cerf in January 1934. Later that month, Random House deposited two copies with the Register of Copyrights and submitted an affidavit attesting to the edition's American manufacture. According to Copyright Office records, a claim of copyright was registered for the edition—registration number A70193—though precisely how the claim was characterized in Random

House's application is not known.[104] Even in Cerf's moment of triumph, however, piracy had its small revenge. In his haste to be the first post-ban publisher to comply with the manufacturing clause, Cerf had inadvertently handed his typesetters a copy of the forged Roth edition of *Ulysses*. He can hardly be blamed; the copy had come from Paris and seemed authoritative enough.[105] For years, the authorized edition bore traces of Roth's error-filled *contrefaçon*, and the claimed copyright in the Random House edition was further complicated by this hapless commingling of authorized and piratical matter.

Cerf's energetic use of the courtesy tradition was nothing short of remarkable; he had done everything he could, legally and morally, to safe-guard the American market for his authorized *Ulysses*. In the manner of nineteenth-century publishers, he had publicly announced his plans to issue the book and then perfected Random House's courtesy title by entering into a contract with Joyce, paying him an advance, and footing the bill for a suc-cessful legal challenge to the customs ban. He had bundled into the volume copyrighted and uncopyrighted material and had inserted prefatory texts that operated on two extralegal levels: on one level, Joyce's authenticating letter urged readers and booksellers to do their moral duty by accepting no substitutes; on another level, Ernst's foreword and Judge Woolsey's opinion reminded vice societies and prosecutors that the book had been cleared by one important court and should not be subjected to further official persecu-tion. Cerf thus transmitted his courtesy appeal over two frequencies, one aimed at securing an informal property right for Joyce and Random House, the other seeking to discourage the recriminalizing of *Ulysses*. With his work complete, Cerf could only wait to see if the publishing and legal communi-ties were cohesive and sympathetic enough to receive his signal and allow the Random House *Ulysses* to circulate unmolested.

He was rewarded beyond his expectations. Except for the harmless skir-mish with the Albatross Press, the pirates that he had thought unavoidable were nowhere on the horizon. Reputable publishers, in a body, embraced the Random House edition. Prominent firms—the Viking Press, Harcourt, Brace, Charles Scribner's Sons, and others—had been among those whose opinions Cerf had previously collected for submission to the court as evi-dence of changing cultural mores.[106] Soon after the announcement of Judge Woolsey's decision, Cerf received letters of congratulation from several houses—Horace Liveright, Inc., Vanguard Press, Fountain Press, Farrar

& Rinehart, Houghton Mifflin, and Knopf—some of which had vied for *Ulysses* in the past.[107] James Henle, president of Vanguard, gushed that Cerf and his publishing partner Donald Klopfer deserved "the thanks of the entire publishing community."[108] Among the many letters of praise that Judge Woolsey received was one from Alfred Knopf, written two days after the *Ulysses* decision was announced: "sincere and hearty congratulations on an Opinion, the rendering of which must have given you no little trouble.... It is superb."[109]

The book trade, too, stood behind Random House. Cerf had contacted the leading bookstores and book departments for opinions that could be included in Ernst's motion papers.[110] Booksellers were impressed by Random House's efforts to legalize *Ulysses* and, according to Cerf, had "voluntarily assured us that they would throw any pirates out of the store who tried to cash in on our victory."[111] A few years earlier, D. H. Lawrence had been surprised to learn that some booksellers would not handle pirated editions of the uncopyrighted *Lady Chatterley's Lover*, out of "sentimental and business scruples."[112] One "semi-repentant" New York bookseller had even sent Lawrence a sum representing a ten percent "royalty" on pirated copies sold in his shop.[113] Siegfried Weisberger, the owner of a bookshop in Baltimore, wrote Cerf that his plan to publish *Ulysses* would be a "good idea" if it had the effect of driving out furtive, expensive bootleg copies.[114] Solomon R. Shapiro, a graduate student who later became a distinguished New York City bookseller, wrote Judge Woolsey of his delight in the liberation of *Ulysses*, "which for twelve years has been available only at very high prices to students and other serious minded people wishing to read the work."[115] The Woolsey decision, which the U.S. Court of Appeals for the Second Circuit later affirmed, united diverse and competitive groups in admiration for the courage shown by Joyce and Cerf. Even the irascible Pound, not given to praising American courts, had to concede that Judge Woolsey was "a cut above the yahoo."[116]

With masterly diplomacy, Cerf had availed himself of both the horizontal and the vertical axes of trade courtesy. By inspiring fellow publishers to respect Random House's informal title to *Ulysses*, he brought stability to what might otherwise have disintegrated into destructive competition for the newly legalized book. Vertically, he had recognized the moral claims of unprotected foreign authors by seeking Joyce's authorization and paying him an advance, and he had won over the booksellers, who were prepared to resist the temptation to stock unauthorized reprints. Just as Henry Holt and the Harpers had done fifty years earlier, Cerf had used courtesy principles to imitate the basic features of copyright law, galvanizing the publishing trade's appreciation for informal rights and duties and filling the legal void created by a protectionist statute that, as Pound put it, favored "the printer at the expense of the author."[117] In the background of all this was the public shaming that Joyce had administered to Roth just a few years earlier. Joyce's negative gossip had targeted the publisher of *Two Worlds Monthly* specifically, but its deterrent effect rippled out from that human bullseye to chasten the conduct of others in the trade. By 1934, no one wanted to look like Samuel Roth.

Within the close-knit community of publishers, and even beyond, Random House had earned the courtesy of rivals. Cerf had labored conspicuously in the Lockean commons, mingling the resources of publishing and litigation with the ownerless materials of genius, and his reward was a peer-recognized ability to "exclude[] the common right of other Men."[118] His efforts brought to completion the work of consensus building that Joyce had so powerfully begun seven years earlier by issuing the international protest. The injunctive relief that Joyce had hoped to win by suing Roth in a New York court, he actually obtained five years later by grace of informal norms working quietly in the publishing trade. Much as he coveted a grand judicial declaration of authors' rights, he had no real need for one. The tradition of courtesy, operating through intricate constellations of professional honor, sentiment, and self-interest, protected *Ulysses* far beyond the pronouncements of courts. With the help of Cerf and Ernst, Joyce had reclaimed his book from the American public domain.

\*   \*   \*

Trade courtesy insulated the Random House *Ulysses* for decades. Then, in the 1960s, an unauthorized version of the novel appeared in the United States, apparently based on the British Bodley Head edition and selling for five dollars a copy. The volume was issued by Collectors Publications of Industry, California, and ran to 933 numbered pages of text and 43 unnumbered pages of advertising. The advertisements, placed at the back, were for assorted paperbacks, nude photographs, and sexual devices. Among the titles that readers could order were *Four Way Swappers* by Carol Klitman,

*Whips Incorporated, Our Lady of the Flowers* by Jean Genet, *The Black Book* by Lawrence Durrell, *It's Fun to Be Irish,* and *The Complete Kennedy Saga.* Also to be had were *The Incestual Triangle, The Whipping Post, Hell Is Filling Up,* and the erotic chestnuts *Fanny Hill* and *Teleny,* along with *The Mad, Mod World of Aubrey Beardsley,* a fin-de-siècle author dressed in a Nehru dust jacket. Lacking a title page and a copyright notice, the Collectors *Ulysses* was printed on newsprint and boasted, misleadingly, that it was the "First American Printing." Collectors Publications advertised the fat paperback in its ADULTS ONLY list; purchasers were required to certify that they were "over 21 years of age."[119]

Here was a *Ulysses* for the swinging sixties, a volume that could take its place beside guides to sexual pleasure, tales of spankings, spouse-swapping, and open marriage, and copies of the magazine *Screw.* The Collectors *Ulysses* carried to a bawdy, hip extreme the whispered promises of erotic gaiety with which Samuel Roth had promoted the novel in the 1920s. By the 1960s, the publishing industry had become honeycombed with paperback subcultures, and the courtesy that had protected *Ulysses* in earlier decades no longer resonated as it had when the heroic efforts of Cerf and Ernst were still fresh in the trade's memory.

Yet, despite the brash, trashy nature of this whips-and-chains *Ulysses,* Random House apparently never tried to bring suit. At $5 a copy, buyers were paying a premium for smutty ambience. In 1967, a paperback *Ulysses* in Random House's Vintage Books series could be had for $2.95: the old courtesy strategy of underselling competitors was quietly protecting the authorized edition. When a college professor complained of the Collectors porno-piracy in 1970, Random House lawyers reportedly told him they had no desire to launch litigation that would generate publicity for the unauthorized edition, particularly when the claimed copyright in the authorized one might not be ironclad.[120] Maintaining the perception of protectibility was more important than putting it to the test in court; it was better to tolerate an obscure outlaw in Industry, California, and to hold down the price of the genuine article, than to risk undoing the long, patient work of courtesy with an ill-advised lawsuit.

Collectors Publications had been founded by Marvin Miller, a versatile entrepreneur, embezzler, and ex-convict. Like others before him, Miller mixed literature and erotica in a list drawn largely from the public domain; many of his titles came from Maurice Girodias's Olympia Press catalogue—victims of the manufacturing clause—and he kept costs down by using cheap materials and working out of his house.[121] He soon had an extensive list and was raking in profits. In 1971, he conducted a mass mailing to advertise books entitled *Intercourse, Man–Woman, Sex Orgies Illustrated,* and *An Illustrated History of Pornography,* together with a film entitled *Marital Intercourse.* A few of the brochures, which contained explicit images of sexual activity and genitalia, were received by individuals who had not requested them, and Miller was convicted of violating California Penal Code Section 311.2(a), a misdemeanor, by knowingly distributing obscene matter. The case might have languished in the appellate courts, but the U.S. Supreme Court selected it as a vehicle for establishing fresh guidelines for separating true obscenity from expression protected by the First Amendment—a distinction that had troubled American courts for years and had failed to find consensus within the nation's highest court.

A five-member majority of the Court adopted what has come to be known as the *Miller* test, a set of loosely interlocking criteria for determining the presence of obscenity in an accused work. The test asks (a) whether the average person, applying contemporary community standards, would find that the work, taken as a whole, appeals to the prurient interest; (b) whether the work depicts or describes, in a patently offensive way, sexual conduct specifically defined by the applicable state law; and (c) whether the work, taken as a whole, lacks serious literary, artistic, political, or scientific value.[122] In the *Miller* test, recognizable fragments of the analysis employed by Judge Woolsey—prurient effect, the average person, serious literary value, holistic context—are fused and constitutionalized so as to balance local community sensitivities with the transcendent values of intellectual seriousness. Today, the *Miller* inquiry remains the governing standard in the United States for determining whether challenged material is legally obscene and may therefore be excluded from First Amendment protection.

In establishing this inquiry, the *Miller* majority discarded an earlier judicial standard—the definition of obscenity as material "utterly without redeeming social importance"—which the Court had first articulated in a case called *Roth v. United States.*[123] The *Roth* decision, handed down in 1957, marked the last time, prior to *Miller,* that a majority of the Court had agreed on a definition of obscenity. In *Roth,* the Court had considered a challenge by Samuel Roth, under the free speech and due process clauses of the U.S. Constitution, to the federal postal statute known as the Comstock

Act, under which he had been convicted for mailing obscene matter. The trial jury had found him guilty on four counts of using the mails to distribute obscene matter concerning his periodicals *Good Times: A Revue of the World of Pleasure* and *American Aphrodite: A Quarterly for the Fancy-Free.* The trial judge had sentenced him to five years imprisonment and fined him five thousand dollars, and a federal appellate court had affirmed.

The Supreme Court agreed to review Roth's challenge to the postal statute and carefully considered his lawyers' written and oral arguments, along with briefs submitted by amici curiae, including one by Morris Ernst, who wrote in vigorous support of Roth's position.[124] In the end, the Court rejected all the constitutional theories that Roth's lawyers and the amici had advanced and upheld his conviction and sentence by a 6–3 vote. Roth, in his sixties, entered a federal penitentiary in Pennsylvania and remained there until 1961.[125]

The periodicals that led to his conviction seem almost absurdly mild by today's standards. *American Aphrodite*, a hardbound quarterly, contained a typical Rothian stew of slightly dated literature and winking erotica, though some of the material, such as Aubrey Beardsley's unfinished novel *Venus and Tannhäuser*, contained stronger sexual content. Woodcuts and drawings of thinly clad or nude women adorned the quarterly's pages, along with frank poems, such as one inquiring of God whether it is wrong to desire "Two women in one affection, / Two vulvas, four breasts."[126] Teasing titles—"Good for Loving," "A Bit of Tale," "Marriage and the Use of Passion," "The Women of Plentipunda"—hinted at more than the stories and poems ever delivered. The promiscuous assortment of recent and older authors included Ruthven Todd, H. A. Manhood, Aleister Crowley, George Sylvester Viereck, Thomas Hardy, and Norman Lockridge (a Roth nom de plume). Roth's editorials chided "Madame Post Office" and other official powers for repressing "our rights as American citizens engaged in interpreting the cultural and emotional motives of our time."[127] *American Aphrodite* was plainly a successor to Roth's *Two Worlds* magazines of three decades before. There was the same edgy, blandishing, defiant editorial tone. The increase of gaiety that Roth had promised in the 1920s had merely given way to more current expressions of the same pledge: a "world of pleasure" for "the fancy-free," sustenance for the intellectually and emotionally liberated.

Ideas of sexual freedom are time-bound. Roth's missionary zeal to disseminate well-wrought erotica was always somehow rooted in the fin-de-siècle decadence that so appealed to him. Marvin Miller's enterprise was shaped by the explosive thrill seeking of an America emerging from social and sexual conformism into Beat beatitudes, happenings, acid tests, and summers of love. Yet both Roth and Miller had the same passion for pressing the boundaries of the printable, and it was this passion, in no small measure, that drew them to *Ulysses* and earned them the title, at least among the high-minded, of pirate-in-chief. They both looked upon the etiquette of courtesy with a cold eye. For them, an uncopyrighted novel was not something to be chivalrously reconstituted as moral property, but rather an opportunity, beyond the pedantic teachings of meum and tuum, to communicate a certain heady freedom and to pocket a few dollars in the bargain. Courtesy principles were for those who could afford them—the accepted, the connected, the prosperous—not for those scrabbling at the margins of respectability, who in some part of their unsocialized souls had never really coveted acceptance anyway. *Ulysses* was an irresistible treasure for such discourteous outsiders—a beautiful, iconic thing that could not be owned, a gem embedded in the mud of the American public domain, waiting to be extracted and held up to the light of famished popular desire.

Whatever its status as property under law or courtesy, *Ulysses* was a work that many still regarded as morally forbidden, and this was part of its allure. Roth and Miller marketed it as an erotic text, a raw, kinetic experience; in doing so, they implicitly reminded readers that it had not always been the monument to aesthetic autonomy that the arguments of lawyers, judges, and literary critics had made it.[128] A passion for communicating the forbidden was what impelled Roth and Miller to carry their challenges to the Supreme Court, and it is really no coincidence that the two greatest pirates of *Ulysses* in America gave their names to two landmark obscenity decisions—cases that are read, every year in courses on constitutional law and the First Amendment, by law students who have scarcely heard of James Joyce or his terrible book.

Communicating the forbidden was one aspect of the modernist project, and Ezra Pound knew it. Long before he was indicted for broadcasting allegedly treasonous tirades over Rome Radio, he praised Henry James as an international communicator of necessary truths. For the same reason, he could never hate Roth with a perfect hatred, not to please Joyce anyway. Pound would have made a poor witness in Joyce's name-misappropriation lawsuit. No sooner would he have begun excoriating Roth as a scoundrel pirate than he would have veered off into equivocal praise for his willingness to print the banned and the scorned. Pound assailed the American public domain—that forcing ground for unprotected works—as the product of unjust laws, but he implicitly accepted the idea of a premature commons in his proposal for overcoming the problem of copyright hoarding by statutorily compelling cross-border dissemination of works.

Without some notion of the unowned there can be no communication. Literary property is instinct with its own death principle. Copyrights are wasting monopolies that must expire, early or late, according to the whims of lawmakers or the memory of communities; they are therefore tolerable in a crowded world of born imitators. The American public domain was sustained, in part, by parochial fears of competition from foreign publishers and book manufacturers, but its inspired byproduct was the early opportunity to distribute valuable public goods. Trade courtesy rose up to meet the challenge of unguarded plenty and fashioned new, fragile forms of property from the teeming commons. Yet the extralegal improvisations of publishers also promoted dissemination by bridging the incentives gap and staving off market failure for uncopyrighted works, thus creating a bankable commons. The specter of the prematurely unowned both haunted and stimulated the consumption of transatlantic modernism in the United States, from Thomas Bird Mosher to Samuel Roth to Marvin Miller. The communication of law-forsaken works, whether through channels of courtesy or acts of so-called piracy, has left its permanent mark on modernism in the American public domain.

# EPILOGUE

## Disturbing the American

## Public Domain

*The statute before us ... does not encourage anyone to produce
a single new work.... [I]t bestows monetary rewards only on
owners of old works—works that have already been created
and already are in the American public domain.*
—Justice Stephen Breyer, dissenting, Golan v. Holder (2012)[1]

The American public domain has made a slow journey from exceptionalism
to internationalism since the first U.S. copyright act of 1790. A chronicler
of this unique commons might view it as falling into several distinct periods. Until 1891, U.S. copyright statutes categorically denied protection to
foreign works and placed them in the public domain ab initio, as a matter of
deliberate protectionist policy. From 1891, foreign authors could obtain U.S.
copyrights but only by complying with often burdensome formalities that,
in practice, ensured that the American public domain would continue to
brim with transatlantic materials. In the mid-1950s, the copyright-stripping
nature of U.S. law changed after the United States joined the Universal
Copyright Convention (UCC) and enacted legislation that exempted
other UCC countries from the requirements of the notorious manufacturing clause.[2] Then, in 1989, after holding out for a century, the United States

joined the international Berne Convention for the Protection of Literary and Artistic Works.[3] As a Berne adherent, the United States was required to abolish statutory formalities, such as mandatory copyright notices, as conditions of legal protection. With America's coming to Berne, the early death sentence for foreign copyrights was commuted by a stroke of the pen of President Ronald Reagan.

In 1994, the United States joined the World Trade Organization (WTO) and the Agreement on Trade-Related Aspects of Intellectual Property Rights (TRIPS).[4] These commitments created pressure to grant further concessions to foreign authors, and Congress responded by enacting Section 514 of the Uruguay Round Agreements Act (URAA),[5] which restored copyright protection to foreign works that had prematurely entered the American public domain for any of several reasons—notably, "noncompliance with formalities imposed at any time by United States copyright law, including ... failure to comply with any manufacturing requirements."[6] In restoring protection to foreign works that had lost copyright because they had not been manufactured on U.S. soil or had run afoul of some other technicality, Congress sought to make belated amends for America's long history of copyright protectionism. The American public domain was forced to give back some of its spoils.

What followed was a quiet revolution in the settled state of the commons. Works that had long existed as free resources were returned to authors, estates, and other owners. Many modernist works made this unfamiliar, inverse journey from public domain back to private dominion. James Joyce's *Ulysses* was one such work. By legislative fiat, the URAA gave to the first Paris edition of *Ulysses*, which had lain in the American public domain since April 1922, what had always eluded Joyce during his lifetime: complete copyright protection in the United States. Under the URAA, the restoration of *Ulysses*, along with thousands or millions of other foreign-origin works, became effective on January 1, 1996.[7]

But protection for *Ulysses* was short-lived. Copyrights restored under the URAA "subsist for the remainder of the term of copyright that the work would have otherwise been granted in the United States if the work never entered the public domain in the United States."[8] Joyce's novel, had it not entered the public domain prematurely, would have enjoyed a U.S. copyright term of seventy-five years running from its French publication in 1922. Thus, under the URAA, *Ulysses*, after many copyright adventures, salvaged two quiet, unremarked years of U.S. copyright protection before passing—this time of natural legal causes—back into the American public domain on January 1, 1998, ten months before the Sonny Bono Copyright Term Extension Act added twenty years to all existing and future copyrights.[9]

Works published before 1923 were untouched by the Sonny Bono Act's generous lengthening of copyright terms; those works remained in the American public domain. But post-1922 works that were eligible for restoration under the URAA received the double benefit of URAA revival and Sonny Bono term enhancement. The combination worked a potent and unprecedented stint upon the American public domain. Many works that had been free resources for Samuel Roth and his contemporaries were now back in private hands, and the shock waves were felt throughout the country. In 2001, a group of orchestra conductors, musicians, and others who had previously enjoyed unfettered access to older foreign works filed a lawsuit in a Colorado federal court assailing the constitutionality of the URAA. Among their allegations was the claim that works by Stravinsky, Prokofiev, Shostakovich, and other composers, which had formerly been available for purchase at modest prices, now cost a thousand dollars or more to rent for a single performance, with additional royalty payments required for every public performance, and mechanical royalties for any recordings based on the restored compositions.[10]

The case was captioned *Golan v. Holder*. In it, the plaintiffs contended that the URAA had done something that no U.S. legislation had ever done on such a vast scale: it had altered the "bedrock principle" that once a work enters the American public domain, it stays there. Section 514 of the URAA, they complained,

> reaches back over 75 years and grants retroactive copyrights to thousands and thousands of foreign works, many of which had been created years ago—potentially dating back to the early 1920s. Under the settled law under the 1909 [U.S. Copyright] Act and later the 1976 Act, these works had unequivocally and unconditionally entered the public domain in the United States because they did not meet the requirements of U.S. copyright law. What § 514 attempts to undo is nearly a hundred years of copyright law retroactively.[11]

The plaintiffs argued that Section 514 violated their First Amendment rights as well as the limitations that the U.S. Constitution places on

Congress's power to adopt copyright legislation. Lawmakers had simply gone too far, they argued. After conflicting decisions in the district and appellate courts, the U.S. Supreme Court agreed to review the case. The parties and numerous amici submitted briefs, and the Court heard oral arguments in October 2011.

In January 2012, Justice Ruth Bader Ginsburg, writing for a six-member majority, rejected the plaintiffs' challenge. Congress had acted rationally, she held, when it exercised its copyright power to accord equitable treatment to formerly disfavored foreign authors. Just as it had done in reviewing the constitutionality of the Sonny Bono Act several years before,[12] the Supreme Court once again showed deference to the legislative branch: "we will not second-guess the political choice Congress made between leaving the public domain untouched and embracing Berne unstintingly."[13] Nor did the URAA alter the traditional contours of copyright protection and thereby transgress the bounds of the First Amendment. The public can still rely, wrote Justice Ginsburg, on the fair use doctrine and the idea/expression dichotomy to make limited unauthorized use of restored works, and the URAA contains certain exceptions that favor users who have come to rely on the public domain status of works. The URAA's "disturbance of the public domain" is simply not a matter of constitutional concern, concluded the *Golan* majority.[14] The threshold of the public domain is one that Congress may traverse in either direction without offending the law of the land.

It was not surprising that the Court upheld the URAA's raid on the American public domain. After the Court's sweeping bow to Congress in *Eldred v. Ashcroft*—the decision that sustained the Sonny Bono Act against constitutional challenge—little else could have been expected from *Golan*. It was not the holding but rather the rhetoric of Justice Ginsburg's opinion that was startling, along with the implications of that rhetoric for U.S. copyright law. She made it clear that the U.S. Constitution does not protect the public domain as an "inviolable" creative resource. The public domain is not "untouchable by Congress," she wrote;[15] it does not even rise to "a category of constitutional significance."[16] After *Golan*, it is hard to imagine any limit to what Congress might choose to withdraw from the endangered commons. The public domain is not a positive legal entity, *Golan* suggests, but rather a negative remnant, an incidental leftover after copyright protection has been subtracted. The public has no vested interest in the legislated commons; the only true vesting of rights occurs when authors or entities create works.

When copyrights end, wrote Justice Ginsburg, "works simply lapse into the public domain."[17] The common pool grows through a slow trickle of ownerless works, but Congress, as long as it makes the least showing of rationality, may dam or redirect those lapsing waters at will.

The *Golan* majority's indifference to the public domain is symptomatic of a shift, amply evidenced by Congress and the Court in recent decades, away from a utilitarian, public-purpose conception of copyrights toward an author-centric, reward-for-labor view. This latter rationale for copyright has not always been dominant in the United States. The legislative drafters of the 1909 Copyright Act observed that the Constitution did not give Congress the power to grant copyrights "primarily for the benefit of the author, ... but because the policy is believed to be for the benefit of the great body of people, in that it will stimulate writing and invention, to give some bonus to authors and inventors."[18] Until recently, the Supreme Court similarly acknowledged that "[c]reative work is to be encouraged and rewarded, but private motivation must ultimately serve the cause of promoting broad public availability of literature, music, and the other arts."[19] The copyright monopoly, the Court stated in 1984, was not "primarily designed to provide a special private benefit" but to stimulate creation for "an important public purpose."[20] The limited monopoly was offered to tempt authors out of silence and indolence, for the nourishment of the public—a sort of noble bait-and-switch that lured authors into exerting themselves for immediate rewards and that gave the public the ultimate benefits.

This is not the vision of copyright that emerges from the majority opinion in *Golan*. Instead, Justice Ginsburg justified the enactment of the URAA, in significant part, on the basis of Congress's rational decision to provide retroactive equity to foreign authors. "Authors once deprived of protection are spared the continuing effects of that initial deprivation," she observed. Section 514 "gives them nothing more than the benefit of their labors during whatever time remains before the normal copyright term expires."[21] This is the language of natural rights, the neo-Lockean view that authorial labor should be rewarded as a matter of elementary entitlement, irrespective of creative incentives or public utility. In his dissenting opinion in *Golan*, Justice Stephen Breyer registered his discomfort with the URAA's seeming indifference to the traditional Anglo-American utilitarian rationale for copyright: "insofar as [Section 514] suggests that copyright should in general help authors obtain greater monetary rewards than needed to elicit new works, it rests upon primarily European, but not American, copyright concepts."[22] Once copyright law becomes focused on the categorical imperative of rewarding authors for their labor in the commons, the public purpose of that labor and the sociocreative role of the commons itself tend to recede from view. Joyce would have applauded *Golan* and the URAA as concessions to authors' natural rights.

In addition to equitable amends for the wrongs done to foreign authors, the *Golan* majority credited another purpose that Congress had advanced for restoring copyrights: Section 514 "continued the trend," wrote Justice Ginsburg, "toward a harmonized copyright regime by placing foreign works in the position they would have occupied if the current regime had been in effect when those works were created and first published."[23] According to this rationale, the URAA furthers the salutary harmonization of U.S. copyright law both with itself and with the laws of most of the rest of the world. The internationalization of American law was also a primary justification for the Sonny Bono Act, by which Congress purportedly brought U.S. copyright terms into parity with those in other countries by adding twenty years to existing and future copyrights. The Sonny Bono Act came just a few years after a directive, issued by the Council of the European Communities, that mandated the harmonization of copyright terms throughout the European Economic Community, as the European Union (EU) was then called.[24] The directive required European lawmakers to enact legislation adding twenty years to existing and future copyrights and to revive copyrights that had recently expired.

The EU revival of copyrights in the mid-1990s caused many public domain works, including Joyce's major writings, to return to private ownership for the remainder of the period they would have been protected had the newly mandated term—the life of the author plus seventy years—been in effect all along in the European Union. The harmonization directive resembled the URAA in its disturbance of the EU public domains and in its upsetting of the expectations of persons who had come to rely on the free availability of uncopyrighted works. Works by Joyce whose copyrights were revived— namely, all editions that had been published during his lifetime—received roughly fifteen years of additional protection. These works reentered the EU public domains at the end of 2011, seventy years after Joyce's death.

What of the harmony that the URAA and the Sonny Bono Act purportedly orchestrated for America's part in the international symphony of copyright?

Simply put, it is an incomplete harmony, because European and American legislators have sought to harmonize copyrights, not public domains. Typically, once lawmakers secure certain copyright benefits for authors, they rest on their oars. The far side of the copyright moon, the unglimpsed public domain, remains untouched by their radio transmissions. The scattered *maria* and rich profusion of craters—including the craters Daedalus and Icarus—appear to lawmakers as dawnless night, mere deficiency, a privation of form. The public learns to say that copyrights expire; they lapse or fall or pass into the public domain, a dim graveyard that blots the fair acres of authorship. The end of copyright is a fall from grace,[25] or, as Alfred de Vigny imagined it, a fatal plunge "dans le gouffre du domaine public."[26] According to Pamela Samuelson, the "public domain has been, for the most part, an uncharted terrain. Sometimes it seems an undifferentiated blob of unnamed size and dimensions.... The public domain is, moreover, different sizes at different times and in different countries."[27] The disharmony of the world's public domains threatens to impede the global spread of creative works. Lawmakers' deafness to this disharmony should concern us all.

Without exaggeration, it can be said that there is no such thing as the public domain. There are only public domains. The public domain is always local.[28]

Joyce's *Finnegans Wake* illustrates the problem. At the end of 2011, the edition of the work that had been published in 1939 reentered the public domains of the United Kingdom, the Republic of Ireland, and other EU countries. Copyright in that edition had already expired in Canada, Australia, and Switzerland twenty years earlier,[29] but the revival of the Joyce copyrights throughout the EU in the mid-1990s fractured the worldwide market for public domain uses of *Finnegans Wake*. Today, despite the *Wake's* return to the public domains of Europe, that global market remains incomplete because the 1939 edition is still protected in the United States by an estate-held copyright that runs to the end of 2034.[30] This artifact of America's long holdout from international copyright norms not only was not cured, but actually was exacerbated by the Sonny Bono Act. The checkerboard effect created by the failure of lawmakers to harmonize public domains together with copyrights may burden the world market for new *Wake*-based projects for decades to come, even though new editions of the work are beginning to appear.[31]

The picture is even more fragmented when we turn to the large, indispensable archive of Joyce's notes and drafts for *Finnegans Wake*. Many of these materials were published in the multivolume *James Joyce Archive* in the late 1970s. Although the *Archive* has entered the public domains of some countries, the volumes will remain protected by estate-held copyrights, in the United States at least, until the latter half of the twenty-first century.[32] In contrast, Joyce materials that remained unpublished as of the end of 2011— including materials relating to *Ulysses* and *Finnegans Wake* held in collections around the world—at that point entered the public domains of the United States and most EU countries.[33] (They had already passed quietly into the Canadian and Swiss public domains at the end of 1991.) But these materials will remain protected by estate-held copyrights in the United Kingdom until 2039[34] and in Australia possibly longer.[35] Adding to the confusion, the copyright law of the Republic of Ireland is ambiguous about when, or whether, copyrights terminate in unpublished works.[36] In this respect, on the worldwide map of copyright, the label for Ireland currently reads, "Hic sunt leones."

The result of all this is a dinning cacophony of laws, an inconsistent, semiprivate world commons. But the copyright babel does not end there. The same European Council directive that compelled the harmonization of copyright terms contained an additional provision:

> Any person who, after the expiry of copyright protection, for the first time lawfully publishes or lawfully communicates to the public a previously unpublished work, shall benefit from a protection equivalent to the economic rights of the author [for] 25 years from the time when the work was first lawfully published or lawfully communicated to the public.[37]

Countries throughout the EU were required to adopt this provision, which grants twenty-five years of economic copyright protection—that is, copyright without moral rights—to the person who first lawfully publishes or makes available a work that has never before been published and whose copyright has expired. On its face, this would appear to be a finders keepers copyright, an invitation to a Fabergé Easter egg hunt. It was adopted as an incentive for making old works available for the first time and to reward the disseminator's investment and sweat of the brow.[38] Here is copyright revival with a difference. An unpublished work no sooner enters the public domains of the European Union than it is restored to copyright by the first industrious disseminator, not as property of the author's estate, but as a new monopoly vested in the disseminator, a transmigration of sole entitlements after a brief sleep of legal death.

Underlying this post-copyright copyright, it seems to me, is a vision of the public domain as passive, inert, unarable, a barren land that will not be irrigated and planted unless an extravagant bounty is offered, to be funded by a tax on culture consumers. It is similar to the vision of the commons suggested by the majority opinion in *Golan v. Holder*, and it is as ready as the URAA to grant a monopoly reward for absolutely no creativity at all: this resurrectionist's copyright seems to require nothing more than digging and delivery; the deliverer need not add a scintilla of new creative expression to the found object. Yet this twenty-five-year entitlement, acquired with little effort in our age of digital reproduction, recaptures the communicated work for further private ownership, substituting new holders for old—copyright after copyright. These EU after-rights are very different from the compulsory licenses of Ezra Pound's proposed statute, which also encouraged publication of neglected works. Pound's licenses were nonexclusive; they allowed for multiple, competitive editions. The EU rights are proprietary and exclusive.

Joyce's unpublished writings no sooner entered the EU public domains than they became the subject of new copyright controversies. In February 2012, the *Irish Times* reported that Ithys Press, a fine-press startup based in Dublin, had announced the publication of a previously unpublished letter by Joyce, written in 1936 to his young grandson, under the title *The Cats of Copenhagen*.[39] This illustrated volume was offered for sale in editions priced at €1,200 and €300 and was based on the original manuscript letter held in the collections of the Zurich James Joyce Foundation. The foundation promptly complained that it had been left "completely in the dark" about the publication and that "it never permitted, tolerated, condoned or connived in this publication."[40] Responding to these criticisms and others, Ithys Press denounced the "hypocrisy" of what it characterized as a cliquish scholarly elite, and argued that the publication of *The Cats of Copenhagen* was both a service to the public and a lawful act of defiance to institutions that purportedly would step into the Joyce estate's recently vacated shoes and arrogate to themselves a "veto over the exploitation of materials under their care."[41] Ithys Press did not deny that it had published *Cats* without seeking the foundation's permission, or that it was setting itself up as the claimant of a new twenty-five-year EU copyright in the text of Joyce's letter.

Then, in early April 2012, another new entity—The House of Breathings, based in the United States—announced that it was issuing *The Dublin Ulysses Papers*, a six-volume edition of previously unpublished Joyce materials that had been acquired by the National Library of Ireland (NLI) some years before at the cost of millions of euro.[42] The volumes could be had for between €75 and €200 each, the complete set for €800. Danis Rose, the editor of the *Papers*, stated on the House of Breathings website, and repeated in prefaces to the six volumes, that he had taken it upon himself to publish the NLI's papers in order to forestall others who might capture the twenty-five-year EU copyright for themselves and reintroduce "restrictive" practices. To show his good faith, he declared himself a temporary trustee of the new copyrights, which he held for the benefit of "[s]cholars, librarians, and artists," and promised that he would conclude his trusteeship by "mak[ing] over to the Irish State such rights in the Joyce text in the *Ulysses* documents" as he had acquired.[43] Rose had not obtained the permission of the NLI before announcing plans to publish these documents.

A few days after this announcement, the NLI placed in its online catalogue digital files containing images of most of the Joyce manuscripts that had been announced for *The Dublin Ulysses Papers* along with numerous other unpublished Joyce materials from its collections.[44] In doing so, the NLI was accelerating its plans for making the Joyce materials digitally available to the public.[45] Rose promptly responded in the press by charging that the NLI had infringed his "copyright," adding that the NLI, by going forward with its online project, had in effect "rejected" his "proposed gift" of the economic rights.[46] Thus, in the space of a few months, the unpublished Joyce had gone from being copyright-free throughout most of the European Union to being the subject of competing monopoly claims.

These post-copyright copyrights raise as many questions as they answer. What constitutes an act of "publication" or "making available" sufficient to trigger the new right? Does a mere announcement of plans to publish trigger the right? (Irish law, for example, appears to require actual issuance of copies of the work to the public.)[47] Must publication occur within the European Economic Area for the new right to be validly acquired? (British regulations say it must.)[48] How are conflicting claims of priority to be resolved? One reason why a term of years running from the author's death has been so widely adopted as a formula for fixing the length of a copyright is that the publication-plus calculus can lead to disputes over when and whether publication actually occurred. The new copyrights abandon this logic.

Moreover, the question of who owns these copyrights is not settled in all EU jurisdictions. Although the language of the harmonization directive appears to vest the right in the first person to disseminate, French law, for example, provides that the right belongs to the owners ("propriétaires") of the manuscript ("oeuvre") who effectuate the publication or cause the publication to be made ("qui effectuent ou font effectuer la publication").[49] This provision, which reflects French law's solicitude for the moral right of divulgation, vests the right in the owners of original manuscripts. In 1993, a French court held, in a case involving certain unpublished manuscripts of Jules Verne, that the publication right belonged to the city of Nantes, which had acquired the manuscripts from Verne's heirs, not to a biographer who had obtained copies and published their contents without securing the city's permission.[50]

The harmonization directive and various EU domestic laws also provide that, to qualify for this right, publication must be undertaken "lawfully." Because the right applies only to works already in the public domain, "lawfully" can hardly mean, without redundancy or contradiction, "with the consent of the author's estate." Some commentators believe it means "with the consent of the owner of the manuscript."[51] In 2003, a German court ruled that publication by news media of photos of the recently unearthed Bronze Age Nebra Sky Disk, without the consent of the German state that owned the disk, did not affect the state's rights under German copyright law.[52] British regulations are explicit on this point. They state that the new right is invalid if it is based on "an unauthorised act ... done without the consent of the owner of the physical medium in which the work is embodied or on which it is recorded."[53] So, are these after-rights intended for finders or for owners? If for owners, does EU law in effect collapse copyright law's hard-won distinction between tangible property and intangible rights? And is this law the best way to incentivize institutions to make or allow productive use of their holdings?

This sampling of puzzles suggests that the EU harmonization initiative is anything but harmonizing at the level of local implementation. When we step back to view the world copyright map, we see profound disharmonies everywhere: a vast patchwork of laws in which the same work is protected in some countries and unprotected in others; laws that restore a century-old work to copyright in some countries and leave it in the public domain in others. I call this state of affairs a tragedy of the uncoordinated commons—a variation on the concept of the tragedy of the anticommons. An anticommons is the antithesis of a commons. It results from a coordination breakdown in which multiple ownership claims in the same resource cause the resource to be underused. In post-Soviet Moscow, for example, several owners typically enjoyed competing rights in the same commercial storefront, with the result that coordination of rights proved difficult or impossible, and many storefronts remained empty.[54] Whereas a commons is threatened with overuse—too many exploiters of a single unowned resource—an anticommons is threatened with underuse—too many owners of a single proprietary resource.

Scholars of modernism are confronted with something that is not exactly a commons or an anticommons problem, but rather a problem of the uncoordinated global commons. As I have noted, a modernist work may occupy the public domains of some or many countries, but it is often simultaneously protected by copyrights or moral rights in other countries. In still other countries, a work will have entered the public domain for a time and then will have been returned to copyrighted status, with ownership vesting in the author's estate, or in a finder, or in a cultural institution, depending on the governing law and the type of work involved—a situation that, as recent events have shown, can give rise to competing claims in the same work in the same countries. We face the nightmarish possibility of a post-copyright modernism being torn to pieces by multiple claimants. Who, then, will gather the limbs of Osiris?

This tragedy of the uncoordinated commons is nothing new, of course. America's copyright isolationism contributed to the fragmentation of the world commons for well over a century. But global copyright congestion seems all the more perverse and antiquated now that digital technology and the Internet have made it easier than ever to distribute texts and scholarship throughout the world. Always on the verge of fully entering history, modernism is repeatedly held back by laws bent on recapturing the past for private interests. Post-copyright copyrights show how reflexive the proprietary model is for legislators and how unnatural the idea of an unowned resource seems to them. The angel of history might desire to make modernism manifest in its fullness and available to all, but a storm is blowing from the public domain. What lawmakers call progress in the free market is really just a single, ongoing catastrophe: the piling up of proprietary ruins, copyright after copyright.

This book has been about the American public domain, a commons that for a century and a half accelerated the demise of foreign and domestic copyrights and made vast quantities of creativity freely available to publishers, book manufacturers, and readers. The production and consumption of transatlantic modernism in the United States were profoundly dependent on a protectionist copyright law that showed little sensitivity to foreign authors' economic or moral rights. The American public domain invented Samuel Roth as the fulfillment of its legal and economic logics. He was reviled as a rogue disseminator, but he was not, for the most part, a copyright infringer and never needed to be one. Joyce's fundamental complaint, just audible above the clamorous lawsuit he launched against him in 1927, was that Roth was a violator of informal norms of reverence for authors. The Romantic conception of the author that underlies justifications for literary property also underlay Joyce's idea of the public domain. It was a realm that should be governed, he believed, by the prerogatives of genius. At the very least, he felt, the old courtesies observed by nineteenth-century publishers should be revived for protecting his uncopyrighted works. Bennett Cerf, B. W. Huebsch, and others obliged.

I confess that when I think of the American public domain I cannot help but feel nostalgia for a system whose legal default was set for the accessibility of creative resources. This protectionist regime was unfair to foreign authors, and it might well have destroyed or at least diminished their incentives to create, had they not been able to look to their own or other markets for legal protection and financial reward. The American public domain was parasitic, aggressive, and insatiable, but it was also a fervent disseminator, and this is why, at a deep level that might have surprised them both, Roth and Pound were kindred spirits, each insisting on the duty of international communication despite the risk of public opprobrium and legal reprisal. The premature commons also sped the fame of many transatlantic authors, and it gave rise to the sometimes touching chivalry and solidarity of businessmen in the midst of chaotic plenty.

The romance of dissemination is intoxicating. I admit that my affection for the old American public domain and for its product, Roth, increaser of the gaiety of nations, has much to do with the wild, open, lawless quality of the law as it then existed, in contrast to today's rights-cluttered culture. Mine is a guilty pleasure, perhaps, made safe by the remoteness of all the human harm the law inflicted: the American public domain took a financial toll on authors even as it gladdened the purses of publishers and readers. For the same reason, I can understand the welcome that some have given to the EU finders keepers copyright, with its plausible incentives for prompt dissemination, though I believe that the costs to the unstinted public domain and to settled institutional and scholarly practices may outweigh the perceived benefits of these after-rights. The cultural commons ought to be a peaceable kingdom for scholars.

Instead of a unified public domain, we now have an uncoordinated global commons. It is certainly one kind of dystopia, this world of checkerboard monopolies, patchwork freedoms, and after-rights, all presided over by the amorphous, often untested promise of fair use. Those who wish or need to make use of authors' works are confronted with a culture of checkmates and obstacles, ambiguous laws, stubborn estates, and orphan works. In a world of copyright gridlock, one response might be to turn pirate out of sheer frustration with encountering endless No Exit signs. In his dissenting opinion in *Golan*, Justice Breyer worried that the "high administrative costs" of obtaining copyright permissions for older works "will tempt some potential users to 'steal' or 'pirate' works rather than do without."[55] Such a response would be something like the inverse of trade courtesy. Where courtesy encouraged lawful behavior in the absence of legal compulsion, obligatory piracy would be the lawless expression of a desperate need to borrow creativity amid a supersaturation of legal rules.

Throughout this book, I have pondered the uses of courtesy in the American public domain. What forms will courtesy take in the uncoordinated global commons? Will the claimants of new EU copyrights declare and carry out trusteeships on behalf of the public? Will institutions that acquire new copyrights in their holdings use those rights to further the spread of knowledge? When modernist copyrights do expire, as they have sporadically begun to do around the world, will adaptive forms of courtesy spring up among scholars, publishers, and libraries—not the self-interested collusiveness of the publishing houses of the nineteenth century, but modes of tolerance and sharing fitted to the needs of communities? The future of modernism is hard to glimpse through the copyright thickets of the present. Yet we can see just enough to feel certain that our progress will take us through many challenges before we reach the delectable mountains and thence arrive at modernism in the global public domain.

# NOTES

Berg        Henry W. and Albert A. Berg Collection of English and American Literature, New York Public Library
C&P         Joyce v. Roth litigation file, Chadbourne & Parke LLP, New York, NY
CR          Contempo Records, Harry Ransom Center, University of Texas at Austin
EP          Ezra Pound Papers, YCAL MSS 43, Beinecke Library, Yale University
HEJ         Hans E. Jahnke Bequest, Zurich James Joyce Foundation
HKC         Papers of James Joyce from the Harley K. Croessmann Collection, 1/4/MSS 073, Special Collections Research Center, Morris Library, Southern Illinois University Carbondale
HSW         Harriet Shaw Weaver Collection, Catalogue 57345–57352, British Library
JJ          James Joyce Collection, Poetry Collection, University at Buffalo, State University of New York
JJ–PL       James Joyce–Paul Léon Papers, National Library of Ireland, Dublin, Ireland
JMP         John M. Price Manuscripts, Lilly Library, Indiana University
JMW         John Munro Woolsey Papers, Special Collections, Yale Law School
JQ          John Quinn Memorial Collection, Manuscripts and Archives Division, New York Public Library
LRR         Little Review Records, UWM Manuscript Collection 1, Archives Department, University of Wisconsin Milwaukee Libraries
MLE         Morris Leopold Ernst Papers, Manuscript Collection MS-1331, Harry Ransom Center, University of Texas at Austin
NYCC        New York County Clerk archives, New York, NY
NYCLA       New York County Lawyers' Association archives, New York, NY
PC          Private Collection
RE          Richard Ellmann Papers, Collection 1988–012, Department of Special Collections and University Archives, McFarlin Library, University of Tulsa

RF–FGM  Robert Frost–Frederic G. Melcher Collection, Accession Number 13024, Albert and Shirley Small Special Collections Library, University of Virginia

RH  Random House Records, MS #1048, Rare Book and Manuscript Library, Butler Library, Columbia University

S&C  Slocum and Cahoon Material, James Joyce Collection, GEN MSS 112, Beinecke Library, Yale University

SB  Sylvia Beach Papers, Call No. C0108, Department of Rare Books and Special Collections, Manuscripts Division, Princeton University Library

SR  Samuel Roth Papers, MS #1463, Rare Book and Manuscript Library, Butler Library, Columbia University

WB–EP  William Bird–Ezra Pound Papers, YCAL MSS 178, Beinecke Library, Yale University

*Archives and libraries are cited parenthetically, directly after the relevant item. With a few exceptions, citations are to archives or libraries generally but not to specific boxes or folders, partly because of space limitations, partly because it has been my experience that materials move about within archives over the years and that today's pinpoint citation may become tomorrow's misdirection.*

## Court Records

*Joyce v. Roth*   James Joyce v. Samuel Roth and Two Worlds Publishing Co. (N.Y. Sup. Ct. filed 3/14/1927; consent decree signed 12/27/1928 and entered in clerk's office 1/2/1929). The trial court record is maintained offsite as file No. 11814–1927 by the New York County Clerk archives, 31 Chambers Street, Room 703, New York, NY, 10007. Printed copies of the appellate papers are kept at the New York County Lawyers' Association, 14 Vesey Street, Third Floor, New York, NY, 10007; and the Appellate Division Law Library, M. Dolores Denman Courthouse, Fifty East Avenue, Suite 100, Rochester, NY 14604.

## Periodicals and Scholarly Journals

| | |
|---|---|
| AM | *Atlantic Monthly* |
| CJT | *Casanova Jr's Tales: A Quarterly Book for Subscribers* |
| CT-P | *Chicago Tribune (Paris)* |
| FR | *Fortnightly Review* |
| H&H | *Hound and Horn* |
| IT | *Irish Times* |
| JJQ | *James Joyce Quarterly* |
| JSA | *Joyce Studies Annual* |
| LR | *Little Review* |
| MM | *Macmillan's Magazine* |
| NA | *The New Age* |
| NS-L | *The New Statesman (London)* |
| NS-NY | *The New Statesman (New York)* |
| NYEP | *New York Evening Post* |
| NYH-NY | *New York Herald (New York)* |

NYH-P      *New York Herald (Paris)*
NYHTB      *New York Herald Tribune Books*
NYT        *New York Times*
PW         *The Publishers' Weekly*
SRL        *The Saturday Review of Literature*
TC         *The Critic*
TD         *The Dial*
TE         *The Exile*
TF         *The Forum*
TLS        *Times Literary Supplement*
TN         *The Nation*
TQ         *This Quarter*
TWM        *Two Worlds Monthly: Devoted to the Increase of the Gaiety of Nations*
TWQ        *Two Worlds: A Literary Quarterly Devoted to the Increase of the Gaiety of Nations*

*Other periodicals are identified by their full names. Periodical citations without page numbers refer to articles found in clipping files or online databases. Dates are abbreviated in the American style; for example, March 4, 1927, is rendered as 3/4/1927; March 1927, as 3/1927; and March–September 1927, as 3–9/1927.*

## PROLOGUE—GROWING THE AMERICAN PUBLIC DOMAIN

1. Parton, "International Copyright," *AM* 20 (10/1867): 443.
2. Thring to James Joyce, 10/15/1919, in Joyce, *Letters*, 2:454.
3. Ibid.; Joyce to Thring, 9/21/1919, in ibid., 452–53.
4. Pretrial Examination of Defendant, 6/7/1927, papers on appeal, 28–29, *Joyce v. Roth*, NYCLA.
5. Roth to William Stanley Braithwaite, 10/20/1919 (transcription by Adelaide Kugel), SR; Donaldson, *Edwin Arlington Robinson*, 336.
6. A British Order in Council, dated February 3, 1915, extended reciprocal protection to the *unpublished* works of American citizens, but to acquire British copyright in their *published* works, Americans had to publish them first or simultaneously in Britain or in a country that had signed the Berne Convention (Howell, *Copyright Law*, 163–64, 252–53). Despite these requirements, it was still less cumbersome for American citizens to obtain British copyright than for British authors to obtain U.S. copyright, as discussed in chapter 2.
7. Handwritten notes composed by Roth in 1933 for his book *Jews Must Live*, SR.
8. Roth, "Count Me among the Missing" (unpublished memoir), 241, SR.
9. For a wide-ranging exploration of the connotations of *pirate* in Britain and the United States from the seventeenth century on, see Johns, *Piracy*.
10. On the importance of historical context for grasping the nuances of the word *piracy*, see Adrian Johns, "Language, Practice, and History," in Bently, Davis, and Ginsburg, *Copyright and Piracy*, 44–52.
11. "American Book Pirates," *NS-NY* (4/16/1927):10–11; reprinted in Pound, *Poetry and Prose*, 4:383.

12. Pound to H. L. Mencken, 4/27/1927, in Pound, *Selected Letters 1907–1941*, 211.
13. "Lecture on Discoveries and Inventions, Jacksonville, Illinois" (1859), in Lincoln, *Selected Speeches and Writings*, 208 (emphasis in original).
14. Tushnet, "Economies of Desire: Fair Use and Marketplace Assumptions," *William and Mary Law Review* 51 (2009): 513, 546.
15. Ibid. See also Dotan Oliar and Christopher Sprigman, "There's No Free Laugh (Anymore): The Emergence of Intellectual Property Norms and the Transformation of Stand-Up Comedy," *Virginia Law Review* 94 (2008): 1787, 1832.
16. See chapter 3 for a discussion of Romantic authorship as justification for copyright protection.
17. "ABC of Economics" (1933), in Pound, *Selected Prose*, 239.
18. Warwick Gould, "W. B. Yeats on the Road to St Martin's Street, 1900–17," in James, *Macmillan*, 195.
19. See, for example, Neil Weinstock Netanel, "Copyright and a Democratic Civil Society," *Yale Law Journal* 106 (1996): 283, 288.
20. See Rainey, *Institutions of Modernism*.
21. Anderson to Pound, ca. 1953, EP.
22. Conan Doyle's 1894 tour of America and Canada is discussed in Redmond, *Sherlock Holmes among the Pirates*, xvi, 20, 61–62. Lawful piracy enabled Dickens and other authors to provide "complementary goods and services, such as readings and lecture tours" (Khan, *Democratization of Invention*, 274).
23. Transatlantic authors were able to exploit "network effects as piracy increased the scale of readership and encouraged the growth of a mass market in the United States" (ibid.).
24. Roth to Dr. H. K. Croessmann, 5/5/1927, HKC.
25. Hyde, *The Gift*, xix.

## CHAPTER 1. THE AMERICAN PUBLIC DOMAIN AND THE COURTESY OF THE TRADE IN THE NINETEENTH CENTURY

1. "The Author's Best Friend," *NYEP* (9/1/1882); reprinted in *PW*, no. 558 (9/23/1882): 430.
2. Holt, "Competition," *AM* 102 (10/1908): 522–23.
3. These authors are included in Mosher, *A List of Books Issued in Limited Editions*.
4. Bishop, *Thomas Bird Mosher*, 1.
5. Lang, letter to the editors, *TC* 28 (1/18/1896): 48. For a discussion of the Mosher–Lang exchange, see Arthur Sherbo, "On the Ethics of Reprinting: Thomas Mosher vs. Andrew Lang," *The New England Quarterly* 64 (3/1991): 100–112.
6. Mosher, letter to the editors, *TC* 29 (7/11/1896): 30–31.
7. Ibid.
8. *Black's Law Dictionary*, 1391.
9. Mosher, letter to the editors, 30–31.
10. A foreign author could obtain a U.S. copyright only by becoming a resident of the United States or by collaborating with a U.S. citizen or resident in whose name the work could be registered. See Peter Jaszi and Martha Woodmansee, "Copyright in

Transition," in Kaestle and Radway, *Print in Motion*, 94. Khan offers examples of the latter strategy, including Harriet Beecher Stowe's idea of partnering with Elizabeth Gaskell (*Democratization of Invention*, 276–77).

11. Mosher, letter to the editors, 30–31.

12. Ibid.

13. Bishop, *Thomas Bird Mosher*, 1.

14. Ray Nash, "Thomas Bird Mosher: His Life and Work," in Hatch, *Check List of the Publications of Thomas Bird Mosher*, 26. See also Warwick Gould, "Yeats in the States: Piracy, Copyright and the Shaping of the Canon," *Publishing History* 51 (2002): 64.

15. Bishop, *Thomas Bird Mosher*, 110, 163–64, 260–61.

16. The Digital Millennium Copyright Act of 1998, S. Rep. No. 105–190, at 8 (1998).

17. For example, *Andersen v. Atlantic Recording Corp.*, No. 07-CV-934-BR, 2009 WL 3806449, at *1 (D. Or. 11/12/2009), discusses the response of record companies to "the problem of massive piracy of their copyrighted works through P2P systems."

18. On *piracy* as a synonym for *infringement* in the nineteenth century, see Catherine Seville, "Nineteenth-Century Anglo–US Copyright Relations: The Language of Piracy versus the Moral High Ground," in Bently, Davis, and Ginsburg, *Copyright and Piracy*, 24–26.

19. *Sheldon v. Metro-Goldwyn Pictures Corp.*, 81 F.2d 49, 56 (2d Cir. 1936).

20. *Gray v. Russell*, 10 F. Cas. 1035, 1038 (C.C. Mass. 1839).

21. "An American Pirate," *The Academy* 49 (6/6/1896): 470.

22. Ibid.

23. Seville, "Nineteenth-Century Anglo–US Copyright Relations," 19–43. On the rhetoric of piracy in the nineteenth century, see also Everton, *Grand Chorus of Complaint*, 103–4.

24. Act of May 31, 1790, ch. 15, § 5, 1 Stat. 124, 125.

25. McGill, *American Literature and the Culture of Reprinting*, 81.

26. Act of May 31, 1790, ch. 15, § 2, 1 Stat. 124, 124–25.

27. Khan, *Democratization of Invention*, 57–58, 254–55.

28. Act of Feb. 3, 1831, ch. 16, § 8, 4 Stat. 436, 438.

29. Act of July 8, 1870, ch. 230, § 103, 16 Stat. 198, 215.

30. Henry Holt, "The Recoil of Piracy," *TF* 5 (3/1888): 27, 35. Everton notes that reformers' rhetoric often targeted both the publishing trade and "the ethical climate of the law itself" (*Grand Chorus of Complaint*, 104).

31. "Remarks on Copyright before the Committee on Patents, United States Senate, Washington, D.C., January 28–29, 1886"; reprinted in Fatout, *Mark Twain Speaking*, 208.

32. Richards, *Author Hunting*, 88–90.

33. Le Gallienne, "Thomas Bird Mosher: An Appreciation," *TF* 51 (1/1914): 125.

34. Drone, *Treatise on the Law of Property in Intellectual Productions*, 383.

35. S. S. Conant, "International Copyright: An American View," *MM* 40 (6/1879): 159.

36. See Johns, *Piracy*, 296–97.

37. Madison, *Book Publishing in America*, 22.

38. Exman, *Brothers Harper*, 7–8.

39. See Archibald, *Domesticity, Imperialism, and Emigration in the Victorian Novel*, 140.

40. Madison, *Book Publishing in America*, 25.

41. Dickens to Henry Austin, 5/1/1842, in Dickens, *Letters*, 3:230. On Dickens's efforts to influence American opinion on international copyright, and the discursive and cultural contexts of his challenges to American piracy, see Seville, *Internationalisation of Copyright Law*, 165–69; McGill, *American Literature and the Culture of Reprinting*, 109–40.

42. Carlyle to Dickens, 3/26/1842, in Dickens, *Letters*, 3:623.

43. "International Copyright," in Lowell, *Complete Poetical Works*, 433.

44. *Democratic Vistas* (1871), in Whitman, *Democratic Vistas, and Other Papers*, 55.

45. Madison, *Book Publishing in America*, 54.

46. Quoted in ibid., 99–100.

47. Dunlap, *The Fleeting Years* (1937); reprinted in Gross, *Publishers on Publishing*, 271–72.

48. Quoted in Frankel, *Oscar Wilde's Decorated Books*, 43.

49. Ellmann, *Oscar Wilde*, 192.

50. See Gould, "Yeats in the States," 63–67. The claim that Yeats consented to the issuance of *The Land of Heart's Desire* appeared in Mosher's 1903 catalogue (Bishop, *Thomas Bird Mosher*, 185).

51. Gould, "Yeats in the States," 66–67, 77, nn.37–38.

52. "The Author's Best Friend," 430.

53. Dunlap, *Fleeting Years*, 272.

54. Madison, *Book Publishing in America*, 22.

55. McGill, *American Literature and the Culture of Reprinting*, 45–75.

56. Khan, *Democratization of Invention*, 286.

57. Madison, *Book Publishing in America*, 55–56; Tebbel, *Between Covers*, 148; Shove, *Cheap Book Production in the United States*, 43–45, 81–82.

58. "The 'Library Publishers' Combination," *PW*, no. 945 (3/8/1890): 354.

59. Goldstein, *Copyright's Highway*, 149. The 1850 U.S. Census reported a literacy rate of approximately ninety percent among white men and women (Brown, *Word in the World*, 10).

60. Exman, *Brothers Harper*, 40.

61. Saunders, *Authorship and Copyright*, 156.

62. Mott, *Golden Multitudes*, 92–93.

63. Royal Commission, *Copyright Commission*, xxxvi.

64. Ibid., xxxvii.

65. Brander Matthews, "Cheap Books," *The Century Magazine* 35 (12/1887): 328–29. Matthews based his figures on data published annually in *The Publishers' Weekly*.

66. "New Books" (Harper & Brothers advertisement), *TN* 42 (3/18/1886): 1.

67. Matthews, "Cheap Books," 329.

68. Shove, *Cheap Book Production in the United States*, 35–37.

69. Khan discusses the United States as a net importer of culture and the role of book tariffs in encouraging the reprinting of foreign titles ("Intellectual Property and Economic Development," 39–41, 44; *Democratization of Invention*, 16–17, 258–87).

70. Act of May 31, 1790, ch. 15, preamble, 1 Stat. 124, 124.

71. *Id.* §§ 1, 3, at 124–25.

72. *Id.* § 5, at 125.

73. Paul A. Samuelson, "The Pure Theory of Public Expenditure," *The Review of Economics and Statistics* 36 (11/1954): 387.

74. Wendy J. Gordon, "Authors, Publishers, and Public Goods: Trading Gold for Dross," *Loyola of Los Angeles Law Review* 36 (2002): 164.

75. Ibid., 164 n.13.

76. On the "piracy wars" among nineteenth-century American publishers, see Robert L. McLaughlin, "Oppositional Aesthetics/Oppositional Ideologies: A Brief Cultural History of Alternative Publishing in the U.S.," *Critique* 37 (1996): 188–204.

77. Quoted in "'The Evening Post's' Libel Suit," *PW*, no. 1100 (2/25/1893): 360.

78. Holt, "Recoil of Piracy," 28.

79. Ibid.

80. Ibid., 30.

81. Harper Brothers to the *London Times*, 5/12/1879; quoted in Harper, *House of Harper*, 428.

82. *New-York Musical Review and Gazette* 6 (6/16/1855): 197; quoted in Scott E. Casper, "Other Variations on the Trade," in Casper et al., *Industrial Book*, 207–8, 451 n.51.

83. *Sheldon v. Houghton*, 21 F. Cas. 1239, 1241–42 (C.C.S.D.N.Y. 1865).

84. Jeffrey D. Groves, "Courtesy of the Trade," in Casper et al., *Industrial Book*, 141. For an excellent discussion of Irish publishing customs in the eighteenth century, see Johns, *Piracy*, 159–64.

85. John Feather, "The Significance of Copyright History for Publishing History and Historians," in Deazley, Kretschmer, and Bently, *Privilege and Property*, 364–65.

86. Khan, *Democratization of Invention*, 280.

87. Feather, "Significance of Copyright History," 361.

88. W.C., "Book Trade," in *Library of Useful Knowledge*, 182 n.*.

89. George Haven Putnam, "Literary Property," in *Cyclopedia of Political Science, Political Economy, and the Political History of the United States*, 3:410.

90. Pammela Quinn Saunders, "A Sea Change Off the Coast of Maine: Common Pool Resources as Cultural Property," *Emory Law Journal* 60 (2011): 1323–88.

91. See generally Acheson, *Lobster Gangs of Maine* and *Capturing the Commons*.

92. Christopher J. Buccafusco, "On the Legal Consequences of Sauces: Should Thomas Keller's Recipes Be Per Se Copyrightable?" *Cardozo Arts and Entertainment Law Journal* 24 (2007): 1121, 1154–55. Buccafusco summarizes the research of Emmanuelle Fauchart and Eric von Hippel into the norms-based conduct of French chefs.

93. Dotan Oliar and Christopher Sprigman, "There's No Free Laugh (Anymore): The Emergence of Intellectual Property Norms and the Transformation of Stand-Up Comedy," *Virginia Law Review* 94 (2008): 1787–1867.

94. Kal Raustiala and Christopher Sprigman, "The Piracy Paradox: Innovation and Intellectual Property in Fashion Design," *Virginia Law Review* 92 (2006): 1687–1777. See also generally Raustiala and Sprigman, *Knockoff Economy*.

95. Sheehan, *This Was Publishing*, 65. Courtesy principles also underlay the system of exchange newspapers in the 1850s, whereby uncopyrighted (and sometimes copyrighted) material from popular American magazines and newspapers could be

reprinted freely by other American newspapers as long as they credited the author of the material and the original publishing source (Homestead, *American Women Authors and Literary Property*, 154–63).

96. Ellickson, "Law and Economics Discovers Social Norms," *Journal of Legal Studies* 27 (1998): 537, 540.

97. Ibid.

98. Ellickson, "Of Coase and Cattle: Dispute Resolution among Neighbors in Shasta County," *Stanford Law Review* 38 (1986): 623, 627–28. For a full elaboration of the norms employed in Shasta County, see Ellickson, *Order without Law*.

99. See Lisa Bernstein, "Private Commercial Law in the Cotton Industry: Creating Cooperation through Rules, Norms, and Institutions," *Michigan Law Review* 99 (2001): 1724–88; Lisa Bernstein, "Merchant Law in a Merchant Court: Rethinking the Code's Search for Immanent Business Norms," *Pennsylvania Law Review* 144 (1996): 1765–1821; and Barak D. Richman, "How Community Institutions Create Economic Advantage: Jewish Diamond Merchants in New York," *Law and Social Inquiry* 31 (2006): 383–420.

100. Holt, "Competition," 522–23.

101. Johns, *Piracy*, 302.

102. Harper, *House of Harper*, 110–11.

103. Sheehan, *This Was Publishing*, 39.

104. For the labor theory of the origins of property, see Locke, *Two Treatises of Government*, 285–302. See also chapter 3 of the present study.

105. Quoted in "'The Evening Post's' Libel Suit," 360.

106. Sheehan, *This Was Publishing*, 71.

107. Groves, "Courtesy of the Trade," 141.

108. Quoted and discussed in ibid., 143.

109. Harper, *House of Harper*, 111–12.

110. The foregoing sketch of trade courtesy is drawn largely from Holt, "Recoil of Piracy," 29–31. Other useful discussions of trade courtesy include Groves, "Courtesy of the Trade," 139–48; Sheehan, *This Was Publishing*, 61–62; Harper, *House of Harper*, 110–11; Johns, *Piracy*, 295–302; Vaidhyanathan, *Copyrights and Copywrongs*, 52–55; and Everton, *Grand Chorus of Complaint*, 44–47, 125–27.

111. Quoted in "'The Evening Post's' Libel Suit," 360.

112. Groves, "Courtesy of the Trade," 141.

113. Sheehan, *This Was Publishing*, 62.

114. Exman, *Brothers Harper*, 116.

115. Ibid., 264–65.

116. Madison, *Book Publishing in America*, 26.

117. Shove, *Cheap Book Production in the United States*, 119.

118. Quoted in Harper, *House of Harper*, 358.

119. *The New World* 6 (5/6/1843): 552.

120. *Harper's New Monthly Magazine* 11 (6/1855): 119.

121. *The Literary World* 2 (1/1/1872): 1.

122. *The Literary News: A Monthly Journal of Current Literature* 1, n.s. (5/1880): 116.

123. *TC* 2 (12/2/1882): 330.

124. Exman, *Brothers Harper*, 58–59.

125. Putnam, *Memories of a Publisher*, 367.
126. Groves, "Courtesy of the Trade," 146.
127. Sheehan, *This Was Publishing*, 69.
128. Tebbel, *Between Covers*, 89.
129. Gilbert, *House of Holt*, 164, 166.
130. Browning, *Dramatis Personae*, 9.
131. De Quincey, *Confessions of an English Opium-Eater and Suspiria De Profundis*, v. For a discussion of Ticknor & Fields' authorized editions, see Winship, *American Literary Publishing in the Mid-Nineteenth Century*, 138–39.
132. Quoted in Martindell, *Bibliography of the Works of Rudyard Kipling*, 33. For a discussion of Kipling's dealings with his American publishers, see Seville, *Internationalisation of Copyright Law*, 296–99.
133. Quoted in Madison, *Book Publishing in America*, 50.
134. Quoted in Gilbert, *House of Holt*, 31.
135. Quoted and discussed in Madison, *Book Publishing in America*, 98.
136. Quoted and discussed in Tebbel, *Between Covers*, 90.
137. Madison, *Book Publishing in America*, 67–68.
138. *PW*, no. 479 (3/19/1881): 316.
139. *PW*, no. 480 (3/26/1881): 322.
140. *PW*, no. 449 (8/21/1880): 216.
141. "'The Evening Post's' Libel Suit," 360.
142. Ibid., 360–61.
143. Ibid., 361.
144. See Richman, "How Community Institutions Create Economic Advantage," 402–3; Richard A. Posner and Eric B. Rasmusen, "Creating and Enforcing Norms, with Special Reference to Sanctions," *International Review of Law and Economics* 19 (1999): 369, 369–70.
145. Ellickson, "Of Coase and Cattle," 677.
146. On refusal to deal and other informal, norms-based sanctions, see Bernstein, "Private Commercial Law in the Cotton Industry," 1745; Oliar and Sprigman, "There's No Free Laugh (Anymore)," 1815.
147. Quoted in Groves, "Courtesy of the Trade," 142.
148. Madison, *Book Publishing in America*, 53–54.
149. Quoted in Gilbert, *House of Holt*, 33.
150. Sheehan, *This Was Publishing*, 62, 217; Madison, *Book Publishing in America*, 53–54; Lehmann-Haupt, *The Book in America*, 167.
151. Harper Brothers to A. D. F. Randolph, n.d. [1879]; quoted in Harper, *House of Harper*, 447. When the Lovell firm published Taine's *History of English Literature* at $1.50 a copy, Holt immediately lowered the price of its authorized edition to $1.25, rendering both editions unprofitable (Shove, *Cheap Book Production in the United States*, 76).
152. Harper, *House of Harper*, 111–12.
153. Quoted in ibid., 344–45.
154. Groves, "Courtesy of the Trade," 145.
155. Bernstein, "Private Commercial Law in the Cotton Industry," 1777–78.
156. Sheehan, *This Was Publishing*, 67.

157. Lehmann-Haupt, *The Book in America*, 166–67.
158. Harper, *House of Harper*, 110–11; Sheehan, *This Was Publishing*, 65.
159. Sheehan, *This Was Publishing*, 69.
160. Tebbel, *Between Covers*, 89.
161. Sheehan, *This Was Publishing*, 65.
162. Bernstein, "Merchant Law in a Merchant Court," 1787–88.
163. Harper, *House of Harper*, 111–12.
164. Day Otis Kellogg, "Copyright," in *New American Supplement to the Latest Edition of the Encyclopædia Britannica*, 2:914.
165. Holt, "Competition," 523.
166. Quoted in Madison, *Book Publishing in America*, 98–99.
167. Quoted in Groves, "Courtesy of the Trade," 143.
168. Johns, *Piracy*, 296–99.
169. Quoted in Madison, *Book Publishing in America*, 10.
170. Quoted in Groves, "Courtesy of the Trade," 143.
171. *PW*, no. 558 (9/23/1882): 430.
172. Raustiala and Sprigman, "Piracy Paradox," 1759.
173. Harper, *House of Harper*, 114.
174. Groves, "Courtesy of the Trade," 145.
175. Dunlap, *Fleeting Years*, 271–72.
176. Quoted in Harper, *House of Harper*, 393.
177. Shove, *Cheap Book Production in the United States*, 26, 32.
178. Ibid., ix, 6, 50.
179. *NYH-NY* (7/7/1889): 21.
180. Shove, *Cheap Book Production in the United States*, 37–38, 130.
181. Quoted in "Views of New York Publishers, From the N.Y. Tribune, Feb. 14," *PW*, no. 629 (2/16/1884): 202.
182. Holt, *Garrulities of an Octogenarian Editor: With Other Essays Somewhat Biographical and Autobiographical* (1923); reprinted in Gross, *Publishers on Publishing*, 97.
183. Quoted in "'The Evening Post's' Libel Suit," 360.
184. John W. Lovell, "The Canadian Incursion" (letter to the editor), *PW*, no. 379 (4/19/1879): 470.
185. See McGill, *American Literature and the Culture of Reprinting*, 76–108.
186. Tebbel, *Between Covers*, 148.
187. Lovell, "Canadian Incursion," 471.
188. I. K. Funk & Co., "Foreign Authors and 'The Standard Series'" (letter to the editor), *PW*, no. 435 (5/15/1880): 499.
189. Holt, "Recoil of Piracy," 35.
190. The book was *The Mystery of Edwin Drood* (Tebbel, *Between Covers*, 89–90).
191. Tebbel, *Between Covers*, 130–31.
192. Act of July 2, 1890, ch. 647, 26 Stat. 209, codified at 15 U.S.C. §§ 1–2.
193. *United States v. Addyston Pipe and Steel Co.*, 85 F. 271 (6th Cir. 1898).
194. The Sherman Act regulates both interstate and foreign commerce. The extent of the latter jurisdiction was not tested until *American Banana Co. v. United Fruit Co.*, 213 U.S. 347 (1909).
195. Quoted in Sheehan, *This Was Publishing*, 59.
196. Quoted in ibid., 59–60.

197. Madison, *Book Publishing in America,* 225–26, describes how Holt eschewed competition for other houses' authors: "'It is utterly opposed to my habits and old-fashioned sense of dignity of the business, and I am pretty old to learn.'"

198. *Fashion Originators' Guild of America v. FTC,* 312 U.S. 457 (1941). On the Guild's attempt to create informal, quasi-property rights in uncopyrighted fashion designs, see Raustiala and Sprigman, "Piracy Paradox," 1697–98.

199. *Straus v. American Publishers' Ass'n,* 231 U.S. 222 (1913).

200. See Michael Winship, "The Rise of a National Book Trade System in the United States," in Kaestle and Radway, *Print in Motion,* 71. For more comprehensive treatments of the history of literary agency, see Gillies, *The Professional Literary Agent in Britain,* and Hepburn, *The Author's Empty Purse and the Rise of the Literary Agent.*

201. Robert Sterling Yard, *The Publisher* (1913); reprinted in Gross, *Publishers on Publishing,* 80.

202. Gillies, *The Professional Literary Agent in Britain,* 3.

203. Quoted in Sheehan, *This Was Publishing,* 75.

204. Holt, "The Commercialization of Literature," *AM* 95 (11/1905): 583.

205. Ibid., 589–90.

206. For much of the nineteenth century, a non-British author could obtain copyright protection in Britain if (1) publication was made in the United Kingdom, (2) there was no previous publication, and (3) the author was within the British dominions at the time of publication. British authors had to comply with the first two conditions but not the third (Drone, *Treatise on the Law of Property in Intellectual Productions,* 230; see also Nowell-Smith, *International Copyright Law and the Publisher in the Reign of Queen Victoria,* 39–40). As Matthew Arnold pointed out in 1880, American authors could obtain British copyright if they visited England or even Canada at the time their book was published in Britain ("Copyright," *FR* 27 (3/1880): 331). However, Homestead, *American Women Authors and Literary Property,* 5, 218, notes how difficult it was, as a practical matter, for American authors to obtain British copyright protection.

207. For the struggle to obtain U.S. copyright protection for foreign authors, see Feather, *Publishing, Piracy, and Politics,* 158, 167; Saunders, *Authorship and Copyright,* 158–61; Seville, *Internationalisation of Copyright Law,* 160–62.

208. Arnold, "Copyright," 331.

209. Act of Mar. 3, 1891, ch. 565, § 4956, 26 Stat. 1106, 1107–8.

210. For brief discussions of the 1891 act's manufacturing clause, see Jaszi and Woodmansee, "Copyright in Transition," 97, 550–51 n.31; Sheehan, *This Was Publishing,* 35; and Gillies, *The Professional Literary Agent in Britain,* 53, 69–70.

211. Exman, *Brothers Harper,* 117; Johns, *Piracy,* 307; Seville, *Internationalisation of Copyright Law,* 29–30.

212. Harper Brothers to Henry C. Lea, 3/13/1884; quoted in Harper, *House of Harper,* 432.

213. Jaszi and Woodmansee, "Copyright in Transition," 550–51 n.31.

214. Putnam, *Memories of a Publisher,* 384.

215. Ibid., 382.

216. Khan, *Democratization of Invention,* 285. See also McGill, *American Literature and the Culture of Reprinting,* 101–2.

217. Shove, *Cheap Book Production in the United States*, 92.
218. While the Berne Convention of 1886 originally made authors' rights subject to any formalities prescribed by the work's country of origin, the 1908 Berlin amendments specified that "[t]he enjoyment and the exercise of such rights are not subject to any formality" (Berne Convention, 11/13/1908, art. 4(2)).
219. Oliar and Sprigman, "There's No Free Laugh (Anymore)," 1791–92.

## CHAPTER 2. TRANSATLANTIC MODERNISM IN THE AMERICAN PUBLIC DOMAIN

1. *Arguments before the Committees on Patents of the Senate and House of Representatives, Conjointly, on the Bills S. 6330 and H.R. 19853 to Amend and Consolidate the Acts Respecting Copyright*, 59th Cong. (12/7–8/1906 and 12/10–11/1906) (Washington: DC: U.S. Government Printing Office, 1906), 48.
2. Yeats to A. P. Watt, 2/8/1902[?], in Yeats, *Collected Letters (1901–1904)*, 154–55.
3. David Weir, "What Did He Know, and When Did He Know It: The *Little Review*, Joyce, and *Ulysses*," *JJQ* 37 (2000): 394–97.
4. Huebsch to Quinn, 12/22/1920; quoted in Robert Spoo, "Copyright Protectionism and Its Discontents: The Case of James Joyce's *Ulysses* in America," *Yale Law Journal* 108 (1998): 633, 643. Huebsch and Joyce gave separate accounts of their Paris meeting, which probably took place in the fall of 1920. For Joyce's side, see Joyce to Ezra Pound, 11/5/1920, EP; Joyce to Quinn, 11/17/1920; quoted in Reid, *Man from New York*, 451–52.
5. Act of Mar. 4, 1909, ch. 320, § 15, 35 Stat. 1075, 1078–79.
6. Howell, *Copyright Law*, 85.
7. Act of Mar. 4, 1909, ch. 320, § 21, 35 Stat. 1075, 1080, as amended by Act of Dec. 18, 1919, ch. 11, § 21, 41 Stat. 368, 369. Under the original 1909 act, applicants had only thirty days from publication abroad to secure ad interim protection, which lasted for thirty days from the date of deposit. Under the 1919 amendment, the time periods were extended to sixty days and four months, respectively. These changes were deemed necessary to alleviate hardships in the postwar period. Under a later amendment, the time periods were extended further to six months and five years, respectively (Act of June 3, 1949, ch. 171, § 2, 63 Stat. 153, 154).
8. Act of Mar. 4, 1909, ch. 320, § 22, 35 Stat. 1075, 1080. See also *Oxford University Press, N.Y. v. United States*, 33 C.C.P.A. 11, 20 (U.S. Ct. of Customs & Patent Appeals, 1945).
9. Burlingame, *Of Making Many Books*, 163.
10. From the start, the Berne principle of national treatment was predicated on publication of a work in any member country (Berne Convention, 9/9/1886, art. 2(1)).
11. Ladas, *International Protection of Literary and Artistic Property*, 899.
12. Fargnoli, "Oral History: B. W. Huebsch," 195.
13. Melcher to Pound, 9/26/1927, RF–FGM.
14. Quinn to Pound, 10/1/1918, JQ.
15. *Oxford University Press*, 33 C.C.P.A. at 20.
16. Melcher to Pound, 9/26/1927, RF–FGM.

17. See Annette V. Tucker, "The Validity of the Manufacturing Clause of the United States Copyright Code as Challenged by Trade Partners and Copyright Owners," *Vanderbilt Journal of Transnational Law* 18 (1985): 577, 588–89.
18. Pound to Quinn, 3/9/1915, in Pound, *Selected Letters of Ezra Pound to John Quinn*, 22.
19. See, for example, Pound's articles "Tariff and Copyright," *NA* 23 (9/26/1918): 348–49, and "Copyright and Tariff," *NA* 23 (10/3/1918): 363–64; reprinted in Pound, *Poetry and Prose*, 3:190–91, 208–9.
20. "American Book Pirates," *NS-NY* 29 (4/16/1927): 10–11; reprinted in Pound, *Poetry and Prose*, 4:383.
21. 17 U.S.C. § 101 (definition of "fixed").
22. Pound to Quinn, 12/30/1917, in Pound, *Selected Letters of Ezra Pound to John Quinn*, 132.
23. Pound, "American Book Pirates," 4:383.
24. Bennett, *Journal* (entry for 10/27/1909), 342.
25. Frederic G. Melcher to Sylvia Beach, 3/4/1927, SB; Parini, *Robert Frost*, 147, 155–56, 171; Frost, *Poems by Robert Frost*, Introduction.
26. Pound to Quinn, 7/27/1916, in Pound, *Selected Letters of Ezra Pound to John Quinn*, 77.
27. Pound to Quinn, 3/9/1915, in ibid., 21.
28. Wordsworth to the *Kendal Mercury*, 4/12/1838, in Wordsworth, *Prose Works*, 3:312.
29. Pound to John M. Price, 1/12/1927, in Barry S. Alpert, "Ezra Pound, John Price, and *The Exile*," *Paideuma* 2 (1973): 437–39.
30. Pound to Lewis, [summer?] 1951, in Materer, *Letters of Ezra Pound and Wyndham Lewis*, 267.
31. Beach, *Shakespeare and Company*, 179–80.
32. Revnes to Lawrence, 5/21/1920, in Lawrence, *Letters* (Boulton et al., eds.), 3:546 n.1.
33. Aldington to Pound, 8/22/1917, in Gates, *Richard Aldington*, 80–82.
34. Lewis to Pound, 1/15/1926, in Materer, *Letters of Ezra Pound and Wyndham Lewis*, 162.
35. Dennison, *Alternative Literary Publishing*, 180–81.
36. Ripp, "Middle America Meets Middle-Earth," 25–33.
37. Laughlin to Leonard Doob, 6/8/1981, PC.
38. Repeal of the manufacturing clause, originally set for July 1, 1982, as provided by the 1976 act (Act of Oct. 19, 1976, Pub. L. No. 94–553, § 601(a), 90 Stat. 2541, 2588), was postponed to July 1, 1986, by congressional amendment (Act of July 13, 1982, Pub. L. No. 97–215, 96 Stat. 178, 178; current version at 17 U.S.C. § 601(a)).
39. "The Exile," *TE*, no. 1 (Spring 1927): 88–92.
40. Pound to Price, 11/30/1926, in Alpert, "Ezra Pound, John Price, and *The Exile*," 435. For accounts of *The Exile*, see ibid., 427–48; Craig Monk, "The Price of Publishing Modernism: Ezra Pound and *The Exile* in America," *Canadian Review of American Studies* 31 (2001): 429–46; and Carpenter, *Serious Character*, 458–60.
41. Pound to Quinn, 3/9/1915, in Pound, *Selected Letters of Ezra Pound to John Quinn*, 21.
42. Pound to Price, 12/2/1926, JMP.

43. Price to Pound, 12/27/1926, EP (carbon copy in JMP).

44. Pound to Price, 1/12/1927, in Alpert, "Ezra Pound, John Price, and *The Exile*," 437.

45. Price to Pound, 12/27/1926, EP (carbon copy in JMP).

46. William Brown, assistant register of copyrights, to Price, 3/2/1927 and 4/7/1927, JMP.

47. Pound to Price, 3/14/1927, JMP.

48. Act of Mar. 4, 1909, ch. 320, § 9, 35 Stat. 1075, 1077.

49. *Id.* § 18, at 1079.

50. *Roy Export Co. v. Columbia Broadcasting System*, 672 F.2d 1095, 1101–2 (2d. Cir. 1982).

51. *United Thrift Plan, Inc. v. National Thrift Plan, Inc.*, 34 F.2d 300, 301 (E.D.N.Y. 1929).

52. *Haas v. Leo Feist, Inc.*, 234 F. 105, 110–11 (S.D.N.Y. 1916).

53. *LR* 6 (5/1919): 1.

54. Quinn to Anderson, 6/30/1919, LRR.

55. *LR* 4 (5/1917).

56. Ibid., 7–11.

57. *TWM* 1 (8/1926): 189–92.

58. In an unpublished letter to Sylvia Beach, dated December 15, 1926, T. S. Eliot stated that he had been unaware that Roth was intending to publish any of his writings, PC.

59. Act of Mar. 4, 1909, ch. 320, § 23, 35 Stat. 1075, 1080.

60. *Russell v. Price*, 612 F.2d 1123 (9th Cir. 1979).

61. Debra L. Quentel, "'Bad Artists Copy, Good Artists Steal': The Ugly Conflict between Copyright Law and Appropriationism," *UCLA Entertainment Law Review* 4 (1996): 39, 47 n.46.

62. *Dastar Corp. v. Twentieth Century Fox Film Corp.*, 539 U.S. 23 (2003).

63. James J. Guinan, Jr., "Duration of Copyright, Appendices A and B," *Copyright Law Revision Study No. 30* (1957); reprinted in *Studies on Copyright*, 473.

64. Roth to James B. Boxley, head, Reference Search Section, U.S. Copyright Office, 4/29/1964, SR.

65. U.S. Copyright Office to Roth, 9/26/1966, SR.

66. Quoted in an undated typescript by Adelaide Kugel, "Joyce—for Article on FW," SR.

67. Overton, *Portrait of a Publisher*, 22.

68. Van Dyke, *National Sin of Literary Piracy*, 5.

69. Sandburg to John M. Price, 7/31/1926, JMP.

70. A. D. Peters, "Mr Roth of New York" (letter to the editor), *NS-L* 28 (3/26/1927): 731.

71. Quinn to Huebsch, 10/30/1917; quoted in Fargnoli, "Oral History: B. W. Huebsch," 213.

72. Quinn to Margaret Anderson, 6/30/1919, LRR. Quinn respected Mosher, however, and corresponded with him frequently before World War I; their letters are preserved in JQ.

73. Pound to Quinn, 2/22/1918, in Pound, *Selected Letters of Ezra Pound to John Quinn*, 143.

74. Fargnoli, "Oral History: B. W. Huebsch," 213.

75. Pound to Homer Pound, 9/2/1927, in Pound, *Ezra Pound to His Parents*, 494.

76. Cerf, *At Random*, 63.

77. Ibid., 95–96.
78. See, for example, Warwick Gould, "Yeats in the States: Piracy, Copyright, and the Shaping of the Canon," *Publishing History* 51 (2002): 64.
79. Quinn to B. W. Huebsch, 11/7/1918; quoted in Fargnoli, "Oral History: B. W. Huebsch," 214.
80. Khan, "Intellectual Property and Economic Development," 42–44.
81. Huebsch, "Cross-Fertilization in Letters," *The American Scholar* (Summer 1942); reprinted in Gross, *Publishers on Publishing*, 299.
82. Shaw, "Preface: Novels of My Nonage," in Shaw, *Cashel Byron's Profession*, xiii–xiv.
83. *TN* 108 (1919): 7.
84. Quinn to Joyce, 6/26/1919, JQ.
85. Beach, *Shakespeare and Company*, 179.
86. Slocum and Cahoon, *Bibliography of James Joyce*, 37–38. See also generally Barnes, Brockman, and Herbert, *James Joyce Bibliography*.
87. See Beach, *Shakespeare and Company*, 182; Fitch, *Sylvia Beach and the Lost Generation*, 315.
88. Barnes, Brockman, and Herbert are therefore mistaken in suggesting that Beach "succeeded in acquiring copyright" for *Pomes Penyeach* by registering a claim with the Copyright Office for the Princeton University Press edition (*James Joyce Bibliography*, n.p. and n.28). A registered claim of copyright is not the same thing as a proven copyright.
89. Unpublished draft version of Sylvia Beach's *Shakespeare and Company*, n.p., SB.
90. Ibid.
91. Roberts and Poplawski, *Bibliography of D. H. Lawrence*, 21. See also Lawrence, *Sons and Lovers*, lix–lxiii.
92. *Sons and Lovers*, lx. The Copyright Office awarded registration number A 357052 to Kennerley's edition (Library of Congress, Copyright Office, *Catalogue of Copyright Entries*, n.s., vol. 12, pt. 1, grp. 1 (Washington, DC: U.S. Government Printing Office, 1915), 254).
93. Lawrence to Thomas Seltzer, 5/24/1923, in Lawrence, *Letters* (Boulton et al., eds.), 4:446.
94. Lawrence to Marian and Aldous Huxley, 12/10/1928, in Lawrence, *Selected Letters*, 420.
95. Ibid.
96. Lawrence to Lady Ottoline Morrell, 4/3/1929, in ibid., 441.
97. Lawrence to Speiser & Speiser, 5/26/1929, in Lawrence, *Letters* (Huxley, ed.), 812–13.
98. Roberts and Poplawski, *Bibliography of D. H. Lawrence*, 749–50, 753.
99. Frieda Lawrence to Edward Titus, 7/15/1931 and 9/2/1931, in Moore and Montague, *Frieda Lawrence and Her Circle*, 33–34. On Roth's claim that he attempted to obtain D. H. Lawrence's permission, see Adelaide Kugel, "Joyce—for Article on FW," undated typescript, SR. For a bibliographic analysis of Roth's editions, see Jay A. Gertzman, "The Piracies of 'Lady Chatterley's Lover': 1928–1950," *D. H. Lawrence Review* 19 (1987): 267–300.
100. Roberts and Poplawski, *Bibliography of D. H. Lawrence*, 750.

101. For example, in discussing Joyce's *Ulysses*, Dennison asserts, without qualification, that "United States law forbids the copyright of an obscene work" (*Alternative Literary Publishing*, 196).
102. In *Hoffman v. Le Traunik*, 209 F. 375, 379 (N.D.N.Y. 1913), the court stated that to be entitled to copyright, a work must be "free from illegality or immorality." On the more relaxed judicial attitude that was in evidence by the 1920s, see Howell, *Copyright Law*, 43–44.
103. Under its rule of doubt, the Copyright Office "will register a claim if some reasonable doubt exists as to the ruling a court would make on validity of the copyright" (Dorothy M. Schrader, "Ad Interim Copyright and the Manufacturing Clause: Another View of the *Candy* Case," *Villanova Law Review* 16 (1970): 215, 218 n.10).
104. The terms *sex pulp* and *gallantiana* designate a range of erotic, salacious, or scatological materials on the borderline of overt pornography. Their avoidance of explicitness did not spare them from the scrutiny of purity societies and legal authorities (Gertzman, *Bookleggers and Smuthounds*, 62–73).
105. Roth's extant correspondence with the U.S. Copyright Office is found in SR.
106. Jay Gertzman ascertained that these titles had been registered with the U.S. Copyright Office ("A Preliminary Checklist of Samuel Roth's Imprints, 1920–40," found at http://home.earthlink.net/~jgertzma/booksite/chk2040.htm (last viewed 12/12/2012)). See also Library of Congress, Copyright Office, *Catalogue of Copyright Entries*, n.s., vol. 28, pt. 1, grp. 1 (Washington, DC: U.S. Government Printing Office, 1932), 2937, 4062, 6161, 6173, 11214.
107. Roth, *Stone Walls Do Not*, 105–6.
108. *CJT* 1 (4/1926): 17–47.
109. For the role of the private edition in this period, see Rainey, *Institutions of Modernism*, 47–49.
110. Beasley to James Joyce, 12/11/1926, SB.
111. *TWQ* 1 (12/1925): 111–14.
112. *TWM* 1 (9/1926): 255–60.
113. *TWM* 1 (10/1926): 408–14.
114. *TWQ* 1 (9/1925): 45–54 (Joyce); *TWM* 1 (9/1926): 299–317 (Lawrence); *TWM* 2 (1/1927): 143–46 (Eliot); *TWM* 3 (5–6/1927): 149–52 (Eliot).
115. *TWM* 1 (9/1926): 290 (Synge); *TWM* 1 (10/1926): 388, 389–95, 398, 472 (Synge, Powys, Davies); *TWM* 2 (12/1926): 44, 45–47 (Synge, Galsworthy).
116. *TWM* 1 (7/1926): 6. Amanda Sigler discussed Roth's strategies of free expression in her talk "Joyce's Magazine Scandals," presented at the Zurich James Joyce Foundation in March 2011.
117. Smithers to Elisabeth Marbury, 1/12/1898; quoted in Mason, *Bibliography of Oscar Wilde*, 415.
118. Nelson, *Publisher to the Decadents*, 199–200. See also Mason, *Bibliography of Oscar Wilde*, 408–9.
119. Nelson points out that, some weeks after the English edition appeared, Wilde's *Ballad* was printed and registered for copyright in the United States (*Publisher to the Decadents*, 208, 389 n.121). This would, at best, have secured copyright in the American edition and left the English edition in the American public domain.

120. Richard J. Finneran, "Yeats and Copyright," paper presented at the 1998 Modern Language Association Conference in San Francisco; Mary Ann Gillies, "Exploitation of Copyright Laws and the Construction of Modernism," paper presented at the 1999 Modernist Studies Association Conference at Penn State University.

121. Warwick Gould, "Yeats in the States," 63. See also Gould, "W. B. Yeats on the Road to St Martin's Street, 1900–17," in James, *Macmillan*, 192–217.

122. Quinn to Yeats, 9/27/1902, in Quinn, *Letters of John Quinn to William Butler Yeats*, 40.

123. Ibid., 2, 13, 39–42, 114, 117, 119; Yeats to Quinn, 10/2/[1903], in Yeats, *Collected Letters (1901–1904)*, 437 and n.13.

124. Quinn to Yeats, 3/21/1905, in Quinn, *Letters of John Quinn to William Butler Yeats*, 70.

125. Quinn to Pound, 7/14/1916, JQ.

126. Pound to Quinn, 7/27/1916, in Pound, *Selected Letters of Ezra Pound to John Quinn*, 77.

127. Pound to Watson, 6/18/1923, in Sutton, *Pound, Thayer, Watson, and The Dial*, 278–79.

128. Pound to Gratia Sharp, 11/30/1927, in ibid., 328–29.

129. Richard Taylor, "Towards a Textual Biography of *The Cantos*," in Willison, Gould, and Chernaik, *Modernist Writers and the Marketplace*, 224.

130. Pound to Eliot, 2/11/1934; quoted in ibid., 225.

131. Eliot to Brace, 12/17/1935, PC.

132. *Night and Day* was published in London on October 23, 1919, according to the *Catalogue of Copyright Entries*, n.s., vol. 17, pt. 1, grp. 1 (Washington, DC: U.S. Government Printing Office, 1920), 816. The same entry indicates that the Doran edition appeared on September 29, 1920, and that Doran registered a copyright claim for that revised text. In November 1919, when Doran first contacted Woolf, the 1909 Copyright Act required foreign editions to be deposited for ad interim protection no later than thirty days after publication abroad. The act was not amended to permit a sixty-day deposit period until December 18, 1919—too late to be of any help to *Night and Day*.

133. Woolf to Strachey, 11/26/1919, in Woolf, *Letters*, 2:401.

134. Briggs, *Virginia Woolf*, 28.

135. Ibid., 25.

136. Quoted in Gilbert, *House of Holt*, 33.

137. Quoted in ibid.

138. See Mason, *Bibliography of Oscar Wilde*, 249–81; Wilde, *Selected Letters*, 36 n.1.

139. Quinn to Huebsch, 10/27/1917 and 11/7/1917; quoted in Fargnoli, "Oral History: B. W. Huebsch," 211, 214.

140. Joyce to Harriet Shaw Weaver, 7/29/1918, in Joyce, *Letters*, 1:115–16.

141. Huebsch to Lawrence, 8/11/1919, in Lawrence, *Letters* (Boulton et al., eds.), 3:546 n.1.

142. Lawrence to Secker, 8/23/1919, in ibid., 3:386.

143. Huebsch to Lawrence, 8/11/1919, in ibid., 3:385 n.2.

144. "Poetry of the Present" appeared in *Playboy*, nos. 4 and 5 (1919). Arens described his magazine as "radically modern" in McCourtie, *Where and How to Sell Manuscripts*, 33.

145. Yeats to Marianne Moore, 4/25/1926, in Yeats, *Collected Letters*, elec. ed. (http://www.nlx.com/collections/130).

146. Pound to Quinn, 7/27/1916, in Pound, *Selected Letters of Ezra Pound to John Quinn*, 77–78.

147. Pound to Quinn, 2/22/1918, in ibid., 143–44.

148. Quinn to Pound, 7/14/1916, JQ.

149. Quinn to Huebsch, 10/30/1917; quoted in Fargnoli, "Oral History: B. W. Huebsch," 213.

150. Act of Mar. 4, 1909, ch. 320, § 3, 35 Stat. 1075, 1076.

151. Pound to Anderson, 2/26/1917, in Pound, *Letters of Ezra Pound to Margaret Anderson*, 9–10.

152. Pound to Quinn, 11/4/1918, in Pound, *Selected Letters of Ezra Pound to John Quinn*, 164.

153. Ibid., 162.

154. Pound to Scofield Thayer, 12/22/1920, in Sutton, *Pound, Thayer, Watson, and* The Dial, 191.

155. Pound to Price, 1/22/1927, JMP.

156. See, for example, *Morse v. Fields*, 127 F. Supp. 63, 64–65 (S.D.N.Y. 1954); *Quinn-Brown Publishing Corp. v. Chilton Co.*, 15 F. Supp. 213, 214 (S.D.N.Y. 1936).

157. The consequences for magazine publication of copyright indivisibility and faulty notice are discussed in *New York Times Co. v. Tasini*, 533 U.S. 483, 494–96 (2001). See also Alfred H. Wasserstrom, "The Copyrighting of Contributions to Composite Works: Some Attendant Problems," *Notre Dame Lawyer* 31 (1956): 381–13.

158. *Mifflin v. R. H. White Co.*, 190 U.S. 260, 264 (1903).

159. Act of Mar. 4, 1909, ch. 320, § 3, 35 Stat. 1075, 1076. *Mail & Express Co. v. Life Publishing Co.*, 192 F. 899, 900 (2d Cir. 1912), reaffirmed that "when a periodical contains articles or pictures made by persons who have not transferred their rights to the publisher the copyright of the periodical does not cover them." For applications of this principle, see *Egner v. E.C. Schirmer Music Co.*, 139 F.2d 398, 399 (1st Cir. 1943), and *Kaplan v. Fox Film Corp.*, 19 F. Supp. 780, 781 (S.D.N.Y. 1937).

160. See *Harper & Bros. v. M.A. Donohue & Co.*, 144 F. 491 (C.C.N.D. Ill. 1905): "if the magazine copyright had been in the name of Holmes [in the *Mifflin* case], the publication of the final chapters would have been protected, but, because the whole work was published serially without any lawful copyright notice whatever, the right to exclusive publication was lost." See also *Goodis v. United Artists Television, Inc.*, 425 F.2d 397, 403 (2d Cir. 1970).

161. *Bisel v. Ladner*, 1 F.2d 436, 436–37 (3d Cir. 1924); *Maurel v. Smith*, 271 F. 211, 215–16 (2d Cir. 1921); *Cohan v. Richmond*, 19 F. Supp. 771, 773 (S.D.N.Y. 1937); *Quinn-Brown*, 15 F. Supp. at 214.

162. *Bisel*, 1 F.2d at 436.

163. *Goodis*, 425 F.2d at 399, 403.

164. *Id.* at 400.

165. Pound to Quinn, 7/27/1916, in Pound, *Selected Letters of Ezra Pound to John Quinn*, 77–78.

166. Quinn to Pound, 7/14/1916, JQ.

167. Pound to Gratia Sharp, 11/30/1927, in Sutton, *Pound, Thayer, Watson, and* The Dial, 328–29.

168. A separate notice was included for one other author, Josef Bard ("Aurea Mediocritas," *TD* 84 (3/1928): 181).

169. *TD* 85 (11/1928): 395.

170. *LR* 5 (1/1919): 1.

171. Wilde to Smithers, 11/19/1897, in Wilde, *Selected Letters*, 318 (emphasis in original).

172. *Carte v. Duff*, 25 F. 183, 186 (C.C.S.D.N.Y. 1885).

173. Quinn, *Letters of John Quinn to William Butler Yeats*, 9, 62–63.

174. Quinn to Yeats, 2/24/1905, in ibid., 66–67.

175. Ibid., 13.

176. Quinn to Yeats, 6/10/1908, in ibid., 119.

177. The steps taken by Joyce's lawyers are summarized in a letter from Chadbourne, Stanchfield & Levy to Joyce, 4/24/1928, JJ. Fitch mischaracterizes these steps in *Sylvia Beach and the Lost Generation*, 269.

178. Joyce to Harriet Shaw Weaver, 9/20/1928, in Joyce, *Letters*, 1:266–67.

179. Slocum and Cahoon, *Bibliography of James Joyce*, 42–43, 46, 47, 50–51. Prior to engaging attorneys to arrange for special copyright editions, Joyce had had another extract, *Work in Progress Volume I*, printed in a special copyright edition of twenty copies by Donald Friede of New York (ibid., 41–42).

180. Joyce to Benjamin Howe Conner, 12/18/1931 (draft), JJ–PL.

181. Invoices for legal work are found in letters to Joyce from Benjamin Howe Conner, 6/5/1930 and 12/23/1932, JJ–PL.

182. Some courts held that the deposit of copies in the Copyright Office was sufficient to establish legal publication (*Cardinal Film Corp. v. Beck*, 248 F. 368 (S.D.N.Y. 1918) (Augustus N. Hand, J.)), while other courts took the opposite view (*Joe Mittenthal, Inc. v. Irving Berlin, Inc.*, 291 F. 714 (S.D.N.Y. 1923) (Learned Hand, J.)). The Copyright Office, however, was unequivocal: "Deposit in the Copyright Office for registration will not be deemed to constitute publication" (*Compendium of Copyright Office Practices (as of July 1, 1970)* (Washington, DC: Copyright Office, Library of Congress, 1970), 3–5; see also Howell, *Copyright Law*, 58–59). Moreover, the plain language of Section 12 of the 1909 act indicated that copyright-securing publication had to take place *outside* of the Copyright Office and *before* any deposit of copies (Act of Mar. 4, 1909, ch. 320, § 12, 35 Stat. 1075, 1078).

183. Pound to Price, 1/20/1927, in Alpert, "Ezra Pound, John Price, and *The Exile*," 439–40.

184. Price to Pound, 2/9/1927, JMP.

185. Gallup, *Ezra Pound*, 271.

186. Price to William Brown, 2/24/1927, JMP.

187. Brown to Price, 3/2/1927, JMP.

188. Pound to Price, 3/14/1927, JMP.

189. Price to Brown, 3/3/1927, JMP.

190. Brown to Price, 4/7/1927, JMP.

191. Gallup, *Ezra Pound*, 271–72.

192. Jeffrey D. Groves, "Courtesy of the Trade," in Casper et al., *Industrial Book*, 147–48. For a similar analysis, see Ellen Gruber Garvey, "Ambivalent Advertising: Books, Prestige, and the Circulation of Publicity," in Kaestle and Radway, *Print in Motion*, 175.

193. Gilbert, *House of Holt*, 3, 18.

194. Ibid., 36–39.

195. West, *American Authors and the Literary Marketplace since 1900*, 23–24.

196. Cerf, *At Random*, 57.

197. Around 1925, Liveright himself extended trade courtesy to the British author Norman Douglas, whose *South Wind* (1917) had long been a public domain text in the United States. Liveright sought Douglas's permission and offered him royalties for including the novel in the Modern Library series, though he discourteously ignored the prior associational claim of Dodd, Mead & Co., Douglas's authorized American publisher (Dardis, *Firebrand*, 225–27).

198. Yeats to A. P. Watt, 4/18/1922, in Yeats, *Collected Letters*, elec. ed.

199. Quoted in Nelson, *Elkin Mathews*, 128.

200. Huebsch to Cornhill Co., 11/9/1917; quoted in Fargnoli, "Oral History: B. W. Huebsch," 214.

201. Huebsch to Quinn, 11/9/1917; quoted in ibid.

202. The Boston volume was reviewed in *The Nation* for October 26, 1918. Huebsch's letter to the editors was dated October 30 of that year (*TN* 108 (1919): 7).

203. Roberts and Poplawski, *Bibliography of D. H. Lawrence*, 140–41.

204. Ibid., 21.

205. Slocum and Cahoon, *Bibliography of James Joyce*, 5–24. Because Joyce's *Exiles* was a play, or what the 1909 act called a "dramatic composition," it was not subject to the requirements of the manufacturing clause (Act of Mar. 4, 1909, ch. 320, §§ 5(d), 15, 35 Stat. 1075, 1076, 1078; see also Howell, *Copyright Law*, 86–87). For that work, Joyce would not have had to comply with the strict time periods imposed by the ad interim and manufacturing provisions, though Quinn may have been unaware of this.

206. Reynolds, *Fiction Factory*, 29–30.

207. Melcher, "Is Publishing a Profession?" *PW* (12/5/1942); reprinted in Gross, *Publishers on Publishing*, 146.

208. Melcher to Beach, 3/4/1927, SB.

209. Bennett, "U.S. Piracy of 'Ulysses,'" *Sunday Express* (London) (photocopied clipping), 3/27/1927, SR.

210. *SRL* 3 (3/5/1927): 630.

211. Burlingame, *Of Making Many Books*, 163.

212. Tolkien, *Fellowship of the Ring*.

213. Tolkien to Michael George Tolkien, 10/30/1965, in Tolkien, *Letters of J. R R. Tolkien*, 364. Tolkien's campaign against unauthorized publication of his writings in America is discussed in Ripp, "Middle America Meets Middle-Earth," 35–42.

214. Pound to Price, 4/16/1927, in Alpert, "Ezra Pound, John Price, and *The Exile*," 443.

CHAPTER 3. EZRA POUND'S COPYRIGHT STATUTE:
PERPETUAL RIGHTS AND UNFAIR COMPETITION
WITH THE DEAD

1. Quinn to Beach, 2/4–6/1922, JJ.
2. Pound to Homer Pound, 11/1/1927, in Pound, *Ezra Pound to His Parents*, 497.
3. The phrase "limited Times" is used in the U.S. Constitution, art. I, § 8, to admonish that U.S. copyrights and patents may not be granted for indefinite periods.
4. Statement of Congresswoman Mary Bono in support of the Sonny Bono Copyright Term Extension Act, 105th Cong., 2d sess., *Congressional Record* 144 (10/7/1998): H 9951–52.
5. Testimony of Professor Peter Jaszi, "The Copyright Term Extension Act of 1995: Hearings on S483 before the Senate Judiciary Committee," 104th Cong., 1st sess. (9/20/1995); available in 1995 WL 10524355, at *6. See also Jaszi, "Caught in the Net of Copyright," *Oregon Law Review* 75 (1998): 299, 303.
6. Carol M. Rose, "Canons of Property Talk, or, Blackstone's Anxiety," *Yale Law Journal* 108 (1998): 601–32. Saint-Amour has catalogued the "memento mori rhetoric" used by proponents of copyright term extension (*Copywrights*, 121–58).
7. Pound to Flint, ca. 5/1912 (draft), EP.
8. Ibid.
9. "Pound for President?" (letter to the editor), *TN* 125 (12/14/1927): 685; reprinted in Pound, *Poetry and Prose*, 4:393.
10. Ibid.
11. See Act of Mar. 4, 1909, ch. 320, § 31, 35 Stat, 1075, 1082–83 (prohibiting importation of certain works not manufactured on American soil), § 32 (seizure and forfeiture), § 33 (empowering the secretary of the treasury and the postmaster general to make and enforce regulations to prevent importation of such works through the U.S. mails).
12. *Booklegging* was a term used to refer to literary piracy and the trade in pornography (Gertzman, *Bookleggers and Smuthounds*, 15, 87).
13. U.S. legislation has been proposed that would mitigate the problem of orphan works. See, for example, Orphan Works Act of 2008, HR 5889, 110th Cong. (2008).
14. Pound to John Quinn, 11/4/1918, in Pound, *Selected Letters of Ezra Pound to John Quinn*, 163. Pound mistakenly referred to John Russell and/or Charles Edward Russell as "George Russel," and to the Committee on Public Information as the "Department of Public Information." On the Committee work of Paul Perry and the Russells, see Creel, *How We Advertised America*, 248, 298; and Mock and Larson, *Words That Won the War*, 296.
15. "Tariff and Copyright," *NA* 23 (9/26/1918): 348; reprinted in Pound, *Poetry and Prose*, 3:190.
16. Pound to Quinn, 9/1/1918, JQ.
17. Pound to Quinn, 9/12/1918, JQ.
18. For details of Pershing's victory, see Zieger, *America's Great War*, 99; Stokesbury, *Short History of World War I*, 286–87.
19. See "A Shake Down," *LR* 4 (8/1918): 9, 11; reprinted in Pound, *Poetry and Prose*, 3:147: "As Armageddon has only too clearly shown, national qualities are the great gods of the present."
20. *Hugh Selwyn Mauberley (Contacts and Life)* (1920), in Pound, *Personae*, 188.

21. "Copyright and Tariff," *NA* 23 (10/3/1918): 363; reprinted in Pound, *Poetry and Prose*, 3:208.

22. Ibid.

23. Ibid., 3:208–9.

24. "Tariff and Copyright," 3:190.

25. Ibid.

26. Atkin, *War of Individuals*, 79.

27. "In Explanation," *LR* 4 (1918): 5; reprinted in Pound, *Poetry and Prose*, 3:143.

28. Ibid., 3:143–44. See also Katz, *American Modernism's Expatriate Scene*, 53–70.

29. "In Explanation," 3:145.

30. Henry James probed American book piracy and cultural tariffs in a witty colloquy, "An Animated Conversation" (1889) (*Essays in London and Elsewhere*, 280–85).

31. "Tariff and Copyright," 3:190.

32. For a concise treatment of Pound's interest in international copyright and efforts to amend U.S. law, see Walkiewicz and Witemeyer, *Ezra Pound and Senator Bronson Cutting*, 28–29.

33. See, for example, Thomas Hood, "Copyright and Copywrong, Letter II," in Hood, *Prose and Verse*, 84.

34. Pound to Quinn, 9/7/1918, JQ.

35. "Copyright and Tariff," 3:208.

36. Pound to Quinn, 8/10–11/1918, in Pound, *Selected Letters of Ezra Pound to John Quinn*, 157.

37. See Susan Eilenberg, "Mortal Pages: Wordsworth and the Reform of Copyright," *English Literary History* 56 (1989): 351–74; and Catherine Seville, "Authors as Copyright Campaigners: Mark Twain's Legacy," *Journal of the Copyright Society U.S.A.* 55 (2008): 283–359.

38. "Copyright and Tariff," 3:208.

39. Pound to Joyce, 12/25/1926, in Pound, *Letters of Ezra Pound to James Joyce*, 226.

40. "The Exile," *TE* 3 (1928): 102; reprinted in Pound, *Poetry and Prose*, 5:17; "Ezra Pound and Will Irwin Denounce Copyright and Boston Censorship," *CT-P* (3/9/1928): 2, in ibid., 5:27; "Das Schone Papier Vergeudet," *LR* 3 (1916): 16–17, in ibid., 2:181; "Newspapers, History, Etc.," *H&H* 3 (1930): 574, in ibid., 5:229.

41. S. S. Conant, "International Copyright: An American View," *MM* 40 (6/1879): 156.

42. "Things to Be Done," *Poetry* 9 (1917): 312–14; reprinted in Pound, *Poetry and Prose*, 2:190.

43. Saunders, *Authorship and Copyright*, 156.

44. For other criticisms of the American book tariff and copyright law, see Putnam, *Memories of a Publisher*, 382; "President's Address, The Tax on Ideas," *Bulletin of the American Library Association* 8 (1–11/1914) (Chicago: American Library Association, 1914), 75; de Bekker, *The Serio-Comic Profession*, 119–24.

45. Pound to Anderson, 1/26/1917, in Pound, *Letters of Ezra Pound to Margaret Anderson*, 9–10.

46. "A Letter from London," *LR* 3 (1916): 7–8; reprinted in Pound, *Poetry and Prose*, 2:150.

47. "Things to Be Done," 2:190.

48. "Copyright and Tariff," 3:208. The quoted phrase in the heading of this subsection comes from Pound to Quinn, 9/12/1918, JQ.
49. Samuel Clemens advocated perpetual copyright in "The Great Republic's Peanut Stand," composed in 1898, and again before a select committee of the House of Lords in 1900 (Vaidhyanathan, *Copyrights and Copywrongs*, 69–79).
50. Berne Convention, 9/9/1886, art. 2(1).
51. U.S. Constitution, art. I, § 8.
52. "A Visiting Card"; reprinted in Pound, *Selected Prose*, 326–27.
53. "Copyright and Tariff," 3:208.
54. Act of Mar. 4, 1909, ch. 320, §§ 12, 21, 35 Stat. 1075, 1078, 1080.
55. The four largest American cities in 1916, according to population size, were, in descending order, New York, Chicago, Philadelphia, and St. Louis (Tarr and McMurry, *World Geographies*, 413). By 1920, Detroit had supplanted St. Louis as the fourth largest city (McMurry and Parkins, *Advanced Geography*, 481).
56. Copyright Act, 1911, 1 & 2 Geo. 5, ch. 46, § 15 (Eng.).
57. "Copyright and Tariff," 3:209 (emphasis in original).
58. Ibid.
59. Wendy J. Gordon, "A Property Right in Self-Expression: Equality and Individualism in the Natural Law of Intellectual Property," *Yale Law Journal* 102 (1993): 1533, 1574 n.204.
60. Property rules permit plaintiffs to obtain injunctive relief; liability rules give plaintiffs noninjunctive, monetary remedies only (Guido Calabresi and A. Douglas Melamed, "Property Rules, Liability Rules, and Inalienability: One View of the Cathedral," *Harvard Law Review* 85 (1972): 1092, 1106–10).
61. "Copyright and Tariff," 3:209 (emphasis in original).
62. Presumably, Pound would have applied the same rule to heirs who did not authorize an affordable translation of a foreign author's work for the American market. Moreover, if the author licensed a translation during her lifetime, her heirs would have the responsibility of keeping the translation in print at affordable rates.
63. "Copyright and Tariff," 3:209.
64. Ibid.
65. Clemens's proposal for perpetual copyright also included a provision for inexpensive books. After twenty years of copyright protection, a work's publisher would be required to issue a cheap edition and keep it in print forever (Vaidhyanathan, *Copyrights and Copywrongs*, 76).
66. In 1918, the British pound sterling was worth $4.8665 in U.S. dollars. There were twenty shillings in a pound (O'Shea, Foster, and Locke, *World Book*, 4802).
67. "Tariff and Copyright," 3:191.
68. Pound to Dorothy Pound, 10/14/1945, in Pound and Spoo, *Ezra and Dorothy Pound*, 131.
69. Pound's focus was on the availability of foreign authors' works in the United States, but nothing suggests that he would not have applied the same rules to the failure of American authors and their heirs to keep works in circulation abroad as well as in the United States.
70. Pound, *Cantos*, 15.
71. Ibid., 16.

72. The story of King Canute and the tide is of ancient origin. One account is found in Dickens, *A Child's History of England*, 25–26.
73. Mary de Rachewiltz, "Mens Sine Affectu," in Saint-Amour, *Modernism and Copyright*, 267–68.
74. Variants of the story exist. See, for example, Carpenter, *Popular History of the Church of England*, 27–28.
75. Pound, *Cantos*, 16.
76. "ABC of Economics" (1933), in Pound, *Selected Prose*, 256.
77. Pound, "The Individual in his Milieu: A Study of Relations and Gesell" (1935), in ibid., 276.
78. Pound to Quinn, 2/29/1916, in Pound, *Selected Letters of Ezra Pound to John Quinn*, 64.
79. Putnam, *Memories of a Publisher*, 365, 370.
80. Pound to Quinn, 7/27/1916, in Pound, *Selected Letters of Ezra Pound to John Quinn*, 78.
81. Quinn to Pound, 10/1/1918, JQ.
82. Birrell, *Seven Lectures*, 206.
83. Saint-Amour, *Copywrights*, 81.
84. "Copyright and Tariff," 3:208.
85. "Tariff and Copyright," 3:228 (emphasis in original).
86. "Copyright and Tariff," 3:208.
87. Locke, *Two Treatises of Government*, 285–302.
88. Ibid., 287–88 (emphasis in original).
89. Ibid., 288.
90. Ibid., 289.
91. Brad Sherman and Lionel Bently discuss Locke's theory as used by courts and pamphleteers to legitimize the concept of literary property in *The Making of Modern Intellectual Property Law*, 23–24.
92. Enfield, *Observations on Literary Property* (1774); reprinted in Parks, *Literary Property Debate*, 21. Over the centuries courts have resorted to the Lockean labor theory to uphold intellectual property. See, for example, *Millar v. Taylor*, 98 Eng. Rep. 201, 252 (K.B. 1769) (Mansfield, L.J.) ("an author should reap the pecuniary profits of his own ingenuity and labor"), *overruled by Donaldson v. Beckett*, 1 Eng. Rep. 837 (H.L. 1774); *Ruckelshaus v. Monsanto Co.*, 467 U.S. 986, 1002–4 (1984) (citing Locke in holding that trade secrets can be "property" under the Fifth Amendment).
93. Conant, "International Copyright," 151.
94. Ibid.
95. In *Donaldson v. Beckett*, 1 Eng. Rep. 837 (H.L. 1774), the British House of Lords overturned a King's Bench decision (*Millar v. Taylor*, 98 Eng. Rep. 201 (K.B. 1769)) that had held that a perpetual common law right survived the limited copyright term for published works imposed by the Statute of Anne. A comparable U.S. decision was *Wheaton v. Peters*, 33 U.S. (8 Pet.) 591, 660–61 (1834). On the myth and reality of common law copyright, see generally Deazley, *Rethinking Copyright*.
96. Conant, "International Copyright," 151.
97. Spencer, *Justice*, 108–9.
98. Birrell observed that it was believed that if authors could claim a "property" right in writings "in the same way as lands, houses, goods and chattels, it followed that this right was one of indefinite duration, and could be disposed of in the market inter

vivos, or bequeathed or left to descend to relatives according to the laws of inheritance" (*Seven Lectures*, 14). For a skeptical view of this argument, see Lawrence Lessig, "The Creative Commons," *Florida Law Review* 55 (2003): 763, 775.

99. Rose, *Authors and Owners*, 121. Scholars have explored how originality "became the watchword of artistry and the warrant for property rights" (Boyle, *Shamans, Software, and Spleens*, 54). In "The Genius and the Copyright: Economic and Legal Conditions of the Emergence of the 'Author,'" *Eighteenth-Century Studies* 17 (1984): 425–48, Martha Woodmansee traces the changing meanings of the author, the book, and writing as property.

100. Wordsworth to the *Kendal Mercury*, 4/12/1838, in Wordsworth, *Prose Works*, 3:312. On Wordsworth's argument for longer copyrights, see Saint-Amour, *Copywrights*, 31–33.

101. Woodmansee, *Author, Art, and the Market*, 145–46. Thomas Hood summarized Wordsworth's argument by noting that "works of permanent value and utility . . . often creep but slowly into circulation and repute" and that "just then, when the literary property is realized . . . the law decrees that then all right or interest in the book shall expire in the author, and by some strange process, akin to the Hindoo transmigrations, revive in the great body of the booksellers" ("Copyright and Copywrong, Letter I," 73, 80).

102. "A Plea for Authors, May 1838," in Wordsworth, *Poems*, 818, ll. 3–4.

103. Ibid., ll. 9, 13–14.

104. Ibid., ll. 5–8.

105. "Copyright and Tariff," 3:208.

106. "In Explanation," 3:144.

107. *A Defence of Poetry* (1821), in Shelley, *Selected Poetry and Prose*, 522.

108. I use *compulsory license* and *royalty scheme* interchangeably, recognizing that they can have different connotations.

109. Nicklin, *Remarks on Literary Property*, 50–54. Adrian Johns briefly discusses Nicklin's tract (*Piracy*, 308).

110. Nicklin, *Remarks on Literary Property*, 54–56.

111. Ibid., 87–89.

112. Ibid., 89.

113. Ibid., 90.

114. For the "republican" view, see Meredith McGill, "The Matter of the Text: Commerce, Print Culture, and the Authority of the State in American Copyright Law," *American Literary History* 9 (1997): 21–59. For the "utilitarian" view, see Rice, *Transformation of Authorship in America*. See also Jaszi and Woodmansee, "Copyright in Transition," in Kaestle and Radway, *Print in Motion*, 548 n.6.

115. The Morton and Elderkin proposals are described by Thorvald Solberg, "International Copyright in Congress, 1837–1886," in *Papers and Proceedings of the Eighth General Meeting of the American Library Association*, 67–68. See also Seville, *Internationalisation of Copyright Law*, 202–3.

116. Smith's proposal was published as "An Olive Branch from America," *Nineteenth Century* 22 (1887): 602–10. It is summarized in Putnam, *Question of Copyright*, 65–76.

117. Putnam, *Question of Copyright*, 66.

118. Ibid., 67–73. Catherine Seville discusses Smith's royalty scheme in *The Internationalisation of Copyright Law*, 226–27.

119. Copyright Act, 1842, 5 & 6 Vict., ch. 45, § 5 (Eng.).

120. Alfred de Vigny, "De Mademoiselle Sedaine et de la propriété littéraire, Lettre à messieurs les Députés," *Revue des deux mondes* (1/15/1841): 87–89.

121. William Briggs discusses the Italian compulsory license system in *The Law of International Copyright*, 114. See also Birrell, *Seven Lectures*, 38.

122. Briggs discusses the 1872 Canadian bill (*Law of International Copyright*, 115).

123. Copyright Act, 1875, 38 Vict., ch. 88 (Eng.), amended by Copyright Act, 1875, 38 & 39 Vict., ch. 53 (Eng.). Discussions of the Canadian bills are found in Feather, *Publishing, Piracy, and Politics*, 185, and Seville, *Internationalisation of Copyright Law*, 103–9.

124. Berne Convention, 9/9/1886, art. 5.

125. Saint-Amour, *Copywrights*, 55 (emphasis in original).

126. For accounts of the Royal Commission on Copyright, see Feather, *Publishing, Piracy, and Politics*, 185–95; Saint-Amour, *Copywrights*, 53–89; and Seville, *Internationalisation of Copyright Law*, 268–78.

127. Farrer's (Board of Trade) Evidence, in Macfie, *Copyright and Patents for Inventions*, 299.

128. Extracts from Report of Royal Commission on Copyright, in ibid., 274.

129. Act of Mar. 4, 1909, ch. 320, § 1(e), 35 Stat. 1075, 1076; Copyright Act, 1911, 1 & 2 Geo. 5, ch. 46, § 19 (Eng.).

130. Copyright Act, 1911, 1 & 2 Geo. 5, ch. 46, §§ 3–4 (Eng.).

131. Modern copyright statutes have added further compulsory or statutory licenses. See, for example, 17 U.S.C. § 111(c)–(d) (secondary transmissions by cable systems), § 114(d) (certain digital transmissions of sound recordings), § 119 (certain secondary transmissions by satellite carriers), § 122 (same) (1994). In the United Kingdom, compulsory licenses exist for the use of works whose copyrights were revived in the mid-1990s as a result of a European Union directive (Council Directive 93/98, 1993 O.J. (L 290) 9) requiring member countries to implement a term of copyright protection equal to the life of the author plus seventy years.

132. Bloom, *Breaking of the Vessels*, 21.

133. Apteryx [T. S. Eliot, pseud.], "Verse Pleasant and Unpleasant," *The Egoist* 5 (1918): 43.

134. "How to Read, or Why: Part III; Conclusions, Exceptions, Curricula," *NYHTB* (1/27/1929): 5; reprinted in Pound, *Poetry and Prose*, 5:117.

135. Pound to Iris Barry, 7/27/1916, in Pound, *Selected Letters 1907–1941*, 90.

136. Pound, *Spirit of Romance*, 222.

137. "Mr. Bennett and Mrs. Brown" (1924); reprinted in Woolf, *Collected Essays*, 1:329.

138. Ibid.

139. "Tariff and Copyright," 3:191.

140. "Copyright and Tariff," 3:208–9 (emphasis in original).

141. Ibid., 3:209.

142. It is beyond my scope here to address the extent to which uncopyrighted works actually undersold copyrighted works in Britain or the United States in 1918. My focus is on Pound's assumptions and the conclusions he drew from them.

143. "A Letter from London," 2:150.
144. "Copyright and Tariff," 3:208.
145. Irving to Henry Brevoort, 8/12/1819, in Irving, *Letters*, 1:554.
146. Quoted in Thomas Bender and David Sampliner, "Poets, Pirates, and the Creation of American Literature," *New York University Journal of International Law and Politics* 29 (1996–97): 255, 262.
147. Quoted in Madison, *Book Publishing in America*, 58–59.
148. Lehmann-Haupt, *The Book in America*, 167. Not all scholars agree that American authors were held back by competition with foreign reprints. See, for example, Khan, "Intellectual Property and Economic Development," 40–41; Khan, *Democratization of Invention*, 267–77.
149. "Copyright and Tariff," 3:209.
150. Pound to Quinn, 10/10/1918, JQ.
151. Ibid.
152. "ABC of Economics," in Pound, *Selected Prose*, 256.
153. The 1911 British Copyright Act protected an author's right to convert a dramatic work into a non-dramatic work, and vice versa, and rights of public performance (Copyright Act, 1911, 1 & 2 Geo. 5, ch. 46, § 1(2) (Eng.)). Similar provisions were included in the 1909 U.S. Copyright Act (Act of Mar. 4, 1909, ch. 320, § 1(b)–(e)). Pound blamed subsidiary rights for Congress's slowness to amend the copyright law: "[T]he welfare of letters is postponed until cinema and radio, and now I suppose talki-o and smellio, rights have been puddled and muddled and strained out to the satisfaction of all the 'parties interested'" ("Newspapers, History, Etc.," 5:229).
154. The British statute defined fair dealing as use of a copyrighted work "for the purposes of private study, research, criticism, review, or newspaper summary" (Copyright Act, 1911, 1 & 2 Geo. 5, ch. 46, § 2(1)(i) (Eng.)). The roughly analogous U.S. privilege of fair use remained an exclusively common law doctrine until it was codified in the 1976 Copyright Act.
155. Saint-Amour, *Copywrights*, 193–98, discusses potentially copyrighted sources that Joyce freely drew upon in *Ulysses*. Pound did feel it necessary to acquire permission for reprinting whole poems or making entire translations. For his study of medieval literature, *Spirit of Romance*, he obtained permission to use lengthy quotations from modern, copyrighted translations of Dante and Michelangelo (Pound, *Spirit of Romance*, 7). He also informed Wyndham Lewis that permission was required to include one of T. S. Eliot's poems in *BLAST* (Pound to Lewis, before 7/1915, in Materer, *Letters of Ezra Pound and Wyndham Lewis*, 12–13). Pound's scrupulousness did not extend to fragments of texts used in his own poems.
156. Eliot's poem quotes from or paraphrases numerous works potentially copyrighted somewhere in 1922, including works by F. H. Bradley, Hermann Hesse, Paul Verlaine, Richard Wagner, and Jessie L. Weston ("Notes on 'The Waste Land,'" in Eliot, *Collected Poems*, 70–76).
157. See, for example, "An Octopus" (1924), in Moore, *Poems*, 167–72, 381–82.
158. Saint-Amour, *Copywrights*, 197.
159. See Landes and Posner, *Economic Structure of Intellectual Property Law*, 52.

160. *The Waste Land* quotes from or echoes Shakespeare at numerous points (*Collected Poems*, 54, 56–57, 59–60, 62; ll. 48, 77–78, 125, 128, 172, 191–92, 257).

161. For "A Study in French Poets," published in *The Little Review* in 1918, Pound had wanted to print a "brief anthology" of modern French poems without commentary, but Alfred Vallette, editor of the *Mercure de France*, pointed out that this would require the permission of authors or their estates. But if Pound interspersed "quelques lignes de commentaires," no permissions would be needed because critics and reviewers enjoyed "le droit de citation" (Pound, "A Study in French Poets," *LR* 4 (1918): 3–4; reprinted in Pound, *Poetry and Prose*, 3:17). Pound followed Vallette's advice, employing what today we would call "transformative" fair use (*Campbell v. Acuff-Rose Music, Inc.*, 510 U.S. 569, 579 (1994)).

162. "ABC of Economics," in Pound, *Selected Prose*, 239.

163. Douglas, *Social Credit*, 48–49.

164. Ibid., 49.

165. Pound, "The Individual in his Milieu: A Study of Relations and Gesell" (1935), in *Selected Prose*, 275.

166. De Rachewiltz, "Mens Sine Affectu," 270.

167. Pound to Quinn, 9/8–9/1916, in Pound, *Selected Letters of Ezra Pound to John Quinn*, 52.

168. Pound to Quinn, 9/3/1918, in ibid., 124.

169. "Letter from Rapallo," *Japan Times & Mail*, Tokyo (8/12/1940): 8; reprinted in Pound, *Poetry and Prose*, 8:63.

170. Solberg to Pound, 4/1/1927, EP.

171. The Vestal bill was H.R. 10434, 69th Cong., 1st sess. (1926).

172. Pound to Price, 4/25/1927, JMP.

173. Pound to Mencken, 4/27/1927, in Pound, *Selected Letters 1907–1941*, 211.

174. "The Exile," *TE* 3 (1928): 102; reprinted in Pound, *Poetry and Prose*, 5:17.

175. See H.R. 12549, 71st Cong., 2d sess. §§ 1–2, 12, 28–29, 34, 41, 61 (1930). See also H.R. 6988, 71st Cong., 2d sess., §§ 1–3 (1929) (authorizing the president to proclaim U.S. adherence to international copyright conventions and providing copyright protection for foreign authors). On Pound's support of Vestal's proposals, see Walkiewicz and Witemeyer, *Ezra Pound and Senator Bronson Cutting*, 28–29, 45–46.

## CHAPTER 4. *ULYSSES* UNAUTHORIZED: PROTECTIONISM, PIRACY, AND PROTEST

1. Shaw to Beach, 12/18/1926, in Joyce, *Letters*, 3:150 n.1.

2. Roth, *Stone Walls Do Not*, 110.

3. "Pound for President?" (letter to the editor), *TN* 125 (12/14/1927): 685; reprinted in Pound, *Poetry and Prose*, 4:393.

4. "Newspapers, History, Etc.," *H&H* 3 (1930): 574; reprinted in ibid., 5:229.

5. James Joyce to Stanislaus Joyce, 9/30/1906 and 11/13/1906, in Joyce, *Letters*, 2:168 & n.4., 189–90; Ellmann, *James Joyce*, 419–20.

6. John M. Price to Ezra Pound, 12/27/[1926], EP (carbon copy in JMP).

7. Heap to Pound, 11/29/1926, EP.

8. Sidney Struble, of Hays, St. John & Buckley, to Heap, 11/17/1926, LRR.

9. Joyce to Pound, 2/23/1927, in Joyce, *Letters*, 3:155.

10. Pound to Price, 1/12/1927, in Barry S. Alpert, "Ezra Pound, John Price, and *The Exile*," *Paideuma* 2 (1973): 437–39.

11. Pound to Joyce, 2/25/1927 (typed copy), C&P. A similar statement by Pound, dated the same day, also exists in C&P. Joyce responded to Pound, "Thanks. That declaration ought to be enough" (Joyce to Pound, 3/2/1927, in Joyce, *Letters*, 3:155.) Richard Ellmann incorrectly assumed that this was a "formal declaration by Pound, made at the American consulate in Genoa, attesting that he had never authorized Samuel Roth to publish Joyce's *Ulysses* in *Two Worlds*" (ibid., 156 n.1). Pound did not travel to Genoa to produce this statement, which concerned only Heap's assertion of copyright ownership, not Roth's claim of authorization.

12. In a note dated December 5, 1918, Joyce acknowledged receipt of £50 from Pound "for the American serial rights of my novel Ulysses." Pound passed this note on to John Quinn in a letter dated October 25, 1919, JQ.

13. *Bisel v. Ladner*, 1 F.2d 436, 436 (3d Cir. 1924).

14. Bruce Arnold discusses *The Little Review* in relation to the American copyright status of *Ulysses*. The discussion is inaccurate on certain legal points but appears to conclude, as I do, that copyright protection for *Ulysses* in the United States was doubtful (*Scandal of* Ulysses, 91–118).

15. Act of Mar. 4, 1909, ch. 320, §§ 10, 12–13, 35 Stat. 1075, 1078.

16. Issues of *The Little Review* for March, April, May, and June 1918—containing the first four episodes of *Ulysses*—were assigned registration numbers B412274, B412276, B413421, and B414990, respectively, by the Copyright Office. An amendment to the 1909 act, effective March 15, 1940, permitted authors or their heirs to renew the copyright in a periodical contribution after the first twenty-eight years of protection, even though no separate copyright had ever been registered in the contribution and no assignment of copyright from the periodical to the contributor had occurred (Howell, *Copyright Law*, 104–5). Renewals of claims in the first four serialized *Ulysses* episodes were registered in the name of Joyce's widow on January 13, 1946 (renewal entries 751 to 755 in the Copyright Office). The Copyright Office typically accepted both original and renewal registrations without questioning the copyright claims contained in them, under its rule of doubt.

17. Act of Mar. 4, 1909, ch. 320, § 12, 35 Stat. 1075, 1078.

18. Vanderham, *James Joyce and Censorship*, 1–2, 28–36.

19. Ibid., 17–18. Paul Vanderham suggests that the authorities may have viewed the issue also as politically subversive.

20. Ibid., 41–53; Ellmann, *James Joyce*, 502–4.

21. Quoted in Vanderham, *James Joyce and Censorship*, 56.

22. Horace Liveright remained interested in publishing *Ulysses* as a book even after the *Little Review* trial, but he backed away after Quinn advised him that prosecution for obscenity would be almost certain (Turner, *Marketing Modernism between the Two World Wars*, 179).

23. Joyce to Quinn, 11/17/1920, JQ.

24. Ellmann, *James Joyce*, 504, 519, 524.

25. Ibid., 519.

26. Defendant's Cross-Interrogatories on Commission, 3/8/1928, at 5, *Joyce v. Roth*, NYCC; a carbon copy with corrections in Joyce's hand is found in EP (Box 26/Folder 1115).

27. Act of Mar. 4, 1909, ch. 320, §§ 15, 21–22, 35 Stat. 1075, 1078–1080, as amended by Act of Dec. 18, 1919, ch. 11, § 21, 41 Stat. 368, 369; Howell, *Copyright Law*, 89–92.

28. On April 11, 1921, Maurice Darantiere, the Dijon printer of *Ulysses*, deposited the work with the Préfecture de la Côte-d'Or Department, in accordance with French law, listing Joyce as the author and Sylvia Beach as the publisher. A typed copy of the registration exists in C&P.

29. Defendant's Cross-Interrogatories, 4.

30. Quinn to Beach, 2/4/1922, JJ. Quinn was replying to Beach's letter dated January 23, 1922.

31. Brown to Beach, 11/28/1931, SB.

32. For the Copyright Office's firm position on the effects of the manufacturing clause, see Dorothy M. Schrader, "Ad Interim Copyright and the Manufacturing Clause: Another View of the *Candy* Case," *Villanova Law Review* 16 (1970): 280–82. *Compendium II of Copyright Office Practices* § 1201.01 (1984) states unequivocally, "Works first published before January 1, 1978, in violation of [the manufacturing] requirements are in the public domain in the United States and cannot be registered under the current [1976] Act." The *Compendium* is not authoritative law, but it forcefully articulates the Copyright Office's view of the law under the 1909 act.

33. In *Eisen, Durwood & Co. v. Tolkien*, 794 F. Supp. 85 (S.D.N.Y. 1992), *aff'd without opinion*, 990 F.2d 623 (2d Cir. 1993), a federal trial court ruled, on summary judgment, that certain portions of J. R. R. Tolkien's *The Lord of the Rings* did not lack American copyright protection just because British-published copies had been circulated in the United States without a copyright notice. The court also suggested, in dictum, that the copyright had not been lost as a result of failure to comply with the 1909 act's manufacturing clause, even though the challengers of the Tolkien copyrights had abandoned that argument. The court offered only superficial remarks about the effects of noncompliance with the ad interim and manufacturing provisions and did not mention the *Candy* decisions. For the views of legal academics, lawyers, and commentators on the manufacturing and ad interim provisions and their effects under the 1909 act, see Robert Spoo, "Copyright Protectionism and Its Discontents," *Yale Law Journal* 108 (1998): 633, 648–50 & nn.82–89.

34. *G. P. Putnam's Sons v. Lancer Books*, 239 F. Supp. 782, 783 (S.D.N.Y. 1965).

35. *Id.* at 784.

36. *Id.* at 787. By the time of the *Candy* litigation, U.S. accession to the Universal Copyright Convention (effective September 16, 1955) had the effect of exempting many foreign works from the manufacturing requirements. But the manufacturing clause still applied to English-language works by *American* authors that were first manufactured and published abroad (Schrader, "Ad Interim Copyright and the Manufacturing Clause," 217–18 & n.9). The *Candy* case thus closely parallels the history of *Ulysses*.

37. *G. P. Putnam's Sons*, 239 F. Supp. at 787.

38. *G. P. Putnam's Sons v. Lancer Books*, 251 F. Supp. 210, 214 (S.D.N.Y. 1966).

39. *Hoffenberg v. Kaminstein*, 396 F.2d 684, 685 (D.C. Cir. 1968) (per curiam).

40. *Id.*

41. Roth to Joyce, 2/12/1921, JJ; Joyce to Roth, 2/18/1921 (negative photostat), S&C (Box 28/Folder 548). The quoted phrase in the heading for this subsection is from a letter of Margaret Anderson to Jane Heap, circa December 1926, LRR.

42. Roth to Joyce, 5/10/1922, SB.
43. Consumer Price Index Calculator, Federal Reserve Bank of Minnesota (http://www.minneapolisfed.org/).
44. Roth to Joyce, 5/10/1922, SB.
45. Symons to Roth, 6/2/1922, SR; Hueffer to Roth, 7/7/1922, SR. Pound's agreement to be a contributing editor is reasonably clear from his letter to Quinn, 7/4–5/1922, JQ.
46. Huxley to Roth, 6/19/1922, SR.
47. Jay Gertzman insightfully discusses Roth's Mocki-Grisball device in an unpublished paper, "James Joyce's International Protest against Samuel Roth, and Roth's Subsequent Career as Pariah Capitalist and First Amendment Hero," 12–13.
48. Roth was not of the "brotherhood" of other insurgent Jewish publishers and "could not afford to be" (Jay A. Gertzman, "Not Quite Honest: Samuel Roth's 'Unauthorized' *Ulysses* and the 1927 International Protest," *JSA 2009*, ed. Philip Sicker and Moshe Gold (New York: Fordham University Press, 2009): 38–39).
49. Gertzman, *Bookleggers and Smuthounds*, 220, 254–55.
50. Roth, "Writing Finis to Volume One of Two Worlds," *TWQ* 1 (6/1926): 565.
51. "Life and Letters," *TWQ* 1 (9/1925): 1–3.
52. Roth, "Two Worlds Will Continue," *TWQ* 2 (6/1927): 305.
53. "Life and Letters," *TWQ* 1 (12/1925): 109–10.
54. "Life and Letters," *TWQ* 1 (3/1926): 253.
55. "Life and Letters," *TWQ* 1 (6/1926): 397.
56. Joyce's extract had first appeared as "Fragment of an Unpublished Work" in *The Criterion* 3 (7/1925): 498–510. Roth reprinted it in *TWQ* 1 (9/1925): 45–54.
57. *TWQ* 1 (9/1925): 45, 54.
58. Joyce to Harriet Shaw Weaver, 11/5/1925, in Joyce, *Letters*, 3:131.
59. One magazine editor publicly complained that Roth had not paid for a "page advertisement" despite "repeated applications" (*NS-L* 28 (3/26/1927): 731).
60. Letters by authors requesting promised payment or contributors' copies are found in SR. See, for example, letters to Roth from Frances Fletcher, 3/31/1927 and 11/23/1927; Patricia Barron, 4/7/1927; Gertrude Diamant, 6/11/1927; and Fletcher McCord, 7/2/1927.
61. Roth discussed his practice of paying contributors "within his means" and "out of unforeseeable profits" in an unpublished memoir, "Count Me among the Missing," 240, 253–54, SR.
62. John M. Price to Pound, 12/22/1925, JMP.
63. Mosher, letter to the editors, *TC* 29 (7/11/1896): 30–31.
64. *TWQ* 1 (12/1925): 111–14; *TWQ* 1 (3/1926): 347–60; *TWQ* 1 (6/1926): 545–60; *TWQ* 2 (9/1926): 35–40.
65. Roth, *Stone Walls Do Not*, 107–8.
66. Ellmann, *James Joyce*, 794–96.
67. This letter has not been located, and Roth later denied having written it ("Count Me among the Missing," 250), but it is discussed in contemporaneous letters of Joyce to Eric Pinker (ca. 10/1925, Joyce, *Letters*, 1:237–38) and to Weaver (11/5/1925, in ibid., 3:131) and in a letter of Sylvia Beach to Roth (12/3/1925, SR).
68. Beach to Roth, 12/3/1925, SR.

69. Roth to Beach, 1/2/1926 (typed copy), C&P. A negative photostat of Roth's $100 check is found in S&C (Box 28/Folder 548).
70. Beach to Roth, 1/21/1926 (typed copy), C&P.
71. Joyce to Weaver, 3/5/1926, Joyce, *Letters*, 3:139.
72. Roth to Beach, 3/18/1926 (typed copy), C&P. Gertzman and Adelaide Kugel, despite some inaccuracies regarding Roth's payments for Joyce's extracts, correctly question the view fostered by Joyce and his supporters that Roth never paid for what he printed except under compulsion (Gertzman, "Not Quite Honest," 52–53; Adelaide Kugel, "'Wroth Wracked Joyce': Samuel Roth and the 'Not Quite Unauthorized' Edition of *Ulysses*," *JSA 1992*, ed. Thomas F. Staley (Austin: University of Texas Press, 1992): 244–47). For his part, Roth exaggerated when he claimed to have sent "checks to Mr. Joyce promptly on the publication of each article" (*Stone Walls Do Not*, 112).
73. Beach to Marianne Moore (editor of *The Dial*), 7/12/1926, in Beach, *Letters*, 110.
74. Joyce to Weaver, 3/18/1926, in Joyce, *Letters*, 1:240.
75. Joyce to Weaver, 9/24/1926, in ibid., 1:245.
76. Roth claimed that he paid Joyce a total of $250 for reprinting five extracts from "Work in Progress" ("'Ulysses' Serial Pirating Is Denied," *NYEP* (11/1/1926)), and his claim is repeated by Kugel ("'Wroth Wracked Joyce,'" 244). Gertzman states that Joyce accepted "$200 for five excerpts" ("Not Quite Honest," 36.) I have found no documentary evidence that Roth paid for the fifth extract. That Joyce was concerned about Roth's use of that extract is suggested by an undated message he drafted for transmission to his attorneys sometime after September 1926, JJ. Beach insisted that Roth gave "two hundred dollars and a promise of more which never came" (letter distributed to various periodicals, 11/18/1926, SB). Joyce himself stated under oath that he had received a total of $200 from Roth for the extracts in *Two Worlds* (Plaintiff's Direct Interrogatories on Commission, 3/8/1928, at 2, *Joyce v. Roth*, NYCC).
77. Roth to Joyce, 2/12/1921, JJ. The quoted phrase in the heading for this subsection is Pound's description of Roth in a letter to H. L. Mencken, 4/27/1927, in Pound, *Selected Letters 1907–1941*, 211.
78. Beach to Weaver, 6/6/1922 (transcription by Adelaide Kugel), SR.
79. Weaver to Roth, 6/8/1922, SR.
80. Weaver to Beach, 7/22/1922 (transcription by Adelaide Kugel), SR.
81. Quinn to Weaver, 7/27/1922 (photocopy), SR.
82. Gertzman, "Not Quite Honest," 37.
83. Weaver to Quinn, 9/15/1922, JQ.
84. "[An agent's a]pparent authority, not otherwise terminated, terminates when the third person [here Roth] has notice ... of a manifestation by the principal [here Joyce] that he no longer consents [to any authorization by the agent]" (*Restatement (First) of Agency* § 125(b) (1933)).
85. Roth to Dr. H. K. Croessmann, 5/5/1927, HKC.
86. Pretrial Examination of Defendant, 6/7/1927, papers on appeal, 31, *Joyce v. Roth*, NYCLA. Roth's claim about Pound's authorization appeared in numerous places, including an article by Robert W. Potter, "T. S. Eliot Reopens Roth 'Piracy' Row," *NYEP* (8/11/1927): 26.

87. Pound, letter to the editor, *CT-P* (5/26/1928): 4; reprinted in Pound, *Poetry and Prose*, 5:30 (emphasis in original). In the original letter, written on May 23 or 24, 1928, Pound was emphatic that his suggestions concerned "the UNPUBLISHED remainder of the book" (Berg). In other correspondence, Pound stressed his recollection that his correspondence with Roth occurred "after" or "just after" the *Little Review* trial (Pound to Price, 1/8/1926, in Alpert, "Ezra Pound, John Price, and *The Exile*," 429–31; Pound to Price, 4/25/1927, JMP).

88. Pound wrote his father around March 1922, "Observer review brought in orders for 136 copies of Ulysses, last Tuesday, 136 in one day at 15 bones the copy. So that for Mr Sumner and his rum-hounds" (Pound, *Ezra Pound to His Parents*, 495).

89. Pound to Quinn, 10/31/1920, in Pound, *Selected Letters of Ezra Pound to John Quinn*, 200.

90. Waverley Lewis Root, a former subeditor of *Two Worlds Monthly*, claimed that Roth "stole" the idea for his *Two Worlds* magazines while visiting England in 1921 ("King of the Jews," *transition*, no. 9 (12/1927): 182–83).

91. After Anderson and Heap were charged with obscenity, Quinn believed it would be better to refrain from publishing *Ulysses* in installments and to issue it as a complete, preferably private, edition; Pound agreed, though he continued to see the virtues of a serialization (Pound to Quinn, 10/31/1920, in Pound, *Selected Letters of Ezra Pound to John Quinn*, 198–201).

92. In an unpublished and undated typescript entitled "The Joyce Incident" (SR), Roth stated that at the time he was negotiating to publish an anthology of American poetry, with Pound as collaborator, Pound "suggested that perhaps I was the very one to carry on, as editor, from where Jane Heap and Margaret Anderson had left off." This would place Pound's suggestion in the spring or early summer of 1921.

93. Kugel states that Pound in July 1922 "supported Roth's proposal to feature a serialization of *Ulysses* in the new journal," but she offers no documentary evidence other than Roth's own assertions ("'Wroth Wracked Joyce,'" 243). Gertzman notes the slim support for her claim ("Not Quite Honest," 36, 43).

94. Pound to Roth, 7/4/1922, SR. Pound's carbon copy of the letter is in WB–EP. Pound's July 4 letter refers to one he wrote Roth the previous day in which he also made suggestions for *Two Worlds*. Kugel was convinced that the July 3 letter, which has never been found, contained Pound's permission regarding *Ulysses* ("'Wroth Wracked Joyce,'" 243). The surviving evidentiary context suggests otherwise.

95. Pound to Lewis, 7/14/1922, in Materer, *Letters of Ezra Pound and Wyndham Lewis*, 133.

96. Replying to a letter from Pound, T. S. Eliot wrote on July 9, 1922, "About '2 Worlds', please let me know about the organizers of it and who the probable star and 2nd star or planetary contributors will be?" (Eliot, *Letters*, 538).

97. Pretrial Examination of Defendant, 28–29.

98. "Count Me among the Missing," 241.

99. Roth's letter, dated April 20, 1927, was originally addressed to Julien Benda, one of the signers of the international protest. He mailed a copy of this letter, with the salutation crossed out, to Dr. H. K. Croessmann on May 5, 1927, HKC.

100. Roth to Anderson, ca. 4/1927, SB. For a similar remark, see Roth, *Stone Walls Do Not*, 111–12.

101. Pretrial Examination of Defendant, 1/12/1928, at 37, *Joyce v. Roth*, NYCC.
102. Roth, *Stone Walls Do Not*, 23.
103. Roth to the editor of *TN*, 3/17/1927 (photocopy), SR.
104. *TWM* 1 (7/1926): 1, 5.
105. Ibid., 6.
106. "American Book Pirates," *NS-NY* 29 (4/16/1927): 10–11; reprinted in Pound, *Poetry and Prose*, 4:383.
107. Pound to Price, 12/2/1926, JMP.
108. *TWM* 1 (7/1926): 3.
109. "James Joyce Makes Deposition against Roth for Pirating Work," *CT-P* (3/20/1928).
110. *TWM* 2 (2/1927): inside front cover.
111. Advertisement for *Tales from Town Topics* in *The Westminster Review* 146 (7–12/1896): advertising section, 16.
112. These authors appeared in various issues of the three volumes of *Two Worlds Monthly*, from July 1926 until the final published issue in September 1927.
113. The twelfth issue of *Two Worlds Monthly* (vol. 3, no. 4), would have completed "Oxen of the Sun," but that issue, though printed, was not published in magazine format and appeared only later when Roth issued all of the *Two World Monthly* numbers in two bound volumes. The quoted phrase in the heading for this subsection is Bennett Cerf's description of the attitude of writers and critics toward Roth after his unauthorized reprinting of *Ulysses*, in a letter to Paul Léon, 12/29/1933, JJ–PL.
114. Roth, *Stone Walls Do Not*, 107–8; Gertzman, "Not Quite Honest," 39.
115. Roth, "Count Me among the Missing," 243–44.
116. Price to Beach, 7/26/[1926], SB.
117. Roth, "Life and Letters," *TWM* 1 (8/1926): 129–30.
118. Joyce to Pound, 11/16/1926, EP.
119. "Not Quite Honest," 53–54.
120. "*Ulysses*: Part Two," *TWM* 1 (8/1926): 210.
121. "*Ulysses* [The Eleventh Instalment]," *TWM* 3 (9/1927): 204. Page 204 omits all of page 402 of the Paris edition.
122. Roth to David Boehm, 8/5/1926 (photocopy), SR.
123. Morris to Beach, 11/1/1925, SB.
124. Price, "1 Roth + 2 Worlds = How Many Suckers?" *Modern S4N Review* (8/1926): 28–29. Price recounted his Roth-sleuthing in two letters to Pound, 12/22/1925 and 3/16/1926, JMP.
125. Price to Pound, 12/22/1925, JMP.
126. Roth to Pound, 12/24/1925, EP; Roth to Beach, 1/2/1926 (typed copy), C&P.
127. Pound to *Vanity Fair*, 2/8/1926, JMP; Pound to Homer Pound, 3/17/[1926], in Pound, *Ezra Pound to His Parents*, 594.
128. "'Ulysses' Serial Pirating Is Denied," *NYEP* (11/1/1926); Beach to *New York Evening Post*, 11/16/1926 (cable), LRR; "Communications: Printed without Permission," *PW* (12/11/1926): 2213; "Letter to the Editor," *TQ* 1 (Spring 1927): 289; "Pirate Publisher of Fake 'Ulysses' is Exposed by Miss Sylvia Beach," *CT-P* (11/20/1926): 1; "Publisher Claims Book is 'Pirated,'" *NYH-P* (11/24/1926).

129. Beach to Kate Buss, 11/22/1926, PC; Fitch, *Sylvia Beach and the Lost Generation,* 245.

130. John B. Overstreet, literary editor of *Mexican Life,* to Beach, 12/7/1926, SB.

131. Pound to Joyce, 11/19/1926, in Pound, *Letters of Ezra Pound to James Joyce,* 226.

132. Helen M. Gifford to Beach, 1/11/1927, SB.

133. Roth to Gifford, 1/19/1927 (typed copy), C&P.

134. Ibid. (note written at the bottom of Roth's 1/19/1927 letter).

135. Arthur Doyle to Roth, 4/27/1927, SR.

136. Dr. H. K. Croessmann to Roth, 5/3/1927, HKC.

137. R. M. Denney to Roth, 5/4/1927, SR.

138. Maurice Samuel to Roth, 4/19/1927; quoted in Gertzman, "Not Quite Honest," 58, 66 n.84; Roth to Untermeyer, 1/7/1927, SR.

139. Beach to Joyce, 9/1/1926, HEJ.

140. Sandburg to John M. Price, 7/31/1926, JMP.

141. Hemingway to Maxwell Perkins, 11/16/1926, in Hemingway, *Selected Letters,* 225.

142. Catherine Seville, "Nineteenth-Century Anglo-US Copyright Relations: The Language of Piracy versus the Moral High Ground," in Bently, Davis, and Ginsburg, *Copyright and Piracy,* 26–27.

143. *LR* 8 (Autumn 1921): 2.

144. Three-page typescript with revisions, SB.

145. The Lewisohn draft is printed in Joyce, *Letters,* 3:151 n.2. A photocopy of this draft, showing annotations and corrections, is in RE.

146. "Statement regarding the piracy of *Ulysses,*" in Joyce, *Letters,* 3:151.

147. Joyce to Weaver, 2/1/1927, in ibid., 1:249.

148. "Printing of 'Ulysses' Here Causes Protest," *NYT* (2/18/1927): 21; Fitch, *Sylvia Beach and the Lost Generation,* 253; Joyce to Harriet Shaw Weaver, 3/2/1927, Joyce, *Letters,* 1:250–51.

149. Canby to Beach, 2/17/1927 (typed copy), C&P.

150. Moore to Roth, 4/25/1927, SR.

151. Quoted in an undated typescript of "The International Protest," a chapter of Adelaide Kugel's unpublished memoir, "In a Plain Brown Wrapper," page PRO-8, SR.

152. Roth to the editor of *The Nation,* 3/17/1927 (photocopy), SR. Gertzman discusses this letter ("Not Quite Honest," 49, 64 n.60).

153. "Count Me among the Missing," 241.

154. Roth, letter to the editor, *NS-L* 28 (3/19/1927): 694–95.

155. Roth, "Mr. Sumner and Beau," *TWM* 2 (3/1927): 360. For Roth as "patron of the public, defender of free speech, and midwife of great literature," see Paul K. Saint-Amour's witty and insightful "Soliloquy of Samuel Roth: A Paranormal Defense," *JJQ* 37 (2000): 461.

156. Roth, "An Offer to James Joyce," *TWM* 3 (9/1927): 181–82.

157. Roth, "Joyce, Ulysses, Roth, The Van Dorens and Villard's 'Nation,'" *TWM* 3 (5–6/1927): 119.

158. Roth, "On Withdrawing Dedications," *TWM* 3 (unspecified month, 1927): 216.

159. In an undated draft letter to George Bernard Shaw, dictated to Beach around January 1927, Joyce remarked that his campaign to discredit Roth had brought

about "in many important instances the rejection of Mr Roth's advertisements," SB (Box 130). Roth remarked a few months later that this "'trouble with Joyce has cost me a lot of money because it has closed many advertising mediums'" (quoted in Potter, "T. S. Eliot Reopens Roth 'Piracy' Row," 26).

160. Quoted in "The Pirated Edition of 'Ulysses,'" *PW* 111 (2/12/1927): 608.
161. *NS-L* 28 (3/19/1927).
162. *SRL* 3 (3/5/1927): 630.
163. John F. Carter Jr., to Beach, 2/18/1927 (typed copy), C&P.
164. *TN* 124 (3/16/1927): 277.
165. Roth attributed this metaphor to Leon Fleischman, the former husband of Joyce's daughter-in-law ("Count Me among the Missing," 241).
166. Scholars have examined the ways in which modernism was marketed to diverse readerships. For example, Catherine Turner has studied the expanding market for modernism in the 1920s and 1930s and the methods by which American publishers appealed to readers and recast authors as celebrities (*Marketing Modernism between the Two World Wars*, esp. ch. 6). Lawrence Rainey has scrutinized various institutions—patronage, limited editions, book collecting, commercial markets, universities—that shaped modernism (*Institutions of Modernism*). A foundational collection of essays is Dettmar and Watt, *Marketing Modernisms*.
167. Pound to Joyce, 12/25/1926, in Pound, *Selected Letters 1907–1941*, 206.
168. Pound to Beach, 1/15/1927, SB.
169. Pound to Homer Pound, 3/17/1926, in Pound, *Ezra Pound to His Parents*, 463.
170. Pound to Beach, 1/15/1927, SB.
171. Pound to John M. Price, 3/14/1927, JMP.
172. Pound to Price, 12/11/1925, in Alpert, "Ezra Pound, John Price, and *The Exile*," 428.
173. Pound to Joyce, 12/25/1926, in Pound, *Selected Letters 1907–1941*, 206.
174. Gertzman suggests that Pound refused to sign the protest "possibly because he had in fact led Roth to believe he could publish the *Ulysses* selections" (Gertzman, *Bookleggers and Smuthounds*, 228; see also Saint-Amour, "Soliloquy of Samuel Roth," 466). More persuasively, Gertzman argues that Pound's refusal was influenced by "a principled opposition to the potential of industrial capitalism for interfering with freedom of expression" ("Not Quite Honest," 44).
175. Joyce to Stanislaus Joyce, 1/8/1927, in Joyce, *Letters*, 3:149.
176. Joyce to George Bernard Shaw (draft dictated to Beach), ca. 1/1927, SB.

## CHAPTER 5. *JOYCE V. ROTH*: AUTHORS' NAMES AND BLUE VALLEY BUTTER

1. John M. Price, "1 Roth + 2 Worlds = How Many Suckers?" *Modern S4N Review* (8/1926): 28–29.
2. Roth, *Stone Walls Do Not*, 109.
3. Pound to Price, 12/11/1925, in Barry S. Alpert, "Ezra Pound, John Price, and *The Exile*," *Paideuma* 2 (1973): 428.
4. Roth to Pound, 11/19/1925, EP.
5. Roth to Pound, 12/24/1925, EP.

6. Roth to Homer Pound, 2/15/1926, JMP. The letter, which is on *Two Worlds* letter-head, is unsigned but plainly composed by Roth.

7. Pound to Homer Pound, 3/4/1926, in Pound, *Ezra Pound to His Parents*, 590.

8. Pound to Homer Pound, 3/4/[1926], in ibid., 591.

9. Pound to John M. Price, 3/4/1926, JMP.

10. Roth to Pound, ca. 3/20/1926, JMP.

11. Pound quoted the "Virgin's Prayer" in a letter to Wyndham Lewis, 1/13/1918, in Pound, *Selected Letters 1907–1941*, 129.

12. *TWQ* 2 (12/1926): 143.

13. *TWM* 1 (8/1926): 195, 252.

14. *TWM* 3 (4/1927): 6, 34.

15. *TWM* 2 (1/1927): 143–46; *TWM* 3 (5–6/1927): 149–52.

16. *TWM* 3 (5–6/1927): n.p.

17. Quoted in Robert W. Potter, "T. S. Eliot Reopens Roth 'Piracy' Row," *NYEP* (8/11/1927): 26.

18. Quoted in ibid.

19. Ibid.

20. Ibid.

21. Eliot to the editor of *NYEP*, 8/22/1927 (typed copy), C&P.

22. *TWM* 2 (12/1926): n.p.

23. Joyce to Harriet Shaw Weaver, 3/5/1926, in Joyce, *Letters*, 3:138–39.

24. *TWM* 2 (12/1926): 1.

25. Hays, *City Lawyer*, 99, 145.

26. Sidney Struble, of Hays, St. John & Buckley, to Jane Heap, 12/6/1926, LRR.

27. Sylvia Beach to Joyce, 10/26/1926, HEJ.

28. Kieffer to Beach, 11/5/1926, SB.

29. *The Albany Law Journal: A Monthly Record of the Law and the Lawyers* 64 (1902): 213–14; *The Brief of Phi Delta Phi: A Quarterly Magazine of the Law* 4 (1903): 189; "France: 'Americans ... reprehensible!'," *Time* 12 (8/6/1928): 18.

30. Joyce to Weaver, 7/26/1927, in Joyce, *Letters*, 3:162.

31. Beach to Jane Heap, 1/17/1927, LRR.

32. Conner to Joyce, 2/12/1930 and 5/1/1930 (enclosing a bill for Chadbourne's and Conner's services, dated 10/30/1929), JJ–PL; Conner to Beach, 11/23/1926, JJ–PL.

33. "Miss Beach Plans to Sue Mutilator of Joyce's Work," *CT-P* (11/23/1926).

34. Neil Loynachan, "Leaf Profile: Paul M. Hahn," *The Tobacco Leaf* 99 (1/5/1963): 2–3.

35. Joyce to Conner, 1/15/1932, JJ. For the conversion to 2012 dollars, I consulted Consumer Price Index Calculator, Federal Reserve Bank of Minnesota (http://www.minneapolisfed.org/).

36. Conner to Beach, 2/1/1927, JJ–PL.

37. Struble to Heap, 11/17/1926, LRR.

38. Price to Pound, 12/27/1926, EP.

39. Beach to Heap, 12/9/1926 (cable), C&P.

40. Hays to Joyce, 1/14/1927 (photocopy of typed copy), SR; Hays to Roth, 1/14/1927 (photocopy), SR; Hays to Roth, 2/26/1927, SR. Joyce discussed the offer in a let-ter to Weaver, dated February 10, 1927, HSW. Adelaide Kugel's claim that Roth

made the thousand dollar offer to Joyce before launching *Two Worlds Monthly* is unsupported by any evidence other than Hays's letter reporting Roth's assurances ("'Wroth Wracked Joyce': Samuel Roth and the 'Not Quite Unauthorized' Edition of *Ulysses*," *JSA* (1992): 246–47).

41. For a similar interpretation of events, see Paul K. Saint-Amour, "Soliloquy of Samuel Roth: A Paranormal Defense," *JJQ* 37 (2000): 465.

42. Hays to Joyce, 2/25/1927 (carbon copy), SB.

43. Hays to Heap, 2/25/1927, LRR.

44. Conner to Paul M. Hahn, 3/8/1927, C&P; Hahn to Conner, 3/10/1927 (carbon copy), C&P; Conner to Beach, 2/1/1927 (carbon copy), C&P.

45. Summons and verified complaint, 3/10/1927 and 3/12/1927, *Joyce v. Roth*, NYCC.

46. N.Y. Civil Rights Law § 50 (Consol. 1922).

47. *Roberson v. Rochester Folding Box Co.*, 64 N.E. 442, 447 (N.Y. 1902).

48. *Weiss v. Herlihy*, 49 N.Y.S. 81, 86 (N.Y. App. Div. 1897). See also Carol Loeb Shloss, "Privacy and Piracy in the Joyce Trade: James Joyce and *Le Droit Moral*," *JJQ* 37 (2000): 450.

49. Roiphe, *1185 Park Avenue*, 17–26.

50. *Ellis v. Hurst*, 128 N.Y.S. 144 (N.Y. Sup. Ct. 1910), *aff'd without opinion*, 130 N.Y.S. 1110 (N.Y. App. Div. 1911).

51. Appellant's brief, n.d., papers on appeal, 8, *Joyce v. Roth*, NYCLA.

52. State courts had jurisdiction over cases involving common law copyrights in unpublished works, but if a work was published, a state court had "no jurisdiction, either on the ground of statutory, or common law, copyright" (Weil, *American Copyright Law*, 172).

53. Padgug, Notice of Appearance, 3/18/1927, *Joyce v. Roth*, C&P.

54. These details were provided by Padgug's son, Jacob ("Jay") Padgug, during a telephone interview (4/23/2010).

55. Roth, *Jews Must Live*, 145.

56. Ibid., 56.

57. Copies of Roth's two motions, Joyce's opposition papers, and the parties' accompanying affidavits are found in NYCC, as is a copy of Joyce's verified amended complaint.

58. Copies of Justice Tierney's orders, documents evidencing Joyce's security bond, and copies of Roth's verified answers and Joyce's Notice of Trial are found in NYCC and C&P. The Chadbourne attorneys expressed their private opinion about a trial date in a letter to Conner, 4/20/1927, JJ.

59. Roth's move to the Hotel Ansonia is described in Adelaide Kugel's unpublished memoir of Samuel Roth, "In a Plain Brown Wrapper," SR.

60. Affidavits of Padgug and Isadore Kupfer in support of order to show cause, 6/7/1927, NYCC.

61. See William E. Nelson, "Civil Procedure in Twentieth-Century New York," *St. Louis University Law Journal* 41 (1997): 1157, 1175–78.

62. Pretrial Examination of Defendant, 6/7/1927, papers on appeal, 21–22, *Joyce v. Roth*, NYCLA.

63. Ibid., 22–23.

64. Ibid., 25–27.

65. Ibid., 28.

66. N.Y. Civil Rights Law § 51 (Consol. 1922).

67. Pretrial Examination of Defendant, 31.
68. Ibid., 32–33.
69. Stipulation by Roth, 6/7/1927, C&P.
70. Pretrial Examination of Defendant, 35.
71. Ibid., 39–40.
72. Ibid., 41.
73. Ibid., 42.
74. Ibid., 44.
75. *TWM* 1 (8/1926): 129–30.
76. Joyce to Pound, 11/16/1926, EP.
77. Pretrial Examination of Defendant, 45.
78. *Gautier v. Pro-Football, Inc.*, 106 N.Y.S.2d 553, 560 (N.Y. App. Div. 1951) (citing *Redmond v. Columbia Pictures Corp.*, 277 N.Y. 707 (N.Y. 1938)).
79. Pretrial Examination of Defendant, 45.
80. Ibid., 45–46.
81. Ibid., 47.
82. Affidavit of Padgug, 6/7/1927, at 2, and Memorandum of Law, 6/9/1927, at 4–7, NYCC.
83. Affidavit of Eugene F. Roth, 6/8/1927, at 2–3, and Memorandum of Law in Opposition to Defendants' Motions to Vacate the Notice for Examination before Trial and Examination before Trial Already Had, 6/9/1927, at 3–7, NYCC.
84. Justice Mullan's order, 6/13/1927, at 1, NYCC.
85. *Joyce v. Roth*, 223 N.Y.S. 878 (N.Y. App. Div. 7/15/1927).
86. Appellant's brief, 9–14.
87. Ibid., 6.
88. Nelson, "Civil Procedure in Twentieth-Century New York," 1170–73, 1199–1200.
89. Respondent's brief, n.d., papers on appeal, 19, *Joyce v. Roth*, NYCLA.
90. Ibid., 3–9.
91. Ibid., 15.
92. *Joyce v. Roth*, 225 N.Y.S. 842 (N.Y. App. Div. 12/9/1927); adjusted bill of costs, 1/5/1928, NYCC.
93. Pretrial Examination of Defendant, 1/12/1928 (continuation of prior testimony), 39, NYCC.
94. Pretrial Examination of Defendant, 1/16/1928 (further continuation of prior testimony), 44, NYCC.
95. Affidavit of Paul M. Hahn, 11/4/1927, at 2, NYCC.
96. Memorandum in Opposition to Plaintiff's Motion for a Commission to Take the Testimony of the Plaintiff, 11/9/1927, at 3–5, NYCC.
97. Commission to Alphonse Gaulin, 2/11/1928, NYCC.
98. Plaintiff's Direct Interrogatories on Commission, 3/8/1928, at 2, NYCC.
99. Ibid., 3.
100. Ibid., 4.
101. Defendant's Cross-Interrogatories on Commission, 3/8/1928, at 6, NYCC; a carbon copy of this document with corrections in Joyce's hand is found in EP (Box 26/Folder 1115).
102. Ibid.
103. Ibid., 7–8.
104. Slocum and Cahoon, *Bibliography of James Joyce*, 31–32.

105. "James Joyce Makes Deposition against Roth for Pirating Work," *CT-P* (3/20/1928).

106. Pound to Homer Pound, 3/21/[1928], in Pound, *Ezra Pound to His Parents*, 652.

107. Joyce to Weaver, 3/28/1928, in Joyce, *Letters*, 3:174.

108. Pound to Joyce, 3/30/1928, in Robert Spoo, "Unpublished Letters of Ezra Pound to James, Nora, and Stanislaus Joyce," *JJQ* 32 (1995): 545–46.

109. Pound's letter is discussed fully in chapter 4.

110. Pound to Joyce, 10/24/1928, in Spoo, "Unpublished Letters of Ezra Pound," 550.

111. Conner to Joyce, 11/26/1928, EP. Scholars have repeated Ellmann's erroneous conclusion that Pound gave testimony in the case (Joyce, *Letters*, 3:156 n.1). See, for example, Pound, *Letters of Ezra Pound to James Joyce*, 227; Jay A. Gertzman, "Not Quite Honest: Samuel Roth's 'Unauthorized' *Ulysses* and the 1927 International Protest," *JSA 2009*, ed. Philip Sicker and Moshe Gold (New York: Fordham University Press, 2009), 42. Kugel even states that Pound "perjured himself before the American consul in Genoa" ("'Wroth Wracked Joyce,'" 245; see also Saint-Amour, "Soliloquy of Samuel Roth," 466). None of this occurred.

112. "Roth's Magazine Accused," *NYT* (3/10/1927): 2.

113. *TWM* 3 (4/1927): 1–2.

114. Roth, *Stone Walls Do Not*, 116–17; copy of clerk's minutes, *United States v. Samuel Roth*, C 53–79 (S.D.N.Y. indictment filed 1/27/1928), C&P.

115. Gertzman, *Bookleggers and Smuthounds*, 229–30; Roth, *Stone Walls Do Not*, 11, 21, 61–62; Henry F. Pringle, "Throwing Mud at the White House," *Outlook and Independent* 159 (12/9/1931): 463.

116. Roth to Pauline Roth, 11/7/1928, 11/14/1928, 11/18/1928, 11/24/1928, and 12/30/1928, SR; Roth to Richard Roth (son), 11/30/1928, SR.

117. Justice Nathan Bijur, order vacating stay of trial, 5/8/1928, NYCC; Joyce to Weaver, 9/20/1928, in Joyce, *Letters*, 1:266–67.

118. Stipulations of the parties, 5/16/1928 and 5/22/1928, C&P; Fulton Brylawski to Chadbourne, Stanchfield & Levy, 5/31/1928, C&P.

119. Copies of witness subpoenas to Moss (6/22/1928) and Hays (n.d.), C&P.

120. David M. Berger to Chadbourne, Stanchfield & Levy, 6/14/1928, C&P.

121. Padgug to Chadbourne, Stanchfield & Levy, 9/5/1928, C&P.

122. Joyce to Weaver, 9/20/1928, in Joyce, *Letters*, 1:266–67; see also Joyce to Conner, 9/1/1928, in ibid., 3:181.

123. Eugene F. Roth to Padgug, 9/25/1928, 11/21/1928, and 12/4/1928, C&P; draft orders, 10/1928, C&P.

124. Copy of signed consent decree, 12/27/1928, C&P. The full text of the decree is reproduced in Joyce, *Letters*, 3:185–86.

125. Scholars sometimes erroneously refer to the "trial" in the Roth case (Fitch, *Sylvia Beach and the Lost Generation*, 281; Kelly, *Our Joyce*, 91). The case never went to trial.

126. See *Miller v. Bond & Mortgage Guaranty Co.*, 188 A. 678, 679 (N.J. Ch. 1936) ("A consent decree of the Court of Chancery cannot be considered as a precedent for like action in a later suit for similar relief.") (syllabus); *Village of Sleepy Hollow v. American National Bank & Trust Co. of Chicago*, 418 N.E.2d 466, 469 (Ill. Ct. App. 1981) ("A consent decree is binding only upon those who consented to its entry."). See also *Black's Law Dictionary*, 410–11.

127. "Injunction," *transition*, no. 16–17 (6/1929): 205–6.
128. Conner to Ould, 11/27/1929 (photocopy), SR.
129. Conner to Ould, 12/6/1929 (photocopy), SR.
130. "Communication de M. James Joyce sur le Droit Moral des Écrivains" (1937), in Joyce, *Critical Writings*, 274–75. My translation.
131. An incomplete draft in English of Joyce's address (probably by Paul Léon) makes this moral rights perspective even more explicit (JJ–PL). On Joyce and moral rights, see Shloss, "Privacy and Piracy in the Joyce Trade," 447–57.
132. See, for example, 17 U.S.C. § 106A (Visual Artists Rights Act) and various state law protections for the works of visual artists. See also Saint-Amour, "Soliloquy of Samuel Roth," 465.
133. Mark Bartholomew, "A Right Is Born: Celebrity, Property, and Postmodern Lawmaking," *Connecticut Law Review* 44 (2011): 301–68.
134. Damages are still awarded for shame, humiliation, and emotional distress in some publicity rights cases. See, for example, *Waits v. Frito-Lay, Inc.*, 978 F.2d 1093, 1103 (9th Cir. 1992).
135. *Fairbanks v. Winik*, 198 N.Y.S. 299 (N.Y. Sup. Ct. 1922), *rev'd*, 201 N.Y.S. 487 (N.Y. App. Div. 1923).
136. Peter Decherney, "Gag Orders, Comedy, Chaplin, and Copyright," in Saint-Amour, *Modernism and Copyright*, 135–54.
137. *Haelan Labs., Inc. v. Topps Chewing Gum, Inc.*, 202 F.2d 866 (2d Cir. 1953).
138. *Lugosi v. Universal Pictures*, 25 Cal.3d 813 (1979); *Groucho Marx Products v. Day & Night Co.*, 689 F.2d 317 (2d Cir. 1982); *Cher v. Forum International, Ltd.*, 692 F.2d 634 (9th Cir. 1982); *Factors Etc., Inc. v. Pro Arts, Inc.*, 652 F.2d 278 (2d Cir. 1981) (Presley); *Eastwood v. Superior Court of Los Angeles County*, 149 Cal. App. 3d 409 (Cal. Ct. App. 1983); *Carson v. Here's Johnny Portable Toilets, Inc.*, 698 F.2d 831 (6th Cir. 1983); *Midler v. Ford Motor Co.*, 849 F.2d 460 (9th Cir. 1988); *Joplin Enterprises v. Allen*, 795 F. Supp. 349 (W.D. Wash. 1992); *Waits v. Frito-Lay, Inc.*, 978 F.2d 1093 (9th Cir. 1992); *White v. Samsung Electronics America, Inc.*, 971 F.2d 1395 (9th Cir. 1992).
139. For an early discussion of trademarks and secondary meaning, see *Apollo Bros., Inc. v. Perkins*, 207 F. 530 (3d Cir. 1913).
140. *TWM* 2 (12/1926): 1.
141. *Sheila's Shine Products, Inc. v. Sheila Shine, Inc.*, 486 F.2d 114, 122–23 (5th Cir. 1973), discusses trademarks and business goodwill.
142. *Sweeney v. Macmillan Publishers Ltd.*, Case No. CH 1997 S 3257 [2001] EWHC Ch B66 (Chancery, 11/22/2001).
143. *Id.*
144. Thomas Jones, "Short Cuts," *London Review of Books* 23 (12/13/2001).
145. 539 U.S. 23 (2003).
146. *Id.* at 34 (quotation marks and citation omitted).
147. Joyce to Weaver, 9/20/1928, in Joyce, *Letters*, 1:266–67.
148. Invoice as of 10/30/1929, enclosed in Conner to Joyce, 2/12/1930, JJ–PL.
149. See http://www.minneapolisfed.org/.
150. Conner to Joyce, 9/27/1930, JJ.
151. Joyce to Weaver, 3/18/1930, in Joyce, *Letters*, 1:291–92.

152. Ibid.

153. The memorandum is reproduced in Fitch, *Sylvia Beach and the Lost Generation,* 308. Fitch states incorrectly that the $2,000 was owed to Conner (rather than the New York firm) and that Joyce finally "accepted his responsibility" for the bill (ibid., 322). He never paid it.

154. Joyce to Conner, 12/18/1931 (draft), JJ–PL; Joyce to Conner, 1/15/1932, JJ.

155. Joyce to Weaver, 12/17/1931, in Joyce, *Selected Letters,* 358–59. See also Beach, *Shakespeare and Company,* 204. Such scholars as Joseph Kelly (*Our Joyce,* 104) have speculated about the reasons for the Joyce–Beach contract but have missed Joyce's primary motive.

156. Fitch, *Sylvia Beach and the Lost Generation,* 322–23; Beach to Paul Léon, 2/4/1932, in Beach, *Letters,* 139.

157. Conner to Joyce, 12/23/1932, JJ–PL.

158. Conner to Joyce, 12/19/1935, JJ–PL.

159. Conner to Joyce, 7/27/1939, JJ–PL.

160. Sommation, 8/24/1939, JJ–PL.

161. Email from James Wiseman, former attorney at Chadbourne & Parke LLP (11/16/1999).

162. Gertzman views Joyce's lawsuit and the protest as an "advertising campaign" ("Not Quite Honest," 41). For diverse treatments of Joyce's celebrity, see Wexler, *Who Paid for Modernism?,* 49–72; Goldman, *Modernism Is the Literature of Celebrity,* 55–80; Maurizia Boscagli and Enda Duffy, "Joyce's Face," in Dettmar and Watt, *Marketing Modernisms,* 133–59.

163. Slocum to Roth, 2/3/1951, SR.

## CHAPTER 6. *ULYSSES* AUTHORIZED: RANDOM HOUSE AND COURTESY

1. Cerf, *At Random,* 95–96.

2. Henle to Klopfer, 12/8/1933, RH.

3. Symons to Beach, 1/11/1927 (photocopy), SR.

4. *TWM* 1 (7/1926): 89.

5. *United States v. One Book Called "Ulysses,"* 5 F. Supp. 182, 185 (S.D.N.Y. 1933), *aff'd sub nom. United States v. One Book Entitled Ulysses by James Joyce,* 72 F.2d 705 (2d Cir. 1934).

6. There is scant record of Roth's involvement in copyright litigation. A rare exception was a 1951 lawsuit brought by the publisher Alfred Knopf over Roth's publication of a translation of a book by André Gide (Leo Hamalian, "Nobody Knows My Names: Samuel Roth and the Underside of Modern Letters," *Journal of Modern Literature* 3 (4/1974): 914).

7. Beach, *Shakespeare and Company,* 179. A typical newspaper account was "'Ulysses' Author Sues Magazine," *NYT* (3/22/1927): 17.

8. Meredith to Mosher, 3/3/1892; quoted in Bishop, *Thomas Bird Mosher,* 214.

9. Cerf to Robert Kastor, 12/30/1931, RH.

10. Joyce to Pound, ca. 3/1932, CR.

11. Pound to the editors of *Contempo,* ca. 3/1932, CR. For a discussion of the *Contempo* contretemps, see Jay A. Gertzman, "Not Quite Honest: Samuel Roth's

'Unauthorized' *Ulysses* and the 1927 International Protest," *JSA 2009*, ed. Philip Sicker and Moshe Gold (New York: Fordham University Press, 2009): 46.

12. Roth to Milton Abernethy, 12/3/1931, SR.

13. There was never a comprehensive legal ban on *Ulysses* in the United States. Rather, the prohibition resulted chiefly from two cases. A portion of *Ulysses* had been deemed obscene by a New York Court of Special Sessions in 1921, as discussed in chapters 2 and 4. In 1928, under the Tariff Act of 1922, the U.S. Customs Court upheld the seizure of seven copies of *Ulysses*, along with ten other titles, at the port of Minneapolis (*Heymoolen v. United States* (Treasury Decision 42907, Cust. Ct. 8/1/1928)). Because the latter decision was the immediate legal obstacle to Ernst's efforts, I find it more accurate to refer to the "customs ban."

14. Ernst to B. W. Huebsch, 10/21/1931, in Moscato and LeBlanc, *United States of America v. One Book Entitled Ulysses*, 98.

15. "Statement regarding the piracy of *Ulysses*," in Joyce, *Letters*, 3:151. The quoted phrase in the heading for this subsection is from a letter of Cerf to Robert Kastor, 3/22/1932, in Moscato and LeBlanc, *United States of America v. One Book Entitled Ulysses*, 103.

16. "The Pirated Edition of 'Ulysses,'" *PW* 111 (2/12/1927).

17. "Defend Joyce," *Times* (St. Petersburg, FL) (2/6/1927).

18. Arnold Bennett, "U.S. Piracy of 'Ulysses,'" *Sunday Express* (London) (3/27/1927).

19. Eric S. Pinker to J. Ralph Pinker, 11/10/1932, JJ–PL.

20. Beach to Jacob Schwartz, 1/31/1931, SB. See also Slocum and Cahoon, *Bibliography of James Joyce*, 51–52.

21. Schwartz to Beach, 12/16/1930 and 2/3/1931, SB.

22. Paul Léon to J. B. Pinker & Son, 11/3/1933, JJ–PL; opinion of Hon. S. O. Henn Collins, K.C., enclosed in Monro Saw & Co. to Léon, 12/5/1933, JJ–PL.

23. Joyce to Harriet Shaw Weaver, 8/6/1932 (typed copy), RE; J. B. Pinker & Son to Léon, 2/28/1933, JJ–PL.

24. Fitch, *Sylvia Beach and the Lost Generation*, 319.

25. Cerf to Morris L. Ernst, 10/20/1932, in Moscato and LeBlanc, *United States of America v. One Book Entitled Ulysses*, 162–63.

26. Lindey, file memo, 11/11/1932, in ibid., 163.

27. *Two Worlds Monthly*, ed. Samuel Roth, vol. 1 (New York: Two Worlds Publishing Co., 1927), n.p.

28. Slocum and Cahoon, *Bibliography of James Joyce*, 28–29; R. F. Roberts, "Bibliographical Notes on James Joyce's 'Ulysses,'" *The Colophon: A Quarterly for Bookmen* 1, n.s. (Spring 1936): 574–75; John J. Slocum to John S. Sumner, 11/25/1950 (typed carbon), SR.

29. Fitch, *Sylvia Beach and the Lost Generation*, 318.

30. Joyce to Weaver, 10/1/1931, in Joyce, *Letters*, 3:229–30; Cerf to Kastor, 12/30/1931, RH.

31. Joyce to Weaver, 12/17/1931, in Joyce, *Letters*, 1:309.

32. Court Injunction, in ibid., 3:185–86.

33. Joyce to Benjamin Conner, 1/15/1932, JJ.

34. Ernst to Huebsch, 10/21/1931, in Moscato and LeBlanc, *United States of America v. One Book Entitled Ulysses*, 99.

35. Lindey to Cerf, 3/31/1932, in ibid., 114–15.

36. Joyce to Weaver, 10/1/1931, in Joyce, *Letters*, 3:229–30.

37. Lindey to Cerf, 3/31/1932, in Moscato and LeBlanc, *United States of America v. One Book Entitled Ulysses*, 114–15.

38. Cerf to Kastor, 12/30/1931, RH.

39. For example, Joseph Kelly refers to the U.S. attorney's decision "to prosecute" (*Our Joyce*, 129). The heading of this subsection echoes the title of chapter 23 in Ernst and Schwartz, *Censorship*, 160.

40. Ernst and Lindey, *Censor Marches On*, 14–16.

41. See generally Walkiewicz and Witemeyer, *Ezra Pound and Senator Bronson Cutting*.

42. Ernst, *The Best Is Yet …*, 160–62; Vanderham, *James Joyce and Censorship*, 90–91.

43. Act of June 17, 1930, ch. 497, § 305, 46 Stat. 688. For an insightful treatment of the *Ulysses* customs case, see Kelly, *Our Joyce*, 106–40.

44. Ernst, *The Best Is Yet …*, 161–62.

45. *Black's Law Dictionary*, 916. Kelly confusingly states that *Ulysses* was "prosecuted for libel by the U.S. Attorney's office" (*Our Joyce*, 132–33). The "libel" in this litigation had nothing to do with the tort of defamation.

46. Léon to Cerf, 4/27/1932, in Moscato and LeBlanc, *United States of America v. One Book Entitled Ulysses*, 129–31.

47. Stephen Gillers, "A Tendency to Deprave and Corrupt: The Transformation of American Obscenity Law from *Hicklin* to *Ulysses II*," *Washington University Law Review* 85 (2007): 237, 259.

48. H. C. Stewart, assistant collector of customs, to Lindey, 5/13/1932, in Moscato and LeBlanc, *United States of America v. One Book Entitled Ulysses*, 142.

49. Stewart to Lindey, 5/24/1932, in ibid., 149.

50. See Anna Pervukhin, "Deodands: A Study in the Creation of Common Law Rules," *American Journal of Legal History* 47 (2005): 237–56; Tamara R. Piety, "Scorched Earth: How the Expansion of Civil Forfeiture Doctrine Has Laid Waste to Due Process," *University of Miami Law Review* 45 (1991): 911, 928–37.

51. Exodus 21:28 (King James Version).

52. For example, the case of *Krimstock v. Kelly*, 306 F.3d 40 (2d Cir. 2002) (Sotomayor, J.), concerned the seizure, as instrumentalities of crime, of motor vehicles driven by individuals arrested for driving under the influence of drugs or alcohol, pursuant to New York City's forfeiture statute, N.Y. City Admin. Code § 14–140.

53. Claimant's Supplementary Memorandum, in Moscato and LeBlanc, *United States of America v. One Book Entitled Ulysses*, 291.

54. Lindey to Ernst, office memorandum, 7/30/1932, in ibid., 157. On the collaboration of the adversaries, see Kelly, *Our Joyce*, 109–10, 130; Vanderham, *James Joyce and Censorship*, 90–93.

55. Ernst, office memoranda, 8/12/1932 and 9/27/1932, in Moscato and LeBlanc, *United States of America v. One Book Entitled Ulysses*, 158, 160; *United States v. One Obscene Book Entitled "Married Love,"* 48 F.2d 821 (S.D.N.Y. 1931); *United States v. One Book, Entitled "Contraception," by Marie C. Stopes*, 51 F.2d 525 (S.D.N.Y. 1931).

56. Ernst to Cerf, 11/11/1932, in Moscato and LeBlanc, *United States of America v. One Book Entitled Ulysses*, 164; Lindey to Ernst, office memorandum, 1/4/1933, in ibid., 172–73.

57. Gillers, "Tendency to Deprave and Corrupt," 280. See also Vanderham, *James Joyce and Censorship*, 90–93.

58. Ernst to Jonas Shapiro, office memorandum, 8/25/1933, in Moscato and LeBlanc, *United States of America v. One Book Entitled Ulysses*, 219.

59. Ernst to J.J.S. [Jonas J. Shapiro], office memorandum, 8/15/1933, in ibid., 217.

60. Lindey, file memo, 10/19/1932, in ibid., 162.

61. Letter to the editor, *CT-P* (5/26/1928): 4; reprinted in Pound, *Poetry and Prose*, 5:30.

62. "Mr. Roth of New York" (letter to the editor), *NS-L* 28 (3/26/1927): 731.

63. Quinn to James Joyce, 4/4/1922 (carbon copy), JQ.

64. Donald S. Friede to Joyce, 5/22/1928 (typed copy), JJ.

65. Joyce to Weaver, 6/3/1928, in Joyce, *Letters*, 3:178.

66. Beach, *Shakespeare and Company*, 201–2.

67. J. Ralph Pinker to Joyce, 3/4/1932, JJ–PL; Luca Crispi, "*Ulysses* in the Marketplace: The Dynamics of the Production and Consumption of a Work of Art," 5–8 (unpublished manuscript).

68. Nowell-Smith, *International Copyright Law and the Publisher in the Reign of Queen Victoria*, 74.

69. Huebsch to Cerf, 12/17/1931, in Moscato and LeBlanc, *United States of America v. One Book Entitled Ulysses*, 100.

70. Huebsch to Ernst, 12/17/1931, MLE.

71. Cerf, *At Random*, 95–96.

72. James B. Pinker & Son to Cerf, 4/4/1932, RH.

73. Kastor to Helen Kastor Fleischman and Giorgio Joyce, 3/23/1932, RH.

74. Consumer Price Index Calculator, Federal Reserve Bank of Minnesota (http://www.minneapolisfed.org/).

75. Kastor to Fleischman and Joyce, 3/23/1932, RH.

76. Cerf to Kastor, 3/22/1932, in Moscato and LeBlanc, *United States of America v. One Book Entitled Ulysses*, 103.

77. Léon to J. B. Pinker & Son, 3/9/1932, JJ–PL.

78. Memorandum of Agreement, ca. 3/1932, in Moscato and LeBlanc, *United States of America v. One Book Entitled Ulysses*, 105.

79. Cerf to Kastor, 3/22/1932, in ibid., 103.

80. Cerf, *At Random*, 95–96.

81. For a brief history of the Albatross Press, see Alistair McCleery, "Collating the Pirate and the Professionals: Preliminary Analysis of the Texts of *Ulysses* 1927–1934," *Genetic Joyce Studies*, No. 6 (Spring 2006) (http://www.geneticjoycestudies.org/GJS6/GJS6McCleery.htm). See also Slocum and Cahoon, *Bibliography of James Joyce*, 29–30.

82. Holroyd-Reece to Cerf, 12/14/1933, JJ–PL.

83. Léon to Wegner, 12/12/1933, JJ–PL.

84. Ibid.

85. Cerf to Holroyd-Reece, 12/26/1933 (carbon copy), JJ–PL.

86. Act of Mar. 4, 1909, ch. 320, §§ 31, 32, 35, Stat. 1075, 1082–83.

87. Ernst noted the possibility of prosecution by state or postal authorities in a letter to Huebsch, 10/21/1931, in Moscato and LeBlanc, *United States of America v. One Book Entitled Ulysses*, 98–99. Léon voiced the same concern in a letter to J. B. Pinker & Son, 2/25/1932, JJ–PL.

88. Ernst to Huebsch, 10/21/1931, in Moscato and LeBlanc, *United States of America v. One Book Entitled Ulysses*, 99.

89. Cerf to Kastor, 12/30/1931, RH.

90. Cerf to Kastor, 3/22/1932, and Memorandum of Agreement, ca. 3/1932, in Moscato and LeBlanc, *United States of America v. One Book Entitled Ulysses*, 103, 105–6.

91. Joyce, *Ulysses*, xv–xvii.

92. Ibid., xvii.

93. Ibid.

94. Cerf to Kastor, 12/30/1931, RH.

95. On the legal, aesthetic, and poststructuralist implications of the prefatory matter in the 1934 edition, see Brook Thomas, "*Ulysses* on Trial: Some Supplementary Reading," in Burt, *Administration of Aesthetics*, 125–48.

96. Cerf to Léon, 10/13/1933, in Moscato and LeBlanc, *United States of America v. One Book Entitled Ulysses*, 234.

97. Ibid.

98. Léon to Cerf, 10/21/1933, in ibid., 278.

99. Cerf to Léon, 10/13/1933, in ibid., 279.

100. Léon to Cerf, 12/5/1933, in ibid., 307.

101. The reply of William L. Brown, acting register of copyrights, to Beach's inquiry is quoted in chapter 4.

102. Léon to J. B. Pinker & Son, 2/25/1932, JJ–PL.

103. Cerf to Holroyd-Reece, 12/26/1933 (carbon copy), JJ–PL.

104. U.S. Copyright Office records show that two deposit copies of the Random House edition were received on January 27, 1934. The affidavit of American manufacture was received on February 23, 1934, with Modern Library, Inc., listed as copyright claimant. Neither the registration application nor a copy of the copyright registration certificate has been located in the records of the Copyright Office.

105. Slocum and Cahoon, *Bibliography of James Joyce*, 28–32.

106. Lindey to Cerf, 5/26/1932, in Moscato and LeBlanc, *United States of America v. One Book Entitled Ulysses*, 150; Alfred Harcourt to Cerf, 6/15/1932, RH; Charles Scribner's Sons to Cerf, 5/11/1932, RH.

107. These letters, written to Cerf and Donald Klopfer in the days following Judge Woolsey's decision, are found in RH.

108. Henle to Cerf, 12/8/1933, RH.

109. Knopf to Woolsey, 12/8/1933, JMW.

110. Lindey to Cerf, 6/6/1932, in Moscato and LeBlanc, *United States of America v. One Book Entitled Ulysses*, 152.

111. Cerf to Holroyd-Reece, 12/26/1933 (carbon copy), JJ–PL.

112. Lawrence, *A Propos of Lady Chatterley's Lover*, 7.

113. Ibid., 8.

114. Weisberger to Cerf, 6/16/1932, RH.

115. Shapiro to Woolsey, 12/7/1933, JMW.

116. Pound to Senator Bronson Cutting, 2/13/[1934], in Walkiewicz and Witemeyer, *Ezra Pound and Senator Bronson Cutting*, 104–5.

117. "American Book Pirates," *NS-NY* 29 (4/16/1927): 10–11; reprinted in Pound, *Poetry and Prose*, 4:383.

118. Locke, *Two Treatises of Government*, 288.
119. Details about the Collectors *Ulysses* are drawn from a copy owned by Michael Groden and from John W. Van Voorhis and Francis C. Bloodgood, "*Ulysses*: Another Pirated Edition?," *JJQ* 9 (1972): 436.
120. Dennison, *Alternative Literary Publishing*, 195–96. The professor who made the inquiry at Random House was my former colleague, the late Darcy O'Brien.
121. Details about Miller are taken from Stephen J. Gertz, "West Coast Blue," in Daley et al., *Sin-A-Rama*, 27–35.
122. *Miller v. California*, 413 U.S. 15, 24–25 (1973).
123. *Roth v. United States*, 354 U.S. 476, 484 (1957).
124. Brief of Morris L. Ernst, as Amicus Curiae Supporting Petitioner, *Roth v. United States*, 354 U.S. 476 (1957) (No. 582), 1957 WL 87528.
125. For a penetrating discussion of the Roth case, see de Grazia, *Girls Lean Back Everywhere*, 273–326.
126. *American Aphrodite: A Quarterly for the Fancy-Free*, vol. 4, no. 13 (1954): 90.
127. Ibid., 3.
128. For critiques of Ernst's and Judge Woolsey's characterizations of *Ulysses* as a modern classic and an autonomous work of art, see Thomas, "*Ulysses* on Trial," 126–36; Kelly, *Our Joyce*, 115–16, 136, 139–40; Vanderham, *James Joyce and Censorship*, 8–12, 94–105, 128–31.

## EPILOGUE—DISTURBING THE AMERICAN PUBLIC DOMAIN

1. *Golan v. Holder*, 565 U.S. ___, 132 S. Ct. 873, 900 (2012) (Breyer, J., dissenting).
2. Act of Aug. 31, 1954, Pub. L. No. 83–743, 83d Cong., 2d Sess., 61 Stat. 655.
3. Act of Oct. 31, 1988, Pub. L. No. 100–568, 100th Cong., 2d Sess., 102 Stat. 2854.
4. Marrakesh Agreement Establishing the World Trade Organization, 4/15/1994, 1867 U.N.T.S. 154.
5. Uruguay Round Agreements Act, Pub. L. No. 103–465, 108 Stat. 4809, 4976–81 (1994) (codified at 17 U.S.C. § 104A).
6. 17 U.S.C. § 104A(h)(6)(C)(i).
7. *Id.* § 104A(h)(2)(A).
8. *Id.* § 104A(a)(1)(B).
9. Act of Oct. 27, 1998, Pub. L. No. 105–298, § 102(d)(1)(B), 112 Stat. 2827, 2828 (codified at 17 U.S.C. § 304(b)). See also *Golan*, 565 U.S. ___, 132 S. Ct. at 903–4 (Breyer, J., dissenting): "[W]orks published between 1921 and 1923 obtained [under the URAA] a 'restored' copyright that expired before the 1998 Sonny Bono Copyright Term Extension Act, and so could have lasted two years at most." Hubert Best has suggested to me that because France was slow in implementing the EU directive that increased copyright terms by twenty years, *Ulysses* may have been in the public domain in France, the work's country of origin, when the URAA became effective in 1996. If this is true, *Ulysses* may not have enjoyed any restored U.S. copyright protection under the URAA.
10. First Amended Complaint at 25–28 (filed 2/18/2003), *Golan v. Holder*, 565 U.S. ___, 132 S. Ct. 873 (2012) (No. 10–545).

11. *Id.* at 38–39.
12. *Eldred v. Ashcroft*, 537 U.S. 186 (2003).
13. *Golan*, 565 U.S. ___, 132 S. Ct. at 887.
14. *Id.* at 882–83.
15. *Id.* at 878, 891.
16. *Id.* at 888 n.26.
17. *Id.* at 892.
18. H.R. Rep. No. 2222, 60th Cong., 2d Sess., 7 (1909).
19. *Twentieth Century Music Corp. v. Aiken*, 422 U.S. 151, 156 (1975).
20. *Sony Corp. of America v. Universal City Studios, Inc.*, 464 U.S. 417, 429 (1984).
21. *Golan*, 565 U.S. ___, 132 S. Ct. at 893.
22. *Id.* at 911 (Breyer, J., dissenting).
23. *Id.* at 893.
24. Council Directive 93/98/EEC, 1990 O.J. (L 290) 9, 9 (EC).
25. Jane Ginsburg, "'Une chose publique?' The Author's Domain and the Public Domain in Early British, French, and US Copyright Law," in Torremans, *Copyright Law*, 154.
26. Alfred de Vigny, "De Mademoiselle Sedaine et de la propriété littéraire, Lettre à messieurs les Députés," *Revue des deux mondes* (1/15/1841): 87–89.
27. Pamela Samuelson, "Mapping the Digital Public Domain: Threats and Opportunities," *Law and Contemporary Problems* 66 (Winter 2003): 147, 148.
28. Larry Lessig suggested to me the formulation that the public domain is "local." See also Brief of Creative Commons Corporation as Amicus Curiae in Support of Petitioners at 9–17, *Golan v. Holder*, 565 U.S. ___, 132 S. Ct. 873 (2012) (No. 10–545).
29. Copyright Act, R.S.C., ch. C-42, § 6 (1985) (Can.); Copyright Act, 1968, § 33(2) (Austl.); Swiss Copyright Act, art. 29(2)(b) (1993); *Neue Schauspiel AG v. Felix Bloch Erben*, Swiss Federal Court, 1/13/1998, ATF 124 III 266 (holding that expired copyrights were not revived under Swiss law).
30. 17 U.S.C. § 304(b) (establishing a term of ninety-five years from the year copyright was originally secured).
31. A newly edited text of *Finnegans Wake*, prepared by Danis Rose and John O'Hanlon and unauthorized by the Joyce estate, was published in London by the Houyhnhnm Press in 2010. A new, estate-authorized text of *Finnegans Wake*, edited by Robbert-Jan Henkes, Erik Bindervoet, and Finn Fordham, appeared in 2012 as a British Oxford World's Classic.
32. 17 U.S.C. § 304(b).
33. *Id.* § 303(a) (establishing a term of the author's life plus seventy years for unpublished works). Throughout much of Europe, Joyce's unpublished works passed out of copyright seventy years after his death in 1941. A term of the author's life plus seventy years had been required in EU countries by Council Directive 93/98/EEC, art. 1, 1990 O.J. (L 290) 9 (EC).
34. Copyright Designs and Patents Act, 1988, sched. 1, par. 12(4) (U.K.).
35. Copyright Act, 1968, § 33(2) (Austl.), provides that a work that is not published or otherwise made available to the public before the author's death is protected for seventy years from the year in which the work is first published or made available to the public.

36. The Irish law states that "copyright in a literary, dramatic, musical or artistic work, or an original database shall expire 70 years after the death of the author, irrespective of the date on which the work is first lawfully made available to the public" (Copyright and Related Rights Act, 2000 (Act No. 28/2000), § 24 (Ir.)). This language, which is ambiguous with respect to unpublished works, is, as of this writing, under review in Ireland and may be revised to encompass unpublished works explicitly.

37. Council Directive 93/98/EEC, art. 4, 1990 O.J. (L 290) 9, 9 (EC).

38. Walter and Lewinski, *European Copyright Law*, 573.

39. Terence Killeen, "Joyce Children's Story Published in Dublin to Dismay in Zürich," *IT* (2/8/2012).

40. Quoted in ibid.

41. Anastasia Herbert, Ithys Press, letter to the editor, *TLS* (5/11/2012): 6.

42. The press release regarding the *Dublin Ulysses Papers* was dated April 4, 2012 (http://joycemanuscriptsdublin.files.wordpress.com/2012/04/pressrelease_dublinulyssespapers_danisrose.pdf).

43. Danis Rose, "The Preface to the Edition" (http://houseofbreathings.com/about).

44. National Library of Ireland website (http://www.nli.ie/en/list/latest-news.aspx?article=3f4bf22c-6dc8-4182-be71-4b09b9df84f2). See also Terence Killeen, "Joyce Collection Published Free on Web," *IT* (4/12/2012).

45. I was a member of the NLI's board of directors at the time of these events.

46. Danis Rose, "A Question of Joyce Copyright" (letter to the editor), *IT* (4/17/2012).

47. Copyright and Related Rights Act, 2000 (Act. No. 28/2000) § 40 (Ir.).

48. Copyright and Related Rights Regs., 1996, S.I. No. 2967, pt. II, 16(4)(a) (U.K.). See also Walter and Lewinski, *European Copyright Law*, 669–70.

49. Code de la propriété intellectuelle art. L 123-4(3). See also Walter and Lewinski, *European Copyright Law*, 577.

50. Cass. 1e civ., 11/9/1993, Bull. Civ. I, No. 319, at 221.

51. See Walter and Lewinski, *European Copyright Law*, 575.

52. Case 7 O 847/03 *Himmelsscheibe von Nebra* [2004] GRUR 672 (LG Magdeburg 10/16/2003). The significance of the word *lawfully* is examined in Walter and Lewinski, *European Copyright Law*, 575–76.

53. Copyright and Related Rights Regs., 1996, S.I. No. 2967, pt. II, 16(3) (U.K.).

54. See Michael Heller, "The Tragedy of the Anticommons: Property in the Transition from Marx to Markets," *Harvard Law Review* 111 (1998): 621–88.

55. *Golan*, 565 U.S. ____, 132 S. Ct. at 906 (Breyer, J., dissenting).

# BIBLIOGRAPHY

*Periodicals, scholarly journal articles, and archival materials, as well as judicial decisions, statutes, and other legal authorities, are cited in full in the notes.*

Acheson, James M. *Capturing the Commons: Devising Institutions to Manage the Maine Lobster Industry*. Lebanon, NH: University Press of New England, 2003.

———. *The Lobster Gangs of Maine*. Lebanon, NH: University Press of New England, 1988.

Archibald, Diana C. *Domesticity, Imperialism, and Emigration in the Victorian Novel*. Columbia: University of Missouri Press, 2002.

Arnold, Bruce. *The Scandal of Ulysses: The Life and Afterlife of a Twentieth Century Masterpiece*, rev. ed. Dublin: Liffey, 2004.

Atkin, Jonathan. *A War of Individuals: Bloomsbury Attitudes to the Great War*. Manchester: Manchester University Press, 2002.

Barnes, Laura, William Brockman, and Stacey Herbert. *James Joyce Bibliography: Pomes Penyeach*. Published for the International James Joyce Symposium, Trieste, Italy, 2002.

Beach, Sylvia. *Letters*. Edited by Keri Walsh. New York: Columbia University Press, 2010.

———. *Shakespeare and Company*. 1956. Lincoln: University of Nebraska Press, 1980.

Bennett, Arnold. *The Journal of Arnold Bennett*. New York: Literary Guild, 1933.

Bently, Lionel, Jennifer Davis, and Jane C. Ginsburg, eds. *Copyright and Piracy: An Interdisciplinary Critique*. Cambridge: Cambridge University Press, 2010.

Birrell, Augustine. *Seven Lectures on the Law and History of Copyright in Books*. London: Cassell, 1899.

Bishop, Philip R. *Thomas Bird Mosher: Pirate Prince of Publishers*. New Castle, DE, and London: Oak Knoll and British Library, 1998.

*Black's Law Dictionary*, 6th ed. St. Paul, MN: West, 1990.

Bloom, Harold. *The Breaking of the Vessels*. Chicago: University of Chicago Press, 1982.

Boyle, James. *Shamans, Software, and Spleens: Law and the Construction of the Information Society*. Cambridge, MA: Harvard University Press, 1996.

Briggs, Julia. *Virginia Woolf: An Inner Life*. Boston: Harcourt, 2005.

Briggs, William. *The Law of International Copyright, with Special Sections on the Colonies and the United States of America*. London: Stephens & Haynes, 1906.

Brown, Candy Gunther. *The Word in the World: Evangelical Writing, Publishing, and Reading in America, 1789–1880*. Chapel Hill: University of North Carolina Press, 2004.

Browning, Robert. *Dramatis Personae*. Boston: Ticknor & Fields, 1864.

Burlingame, Roger. *Of Making Many Books: A Hundred Years of Reading, Writing, and Publishing*. New York: Charles Scribner's Sons, 1946.

Burt, Richard, ed. *The Administration of Aesthetics: Censorship, Political Criticism, and the Public Sphere*. Minneapolis: University of Minnesota Press, 1994.

Carpenter, Humphrey. *A Serious Character: The Life of Ezra Pound*. Boston: Houghton Mifflin, 1988.

Carpenter, William Boyd. *A Popular History of the Church of England from the Earliest Times to the Present Day*. London: John Murray, 1900.

Casper, Scott E., Jeffrey D. Groves, Stephen W. Nissenbaum, and Michael Winship, eds. *The Industrial Book, 1840–1880*. Vol. 3 of *A History of the Book in America*, ed. David D. Hall. Chapel Hill: University of North Carolina Press, 2007.

Cerf, Bennett. *At Random: The Reminiscences of Bennett Cerf*. 1977. New York: Random House, 2002.

Creel, George. *How We Advertised America: The First Telling of the Amazing Story of the Committee on Public Information That Carried the Gospel of Americanism to Every Corner of the Globe*. New York: Harper & Brothers, 1920.

*Cyclopedia of Political Science, Political Economy, and the Political History of the United States*. Edited by John J. Lalor. 3 vols. New York: Charles E. Merrill, 1890.

Daley, Brittany A., Adam Parfrey, Hedi El Kholti, and Earl Kemp, eds. *Sin-A-Rama: Sleaze Sex Paperbacks of the Sixties*. Los Angeles: Feral House, 2005.

Dardis, Tom. *Firebrand: The Life of Horace Liveright*. New York: Random House, 1995.

Deazley, Ronan. *Rethinking Copyright: History, Theory, Language*. Cheltenham, UK: Edward Elgar, 2006.

Deazley, Ronan, Martin Kretschmer, and Lionel Bently, eds. *Privilege and Property: Essays on the History of Copyright*. Cambridge, UK: Open Book, 2010.

De Bekker, Leander Jan. *The Serio-Comic Profession: A Book for Writers, and for such Readers as May Be Interested in Them and Their Craft*. Brooklyn: Writers' Publishing Co., 1915.

De Grazia, Edward. *Girls Lean Back Everywhere: The Law of Obscenity and the Assault on Genius*. New York: Random House, 1992.

Dennison, Sally. *Alternative Literary Publishing: Five Modern Histories*. Iowa City: University of Iowa Press, 1984.

De Quincey, Thomas. *Confessions of an English Opium-Eater and Suspiria De Profundis*. Boston: Ticknor & Fields, 1864.

Dettmar, Kevin J. H., and Stephen Watt, eds. *Marketing Modernisms: Self-Promotion, Canonization, and Rereading*. Ann Arbor: University of Michigan Press, 1996.

Dickens, Charles. *A Child's History of England*. London: Chapman & Hall, 1870.

———. *Letters*. Edited by Madeline House and Graham Storey. 12 vols. Oxford: Clarendon, 1965–2002.

Donaldson, Scott. *Edwin Arlington Robinson: A Poet's Life*. New York: Columbia University Press, 2007.

Douglas, Clifford Hugh. *Social Credit*, 3d ed. London: Eyre & Spottiswoode, 1933.

Drone, Eaton S. *A Treatise on the Law of Property in Intellectual Productions in Great Britain and the United States.* Boston: Little, Brown, 1879.

Eliot, T. S. *Collected Poems: 1909–1962.* New York: Harcourt, Brace & World, 1963.

———. *Letters, 1898–1922,* vol. 1. Edited by Valerie Eliot. New York: Harcourt Brace Jovanovich, 1988.

Ellickson, Robert C. *Order without Law: How Neighbors Settle Disputes.* Cambridge, MA: Harvard University Press, 1991.

Ellmann, Richard. *James Joyce,* rev. ed. New York: Oxford University Press, 1982.

———. *Oscar Wilde.* New York: Alfred A. Knopf, 1988.

Ernst, Morris L. *The Best Is Yet ...* New York: Harper & Brothers, 1945.

Ernst, Morris L., and Alexander Lindey. *The Censor Marches On: Recent Milestones in the Administration of the Obscenity Law in the United States.* 1939. New York: Da Capo, 1971.

Ernst, Morris L., and Alan U. Schwartz. *Censorship: The Search for the Obscene.* New York: Macmillan, 1964.

Everton, Michael J. *The Grand Chorus of Complaint: Authors and the Business Ethics of Publishing.* New York: Oxford University Press, 2011.

Exman, Eugene. *The Brothers Harper: A Unique Publishing Partnership and Its Impact upon the Cultural Life of America from 1817 to 1853.* New York: Harper & Row, 1965.

Fargnoli, A. Nicholas, ed. "Oral History: B. W. Huebsch," in *Dictionary of Literary Biography Yearbook 1999,* ed. Matthew J. Bruccoli. Detroit, MI: Gale, 2000.

Fatout, Paul, ed. *Mark Twain Speaking.* Iowa City: University of Iowa Press, 1976.

Feather, John. *Publishing, Piracy, and Politics: An Historical Study of Copyright in Britain.* London: Mansell, 1994.

Fitch, Noel Riley. *Sylvia Beach and the Lost Generation: A History of Literary Paris in the Twenties and Thirties.* New York: W. W. Norton, 1983.

Frankel, Nicholas. *Oscar Wilde's Decorated Books.* Ann Arbor: University of Michigan Press, 2000.

Frost, Robert. *Poems by Robert Frost: A Boy's Will and North of Boston.* Introduction by William H. Pritchard. New York: New American Library, 1990.

Gallup, Donald. *Ezra Pound: A Bibliography.* Charlottesville: University Press of Virginia, 1983.

Gates, Norman T., ed. *Richard Aldington: An Autobiography in Letters.* University Park: Pennsylvania State University Press, 1992.

Gertzman, Jay A. *Bookleggers and Smuthounds: The Trade in Erotica, 1920–1940.* Philadelphia: University of Pennsylvania Press, 1999.

Gilbert, Ellen D. *The House of Holt 1866–1946: An Editorial History.* Metuchen, NJ: Scarecrow, 1993.

Gillies, Mary Ann. *The Professional Literary Agent in Britain, 1880–1920.* Toronto: University of Toronto Press, 2007.

Goldman, Jonathan. *Modernism Is the Literature of Celebrity.* Austin: University of Texas Press, 2011.

Goldstein, Paul. *Copyright's Highway: From Gutenberg to the Celestial Jukebox,* rev. ed. Stanford, CA: Stanford University Press, 2003.

Gross, Gerald, ed. *Publishers on Publishing.* New York: Grosset & Dunlap, 1961.

Harper, J. Henry. *The House of Harper: A Century of Publishing in Franklin Square.* New York: Harper & Brothers, 1912.

Hatch, Benton Le Roy. *A Check List of the Publications of Thomas Bird Mosher of Portland, Maine, MDCCCXCI [to] MDCCCCXXIII.* Northampton, MA: Gehenna, 1966.

Hays, Arthur Garfield. *City Lawyer: The Autobiography of a Law Practice.* New York: Simon & Schuster, 1942.

Hemingway, Ernest. *Selected Letters 1917–1961.* Edited by Carlos Baker. New York: Scribner's, 1981.

Hepburn, James. *The Author's Empty Purse and the Rise of the Literary Agent.* London: Oxford University Press, 1968.

Homestead, Melissa J. *American Women Authors and Literary Property, 1822–1869.* Cambridge: Cambridge University Press, 2005.

Hood, Thomas. *Prose and Verse,* vol. 2. New York: Wiley & Putnam, 1845.

Howell, Herbert A. *The Copyright Law: An Analysis of the Law of the United States Governing Registration and Protection of Copyright Works, Including Prints and Labels,* 2d ed. Washington, DC: Bureau of National Affairs, 1948.

Hyde, Lewis. *The Gift: Creativity and the Artist in the Modern World,* rev. ed. New York: Vintage, 2007.

Irving, Washington. *Letters.* Edited by Ralph M. Aderman. 4 vols. Boston: Twayne, 1978–1982.

James, Elizabeth, ed. *Macmillan: A Publishing Tradition.* Houndmills, Basingstoke, Hampshire, UK: Palgrave, 2002.

James, Henry. *Essays in London and Elsewhere.* New York: Harper & Brothers, 1893.

Johns, Adrian. *Piracy: The Intellectual Property Wars from Gutenberg to Gates.* Chicago: University of Chicago Press, 2009.

Joyce, James. *The Critical Writings.* Edited by Ellsworth Mason and Richard Ellmann. New York: Viking, 1959.

———. *Letters.* Edited by Stuart Gilbert and Richard Ellmann. 3 vols. New York: Viking, 1957, 1966.

———. *Selected Letters.* Edited by Richard Ellmann. New York: Viking, 1975.

———. *Ulysses.* New York: Random House, 1934.

Kaestle, Carl F., and Janice A. Radway, eds. *Print in Motion: The Expansion of Publishing and Reading in the United States, 1880–1940.* Vol. 4 of *A History of the Book in America,* ed. David D. Hall. Chapel Hill: University of North Carolina Press, 2009.

Katz, Daniel. *American Modernism's Expatriate Scene: The Labour of Translation.* Edinburgh: Edinburgh University Press, 2007.

Kelly, Joseph. *Our Joyce: From Outcast to Icon.* Austin: University of Texas Press, 1998.

Khan, B. Zorina. *The Democratization of Invention: Patents and Copyrights in American Economic Development, 1790–1920.* Cambridge: Cambridge University Press, 2005.

———. "Intellectual Property and Economic Development: Lessons from American and European History." Study Paper 1a. London: Commission on Intellectual Property Rights, 2002.

Ladas, Stephen P. *The International Protection of Literary and Artistic Property.* New York: Macmillan, 1938.

Landes, William M., and Richard A. Posner. *The Economic Structure of Intellectual Property Law.* Cambridge, MA: Harvard University Press, 2003.

Lawrence, D. H. *A Propos of Lady Chatterley's Lover*. 1930. New York: Haskell House, 1973.

———. *Letters*. Edited by James T. Boulton et al. 8 vols. Cambridge: Cambridge University Press, 1979–2001.

———. *Letters*. Edited by Aldous Huxley. New York: Viking, 1932.

———. *Selected Letters*. Edited by James T. Boulton. Cambridge: Cambridge University Press, 1997.

———. *Sons and Lovers*, pt. 1. Edited by Helen Baron and Carl Baron. Cambridge: Cambridge University Press, 1992.

Lehmann-Haupt, Hellmut. *The Book in America: A History of the Making, the Selling, and the Collecting of Books in the United States*. New York: R. R. Bowker, 1939.

*Library of Useful Knowledge, Being a Reprint Entire of the Last (1879) Edinburgh and London Edition of Chambers Encyclopedia*, vol. 3. New York: American Book Exchange, 1879.

Lincoln, Abraham. *Selected Speeches and Writings*. New York: Vintage, 1992.

Locke, John. *Two Treatises of Government*. Edited by Peter Laslett. Cambridge: Cambridge University Press, 1988.

Lowell, James Russell. *The Complete Poetical Works*. Boston: Houghton, Mifflin, 1896.

Macfie, R. A. *Copyright and Patents for Inventions: Pleas and Plans for Cheaper Books and Greater Industrial Freedom, with Due Regard to International Relations, the Claims of Talent, the Demands of Trade, and the Wants of People*, vol. 1. Edinburgh: T. & T. Clark, 1879.

Madison, Charles A. *Book Publishing in America*. New York: McGraw-Hill, 1966.

Martindell, Walter. *A Bibliography of the Works of Rudyard Kipling (1881–1921)*. London: Bookman's Journal, 1922.

Mason, Stuart. *Bibliography of Oscar Wilde*, new ed. London: Bertram Rota, 1967.

Materer, Timothy, ed. *The Letters of Ezra Pound and Wyndham Lewis*. New York: New Directions, 1985.

McCourtie, William B., comp. *Where and How to Sell Manuscripts: A Directory for Writers*. Springfield, MA: Home Correspondence School, 1920.

McGill, Meredith L. *American Literature and the Culture of Reprinting, 1834–1853*. Philadelphia: University of Pennsylvania Press, 2003.

McMurry, Frank M., and A. E. Parkins. *Advanced Geography*. New York: Macmillan, 1921.

Mock, James Robert, and Cedric Larson. *Words That Won the War: The Story of the Committee on Public Information, 1917–1919*. New York: Russell & Russell, 1968.

Moore, Harry T., and Dale B. Montague, eds. *Frieda Lawrence and Her Circle: Letters from, to, and about Frieda Lawrence*. Hamden, CT: Archon, 1981.

Moore, Marianne. *The Poems*. Edited by Grace Schulman. New York: Viking, 2003.

Moscato, Michael, and Leslie LeBlanc, eds. *The United States of America v. One Book Entitled Ulysses by James Joyce: Documents and Commentary*. Frederick, MD: University Publications of America, 1984.

Mosher, Thomas. B. *A List of Books Issued in Limited Editions*. Portland, ME: Thomas B. Mosher, 1897.

Mott, Frank Luther. *Golden Multitudes: The Story of Best Sellers in the United States*. New York: Macmillan, 1947.

Nelson, James G. *Elkin Mathews: Publisher to Yeats, Joyce, Pound.* Madison: University of Wisconsin Press, 1989.

———. *Publisher to the Decadents: Leonard Smithers in the Careers of Beardsley, Wilde, Dowson.* University Park: Pennsylvania State University Press, 2000.

*New American Supplement to the Latest Edition of the Encyclopædia Britannica.* Edited by Day Otis Kellog. 5 vols. New York: Werner, 1897.

Nicklin, Philip H. *Remarks on Literary Property.* Philadelphia: P. H. Nicklin & T. Johnson, 1838.

Nowell-Smith, Simon. *International Copyright Law and the Publisher in the Reign of Queen Victoria.* Oxford: Clarendon, 1968.

O'Shea, Michael Vincent, Ellsworth D. Foster, and George Herbert Locke, eds. *The World Book: Organized Knowledge in Story and Picture.* Chicago: Hanson-Roach-Fowler, 1918.

Overton, Grant. *Portrait of a Publisher and the First Hundred Years of the House of Appleton, 1825–1925.* New York: D. Appleton, 1925.

*Papers and Proceedings of the Eighth General Meeting of the American Library Association, Held at Milwaukee, July 7 to 10, 1886.* Boston: Rockwell & Churchill, 1886.

Parini, Jay. *Robert Frost: A Life.* New York: Henry Holt, 1999.

Parks, Stephen, ed. *The Literary Property Debate: Eight Tracts, 1774–1775.* New York: Garland, 1974.

Pound, Ezra. *The Cantos,* 13th prtg. New York: New Directions, 1995.

———. *Ezra Pound to His Parents: Letters 1895–1929.* Edited by Mary de Rachewiltz, A. David Moody, and Joanna Moody. Oxford: Oxford University Press, 2010.

———. *The Letters of Ezra Pound to James Joyce, with Pound's Essays on Joyce.* Edited by Forrest Read. New York: New Directions, 1967.

———. *The Letters of Ezra Pound to Margaret Anderson: The Little Review Correspondence.* Edited by Thomas L. Scott and Melvin J. Friedman. New York: New Directions, 1988.

———. *Personae: The Shorter Poems,* rev. ed. Edited by Lea Baechler and A. Walton Litz. New York: New Directions, 1990.

———. *Poetry and Prose: Contributions to Periodicals.* Edited by Lea Baechler, A. Walton Litz, and James Longenbach. 11 vols. New York: Garland, 1991.

———. *Selected Letters 1907–1941.* Edited by D. D. Paige. New York: New Directions, 1950.

———. *Selected Letters of Ezra Pound to John Quinn, 1915–1924.* Edited by Timothy Materer. Durham, NC: Duke University Press, 1991.

———. *Selected Prose 1909–1965.* Edited by William Cookson. New York: New Directions, 1973.

———. *The Spirit of Romance.* 1910. New York: New Directions, 1968.

Pound, Omar, and Robert Spoo, eds. *Ezra and Dorothy Pound: Letters in Captivity, 1945–1946.* New York: Oxford University Press, 1999.

Putnam, George Haven. *Memories of a Publisher, 1865–1915.* New York: G. P. Putnam's Sons, 1915.

———, comp. *The Question of Copyright: Comprising the Text of the Copyright Law of the United States, a Summary of the Copyright Laws at Present in Force in the Chief Countries of the World,* 2d ed. New York: G. P. Putnam's Sons, 1896.

Quinn, John. *The Letters of John Quinn to William Butler Yeats*. Edited by Alan Himber. Ann Arbor, MI: UMI Research Press, 1983.

Rainey, Lawrence. *Institutions of Modernism: Literary Elites and Public Culture*. New Haven, CT: Yale University Press, 1998.

Raustiala, Kal, and Christopher Sprigman. *The Knockoff Economy: How Imitation Sparks Innovation*. New York: Oxford University Press, 2012.

Redmond, Donald A. *Sherlock Holmes among the Pirates: Copyright and Conan Doyle in America 1890–1930*. Westport, CT: Greenwood, 1990.

Reid, B. L. *The Man from New York: John Quinn and His Friends*. New York: Oxford University Press, 1968.

Reynolds, Quentin. *The Fiction Factory or from Pulp Row to Quality Street*. New York: Random House, 1955.

Rice, Grantland S. *The Transformation of Authorship in America*. Chicago: University of Chicago Press, 1997.

Richards, Grant. *Author Hunting: Memories of Years Spent Mainly in Publishing*. London: Unicorn, 1934.

Ripp, Joseph. "Middle America Meets Middle-Earth: American Publication and Discussion of J. R. R. Tolkien's *Lord of the Rings*, 1954–1969." Master of Science in library science paper, University of North Carolina at Chapel Hill, 2003.

Roberts, Warren, and Paul Poplawski. *A Bibliography of D. H. Lawrence*, 3d ed. Cambridge: Cambridge University Press, 2001.

Roiphe, Anne. *1185 Park Avenue: A Memoir*. New York: Simon & Schuster, 1999.

Rose, Mark. *Authors and Owners: The Invention of Copyright*. Cambridge, MA: Harvard University Press, 1993.

Roth, Samuel. *Jews Must Live: An Account of the Persecution of the World by Israel on All the Frontiers of Civilization*. New York: Golden Hind, 1934.

———. *Stone Walls Do Not: The Chronicle of a Captivity*. New York: William Faro, 1930.

Royal Commission on Copyright. *Copyright Commission: The Royal Commissions and the Report of the Commissioners, Presented to Both Houses of Parliament by Command of her Majesty*. London: Eyre & Spottiswoode, 1878.

Saint-Amour, Paul K. *The Copywrights: Intellectual Property and the Literary Imagination*. Ithaca, NY: Cornell University Press, 2003.

———, ed. *Modernism and Copyright*. New York: Oxford University Press, 2011.

Saunders, David. *Authorship and Copyright*. London: Routledge, 1992.

Seville, Catherine. *The Internationalisation of Copyright Law: Books, Buccaneers, and the Black Flag in the Nineteenth Century*. Cambridge: Cambridge University Press, 2006.

Shaw, George Bernard. *Cashel Byron's Profession*, rev. ed. Chicago: Herbert S. Stone, 1901.

Sheehan, Donald. *This Was Publishing: A Chronicle of the Book Trade in the Gilded Age*. Bloomington: Indiana University Press, 1952.

Shelley, Percy Bysshe. *Selected Poetry and Prose*. Edited by Carlos Baker. New York: Random House, 1951.

Sherman, Brad, and Lionel Bently. *The Making of Modern Intellectual Property Law: The British Experience, 1760–1911*. Cambridge: Cambridge University Press, 1999.

Shove, Raymond Howard. *Cheap Book Production in the United States, 1870 to 1891.* Urbana: University of Illinois Library, 1937.

Slocum, John J., and Herbert Cahoon, comps. *A Bibliography of James Joyce.* 1953. Westport, CT: Greenwood, 1971.

Spencer, Herbert. *Justice: Being Part IV of the Principles of Ethics.* London: Williams & Norgate, 1891.

Stokesbury, James L. *A Short History of World War I.* New York: HarperCollins, 1981.

*Studies on Copyright: Arthur Fisher Memorial Edition.* Hackensack, NJ: Fred B. Rothman; Indianapolis: Bobbs-Merrill, 1963.

Sutton, Walter, ed. *Pound, Thayer, Watson, and* The Dial: *A Story in Letters.* Gainesville: University Press of Florida, 1994.

Tarr, Ralph S., and Frank M. McMurry. *World Geographies: Second Book,* rev. ed. New York: Macmillan, 1919.

Tebbel, John. *Between Covers: The Rise and Transformation of Book Publishing in America.* New York: Oxford University Press, 1987.

Tolkien, J. R. R. *The Fellowship of the Ring.* New York: Ballantine Books, 1965.

———. *Letters of J. R. R. Tolkien: A Selection.* Edited by Humphrey Carpenter. London: George Allen & Unwin, 1981.

Torremans, Paul, ed. *Copyright Law: A Handbook of Contemporary Research.* Cheltenham, UK: Edward Elgar, 2007.

Turner, Catherine. *Marketing Modernism between the Two World Wars.* Amherst: University of Massachusetts Press, 2003.

Vaidhyanathan, Siva. *Copyrights and Copywrongs: The Rise of Intellectual Property and How It Threatens Creativity.* New York: New York University Press, 2001.

Van Dyke, Henry. *The National Sin of Literary Piracy: A Sermon.* New York: Charles Scribner's Sons, 1888.

Vanderham, Paul. *James Joyce and Censorship: The Trials of "Ulysses."* New York: New York University Press, 1998.

Walkiewicz, E. P., and Hugh Witemeyer, eds. *Ezra Pound and Senator Bronson Cutting: A Political Correspondence, 1930–1935.* Albuquerque: University of New Mexico Press, 1995.

Walter, Michel M., and Silke von Lewinski, eds. *European Copyright Law: A Commentary.* Oxford: Oxford University Press, 2010.

Weil, Arthur W. *American Copyright Law, with Especial Reference to the Present United States Copyright Act.* Chicago: Callaghan, 1917.

West, James L. W. *American Authors and the Literary Marketplace since 1900.* Philadelphia: University of Pennsylvania Press, 1988.

Wexler, Joyce Piell. *Who Paid for Modernism? Art, Money, and the Fiction of Conrad, Joyce, and Lawrence.* Fayetteville: University of Arkansas Press, 1997.

Whitman, Walt. *Democratic Vistas, and Other Papers.* London: Walter Scott, 1888.

Wilde, Oscar. *Selected Letters.* Edited by Rupert Hart-Davis. Oxford: Oxford University Press, 1979.

Willison, Ian, Warwick Gould, and Warren Chernaik, eds. *Modernist Writers and the Marketplace.* London: Macmillan, 1996.

Winship, Michael. *American Literary Publishing in the Mid-Nineteenth Century: The Business of Ticknor and Fields.* Cambridge: Cambridge University Press, 1995.

Woodmansee, Martha. *The Author, Art, and the Market: Rereading the History of Aesthetics.* New York: Columbia University Press, 1994.

Woolf, Virginia. *Collected Essays.* Edited by Leonard Woolf. 4 vols. London: Hogarth, 1966–1967.

———. *Letters.* Edited by Nigel Nicolson and Joanne Trautmann. 6 vols. New York: Harcourt Brace Jovanovich, 1976.

Wordsworth, William. *The Poems.* Edited by John O. Hayden. New Haven, CT: Yale University Press, 1977.

———. *The Prose Works.* Edited by W. J. B. Owen and Jane Worthington Smyser. 3 vols. Oxford: Clarendon, 1974.

Yeats, W. B. *Collected Letters (1901–1904),* vol. 3. Edited by John Kelly and Ronald Schuchard. Oxford: Clarendon, 1994.

———. *Collected Letters,* elec. ed. Charlottesville, VA: InteLex; at http://www.nlx.com/collections/130.

Zieger, Robert H. *America's Great War: World War I and the American Experience.* Lanham, MD: Rowman & Littlefield, 2000.

# INDEX